THE PRODUCER'S MANUAL

ALL YOU NEED TO GET PRO RECORDINGS AND MIXES IN THE PROJECT STUDIO

BY PAUL WHITE

Sample
Magic

GETTING THE MOST FROM THIS BOOK

You can use this book in a number of ways. On first reading it is probably worth starting at the beginning and reading through to the end – later chapters refer back to earlier ones and you will get considerably more out of **The Mixdown** (Chapter 19) if you've read through the earlier 101-style guides. The overall shape of the book is also governed by the workflow of a typical project: from setting up your mixing room to the final mastering process.

But real-life studio situations rarely allow the luxury of a full sitting. On these occasions the book has been purposefully designed to be dipped into; so if you have a guitar session you can read **Recording Electric Guitar & Bass** (Chapter 7) alongside **Electric Guitar Production** (Chapter 15) – as well as **Compression & Dynamics 101** (Chapter 11) and **Reverb & Ambience 101** (Chapter 12) if applicable. You will probably find some overlap when you read the book in this way: this is both intentional and inescapable – each decision made during recording inevitably impacts on what you do during mixdown, with decisions on compression, for example, occuring at any number of stages during both recording and mixing.

To make using this book even easier we've provided not only an exhaustive index, but also a comprehensive easy-read glossary. If you're confused by a term then make that your first call.

Finally some notes on references to DAWs and kit: my view – stated many times in these pages – is that making great recordings and mixes is less to do with individual equipment than the talent behind the mic, the arrangement, the quality of performance and the musical instincts of the producer.

Where I do reference specific equipment, DAWs or plug-ins I try also to indicate alternatives. My DAW of choice is Logic – which is used in many of the walkthroughs – but the techniques discussed are universal. Most DAWs offer very similar overall functionality; if you don't know if your own DAW supports a particular feature then a quick check in the manual should tell you what you need to know.

Written by **Paul White**
Edited by **David Felton**
Design by **Andrew Chapman**
Illustrations by **Paul White** and **Jonathan Edmund-Jones**
Photography by **Jamie Trounce**
Additional walkthrough images by **Sharooz Raoofi**
Additional indexing and proofreading by **Ali Jamieson** and **Sharooz Raoofi**

Print by Captiv8
www.captiv8uk.co.uk

Published by **Sample Magic**
145–157 St John Street
London, EC1V 4PA
www.samplemagic.com

First published in the UK, September 2011
Second Edition (revised), May 2012

ISBN: 978-0-9564460-1-5

Acknowledgements
Special thanks to Gary Pitts at Manatee Audio for the use of studio locations for photography.

Printing
Sample Magic cares about the world we live in. This book is printed in the UK on FSC-certified paper, using wood sourced from sustainably managed forests.

FSC
www.fsc.org
MIX
Paper from responsible sources
FSC® C006509

CONTENTS

INTRODUCTION
THE MODERN PRODUCER

What does the modern music producer do?

Set up mics? Press record? Tweak levels? Balance the tracks? Spot an ill-tuned guitar? Help keep the band's spirits up? Get the best performance they can from the performer?

There's no right answer. Sometimes it can be a handful of the above, leaving other people — from engineers to arrangers — to do the rest. And sometimes it is the whole lot, the producer forging a role that combines musical director, project manager, mediator and engineer.

Many of today's biggest producers started out as engineers. Others came into production from a musician's background. In the dance music world, a good number were DJs before they became producers.

What unites them all is a genuine empathy for the musical genres in which they work, exceptionally good ears and an understanding of the capabilities (and limitations) of audio engineering. They also have well-developed interpersonal skills and a head for business and marketing.

Ultimately, all of these skills are employed with one overriding purpose: to realise the artistic vision of the project.

This book aims to give you the tools to do that — whether you're producing your own music or recording and mixing for others.

It straddles both production and engineering, mirroring the dual role of the small studio owner, and acknowledging that it isn't possible to gain a full understanding of one without the other.

The techniques outlined in these pages have been picked up over the many years I have spent editing Sound On Sound magazine. Talking to some of the world's most exceptional producers and engineers has reinforced the simple truth that there are no golden rules for producing magic mixes. There are no secrets. There are no pieces of equipment that deliver audio gold.

Nor is there a single way to mix a hit record: there are as many approaches to production as there are producers. Any attempt to pin down a set process is as futile as laying down the rules of impressionist painting.

Instead, over the following pages I share a wide range of common and more creative approaches to recording and mixing. These are supported by 101-style guides on how to get the most from the kit we use — from mics to compressors. Hundreds of strategies, solutions, techniques and tips flesh out the theory.

I can't guarantee you'll turn out a number one after reading this book, but I'm confident you'll gain the knowledge to bring out the best in any song.

Paul White

THERE ARE NO GOLDEN RULES FOR PRODUCING MAGIC MIXES. THERE ARE NO SECRETS. THERE ARE NO PIECES OF KIT THAT DELIVER AUDIO GOLD.

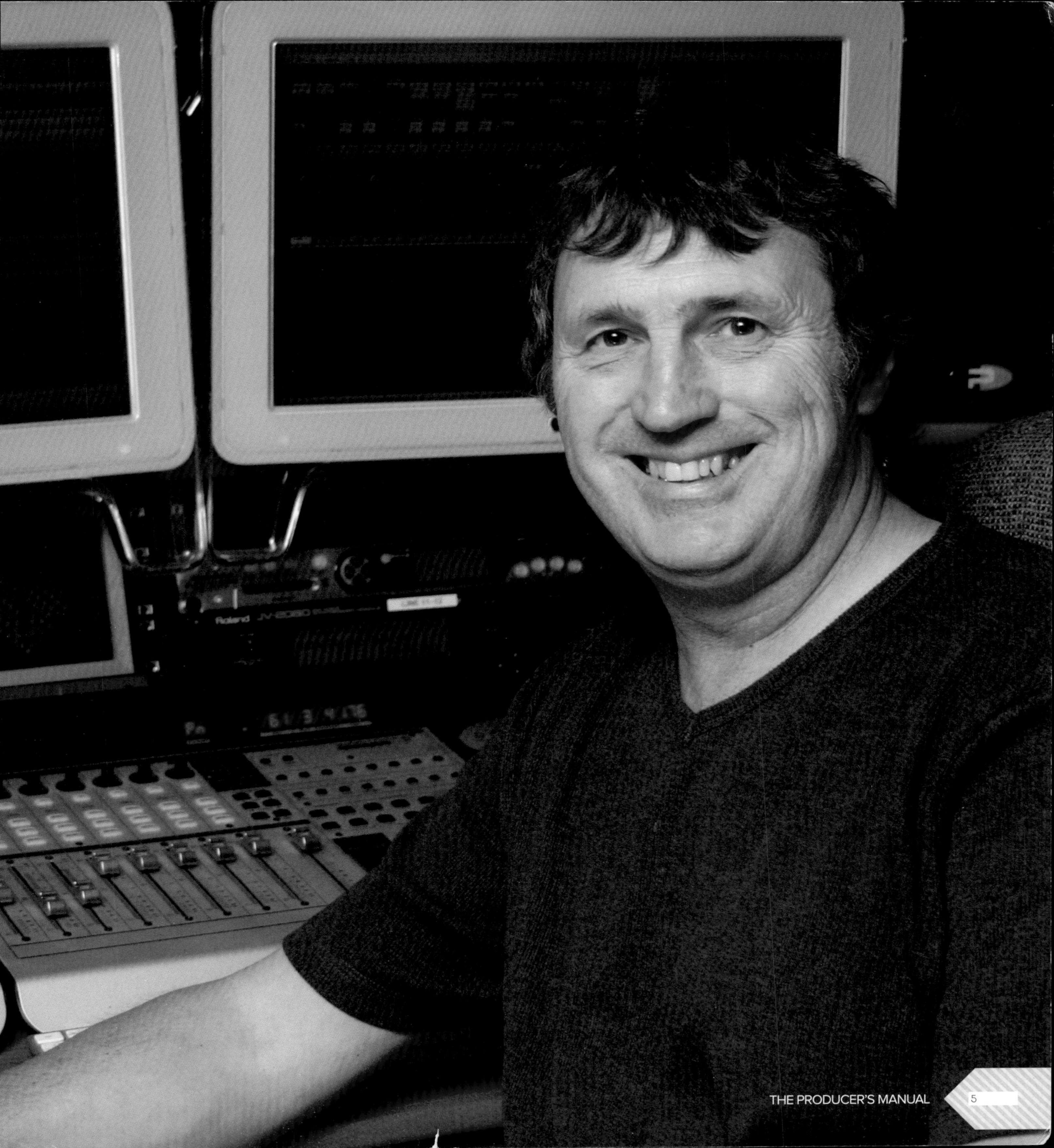
Roland JV-2080

SECTION ONE

ON THE SHOULDERS OF GIANTS

- The History of Recording
- Classic Kit

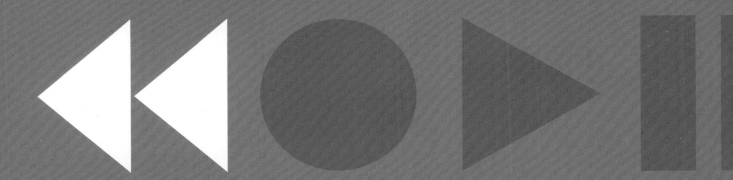

1
THE HISTORY OF RECORDING

150 YEARS OF CHANGE

Today we take accessible high-end recording systems for granted, but everything has to start somewhere, and in the case of audio recording a lot has happened over the last 150 years.

The earliest documented example of a mechanical device able to record sound dates back to 1857, when Edouard-Léon Scott de Martinville created his **phonautograph** – a mechanical pen recorder that traced sound vibrations collected via a diaphragm at the end of a horn onto a paper roll. At the time there was no practical playback mechanism so he must have felt rather like the inventor of the first television set who switched on to discover there was nothing to watch!

Twenty years later Thomas Edison had more success with his **phonograph**, which again used a mechanical horn and diaphragm to collect the sound. Edison experimented with metal foil, lead, and wax as recording media, but all of them suffered significant degradation when replayed.

A decade later Emile Berliner's **gramophone** tackled the problem of degradation using the familiar flat disk with its familiar spiral groove. In this design the sound vibrations were stored as side-to-side movements of the stylus rather than vertical. While the sound quality was little different from that of Edison's cylinder machine, the discs were much easier to duplicate – allowing the pressing of records on a mass scale for the first time.

By the 1930s, all-electronic playback devices had become the norm. Clockwork gave way to electric motors and the horn was replaced by an amplifier and loudspeaker. Further developments allowed stereo recording and playback. Eventually the gramophone evolved into the **hi-fi transcription turntable**. Its market dominance was sealed by the mass distribution of **vinyl**.

THE GENESIS OF TAPE

Recording tape, and its associated recording and playback machines, came into use during World War 2 as a result of German developments. Tape works by storing the changing electrical source signal from a microphone as corresponding changes in magnetic charge along the length of a flexible tape coated with magnetic metal oxide. A pickup head designed to convert these back into an electrical output is used to replay the tape via an amp and speaker.

IN THE CASE OF AUDIO RECORDING A LOT HAS HAPPENED OVER THE LAST 150 YEARS.

HISTORY OF RECORDING

1857
Léon Scott de Martinville's Phonautograph

1877
Edison's phonograph

1897
A Berliner disc for the gramophone

It was the American singer Bing Crosby who recognised the potential of the **tape recorder** for the entertainment business. Tape made it possible for him to pre-record radio shows to a high standard rather than having to do everything perfectly live every time. So enthused was he by the emerging technology that he became one of the original investors behind Ampex – putting $50,000 into the company in 1947 and helping it to become a major player in the manufacture of both tape recorders and tape.

Recording as we know it today relies heavily on **multitrack recording**, the invention of which is credited to the late Les Paul, who was both a musician and a prolific inventor. He had Ampex build him a custom eight-track recorder to his own specification so that he and his singer wife Mary Ford could create multi-layered harmonies and instrumental parts.

In the very early days of multitrack recording, Ampex produced a commercially available **three-track recorder**, which seems like an odd format, but it allowed the band to be recorded in stereo to two of the tracks leaving space for the lead vocal to be added later on the third. These three-track machines were behind countless classic records, including many Tamla Motown recordings as well as Phil Spector's huge soundscapes.

When you listen to a Phil Spector production it sounds as though it must have been made using extensive overdubbing. Not so. The truth is that this layering was done by multiple session musicians playing the parts live. The mixers at the time had either no EQ or very basic EQ, so the secret to making a great-sounding record was getting the sound right at source, capturing it using the right types of mics set up in the right places. The different elements were balanced using the mixer before committing them to tape. Reverb came from echo rooms, not machines.

By the 1960s **four-track recording** was commonplace and it is on those lumbering machines that many of the memorable hits of the '60s were made, including classics by The Beatles and the Rolling Stones. If you needed more tracks, you had to mix or 'bounce down' to a fresh track on a second machine, or to a free track on the first machine.

HISTORY OF RECORDING

1940
Vinyl becomes storage medium of choice for recorded music.

1967
The Beatles' historic Sgt. Pepper's Lonely Hearts Club Band brings about a new era in multi-track recording.

This meant getting the balance perfect at each stage of the mix – there was no going back. The Beatles' seminal masterpiece, 'Sgt Pepper's Lonely Hearts Club Band', is probably the most famous recording project made possible by bouncing recordings between two four-track machines.

It didn't take long for developers to up the track count. Studios went from four to eight, then to 16 and 24 tracks, in a relatively short space of time. The standard format for 24-track recording was two inch wide tape running at either 15 or 30 inches per second. The reason for selectable tape speeds was that the recording quality was generally better at higher tape speeds, with the inevitable trade-off that you got less recording time per reel. Editing was done by cutting and splicing the tape using razor blades, a splicing block and splicing tape.

Meanwhile, in the world of the consumer, analogue **tape cassettes** or '**Compact Cassettes**' had become popular because of their convenience and portability. After some negotiation with Phillips over licensing terms, which initially specified that cassettes had to be used only for stereo recording, Tascam created the **Portastudio**, which recorded four tracks all running in one direction, at double speed. This was quickly emulated by other companies and before long these **portable four-tracks** had introduced a whole generation of musicians to the previously unaffordable world of recording.

DIGITAL RECORDING

The development of **digital recording** caused a paradigm shift in the recording process.

Unlike analogue media, which can't be copied without some loss of quality, digital audio recording systems represent the audio data as a string of discrete numbers that can be copied indefinitely. As long as the numbers are copied correctly, the copy is in every way identical to the original.

Digital tape recorders first appeared in the 1970s, but it was Sony's all-in-one stereo **Digital Audio Tape (DAT)** format, introduced in 1987, that became the industry standard. DAT machines recorded at 16-bit resolution with sample rates of 44.1kHz (the same as **Compact Disc**) or 48kHz for use in the video and film industries. Before long there were few professional studios that didn't own at least one DAT device.

HISTORY OF RECORDING

1979
Release of Tascam Portastudio 144.

1987
DAT enters the market.

1992
The ill-fated DCC makes its short-lived appearance.

NOW
Desktop and laptop computers, like the MacBook Pro, now offer full studios in a box.

Open-reel digital multitrack machines were always expensive, but at the start of the '90s Los Angeles-based Alesis launched their revolutionary eight-track **ADAT (Alesis Digital Audio Tape)** digital recorder, based around a modified consumer VHS tape transport system.

Tascam came up with their own digital 8-track machine in the form of the **DA88**, which was a little more expensive but more readily accepted in professional circles than the ADAT. Although the ADAT is now officially obsolete, the optical 8-channel format developed for linking multiple ADAT machines has become an industry standard for connecting multi-channel digital devices, especially in the project studio sector of the market.

While the consumer industry flirted with the ill-fated **DCC** digital cassette and **MiniDisc**, the expanding computer market meant that hard drives were getting bigger in capacity and lower in cost every year and the whole landscape of digital recording was changing forever — finally moving from outside to inside the box.

RECORDING TODAY
And so to now. The majority of today's small studios are based on conventional **Windows PC** or **Apple Mac** **computers** running DAW (Digital Audio Workstation) software. Audio interfacing is taken care of by a soundcard or external audio interface, usually connected by USB, Firewire or a specialised PCI card, that can provide anything from two to 64 or more inputs.

Most of the affordable interfaces designed for multi-musician use offer eight analogue inputs, often with the option to expand the count to 16 or even 24 with the addition of extra eight-channel pre-amp extender units, usually connected using the ADAT optical interface.

For those who prefer not to use computers there are **hardware recording systems** based on hard drive technology, such as the 24-track Alesis HD-24 and a number of combined recorders and mixers, offering upwards of eight tracks, from companies such as Yamaha, Roland, Korg, Tascam and Zoom.

From single tracks on unstable media to hundreds of tracks on computers you can carry around, the history of recording has been one of ever-increasing amounts of power on ever-smaller and more affordable pieces of kit. As an indication of how technology has fallen in price, a hard drive to go with an early Digidesign system cost well over £2,500 for a lowly 600MB worth of storage (I know because I bought one!). Today you can buy finger-sized USB sticks with ten times the amount of storage space for less than the price of a take-away pizza.

CONSUMING MUSIC TODAY: THE MP3
Mp3 (MPEG3 to give it its full title) and other audio data compression formats are designed to reduce the amount of storage space (and internet bandwidth) a piece of audio takes up. They generally do this by leaving out anything that the human hearing system can't hear because it

> **THE HISTORY OF RECORDING HAS BEEN ONE OF EVER-INCREASING AMOUNTS OF POWER ON EVER-SMALLER AND MORE AFFORDABLE PIECES OF KIT.**

▲ In the consumer music landscape programs like iTunes have taken the place of CD stacks and vinyl shelves.

or for playback on mp3 players. Creating this mp3 master (page 326) involves encoding the final mix using an mp3 data compression algorithm — a quick, painless process in all modern DAWs.

But there are some important considerations. If you start out working with compressed audio and then it gets compressed again when you put it on the internet, the quality can suffer noticeably. What's more, if you send an mp3 to a radio station to play they may send it through the encoding process yet again — causing further degradation.

Remember that every time an audio file is subjected to data compression it loses quality, and a file that has been compressed at several stages can really suffer.

The lesson here is to use high quality, uncompressed audio at all stages of the writing and mixing process (including when using samples) up until the finished master. That way you end up with the highest possible quality master mp3. Of course, you have little control over what happens to it after you hand it over — but at least you've done your job.

is hidden or masked by something louder. As long as the data isn't compressed too much the end result can sound very good — despite the audio file only being around one tenth the size of the original high-resolution recording.

It is likely that the end result of your work will need to be made available in compressed formats for use on the internet

THE BENEFIT OF 1s AND 0s

Digital recording systems convert the incoming analogue signal into a stream of numerical values that are stored as 1s and 0s on the storage medium — usually a hard drive in modern systems, although portable stereo recorders tend to record to solid-state flash memory cards.

These digital measurements are taken at regular intervals controlled by a sampling clock. Providing the sampling clock runs

at least twice as fast as the highest audio frequency being recorded, the original waveform can be reconstructed with far greater accuracy, and with far lower noise, than was ever possible using analogue recording methods.

A major advantage of digital recording is that digital data — samples, individual audio tracks, final masters and so on — can be copied by simply duplicating the stream of numbers used to describe a

piece of audio. As long as the numbers are copied correctly, there is no quality loss, unlike analogue copies which lose quality with every generation.

You can visualise analogue copying as being similar to photocopying, where the copy is never quite as good as the original. Digital copying, on the other hand, is more like duplicating a word processor document, where the copy is identical in all respects to the original.

ANALOGUE ARTEFACTS
(OR, DOES TAPE REALLY SOUND BETTER?)

Why do so many engineers and producers talk so passionately about the benefits of analogue tape when it is noisy compared to digital, adds a lot more distortion and you can't make copies without losing quality each time?

The short answer is that, shortcomings aside, analogue tape does something to the sound being recorded that can make it punchier, smoother and warmer.

THE SHORTCOMINGS

The key difference between digital and analogue recording is that, unlike with digital, nothing ever comes back sounding quite the way you heard it when recording to tape. This is down to a number of factors:

> Recording to tape introduces **noise**, specifically **hiss**, that gets worse as the tape speed is lowered and/or the track width reduced. A number of noise reduction systems – Dolby A, B, C and later S – were developed to minimise noise but they all introduced side effects of their own.

> **Mechanical imperfections** cause the tape speed to vary, generating low frequency variations ('wow') and faster variations ('flutter').

The result of these variations is that instruments such as pianos, which produce very precise fixed pitches, tend to play back sounding as though they've been treated to a very mild chorus effect.

> And... **distortion**. The most significant side-effect of recording onto analogue tape is distortion. Unlike digital systems, which remain clean-sounding until you exceed their input range, analogue tape reacts in a non-linear way, subtly altering the waveforms as they are recorded.

The higher the level you record onto tape, the more squashed the waveform peaks become. High frequency sounds distort especially badly, which means that particular care has to be taken when recording hi-hats and female vocal parts.

As if the noise, distortion and unreliability of the medium isn't enough to deal with, there's the not insignificant amount of **maintenance** a multitrack tape machine requires – even before you consider the high price and limited availability of wide format recording tape. The moving parts and brakes are subject to wear, as are the tape heads, and to keep a machine in top condition it is necessary to regularly align the physical position of the heads and settings of the record and playback electronics while running a professionally prepared (and expensive) test tape.

Oh, and they're **big**.

Which is all to say that the myths surrounding tape should all be taken with a liberal sprinkling of salt, although it would be remiss – and a lie – not to concede that tape can, and does, sound very good in certain situations.

THE BENEFITS

Ironically, the single biggest drawback of tape also explains its appeal. The non-linear distortion that changes the sound also turns out to bestow a certain warmth. The more squashed the signal becomes at high input levels, the richer it is in additional (and nice sounding) harmonic distortion components. Well, up to a point anyway. Indeed you can drive the level meters several dBs into the red before the sound gets too obviously distorted – a fact (and sound) exploited by many producers (see Levels, page 34).

The new harmonics generated by distortion are not the only changes made to the sound when tracking to tape. The audio signal is equalised prior to recording and then the reverse EQ curve applied on playback. The frequency characteristics of tape saturation and distortion are skewed by this EQ curve – giving a further flavour to the sound.

Music 'likes' tape because the sound can be made to seem bigger and more punchy: audio peaks are reduced in level due to tape saturation producing an effect not unlike compression. Genres from rock to dance can benefit from obvious tape overdrive, while a more subtle push can warm vocal and guitar performances.

Where an original recording was made using digital technology, some mastering engineers choose to copy their digital masters to a stereo tape machine and then output back to digital again to add a sheen of analogue gold-dust.

TAPE: THE PLUG-IN WAY

The complex way in which tape modifies audio signals is difficult to replicate by digital modelling as there are so many different variables to consider. There's distortion in the analogue tape recorder circuitry

and the non-linear characteristics of both the recording machines and tape types (which also vary according to tape speed); then there's the EQ used during recording and playback to take into account. Over and above this, all these factors also have to respond correctly to changes in input level – something very hard to model with genuine accuracy.

But there are a few plug-ins on the market that do the job remarkably well. One of the first to market was Universal Audio's Studer A800 plug-in (below), which replicates a specific Studer multitrack machine. It warms up the low end, adds density and smooths out the highs in a subtle but musical way.

A major benefit of the plug-in approach, other than the cost saving over real tape, is that the effect of tape compression can be applied solely to those tracks that benefit from it. Tape can distort unpleasantly on high level, high frequency sounds such as hi-hats; with plug-ins you can choose to leave those channels unprocessed or use lower drive levels on them. Less aggressive drive settings can also be used to process final stereo mixes.

MUSIC 'LIKES' TAPE BECAUSE THE SOUND CAN BE MADE TO SEEM BIGGER AND MORE PUNCHY.

CHANGING ROLES IN THE STUDIO

It's not just studio kit that has changed over the decades; the way in which recordings are made has changed dramatically too.

Talk to old-time engineers and you'll hear tales of them having to wear suits, ties and white coats while working. They weren't even allowed to touch the mics – they had technicians in brown coats for that! Look at the books documenting the early Beatles sessions and you'll see George Martin in his suit and tie, although it seems that as producer he was spared the white coat.

In the early commercial studios regulations were rife. A studio would have documented setups for recording specific instruments, including mic types and position. Engineers could be disciplined for deviating from the rules. Recording was scheduled in strict shifts too, which rarely continued past six o'clock. It was only around the time of The Beatles, when artists wanted to do things their own way, that the rules started to relax, with artists taking a more active studio role and bands finally being allowed to record through the night.

The role of the producer has changed too. In the early days of recording the producer's role as it is now didn't exist; the arranger looked after the music, the engineer looked after capturing the performance as accurately as possible, and that was pretty much the end of the story.

The advent of multitrack recording created an opening for the kind of producer we recognise today – a multi-faceted individual who often has to wear several hats, including those of arranger, creative ideas generator, keeper of the purse-strings and – often most crucially – peacemaker!

TODAY'S PRODUCER

In broad terms, the role of the modern music producer is to work with the artist(s) and engineer(s) to produce a commercially viable recording. Their job can extend to choosing and booking a studio, employing session players and organising mastering.

A successful producer needs to know what is possible in the studio – even if they aren't an experienced engineer. They need to have good ears in a musical sense, and, somewhere close to the top of the list, they must be good with people, as friction often arises during recording sessions.

Beyond that the producer can shape the role to fit their own skills and passions. Some take a back seat and let the band get on with it, offering the occasional suggestion on arrangement and mixing (although the skilled ones wield a lot of influence without the band realising how great their contribution really is). Others are known for micromanaging every stage of the process.

Some, like Trevor Horn in his 'Frankie' days, build the actual arrangements themselves, sequencing large sections of songs using samplers and programmers rather than the original musicians. Others, like Mark Ronson, are multi-instrumentalists who are able not just to mix a track but also supply many of the musical elements.

The pro-active producer will have their own distinctive style and approach that makes their work almost as recognisable as that of the musicians they work with. And while many producers remain unsung heroes in the industry – shadowy names eclipsed by the artists they produce – an increasing number are breaking from anonymity to become big names themselves, with equally big bank balances. ●

A SUCCESSFUL PRODUCER NEEDS TO KNOW WHAT IS POSSIBLE IN THE STUDIO – EVEN IF THEY AREN'T AN EXPERIENCED ENGINEER.

TIPS FOR A BETTER MIX

Arrangement is key.
Not every part should play all the time. Music comprises both notes and spaces. If you lose all the spaces, you lose the music.

COMMON MIX MISTAKES AND HOW TO AVOID THEM

Too many tracks.
In the days of the eight-track, if you finished a song using only seven tracks somebody would always think of something to add on the eighth! In the era of the near-limitless track count it's easy to keep on adding. Too many productions have too many parts fighting for the same frequency real-estate. Examine the arrangement and ask what the song really needs; less is often more.

2
CLASSIC
KIT

> MUCH CLASSIC KIT DOES SOMETHING FLATTERING TO THE SOUNDS IT TREATS.

BACK FOR GOOD

It is human nature to look backwards fondly, and to believe that our ancestors had some knowledge – some secret awareness – that evades us today. A similar view prevails in production circles around classic recording gear, even when rational thought tells us audio technology must have improved over the past century. Why is it, then, that we persist in looking back through rose-tinted glasses (or listening through rose-backed headphones)?

There's no doubt that some of the early recording gear was very well designed, making the best use of the limited technology available at the time. But it wasn't perfect. Early valve gear suffered from distortion, while audio transformers introduced phase shift and further distortions into recordings. Analogue tape added its own considerable number of imperfections (page 14).

Of course great records – some of the greatest – were made using this classic kit. But its modern-day veneration is an odd thing. It doesn't extend to the wider consumer music market; how many music listeners are still investing in tape players, for example? Yet in the pro-audio world the respect for the machines of the past continues to spawn remodels, both physical and digital, and assures sky-high resale prices for some of the rare pieces that make it onto the second hand market.

My own view is that the tonal imperfections exhibited by some of the early equipment have become familiar to us as producers and music lovers because so many great records were made using it. We think of the sound of the records we like as being sonically 'right' – an association that extends to the kit used to make them.

Over and above that, much of this equipment does something flattering to the sounds it treats; the vast majority of these old devices sound the way they do because of their imperfections, not because of some hidden magic.

In some cases these imperfections produce a musically pleasing result – essentially a form of musical flattery. In the case of compressors, many recording engineers adopted them as much for the sonic colouration they bestowed as their ability to control levels.

Knowing a little about the kit that has gone before – and that shaped the sonic landscape of today – can help us get more from the range of tools and emulations we have at our disposal in the studio today.

EVOLUTION OF A GUITAR SOUND

The most obvious example of the shortcomings of equipment shaping our tonal expectations is the electric guitar amplifier.

Early amps were relatively low in power and used valve circuitry because that's all that was available at the time. They also employed loudspeakers that didn't reproduce high frequencies well and couldn't handle high power levels without distorting. If you played them too loudly they noticeably distorted.

Blues players soon found a way to exploit this unintended distortion and incorporate it into their style of playing. The limited frequency range of the speakers helped by smoothing away the more unpleasant harmonics introduced by distortion. And so a sound was born.

Today some form of distorted guitar sound plays an essential part in any form of rock, metal or blues music and a lot of technology has been thrown at the problem of emulating the sound of the early valve amps in today's solid stage designs, digital pre-amps (such as the Line 6 POD) and software plug-ins.

▲ **The 1963 Fender Champion: An essential part of the blues legacy.**

Who knows what would have happened if the technology to build high power, distortion-free amps had been available at the time the electric guitar was invented? We might be listening to very different guitar sounds today.

MIC: THE NEUMANN U47

Neumann's legendary U47 (right) is a large-diaphragm, valve condenser microphone manufactured between 1949–1965 and based around the company's M7 capsule originally developed for their 'Bottle' CMV3. It has the distinction of being the first capacitor mic to go into commercial production. Prior to this, most vocals were recorded using ribbon mics, which had a much less well-defined high end.

The U47 was equipped with a dual-diaphragm capsule that could be switched between cardioid and omni polar patterns (page 64), but unlike today's capacitor mics, most of which use mylar diaphragms sputtered or evaporated with gold to form a conductive layer, the M7 capsule used PVC, which tended to deteriorate with age.

In 1960 the M7 capsule was replaced by the K47, a similar capsule fitted with a more durable PET film diaphragm.

The U47's internal pre-amp circuitry was based on Telefunken's VF14 valve or vacuum tube. A similar U48 model was also available with a choice of cardioid or figure-of-eight polar patterns. When Telefunken ceased production of the VF14, Neumann had to redesign the U47, the result being the well-known U67, which offered omni, figure-of-eight and cardioid polar patterns. This model is the forerunner of the Neumann U87 – still available today and found in leading studios all over the world.

Original U47s are still popular in some top studios, despite the incredibly high cost of maintenance, especially when sourcing original VF14 pre-amp valves. The mic has a well-balanced, clear sound with emphasis in the upper mid-range giving it a useful presence characteristic when used on vocals – even though many engineers at the time perceived it as being somewhat strident, presumably because they were used to the sound of their ribbon models.

Whether the U47 possessed any real magic beyond good quality German design and engineering I'll leave others to debate, but it was certainly the mic of choice on countless classic records, including many Beatles hits.

Today several companies produce mics 'inspired by' both the original valve and later FET (Field Effect Transistor) versions of the U47, some of which come close to resurrecting 'that' sound of the original.

▼ **The Neumann U47 – used on countless classic recordings, including many Beatles hits.**

MIC: AKG'S LEGACY

Based in Vienna, AKG produced its first C12 model in 1953, the capsule of which was used in a number of subsequent mics including the C412 and several incarnations of the perennially popular C414 (below left). Although similar in principle to the capsules used by Neumann, the C12 diaphragm was edge-terminated (Neumann preferred a centre-terminate approach), which in conjunction with AKG's specially tuned backplate gave their mics a different tonal character. Early versions of the capsule had a fairly flat frequency response but later revisions added some high-end sparkle.

In 1964 AKG launched the softer-sounding C-12a using a Nuvistor tube as an impedance converter in a body not unlike that of the 414. This was superseded in 1971 by the C412, which used a FET rather than a valve as the amplification device. Next came the C414, a mic popular in classical recording and pop work, both on vocals and instruments.

The best AKG capacitor mics are regarded as having an enhanced high-end that helps pop vocals sit well in a mix. They are also extensively used as drum overheads and for mic'ing the acoustic guitar.

Although the C12 and C414 model names remain in the catalogue, there have been so many design revisions that the current C414 bears little resemblance to its forebears other than in general shape. Similarly, today's C12VR is a very different beast to the original C12; its smoother sound is probably closer to that of the C12a. I have a C12VR in my studio, and if anything the high end is smoother and more recessed than one might expect from a typical capacitor model — and certainly much less forward sounding than the older C12 models.

While it can be argued that older C12s and C414s represent AKG's most famous studio mics, their D12 and subsequent D112 large diaphragm dynamic models have also earned a place in audio history, predominantly as kick drum mics.

MIC: THE ELECTRO-VOICE RE20

Another classic dynamic mic, the Electro-Voice RE20 has applications in broadcast, live sound and the recording studio where its high resistance to both handling noise and electrical interference makes it very useful in difficult situations.

It boasts a sensibly flat response up to 18kHz with good transient handling. And being dynamic, it isn't susceptible to the same humidity problems that can knock out a capacitor mic (page 62).

It is physically larger than most of its contemporaries and can handle very high SPLs, making it particularly suitable for close mic'ing brass instruments. It is also the vocal mic of choice for some high-profile hip hop and rap vocalists.

MIC: SHURE SM57

No discussion of dynamic mics would be complete without a mention of the Shure SM57, an inexpensive, cardioid pattern dynamic mic that is a firm studio favourite for recording guitar amps and close-mic'ing drums. Introduced in 1965, the SM57 uses the same capsule developed for the Shure Unidyne III model six years before, in itself similar to that used in the ubiquitous SM58 live vocal mic. The only difference is that the SM58 has a built-in low frequency roll-off to counter the proximity effect when the mic is used very close to its sound source. Some engineers use the SM58 to mic the snare drum.

MIC: SENNHEISER 421

Almost as well-known and certainly as distinctive in appearance is the Sennheiser 421 (right), a large diaphragm dynamic mic brought to market in the early 1960s.

The 421 is the perfect desert island mic: it makes a good stab at anything from vocals to drums, it sounds good on kick drums, it takes guitar amps in its stride and can handle very high SPLs before distorting. Indeed, in the decades I've been using 421s I haven't found anything they do badly; no wonder they are found in just about every studio in the world (I have two in mine). The mic features a five position bass roll-off dial and an in-built mic stand clip that works perfectly well – until you break it!

COMPRESSOR: TELETRONIX LA-2A

A compressor includes a side-chain for following the level of the audio being treated and a gain control that is driven by the electrical output from the side-chain circuitry. Today we have low-distortion, low-noise electronic gain devices known as Voltage Controlled

Amplifiers (VCAs) that can be used to make high-spec compressors, but in the early days of audio circuit design engineers tried all manner of circuit topologies to create a variable gain element.

One of the enduring classics is the LA-2A (above), first built by Teletronix in 1965, and still being manufactured today – to the original specification – by Universal Audio.

The LA-2A uses the side-chain signal to control the brightness of a lamp which shines on a photocell to adjust the gain of the main audio path. This optical system is far from technically perfect and it's hard to find two original LA-2As that work in exactly the same way, but the effect it produces is very musical, making it one of the best loved compressors ever produced.

The simple photocell circuitry, based around a combined lamp and photocell module called a T4, also has the benefit of low noise and a reasonably wide, flat frequency response.

Rather than having a conventional threshold control, the LA-2A simply has a control labelled Peak Reduction. The higher the setting, the more the signal is compressed. A Gain control is

▲ Univeral Audio's LA-2A: Just two controls on a compressor that can be used to great effect on vocals, electric bass, guitar and drums. Note the 'Limit' and 'Compress' switch on the far left.

> THE LA-2A'S OPTICAL SYSTEM IS FAR FROM TECHNICALLY PERFECT AND IT'S HARD TO FIND TWO ORIGINAL MODELS THAT WORK IN EXACTLY THE SAME WAY. BUT THE EFFECT IT PRODUCES IS VERY MUSICAL.

used to restore any level lost due to compression.

While a modern compressor may have a wide range of compression ratios, the LA-2A can only be set to 'Compress' or 'Limit', with the amount of gain reduction shown on a moving coil meter. The Compress setting has a lower ratio than the Limit setting and a softer 'knee', or compression curve.

The LA-2A's attack time is preset to a very fast 10ms, while the release has a dual slope characteristic that only takes around 40–80ms to achieve 50 per cent release, and then a further 0.5–5 seconds for the gain to fully return to normal.

The reason for this dual slope is that the photocell has a memory that persists for a few seconds after the lamp has been extinguished. While this was probably viewed as an unavoidable design flaw when the unit was originally designed, there's no doubt that this happy accident contributed to its musical sound.

The LA-2A doesn't just compress. It also adds a distinct sonic character to any signal that passes through it, best described as a warmth without any obvious distortion (unless deliberately overdriven!).

It is popularly used to great effect on vocals, where it can keep a voice up-front and smooth, and to a lesser extent on electric bass, guitar and drums (notably the kick). The truth is, it can sound good on a whole range of sounds – including buses. Using the transformer and amp without any gain reduction can also be useful for warming up harsh digital signals, adding a certain smooth swell to the low end.

COMPRESSOR: UREI (OR UNIVERSAL AUDIO) 1176

Developed in 1966 by Bill Putnam, the founder of Universal Audio, the 1176 was available under both the Universal Audio and UREI banners.

Using a FET as the gain control element, the 1176 features discrete class A circuitry and is designed to process line-level signals. A quieter version, the 1176LN, used lower noise circuitry and components.

The character of the compressor is embodied in its ability to even out the level of vocals while preserving their definition and presence, although it works well on many other instruments too.

The compression ratio is selected via four push-button switches labeled 4, 8, 12 and 20dB, although these can be used in combinations, where all four buttons pressed in (famously described as 'all buttons in', Nuke or British mode) produces a seriously assertive limiting effect.

There are controls for input and output gain, where the input essentially pushes the signal up against a preset internal threshold. A moving coil VU meter can be switched to show the output level or the amount of gain reduction. Both the attack and release times are adjustable.

Some engineers favour an 1176 followed by an LA-2A: a sublime double act that can tame and smooth a vocal line while adding a useful presence and depth.

COMPRESSOR: FAIRCHILD 670

Weighing in at around 65lbs, the Fairchild 670 'limiting amplifier' is one of the heaviest – and most revered – dynamic processors ever built. A used one can cost you as much as a decent new car.

It uses tubes or valves as gain control elements wired in a so-called 'variable mu' configuration. A DC bias control is used to adjust the compression ratio and compression knee. In all, the Fairchild contains 14 transformers and 20 tubes, meaning that – if nothing else – it's useful for keeping the studio warm during long winter sessions!

The compressor is known for its warm, fat sound and ability to add a pumping energy to a mix when pushed hard. Countless classic records were mastered with a Fairchild 670 in the signal chain.

Few people have access to working units these days but some companies are building replicas claiming to use the same parts and circuitry.

The Fairchild is also a usual suspect for chaining: in a Sound On Sound feature about favourite processors used by A-list engineers, both Steve Churchyard and Tom Elmhirst suggested combining the Urei 1176 with the Fairchild 670 on vocals.

COMPRESSOR: DBX 160

Introduced in the mid '70s, the original (and diminutive) dbx 160 compressor became popular for its ability to add an assertive character to drums and bass when pushed hard. It can sound great on a kick/snare drum bus mixed low to add punch to a mix.

Its so-called 'Over Easy' ultra-soft-knee compression curve causes the compression ratio to increase gradually with the level of the input signal. The attack and release times are preset. All the user has to do is set a threshold level then dial in more or less compression.

Later models of the 160 allowed the operator to select between dbx's Over Easy mode and traditional hard knee compression. The dbx 160A model also included a novel Infinity mode that allowed the output level to decrease when the input rose above the threshold.

However, it's the original dbx 160 – the first commercial VCA-based compressor – that today's engineers remember most.

EQ: PULTEC EQP-1A

One of the most revered high-end EQs among recording and mastering engineers, the Pultec EQP-1A equaliser (far right), is a so-called passive design, where the passive EQ filters are followed by active valve make-up gain to compensate for level losses in the passive circuits. It is known for its silky-smooth top end, and a warm, fat bottom.

Its two-band (plus shelving high cut) design offers low shelving filters at 20, 30, 60 and 100Hz. Because the filters are passive, the low cut ('Atten') control interacts with the low boost ('Boost') so that when both are turned up there is a resulting dip in the response above the filter turnover frequency combined with boost below. It may seem

▲ An original ad for the 160 series of dbx comressors.

▲ The Pultec EQP-1A:
All about the curves.

> **THE PULTEC IS WIDELY CONSIDERED TO BE ONE OF THE MOST MUSICAL SOUNDING EQS AROUND.**

strange for an EQ to have separate controls for cut and boost at the same frequency, but it makes sense given the passive circuit filter design. The unique curve generated by the boost and cut combined is a large part of the unit's charm.

The high boost section has a parametric-style bell curve filter with seven switchable frequencies between 3–16kHz, where the bandwidth control interacts with the boost knob (providing more boost at narrower bandwidths with a maximum of 20dB of boost available).

The high-cut shelving filter offers three frequency settings at 5, 10 and 20kHz.

Pultec EQs don't offer the degree of forensic control we've come to expect from a modern parametric equaliser, but their gentle filter curves and the lack of active circuitry around the filters give them a musical sound – even when adding a lot of boost.

Typically used on the kick drum (to add bite), bass line (to help it sit), vocals (for air), and during mastering, the Pultec is widely considered to be one of the most musical sounding EQs ever conceived.

Several modern equivalents are available based on the original circuit, as well as some excellent plug-in emulations.

REVERB: EMT 140 PLATE REVERB

Early engineers used natural reverb created in specially designed reflective rooms to give sounds space in the mix (page 181). Their options increased considerably in 1957 when EMT developed its 140 plate reverb.

The EMT Model 140 features a metal plate suspended by springs in a metal frame (below). Vibrations are generated by an audio transducer, which are then picked up from other parts of the surface by contact mics. Sound reflects back and forth between the edges of the plate producing a dense, musical reverb that can be adjusted by applying mechanical damping pads to the plate to reduce the decay time.

The EMT 140 Plate Reverb was large, expensive and had to be isolated from vibration and external noise. Why then the enduring love for this early reverb sound?

Part of it was practical: the plate reverb was considerably cheaper than building a dedicated acoustic chamber. But the main reason was its sound; one of the explanations for why plate reverb works so well is the fact that it doesn't conjure any

particular acoustic environment in the mind of the listener. Often vocals (and drums) don't need to sound as though they are in a concert hall, a tiled room or a cave – they just need a dash of reverb to bring them to life. Plate reverb provides this. Its slightly brighter-than-life sound – bestowed by the colouration of the vibrating plate – also lends a natural presence that has become part of our musical heritage.

There are few mechanical plates still in use today, but most digital reverbs include generic plate emulations of some kind.

In the years following the arrival of the 140 a range of other companies developed their own plate reverbs, but the EMT140 was always considered to be 'the one'.

REVERB: LEXICON 224

While EMT busied itself developing its first digital reverb (the model 250), the Lexicon 224, launched in 1978, became the first truly high-end digital reverb processor.

Its designer, Dr David Griesinger, would demonstrate his reverbs at trade shows by playing his recorder through them. He was trained as both a physicist and a musician – a double skill set that helped him bring the maths and art of digital reverb together. His algorithms included time modulation (the famous Lexicon Spin and Wander parameters) that, although not present in nature, gave the reverbs a lush, dense sound and also helped avoid metallic resonances.

The 224 had a separate control unit for adjusting the reverb sound and could simulate chambers, plates and rooms. The later 224X and 224XL models came with the LARC (Lexicon Alphanumeric Remote Control) desktop control unit sporting six faders, a few buttons and a display.

Because of the limited computing power available in the late '70s, the reverb the 224 produced had a coarser sound than a plate or natural reverb, but it sounded wonderfully musical.

The much-loved Rich Plate and Rich Chamber presets can work beautifully on vocals, generating anything from a subtle halo to the long, lush trademark tail that has graced thousands of hit records.

DELAY: ECHOPLEX TAPE ECHO

The Echoplex was one of the first commercially successful tape-based echo devices, although many companies had come out with their own take on the concept in the late '50s and early '60s – not least the UK-based Watkins Copycat (originally valve, then transistor) and the Meazzi unit used by Hank Marvin.

These devices all work by recording a signal onto tape, then replaying it a short time later using one or more playback heads to create a series of delays that can be further extended by feeding some of the output signal from the playback heads back to the input.

Varying the tape speed varied the delay time on many models, where the tape was usually in the form of an endless loop to prevent it running out mid-performance.

The first Echoplex used valve circuitry, and, rather than a variable tape speed, employed a single moving playback head to allow the delay time to be changed.

In 1962 Echoplex machines were made available through distributor Maestro, the first model being the EP-1, though this designation was only applied when it was time to update the design. An upgraded

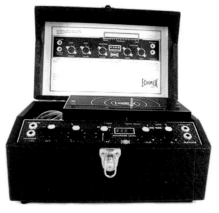

▲ The solid state Echoplex EP-3: An older (though not necessarily wiser) brother of the original valve tape-based echo device.

EP-2 followed and there are still some of these units around today where studios can afford to keep them maintained.

A solid state EP-3 (left) appeared at the start of the '70s and stayed in production until the early '90s, although true Echoplex aficionados prefer the warmer sound of the older valve units.

Maestro was eventually bought out by Norlin and in the mid '70s the company unveiled the EP-4 with added features in the form of LED level metering, tone controls, and a simple tape noise reduction system to reduce audible tape hiss.

Although they are no longer made, there are some very accurate digital emulations of the EchoPlex alongside other notable tape echo machines, such as the popular Roland RE-201 Space Echo.

Although perceived mainly as a guitar effect — and employed by guitarists from Brian May and Joe Satriani to Jimmy Page, David Gilmour and The Edge — tape delay has come to be viewed as a general studio effect, used in a range of situations.

PRO TIP

Tony Visconti once told me that he used an early Harmonizer to create the deep snare sound on David Bowie's 'Let's Dance', but when asked how he did it he'd send people in the wrong direction by telling them he had the tape op turn down the tape speed for each snare hit!

PROCESSOR: EVENTIDE HARMONIZER

Eventide started out building utilitarian tape locator devices in the corner of a New York studio before progressing to RAM-based digital delay devices. But it was engineer Tony Agnello's arrival at the company in the early '70s, and his subsequent work on what would eventually become the H910 Harmonizer, that would seal the company's reputation in the pro audio market.

The Harmonizer was a device that could change the pitch of an audio signal without changing its speed — something that, at the time, was all but impossible without introducing very obvious side effects.

The rapid success of this miraculous device enabled the company to develop the H949 model Harmonizer, which included adjustments for the creation of detuning effects, including cosmic delay, pitch-shifting and ultra-rich flanging. In addition to vocals, Harmonizers can be applied to guitar, pads, keyboards — even drums.

EXCITER: APHEX AURAL EXCITER

Like a surprising number of audio devices, the Aphex Aural Exciter was reportedly invented by accident.

Speaking with Aphex co-founder Marvin Caesar many years ago, he told me it all started with a wrongly wired valve amp kit. One channel worked properly but the other produced a nasty, thin distorted noise. However, when both signals were mixed, the result was an improvement in clarity and intelligibility.

What was going on here? It turns out that if you high-pass filter an audio signal then subject it to some pretty severe

▲ Classic processors: The Eventide Harmonizer (top) and the Aphex Aural Exciter (Type C). Both boxes are known for bestowing a certain sonic gold-dust on an audio signal — but are best used sparingly!

distortion and level compression, the newly generated harmonics can be mixed with the original clean signal in relatively small amounts to create a musically appealing sparkle. Realising they were onto something good, Aphex stuck the electronics in a single box and started renting it out to studios.

Originally Aphex only rented their magic box for $30 per minute – you couldn't buy one – but eventually a series of affordable Aural Exciter hardware went into production and Aphex became a recording hardware company, starting out with its Model B, then C.

A later version integrated a 'Big Bottom' circuit to add low end girth to a sound in addition to the familiar airiness up top. The Big Bottom process is based around a low-pass filter and compressor plus a little delay so that the effect is most noticeable on lower level signals but doesn't significantly increase the level of louder sounds. In many ways it replicates what many engineers now achieve using parallel compression.

Today, competing devices offer variations on the Aural Exciter theme and tend to be tagged psychoacoustic processors. Plug-ins are now available to replicate many of these processes while SPL's Vitalizer achieves similar results but by different means.

The musically-related harmonics generated by the Aural Exciter can be used to brighten up sounds that have little in the way of naturally occurring high-end harmonics. While EQ can only boost frequencies that already exist in a signal, the Aural Exciter can extend the high end of a sound by over an octave.

Used sparingly the Aural Exciter can do great things with vocals, as exemplified in The Buggles' 'Video Killed the Radio Star', but it is also useful for adding bite to dull snare drums or lifeless steel-strung acoustic guitars.

FUTURE CLASSICS

Sometimes it is difficult to think of our pro-audio future as little more than an ongoing attempt to recreate the past. But the passions of our forebears still exist, both among a generation of new software engineers and a small, but hugely talented, community of hardware manufacturers building high-end devices that are engineered to last for decades.

It's difficult to gamble on which of these will go on to become classics themselves, but I'd suggest the hall of fame might include units such as Manley's Massive Passive equaliser, Vic Keary's Thermionic Culture bird-inspired boxes, Tube-Tech's CL1B compressor, some of Empirical Labs' boxes and pretty much any of the units made by Summit Audio. TL Audio's valve mixer range is also a strong contender.

It remains to be seen whether any modern solid-state mixers will become desirably vintage, but already analogue mixers built in the latter part of the 20th century are in demand.

The market for hardware may continue to shrink as the quality of in-the-box processing improves, but for many engineers high-end analogue hardware will always hold an attraction. ●

▲ Future classics? (from top): Empirical Labs' Distressor, Thermionic Culture's Culture Vulture (Anniversary Edition), Summit Audio's Everest channel strip and Tube-Tech's CL 1B.

SECTION TWO
THE STUDIO AND ITS KIT

- The Studio and its Kit
- The Microphone
- Studio Acoustics

3
THE STUDIO AND ITS KIT

THE MIXER

Like reel-to-reel tapes and precariously balanced piles of floppy discs, mixing desks are now rarities in the smaller studio, their role and place usurped by the laptop or desktop computer. But their legacy survives in every DAW, and in every step of the mixing process.

Where recording is about capturing performances as audio signals, mixing is about treating, balancing and shaping these signals in all kinds of ways to create the final 'mixed' track. The mixer, whether real or virtual, is the nerve centre of the production process and is arguably the single most important piece of kit in the studio.

All multitrack recording software packages – from Logic to Ableton Live, Pro Tools to Reason, Cubase to Cakewalk – include virtual mixers that combine individual audio and instrument tracks into a single mix. In addition to combining signals, the mixer allows signals to be routed from one place to another and provides buses, insert points and aux sends that can be used to connect effects (like delays and reverb) and signal processors (like equalisers and compressors).

The majority of DAW mixers are based on the analogue console paradigm, as indeed are the mixers built into most hardware-based, hard disk or memory card multitrack recorders. Knowing how a mixer works, and understanding the geography of a mixer's signal flow, is fundamental to both recording and mixing.

MIC AND LINE LEVELS

A mixer's signal flow starts at the inputs. The first job of the mixer is to bring all signals up to its internal operating 'line' level (page 34).

In traditional mixers, the input channels usually accept both **mic** (very low level) and **line level** signals (higher level, of a few volts) with a **gain** knob to adjust the input level. Although electric guitars and basses produce outputs that are in the same range as line level signals, they require a different kind of input stage – specifically one with a **high input impedance**.

In the modern DAW these inputs are usually found on the soundcard or external audio interface as software has, by definition, no 'hard' physical inputs.

INSERT POINTS

Once the signal has been brought up to the correct level it can be routed in all kinds of ways within the mixer. Usually the first port of call is the channel's **insert** point.

An analogue mixer channel's insert point allows an external processor, like a compressor, limiter or noise gate, to be inserted into the signal path to process all of the signal passing through that particular channel or bus. It usually comes before the channel EQ section, although on some mixers it can be switched **pre- or post-EQ** (page 37).

When a connection is made at the insert point, the signal is routed via the external device and then back into the channel to continue its journey. When nothing is plugged into it, the signal is routed as normal.

DAW mixers also have insert points that allow software plug-ins to process the track's signal. Multiple plug-ins – from compressors to bit-crushers – can be inserted into the same channel, the signal passing through them in the order in which they are arranged.

> **THE MIXER IS THE NERVE CENTRE OF THE PRODUCTION PROCESS AND ARGUABLY THE SINGLE MOST IMPORTANT PIECE OF KIT IN THE STUDIO.**

As on larger analogue consoles, insert points are also available on the buses and master outputs to allow sub-groups and entire mixes to be processed using plug-ins.

EQ

The EQ (short for **equalisation**) section allows the signal to be tonally shaped in all kinds of ways using a variety of filters to remove low end or high end, and boost (or cut) chosen frequencies. EQ might be used to remove unnecessary low-end rumble from a drum part, or unpleasantly honky frequencies from a guitar line, or to reduce the harsh mids from a vocal.

EQUALISERS AND THEIR USES

The term equalisation – like so many terms in the pro audio world – is a throwback to the pioneering days of the telephone, when filter circuits were used to correct or 'equalise' tonal changes caused by losses in long telephone lines. Since then EQ has become an integral part of the creative process of making music.

In the studio, the term EQ relates to any device that selectively alters the relative levels of different parts of the audio spectrum. Early EQ circuits could only cut frequencies – not boost them – but today's active designs can boost and/or cut selected frequencies in a variety of surgical ways.

High cut and low cut filters: The simplest filters are the so-called **high cut** and **low cut filters** that we use to reduce the levels of extreme highs and lows in a signal.

A high cut (sometimes known as a **low pass** filter), passes frequencies below its **cutoff point** and attenuates (reduces)

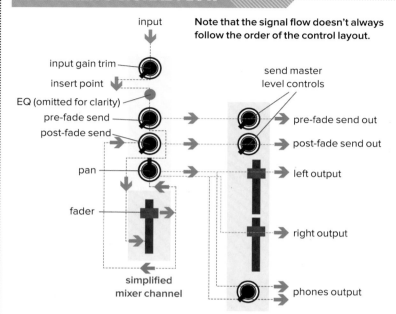

THE MIXER'S SIGNAL FLOW

input

Note that the signal flow doesn't always follow the order of the control layout.

input gain trim

insert point

EQ (omitted for clarity)

pre-fade send

post-fade send

pan

fader

send master level controls

pre-fade send out

post-fade send out

left output

right output

phones output

simplified mixer channel

simplified master section

Fig 1: Basic mixer signal flow diagram

those above. On the flip side, a low cut filter (sometimes called a **high pass** filter) passes frequencies above its cutoff point.

These filters can be designed with varying steepnesses of cutoff, usually expressed in terms of dBs/octave. The more dBs per octave, the steeper the filter. The most basic filter design has a 6dB per octave slope (sometimes called a first order filter). A second order filter has a slope of 12dB/octave, a third order filter 18dB/octave and so on.

Shelving equaliser: A more practical filter design when boosting is required is the **shelving equaliser**. Here the filter slope doesn't rise or fall indefinitely after the cutoff point but instead flattens out, its graph somewhat like a shelf or plateau (below right). There's a slope as the filter starts to come into operation, then it levels out so that all the low frequencies affected by, for example, a low shelving filter set at 100Hz (that is everything below 100Hz) will be cut or boosted by the same amount when you turn the EQ gain control, a typical range being around 12–18dB of cut or boost depending on the design.

Band-pass EQ: Cutting or boosting the extreme highs or lows is OK if you only need a simple bass or treble control, but we often need to be able to get at the mid range too. That's where the **band pass equaliser** comes in – a type of tuned filter offering both cut and boost that operates on a specific range of frequencies either side of its centre frequency. The range of frequencies affected is determined by the **bandwidth** of the filter, where the narrower the bandwidth, the tighter the focus of

the filter. Analogue filters can usually be tuned over a frequency range of at least 10:1. Digital filters can be designed to be adjusted over a much wider range.

The shape of the band-pass EQ curve is often likened to a bell. The maximum cut or boost happens in the centre of that bell. The term '**Q**' refers to the the tightness or focus of the filter. The higher a filter's Q, the narrower the filter band. Resonant synth filters and wah wah pedals have very high Qs, which give them their characteristically peaky sounds.

On some analogue mixers the mid filter operates at a fixed frequency, but in the DAW world pretty much everything can be adjusted: the frequency, the Q and the amount of cut and boost. If you can adjust all three, the equaliser is known as a **parametric EQ** (below). If you can only adjust the frequency it is known as **sweep EQ**.

HOW EQ LOOKS

(Left) Parametric EQ with a high Q boost. (Middle) Parametric EQ with a low Q boost. (Right) High shelf boost.

STUDIO ESSENTIALS: LEVELS

The term **line level** refers to the amplitude of an audio signal that conforms to a standard nominal level, usually -10dBv for consumer and semi-pro equipment, and +4dBu for professional equipment.

Most electronic keyboard instruments, hardware signal processors and sound modules provide a line level output, although some cheaper ones adopt the -10dBV standard rather than the +4dBu professional standard. However, the gain control on a typical line input has more than enough range to accommodate either.

Microphones generate weak electrical signals in comparison to line level, and can require up to 60dB of gain to bring them up to a mixer's normal operating level.

Amplification is performed by a pre-amp, either housed in the audio interface or as a dedicated external pre-amp. The pre-amp will also normally provide **phantom power** to connected capacitor mics (other than tube models), active ribbon mics or active DI boxes (**The Microphone, Chapter 4**).

Instrument levels are close to line levels, typically just a few volts maximum, but require a higher input **impedance** (page 335), typically around 1mOhm.

OPERATING LEVELS

As with all electronic circuitry, mixers are designed to work within a specific range of signal levels. The **low end** is determined by the **background electrical noise** of

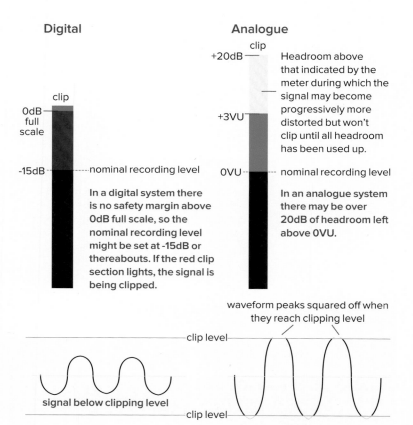

Digital

clip
0dB full scale
-15dB ---- nominal recording level

In a digital system there is no safety margin above 0dB full scale, so the nominal recording level might be set at -15dB or thereabouts. If the red clip section lights, the signal is being clipped.

Analogue

clip
+20dB ----
+3VU ----
0VU ---- nominal recording level

Headroom above that indicated by the meter during which the signal may become progressively more distorted but won't clip until all headroom has been used up.

In an analogue system there may be over 20dB of headroom left above 0VU.

waveform peaks squared off when they reach clipping level

clip level
signal below clipping level
clip level

clip level
signal above clipping level

the mixer. The **high end** is set by the level at which the system starts to seriously **distort the waveform** – a process known as **clipping**. Clipping is essentially a squaring off of the tops and bottoms of the waveform caused when the circuitry can't deliver any more level, regardless of how much the gain control is turned up (above).

EXPLAINED: DITHER

A mathematical process known as 'dither' is employed by algorithm designers to reduce low level distortion in digital systems at the expense of adding a little noise. This added noise is so trivially small as to be negligible.

With a correctly dithered signal, low level audio can be heard below the level of the noise, much as it can with analogue tape.

Without dither, the signal simply disappears when its level falls below that required to activate the least signifiant single digital bit.

Dithering is also used as the final process in mastering when a 24-bit signal is reduced to 16-bit for CD release.

What this means in practice is that when the input level gets too low, the sound is overwhelmed by the mixer's own background noise, while if it gets too high, it becomes distorted. In theory, the optimum performance is delivered when the signal level is **as high as possible but still with enough safety margin (or 'headroom') left over to handle unexpected signal peaks without clipping**.

Maintaining this optimum level — so that each piece of equipment or circuitry in the signal chain is working in its 'happy range' — is referred to as optimising the **gain structure** and applies equally to analogue and digital systems.

In the days of tape, compressors were often used during tracking to help keep the signal above the noise floor while controlling the peaks to reduce the risk of clipping. Digital technology offers such a wide dynamic range that we no longer need to compress signals on the way in for dynamic range reasons — although we may still choose to do so for artistic ones.

Analogue equipment can often handle signals that exceed the nominal operating level set by the manufacturer by 15dB or more before clipping occurs. If a mixer shows 0dB on the meters at a signal level of +4dBu, for example, the circuitry may not actually clip until the signal level reaches +19dBu or above.

Analogue circuitry can introduce a progressive increase in distortion above its nominal operating level and prior to clipping. This distortion may be used to inject a signal with analogue warmth. In extreme cases analogue gear can give useful results when driven all the way into clipping, for example, to sharpen up the sound of a snare drum.

Digital mixers have slightly different constraints from their analogue forebears. They have a wider dynamic range, allowing the engineer to leave around 12–18dB of headroom when recording without compromising on audio quality or risking excessive noise.

And where unduly low level signals suffer from noise in analogue mixers, the tradeoff in the digital domain is that very low level signals are represented by fewer 'bits' and so suffer more distortion instead of noise, although noise may be added from the analogue circuitry used prior to digital conversion.

Importantly, a digital meter shows no safety margin above the full scale line.

This is different from an analogue meter, which tends to have a nominal 'maximum level' marked as 0dB — but with space for the meter to move further. Indeed when recording in the analogue domain you can set the level so the signal peaks around the 0dB mark and know you still have some safety margin beyond.

With digital systems you have to decide for yourself how much safety margin to leave in order to avoid accidental clipping. Typically, a nominal maximum level of -15dB on the meter should leave around the same safety headroom as an analogue system provides.

Despite these technical differences, the same operational philosophy applies when recording digitally: the signal level should still be kept reasonably high while leaving a sensible safety margin of headroom to allow for unexpected signal peaks — like a particularly loud vocal phrase or drum fill.

A typical **parametric EQ** has around 15dB of cut or boost range, and features several bands of band pass filters that can work at the same time to cut or boost problem frequencies right across the audio spectrum.

▲ The Alesis DEQ230 2-Channel Digital Graphic EQ: note the EQ curve.

Graphic EQ: A **graphic equaliser** (above, right) is essentially a set of fixed frequency bell filters spaced at intervals across the audio spectrum, for example, one third of an octave apart. The bandwidth of each filter is usually set so that each filter merges smoothly with the one next to it .

The term 'graphic' comes about because the vertical sliders used to control the filter cut or boost form a curve that is essentially a graph of the overall EQ response. Live sound engineers like graphic equalisers as they are fast and intuitive to set up, whereas most studio engineers opt for more flexibile parametric EQ. You'll occasionally see high-end graphic EQs in mastering suites alongside parametrics.

EQ AND PHASE

All analogue EQs cause **phase changes** in the original signal when EQ is applied; some harmonics are delayed more than others according to their frequency. These phase shifts are often thought to contribute to the sound of a specific equaliser circuit.

Digital equalisers can be designed to emulate existing analogue hardware with all their imperfections and phase shifts. These are known as '**minimum phase**' designs. However, digital equalisers can also be designed to have a '**linear phase**' characteristic – where no phase shift is introduced between the low and high frequency harmonics of a signal when cut or boost is applied, something that is

virtually impossible with analogue circuitry. This allows them to change the spectral balance of a piece of audio without bringing about the additional changes in character caused by phase shifts.

For technical reasons, linear phase equalisers introduce a lot of delay and so increase the latency (page 42) of the DAW by a significant amount. They can also sound clinical – try one to see how its sound differs from that of a conventional minimum phase equaliser.

They can occasionally be useful for balancing the frequencies within a mix without changing the overall sound too much.

WHERE TO CUT AND WHERE TO BOOST

Listen to the results of narrow EQ cuts and boosts at different parts of the frequency spectrum and you'll soon realise that your ears interpret narrow deep cuts as sounding a lot less obvious than narrow high boosts. EQ boost is certainly useful, but it sounds most natural when the bandwidth is wide (low Q) and where the amount of boost is kept to a practical minimum.

It's also worth saying that if you feel something needs to be made brighter, before you reach for the high boost knob, try cutting the lows instead. This can have a similar effect.

You can sometimes help instruments sit better in a mix by using low and high-cut filters to '**bracket**' the sound, in other words,

EXPLAINED: MODELLED EQ

Some vintage equalisers have their own tonal character because of the shape of their EQ curves, and possibly because they also add subtle distortions.

Digital models of analogue gear often model the sound of the analogue signal path, including any distortion.

PRE- OR POST-FADE

The terms pre- and post-fade refer to functions that happen either before or after the level fader (Fig 1, page 32).

In the hardware world pre- and post-fade aux sends typically provide feeds to effects units (post-fade) and for performer monitoring purposes (pre-fade).

In a DAW mixer, the pre-fade aux sends are commonly used to feed outputs on the audio interface to set up individual monitor mixes for performers, while post-fade aux sends are used to feed effects or signal processing plug-ins (such as reverb) inserted on aux buses.

The reason effects are normally fed post-fade is to maintain the relative balance between dry signal and effect, meaning the effect level changes in relation to the track's volume when the fader is moved.

In most DAWs you can manually select whether effects sends are routed pre- or post-fade.

KIT LIST: SAVING

One practical benefit of using plug-in instruments is that when you save a song all settings for that project are saved, including all plug-in effect and instrument settings. This means that if you've tweaked a software synth to create the perfect bass sound then it will be recalled exactly as you set it next time you open the song.

remove some of the highs and lows so that what is left fits into a narrower part of the audio spectrum. High and low cut filters with an 18dB/octave slope are good for this.

A common technique to locate the parts of the spectrum that need tweaking is to set a parametric EQ to a Q of around 1 and turn the boost way up. Next sweep the frequency through the spectrum and listen as the filter picks out different things – some of them good, some less so. Keep the master volume low enough to avoid clipping when doing this as EQ boost can add a lot of gain. The areas that contain too much activity, and any rogue frequencies, should clearly stand out as you sweep through. Once you've found them you can apply however much cut is needed to tame them (Walkthrough, page 38).

All DAWs include at least one basic equaliser as standard, typically offering high and low pass filters and one or more parametric bands. Some offer more comprehensive EQ as standard, such as the Channel EQ in Logic Pro. There are also numerous third party plug-in equalisers that can be used as alternatives to your DAW's native EQ, depending on your needs and tastes. They are invariably used as inserts on the relevant channel or bus.

In the analogue world, a hardware mixer rarely offers the same number of equaliser controls, typically supplying just high and low shelving controls at fixed frequencies and one or two sweep mid controls where the frequency can be varied but the Q or bandwidth may be fixed. Yet what the analogue mixer omits in terms of quantity it often makes up for in quality – see Other kit in the recording chain, page 50.

VOLUME AND PAN

After EQ, the channel signal passes through a level control fader and a pan control. The **level fader** determines the volume of the signal. **Pan** determines how much signal is fed to the left mix bus and how much to the right, allowing sounds to be positioned anywhere between the left and right speakers. This creates the illusion of stereo placement, and although it is really just panned mono it is very effective.

A true stereo signal is recorded using two mics set up in a stereo array and then sent via a stereo DAW mixer channel (page 69). In an analogue mixer, a stereo signal requires two mono channels, one panned fully left and the other fully right.

Most contemporary mixes include a combination of true stereo sources and panned mono sources.

SOFTWARE INSTRUMENTS

In the analogue world there were no software instruments. In a DAW, software instruments are offered as plug-ins, usually via specially designated DAW instrument tracks. These are functionally the same

EQ 'boost and sweep' technique

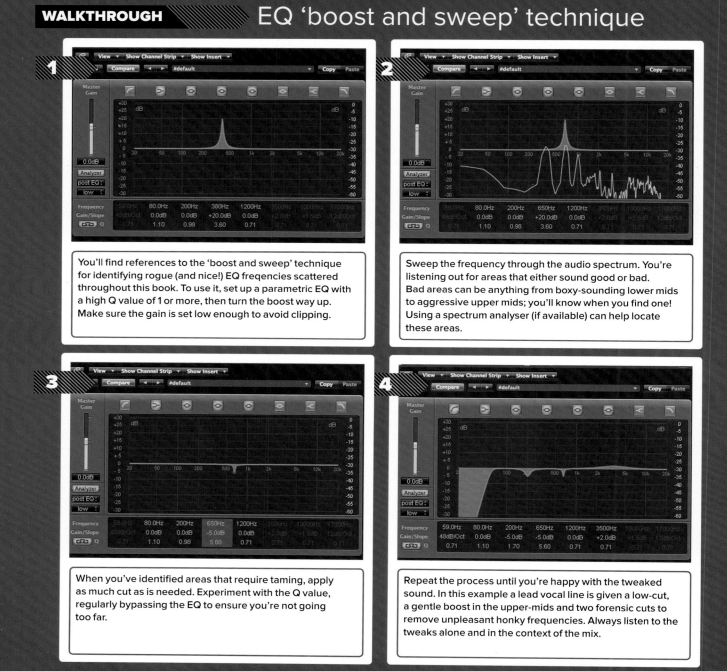

1 You'll find references to the 'boost and sweep' technique for identifying rogue (and nice!) EQ freqencies scattered throughout this book. To use it, set up a parametric EQ with a high Q value of 1 or more, then turn the boost way up. Make sure the gain is set low enough to avoid clipping.

2 Sweep the frequency through the audio spectrum. You're listening out for areas that either sound good or bad. Bad areas can be anything from boxy-sounding lower mids to aggressive upper mids; you'll know when you find one! Using a spectrum analyser (if available) can help locate these areas.

3 When you've identified areas that require taming, apply as much cut as is needed. Experiment with the Q value, regularly bypassing the EQ to ensure you're not going too far.

4 Repeat the process until you're happy with the tweaked sound. In this example a lead vocal line is given a low-cut, a gentle boost in the upper-mids and two forensic cuts to remove unpleasant honky frequencies. Always listen to the tweaks alone and in the context of the mix.

FOCUS: GROUPS

On a typical hardware mixer the group signals can be sent out separately and at the same time recombined by routing them to the main stereo mix.

The Group faders are then used to control the levels of individually submixed sections feeding the main mix. On the left, the signal flow is shown in mono for clarity.

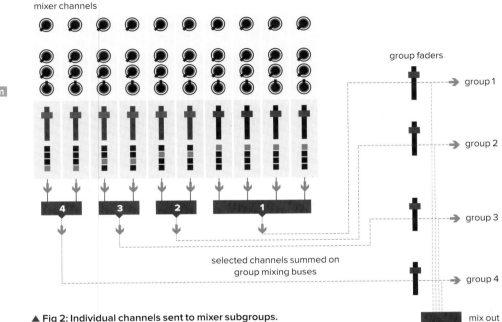

mixer channels

group faders

group 1

group 2

selected channels summed on group mixing buses

group 3

group 4

mix out

▲ Fig 2: Individual channels sent to mixer subgroups.

as normal audio tracks, except the input source is a software instrument rather than an audio input. Instrument tracks can be processed using effects plug-ins via insert points or aux sends in the same way as regular audio tracks.

Some software instruments, such as samplers, drum plug-ins or multi-timbral synths, include the option to route different outputs to different DAW mixer channels so that they can be processed separately. This is particularly useful in the case of drum plug-ins, where the kick drum and snare, for example, can be treated with different compressors, equalisers and so on.

BUSES

In a simple mixer all tracks feed the same stereo mix bus, on which all the channel outputs are combined according to

their individual fader settings. In more sophisticated mixers, and in most DAWs, there is more than one bus. The additional buses can be used either to **feed multiple outputs** on the audio interface or to **create subgroups** within the mix (Fig 2, above).

Subgroups are used to group related tracks, such as the those for the multiple mics used on a drum kit, on a single stereo mix bus.

There are two significant benefits of routing multiple mixer channels to a single mix bus:

› 1. A single bus fader can be used to control the volume of an entire group (like the drum kit) once it has been balanced, rather than having to readjust multiple channel faders every time you want to change the volume of the group.

❯ 2. You can process all tracks on the subgroup using the same set of plug-in processors like compressors or equalisers inserted into the bus insert points. In the example of a drum kit, you might choose to compress the drum bus to gel the different parts, and perhaps EQ it to reduce some of the highs across the whole kit. Bus mixing both simplifies mixing and allows the application of more sophisticated mixing techniqes like parallel bus compression.

Buses can also be used to feed **submixes** of DAW tracks **to different physical outputs** on the audio interface if necessary, for example, to set up monitor mixes or to route signals via external hardware.

USING EFFECTS: INSERTS AND AUX BUSES

There are two main ways that effects can be added to an audio channel using a hardware or DAW mixer. The simplest is via the channel **insert point**. The insert points on a hardware mixer add effects 'in-line', processing all of the signal rather than part of it. EQs, compressors, gates and pitch correctors are the most common insert processors, although there's no reason not to insert effects such as reverb if they're only needed on a single channel.

The second way to add effects is to use an **aux (auxiliary) bus**. The send takes a feed from the audio channel (post fader) and routes part of the signal to the aux bus determined by how high you turn up the channel's send control. You can send as much signal as you want to be effected and several different channels can be sent to the same bus, at different levels, to add differing amounts of the same effect. The key point to note here is that the dry channel signal still goes to the main mix as normal. The desired proportion of 'wet' effect signal is

then added to it. This is very different from a channel insert, where the entire channel signal is processed by whatever plug-in/s you place there.

The aux return on a typical analogue desk is essentially just another audio channel on the mixer, fed from the effect output and then returned to the main mix. In a DAW mixer this usually takes the form of a bus, fed from the aux sends assigned to it and with any required effects dropped into its insert points.

The main benefit of using effects on the bus is that multiple signals can be sent to the same bus for treatment, allowing every vocal track, for example, to share a common room reverb treatment. This sharing can help save CPU resources as well.

Note / Where an effect, such as reverb, is added via a channel insert point, the wet/dry balance is set using the mix control on the plug-in itself. By contrast, when the same effect is used in an aux send configuration, the effect is set to 100 per cent wet and the amount of effect added adjusted by means of the individual channel send control.

MUTE AND SOLO

A typical DAW mixer channel includes a **Channel On** or **Mute** switch and a **Solo** button.

Muting a channel stops you from hearing it in the mix without having to pull down the channel fader. Unmuting it brings it back in.

Solo leaves the solo'd channel audible but mutes all others, allowing a signal to be checked in isolation – useful for checking individual tracks. There are two common

insert points

aux sends

pan

peak hold

level fader

mute

solo

BACK TO THE FUTURE: THE RESURGENCE OF THE MIXING DESK

A number of DAW users still prefer the sound of a mix made using an analogue desk over one mixed in the box.

As long as you have an audio interface with enough analogue outputs it's easy enough to mix this way – it's just a case of routing the relevant DAW outputs (often subgroups you've already set up in the DAW to simplify the mix) from the interface to the relevant mixer inputs and then patching the mixer output back into a couple of spare interface inputs so that your final mix can be recorded on a new DAW track.

An alternative is to record the mix to an external hardware recorder, although there's little need for this any more.

Good used analogue consoles come up on eBay regularly at bargain prices and there's also a wide choice of small to medium-sized new consoles built and priced for the project studio market.

▲ The Black Lion Audio PM8 summing mixer.

While I would agree that the sonic character of an analogue mix is a little different from what you get mixing in the box (and mixing externally makes it much easier to patch in your favourite hardware processing boxes), the downside of using an external mixer – aside from the size – is that it is considerably more difficult to recall the individual settings used on a project if you need to revisit it at a later date, especially if you have hardware processors hooked up to the mixer as well. When working on a number of projects at once this downside can become a serious stumbling block.

A halfway house approach is to use an external **summing mixer**, which is essentially a simplified mixer designed only to adjust the levels and pan positions of the sources feeding it before combining them.

This can produce a nicer sounding mix than mixing in the box – although the jury is still out on why this should be.

All effects and processors in a summed mix are normally still applied using plug-ins, making the session easier to keep track of.

Solo modes, PFL and Solo In Place:

> **PFL** solos the channel signal before the fader so that you can hear the channel signal when solo'd even though the channel fader may be turned right down.

> **Solo In Place**: the most common mode used in DAW mixers. Solos the channel signal after the fader so that the signal is heard at the level it would be in the mix.

You may also find a **Solo Safe** function that allows certain channels to remain audible even when Solo is activated. This is useful when you want to solo a channel but still need to hear the effects being fed from it.

MASTER CHANNEL/S
The final stage in the mixer is the master channel/s. While many analogue mixers

have a busy master section containing everything that doesn't fit comfortably elsewhere – like talkback mics and monitor controls – the DAW world tends to be a little tidier, often with nothing but a stereo output channel offering the ability for the producer to add plug-ins to effect the master bus. Aux return buses usually appear alongside, as do any additional output buses that have been set up to feed monitor mixes or external hardware.

USING HARDWARE WITH SOFTWARE
Although plug-ins replicate almost every studio function, many producers still choose to incorporate at least some outboard kit into their setup. The only precondition for doing so (other than when routing the signal through hardware processors prior to recording them) is

having enough spare inputs and outputs on the audio interface to handle the extra connections.

Using outboard for an insert effect:
Set up a physical output from the audio interface to feed the hardware device and route the desired audio channel to that output. The output from the device is then routed back into a spare interface input which you route back into the main DAW mix. This does roughly the same job as a traditional insert point, although the hardware actually comes after the channel fader rather than before it as with a conventional insert point. Some DAWs make this even easier by providing a type of dummy insert plug-in that handles the routing to and from the interface outputs of your choice. Once you load this plug-in, the signal is automatically routed via the appointed DAW ins and outs and through the connected hardware.

Using outboard for an aux bus effect:
To set up an external send effect, such as a reverb unit, you need to set up a physical interface output fed from a post-fade aux send bus. The rest of the setup is the same as before – feeding the reverb's output to an interface input routed back into the main DAW mix. If the reverb is mono-in, stereo-out, then the outputs from the reverb unit, which should be set to 100 per cent effect, will need to feed two inputs (an odd/even numbered pair) on the audio interface.

The inherent problem with using hardware kit in a software environment is that bugbear of music computer users everywhere – **latency** (below), which may be negligible with effects such as reverb or echo (which already incorporate a lot of delay) but that can cause problems where sample accuracy is required, such as when

THE 'L' WORD – LATENCY

You won't get far in computer recording before coming across the term latency.

A modern computer is a multitasking device. It operates rather like a team of builders where the guy mixing the cement makes a bit extra, then goes off for an hour or two to finish a previous job or to deliver an estimate while hoping his mate doesn't run out of cement.

Because computers multitask, they sort out their tasks into little blocks and do a bit of each job before moving on to the next. Data buffers, the software equivalent of the builder's cement mixer, are used to store up data in advance so that the flow doesn't stop while the computer is attending to something else, such as accessing a hard drive or redrawing a screen.

When applied to audio, this means that anything you feed into the computer will emerge from it after a short time delay

related to the size of the data buffer (usually a few thousandths of a second), and while a modern system can run with a very small delay, it is always present to some extent.

This delay is what we refer to when we speak of latency, and it can be adjusted in your DAW's settings by choosing a larger or smaller data buffer size.

A **smaller buffer** means less delay, but when the computer is working hard it increases the risk of **audio glitches** if the computer can't keep up. The analogy for this situation would be a fast bricklayer teamed with a small cement mixer.

Latency only becomes a problem when the physical and the digital worlds need to interact – for example when overdubbing parts while monitoring the performance – because although what you record is kept in sync with the tracks already recorded,

the part you're overdubbing will be heard coming back over the speakers or headphones after the latency delay, which – if significant – can put a performer off playing or singing in time.

Even a few milliseconds is enough to upset some performers, although the majority of musicians can live with anything up to 10ms.

DIRECT MONITORING
To get around this problem, some audio interfaces provide what is known as Latency-Free or Direct Hardware Monitoring (see Walkthrough, right).

This work-around means that when recording a new part, the audio is sent to the DAW in the normal way, while the voice or instrument is routed directly to the headphones for monitoring purposes, bypassing the computer altogether.

Direct monitoring with DAW reverb

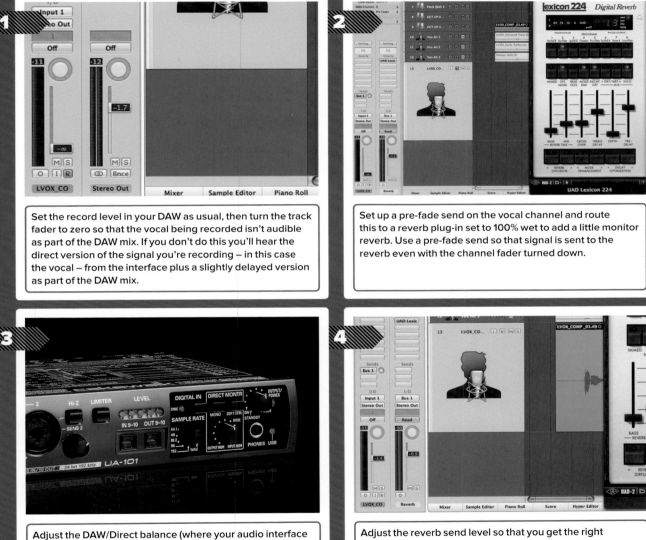

1 Set the record level in your DAW as usual, then turn the track fader to zero so that the vocal being recorded isn't audible as part of the DAW mix. If you don't do this you'll hear the direct version of the signal you're recording – in this case the vocal – from the interface plus a slightly delayed version as part of the DAW mix.

2 Set up a pre-fade send on the vocal channel and route this to a reverb plug-in set to 100% wet to add a little monitor reverb. Use a pre-fade send so that signal is sent to the reverb even with the channel fader turned down.

3 Adjust the DAW/Direct balance (where your audio interface offers this facility) so you hear the right mix of vocal and reverb DAW mix in the cans.

4 Adjust the reverb send level so that you get the right amount of reverb. Record the track as normal, then bring the track fader back up so you can hear what you've recorded when you play it back. The temporary 'comfort reverb' send can then be switched to post-fade for mixing or simply bypassed.

adding a processed and unprocessed signal as with parallel compression.

If you want to use external processors as inserts then you need to check that your DAW hasn't introduced any appreciable delay. The easiest way to do this is to record the processed track alongside the original, then zoom in on the waveform displays to see that they are aligned. Invariably the track processed via the external analogue gear will be delayed very slightly. If so, simply shift the track to line it up with the original.

When using parallel compression (page 172) or another technique that requires a processed signal to be added to the original dry sound, **it is important that the compressed track be lined up perfectly** (accurate to within a single sample) **with the original**, otherwise colouration caused by phase differences will occur.

Tip / One surefire way of increasing the DAW's latency is to run a load of CPU-intensive effects in a project. As a consequence it is good practice when recording or overdubbing to bypass as many of these effects as you can. Logic has a 'low latency button' that bypasses the worst offenders for you.

Tip / If you use a mixer as a mic pre-amp, you can usually hook up a hardware effects unit (or use a mixer with built-in effects) and use that to add comfort reverb to the headphone mix. This reverb is not normally recorded into the DAW: you need the freedom to choose the right type and amount of reverb once the track is ready to mix. The track direct output or the pre-fade aux send can be used to create a recording feed free from effects.

RECORDING THE MIX

In the all-analogue world a second tape machine or digital recorder was required to record the final stereo mix, but in DAW land the most common approach is to allow the final mix to be created in the computer and stored as a new audio file, usually by way of a **Bounce** command that starts the process.

Bouncing can be done in real time – where you can listen to the song as it mixes – or offline to save time.

If **external hardware processors** or instruments are being used in the mix, this 'bounce' has to happen in real time. If, on the other hand, you want to process the entire mix via external hardware by passing it through a good compressor and maybe an EQ, then the outputs from the external processing chain must be fed back into the audio interface to be recorded on a new stereo track. In this scenario you simply play the mix while recording onto a new stereo mix track rather than using the Bounce function.

BASIC STUDIO HARDWARE

It's all too easy to think of the modern studio as a computer-based DAW and not much more. But even the most basic setup will include speakers and/or headphones for monitoring, maybe a music keyboard and potentially a mic or two. Other niceties include a DI box, a physical control surface and a good seat – it all depends on your needs and budget (see Areas for Investment, page 57).

An early essential is a suitable **audio interface** – the physical interface between the analogue and digital worlds. Which one you choose depends on your requirements. The most important consideration is the

THE PRICE YOU PAY FOR AN AUDIO INTERFACE FOLLOWS THE LAW OF DIMINISHING RETURNS: THE MORE YOU PAY, THE SMALLER THE IMPROVEMENTS GET BETWEEN SUCCESSIVE MODELS.

▲ The MOTU 896mk3
FireWire audio interface.

number of physical inputs and outputs, both analogue and digital. The home-based dance producer who has no intention of recording won't need many inputs or outputs (until they start investing in outboard!), while those planning on recording full bands will need a good number of both; inputs to record using multiple mics at once, and outputs to allow the setting up of different headphone balances.

If you're a guitar player a combined interface/guitar pre-amp device, such as the Line 6 POD or Toneport series of devices may be more appropriate.

Another alternative is to use one of the growing range of analogue or digital hardware mixers that have in-built digital connectivity for recording. Some keyboard workstations also feature audio interfacing capabilities, as do USB mics.

Note / While your computer may come with a built-in sound card, this is unlikely to give as good a result as a dedicated external audio interface.

Note 2 / Not all interfaces offer mic inputs on all channels and some may be line only (page 34). Ensure you have enough mic inputs for your needs, although a stand-alone pre-amp can always be plugged into the line input of an audio interface – a good option if you have an especially nice mic pre-amp you like to use. If the pre-amp has a balanced XLR line output you may need to buy an adaptor cable to convert

it to a balanced jack as that's what most interfaces use for their line inputs.

Note 3 / Not all audio interfaces are built equal. High-end interfaces are different beasts from budget ones – providing generally clearer separation, lower noise levels and more accurate A/D conversion. Although interfaces are some of the least sexy pieces of kit in the studio, money invested in a good quality one is generally money well spent. That said, the price you pay follows the law of diminishing returns: the more you pay, the smaller the improvements get between successive models. In a typical project studio a mid-priced interface from the likes of MOTU (above left), Presonus, M-Audio or RME is likely to be perfectly adequate and you'll almost certainly find that you have weaker links elsewhere in the recording chain.

DI BOXES
A DI (Direct Inject) box serves two purposes:

❯ Firstly, it has an **input impedance suited to specific signal sources**, where the active type usually has a high input impedance to match electric guitars and basses.

❯ Secondly, it offers **a balanced output – usually a balanced XLR – that connects directly to the mic input of a mixer or mic pre-amp**. It is commonly used to connect electric guitars and basses to an audio interface's mic input, although it can also be used to run other line level signals over long distances.

The DI box can be thought of an essential translation device between the electric guitar/bass and the audio interface, matching the impedance between the two and converting the level to match the requirements of a mic input stage.

▲ The Meridian NDI100
Active DI Box: note the
different input options.

The majority of active DI boxes are run on standard phantom power (page 63), although some also run on 9 volt batteries. Those designed for use with instruments usually include a link jack so that the input signal can be split to feed both the DI box and a local guitar amp.

In addition to their connectivity benefits, most DI boxes include a ground lift switch, which can help solve ground loop hum problems in some situations.

SPEAKERS AND HEADPHONES

High quality headphones are good for working late at night when you don't want to upset the neighbours / significant other. They can also help you pick out problems in a mix – they're good on detail – that you might otherwise miss when listening on speakers (page 288).

But it is rarely a good idea to mix entirely on headphones. Stereo imaging sounds very different on headphones than it does on speakers. You may also find that the bass end on headphones varies according to how the headphones fit your ears.

As a general rule use **open or semi-open back phones for mixing**, where the low end is likely to be more accurate, and **fully enclosed headphones for recording**, as they allow less sound to bleed into the mic.

Mixing proper, though, is the domain of the studio **speaker**.

Hi-fi speakers are generally designed to flatter the music fed to them, and therefore make poor choices for studio monitors. The same is true of computer speakers, which are generally engineered to make games sound exciting.

Studio speakers (or **monitors**), on the other hand, are generally designed to be as accurate (and unforgiving!) as possible to give you a true picture of the mix and create a master that sounds acceptable on other sound systems; if the mix is bad, you need a speaker that will let you know.

If the speakers you mix with aren't accurate, you can end up making adjustments to iron out perceived problems in the mix that are actually problems caused by the speakers. If your speakers produce too much low end, for example, it's natural to compensate by reducing the amount of low end in the mix. The result is a mix that sounds bass-light when played back on more accurate systems (page 79).

When investing in speakers you have two choices: either **passive speakers**, that team up with a suitable hi-fi amp; or **active speakers** that have their own built-in amps. My preference is active models: they take the guesswork out of choosing a suitable amp, and some form of driver protection is also built in. But if you already have a good quality, reasonably powerful hi-fi amp, then by all means consider passives.

When deciding what speakers to buy, the main consideration – other than an accurate sound – is how much bass extension they have. As a rule, bigger monitors reproduce lower frequencies more efficiently. Never buy anything that is too big for the room or you'll invite bass problems (page 84). For a typical domestic room used as a studio, speakers that have a main driver of between 5–8 inches in diameter is fine.

Ensuring the monitors sound as they should is largely down to the acoustics of the room and where you place the monitors in that room (page 87).

▲ KRK's ROKIT 8 monitors: highly regarded speakers for the project studio.

It helps to have a pair of cheap, nasty 'grot-box' consumer speakers set up alongside your good monitors so you can double-check how a mix might sound on the radio and other small consumer systems.

/ **Know speakers. Studio Acoustics, Chapter 5.**

▲ The Mackie Big Knob Studio Command System: includes talkback function.

MICROPHONES

The microphone captures the sound of the guitar, singer, drummer or kazoo player and translates it into an electrical signal to feed the audio interface.

While you can record almost anything using a cheap **dynamic mic**, such as the ever-popular Shure SM58 (left), you won't always get the best possible results.

This kind of mic is designed to help the human voice project in the upper mid-range but its moving-coil mechanism struggles to capture high frequencies, so things like acoustic guitar recordings (and the high end of vocals) may lack sparkle.

To capture the entire audio spectrum you need a **capacitor mic**. At one time these were priced out of the budget of many project studio owners. However, thanks to the increasing size of the project studio market and a downward pressure on prices brought about by overseas manufacturing, there is now a wide choice of high-end capacitor mics available at ever more affordable prices.

Selecting the right mic for the job and putting it in the right place can make all the difference between an OK recording and a great one.

/ **Know mics. The Microphone, Chapter 4.**

MONITOR CONTROLLER

If you have active speakers, you need a physical control to turn the volume up or down. While you can often adjust the volume in the DAW, this isn't the best way and you could be in for some loud bangs and pops if the software crashes while the speakers are connected.

Some audio interfaces include a physical volume control, in which case you can use that. Otherwise you need a desktop monitor control box with a volume control installed between the DAW output and the speakers.

While there are some products that are as simple as a volume knob mounted on a box, the majority also include a headphones output with its own level control and a switch to allow the engineer to choose between two or three different sound sources, such as the DAW, an mp3 player, CD player and so on. They may also offer the option of switching between two or three sets of speakers: from your main studio monitors, through hi-fi style speakers to a small radio.

More sophisticated monitor controllers, such as the Mackie Big Knob (above), also include a **talkback mic** and talkback button so that you can interrupt the headphone feed to the musicians to pass on instructions.

Talkback is incredibly useful where you have the studio in one room (the control room) and the performers in a second one (the live room). With this kind of setup you need some way of allowing communication between both rooms, a function covered by talkback.

In two-room setups you also need to budget for a **headphone amp** for the live room to allow the musicians to hear each other as well as the output from the DAW.

The simplest type of headphone amp has two or more headphone outputs, each with its own volume control. If you have a small mixer that you use for live work you could press that into service as a monitor controller and headphone amp instead.

More sophisticated headphone amps have separate inputs for each performer so that each can have their own monitor mix. This is a little more complicated to set up as you need to create the monitor mixes in the DAW and send each to a separate physical output of the audio interface.

Setting up the different monitor mixes is done by using different pre-fade sends routed to different buses that are then routed to different interface outputs (Walkthrough, page 103).

DAW CONTROLLER

While you can operate a DAW using nothing more than a mouse and get perfectly good results, it can be hard on the hand and wrist, with a risk of repetitive strain injury in the long-term. It is also less than ideal creatively, lacking the hands-on feel associated with the mixer faders and knobs of old.

This hands-on feel can be recaptured using a **hardware control surface**. Many

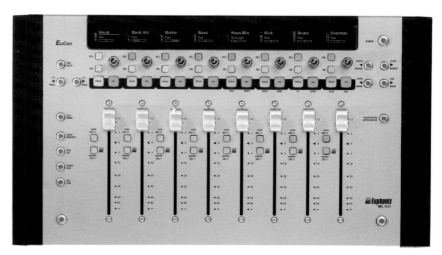

▲ The Avid Artist Mix: Eight channel control surface.

people find that a control surface improves workflow and makes the recording and mixing process quicker and more enjoyable.

The simplest DAW controllers are around the size of a paperback book and feature a single moving fader that follows the channel selected in the DAW. Most also include a small LCD display, transport buttons similar to those on a tape recorder and a few other controls to access key features and move the playback position in the song.

The next step up is a controller with multiple faders that allow several channels to be adjusted at the same time. It may also have rotary controls for altering pan, EQ and plug-in settings, as well as Mute and Solo buttons. These more expensive controllers have the feel of a traditional mixer, with the Mackie Control and Avid (formerly Euphonix) Artist Series (above) probably the best-known.

At the top of the range are large-scale surfaces such as Avid's D-Control, or mixing consoles – usually digital – that also double as DAW controllers. These are most

QUICK TIP

A good control surface has motorised faders that follow the on-screen fader movements when automation is being played back. The same faders may also be used to record new automation.

often found in professional studio facilities, their price point pushing them out of reach of most project studio owners.

MUSIC KEYBOARD

Even if you're not a natural keyboard player, some form of music keyboard is useful for tapping in drum rhythms and playing simple melody lines. Smaller portable keyboards connect via MIDI and/or USB and can be all you need to provide at least one tactile input and a creative springboard to jot down musical ideas.

Keyboards come in all sizes, from a couple of octaves to full 88-note piano scale. Most budget models have simple sprung keys like an organ. They won't satisfy a concert pianist, but if you want the feel of a traditional weighted piano keyboard you can expect to pay a lot more for it.

Any model worth having will be velocity sensitive, allowing you to produce louder sounds by pressing the keys harder. It might also include physical control levers or wheels for controlling pitch bend and vibrato depth.

The majority of controller keyboards are 'dumb' – that is to say they produce no sound – but in the era of the software instrument that's not a problem; the keyboard is only used to generate MIDI data that controls 'virtual' plug-in instruments within the DAW.

THE PRE-AMP

While a theoretically perfect mic pre-amp adds nothing but gain, many of the vintage pre-amps sought after today did add some tonal coloration – usually as a result of the technology used at the time rather than as a deliberate design feature.

▼ M-Audio Oxygen 8 V2 MIDI Controller Keyboard.

This colouration comes mainly from the valve circuitry and the magnetic properties of the audio transformers. Both valves and transformers are slightly non-linear when pushed hard, introducing distortions of a type that many people find pleasing.

A typical valve product will add density to the lower end of a signal and also keep the high-end detail sounding smooth. The Neve 1081 is a classic example, originally a combined mic pre-amp and equaliser but now re-released as the 1073DPA mic pre-amp without the EQ section (above).

Designs by Telefunken, Siemens and Neumann are also treasured for their slightly larger-than-life sound, but a genuine vintage pre-amp can be expensive to maintain and replacement valves may be difficult (and expensive) to find.

Modern valve mic pre-amps are available, some at a much lower cost. Companies such as Manley, Summit and Tube-Tech build excellent valve-based pre-amps and processors, although they tend to be rather expensive in comparison with solid-state designs. A less costly approach is to choose a pre-amp that uses hybrid valve/solid-state circuitry; SPL's surprisingly inexpensive Gold Mic, for example, delivers excellent results.

Beware of budget valve products that run from low voltage power adaptors though, as this often means the valves are run at lower than their normal operating voltage. While they will still work, they won't have the same sonic characteristics as a valve run from the correct high voltage source. Also beware of valve pre-amps that are specifically designed to add distortion. The best valve mic pre-amps had very subtle distortion characteristics and it is these that created the magic.

Of course a pre-amp doesn't have to be based around valves to sound good. Indeed combining a valve mic with a valve pre-amp might result in too much sonic colouration. There are numerous excellent solid state designs around and many engineers prefer them specifically because they don't colour the sound – Grace Designs and Broadhurst Gardens both build pre-amps that are valued for their clarity and transparency. As with almost everything in the wider music and mixing world, the choice of pre-amp ultimately comes down to artistic preference.

OTHER KIT IN THE RECORDING CHAIN: EQUALISERS, COMPRESSORS AND BEYOND

Other than pre-amps, **compressors** and **equalisers** are the most likely additions to the recording chain, especially if the engineer has access to classic hardware units – like those profiled in Classic Kit, Chapter 2 – that they feel don't have acceptable software equivalents.

Modern high-end hardware **EQ** units such as those from Manley, Tube-Tech and Summit are deservedly popular but there are also numerous new models that attempt to clone 'out-of-copyright' vintage hardware – with a host of Pultec and Neve derivatives available.

Equalisers can sound very different from each other for many reasons. Some even change the character of a sound fed through them slightly when their controls are flat.

Those built around valves and transformers introduce the same subtle distortions as valve pre-amps, most notably a tendency to compress and round off signal peaks.

The shape and steepness of their EQ curves also affects the sound, as any analogue EQ circuitry also introduces complex phase shifts that can be pleasing to our ears. Indeed it's the shapes of these curves that make the really prized classics – like the Pultec (page 24) – what they are.

A good equaliser will make a useful difference even if you only apply one dB or less of boost. The highs will also still sound smooth when boosted. By contrast, a cheaply-designed equaliser may leave you with flabby sounding lows and harsh highs.

Compression was used extensively when recording to tape. Indeed it was almost essential, as the levelling effect of the compressor helped keep the signal level above the noise floor while preventing signal peaks pushing the meters too far into the red (pages 34–35).

Today, with the much lower noise floor of digital recording, we routinely leave both EQ and compression to the mixing stage where plug-ins take the place of hardware, but there's no denying that certain pieces of hardware, used carefully, produce results that are difficult – if not impossible – to recreate exactly using plug-ins.

Although the concept of a compressor is simple – a device that adjusts the gain according to the incoming signal level – there are many elements that can affect the subjective sound, including the shape of the attack and release curves, distortion introduced by the gain control element, non-linearities in the compression curve

▲ Potential candidates for the recording chain: The Manley Massive Passive EQ (top) and LA-2A compressor / limiter.

itself and any valves and transformers in the audio path. A FET compressor, such as the UA 1176 for example (page 23), distorts in a slightly different way to a valve compressor, while opto designs, such as the LA-2A (page 22) and LA-3A, which rely on a lamp and photocell, introduce some very strange distortion and linearity artefacts that are difficult to model in software but which are essential to their unique sound. Then there are VCA compressors, the best of which control the signal level while introducing extremely low levels of distortion.

> "THE BEST SOFTWARE COMPRESSORS NOW COME SO CLOSE TO THEIR HARDWARE COUNTERPARTS THAT ANY REMAINING DIFFERENCES ARE NOT GOING TO AFFECT RECORD SALES."

As with equalisers, pro engineers tend to have a go-to rack of their favourite compressors that they may employ during tracking. By all means try one if you're lucky enough to have one around, although it's worth repeating my earlier warning that **if you record via any form of hardware processing, take great care not to over-process the signal or you may not be able to get the part sounding right in the final mix**. You can always add a little more EQ or compression using plug-ins if you need to, but you can never undo the original processing if you apply it too heavily prior to recording.

In my view, the best software compressors now come so close to their hardware counterparts that any remaining differences are not going to affect record sales. Which is not to devalue the sound of the classics — some of them will always merit the hype.

WIRING

Even a minimalist studio has its fair share of cables. Getting this wiring – either electrical or audio – wrong can result in buzzes and hums that, unless remedied, may render a studio setup useless. Fortunately most common problems are relatively easily solved, and a few good-practice tips should help keep you out of trouble:

> Where possible, **feed all recording gear from a single power socket** (or double wall socket) using distribution blocks to fan out the power feeds from that single initial point. A typical home studio requires relatively little current so overloading the socket shouldn't be an issue. A surprising number of hum problems are solved by following this simple step.

> **Avoid sharing your studio equipment with a ring main that has anything on it that generates electrical noise,** such as a fridge, freezer or other similar appliance.

> **Keep mains cables away from signal cables,** especially unbalanced cables such as guitar leads. You should also **use balanced leads to connect any equipment that is designed for balanced operation**. While I've never experienced any discernible benefit from using expensive, exotic studio cables over cheaper ones (other than guitar cables, which do sound slightly different), **avoid the cheapest cables**; they are often fitted with cheap connectors that are more likely to fail than decent ones. Cheaper cables may also be less effective at screening interference.

> If you've ever tried to record an electric guitar while sitting in front of a laptop, you've probably experienced buzz. Buzz arises when sensitive audio equipment is placed too close to computer hardware or lighting dimmers. Buzz problems can only be solved by **replacing dimmers with low interference types** (or better, no dimmers at all!) and by **keeping audio gear away from the source of interference**.

If you can hear a hum from your monitors (and I mean hum, not buzz!), then you may be suffering from a problem known as a 'ground loop'.

A ground loop occurs when different pieces of interconnected equipment grounded by two or more paths (for example, the signal cable screen and the mains cable ground) result in a mains frequency hum being introduced onto the audio signal ground conductor. If you were to draw out the wiring you'd see that the mains ground and the signal ground form a closed loop; it is this loop that picks up electromagnetic hum from transformers and nearby mains wiring.

Well-designed equipment connected via balanced cables rarely suffers from ground loops, but if you do find yourself with a ground loop hum, start by searching soundonsound.com for articles on tracing and curing the problem. The solution sometimes requires resorting to **specially wired signal cables**, especially when an unbalanced signal source needs to feed into something with a balanced input. If you find yourself in this situation, learning to solder can save you a fortune. If you don't know how to solder, check out YouTube for many videos on the subject.

Warning / Although a ground loop can sometimes be cured by disconnecting a mains ground, **don't be tempted to do this as there could be adverse safety implications**. Fix ground loops by modifying audio wiring, **not the mains wiring**.

BALANCED WIRING

Because mics produce relatively small output signals and can be connected via cables many metres in length, they are especially susceptible to external noise.

GOING TO GROUND

While having too many grounds in a system can aggravate ground-loop hum, having no grounds at all – a situation you may find yourself in if all your studio gear runs from external power adaptors – is also a recipe for hum. This is increasingly likely in the modern studio, where everything from laptops to guitar pre-amps and HD recorders seem to come with their own adaptors.

You must have at least one grounded device in the system to keep hum at bay, especially when recording electric guitar via a DI pre-amp such as a Line 6 POD, which also uses an external power supply.

A ground wire connecting one of the metal parts of your audio interface case to the metal case of another item that you know is grounded, such as the metal case of a hi-fi system, should cure the problem.

Unless you know what you're doing, get a qualified electrician to do the job.

This makes them ideal candidates for **balanced wiring**, a type of connection designed to minimise electromagnetic interference.

Balanced wiring is a three-wire system, which in the context of audio cables means a screened cable with two cores and a conductive outer sleeve or sheath to provide an electrostatic screen. The two inner cores, if fed from a balanced device, carry the same electrical signal as each other. The signal fed to one of the cores, usually known as the 'cold', has its signal polarity inverted with respect to the other conductor, which is referred to as 'hot'.

The **XLR connector** wiring standard adopted by the vast majority of pro-audio equipment specifies that pin one is ground, which is what we connect to the screen. Pin two is hot and pin three is cold. Where the balanced signal travels along a **jack cable**, this must again have three conductors and be fitted with TRS jacks (tip, ring, sleeve) of the type often also used on stereo headphones.

tip   ring   sleeve

▲ A jack cable with a TRS jack (above) and (below) a cable fitted with XLR connectors at both ends.

Why this hot/cold arrangement? Any interference making it through the outer screen will affect the hot and cold signal cores equally as they are in very close proximity to each other. To exploit this, the receiving piece of equipment inverts the cold signal to put it back in phase with the hot signal, but in doing so it also inverts the polarity of any interference picked up by the cold conductor. The outcome of this simple but effective strategy is that when the hot signal is recombined with an inverted version of the cold signal, the wanted signal doubles in level but the interference components cancel each other out.

DC blocking filters built into the devices at either end of the cable mean that 48v phantom power can be applied to both cores without affecting the audio signal. It is this DC voltage that is separated out in the mic (or active DI box) to power the internal electronics.

PATCHBAYS

Back when recording studios were centred around analogue mixers and multitrack tape recorders with racks of outboard gear, patchbays – often housed on or near the mixing desk – were essential components, allowing the engineer to connect the various pieces of gear in different orders for different projects without endlessly reaching behind equipment with a torch to hunt for and re-arrange leads. Patchbays can make life significantly easier in the studio, saving time and muscle strains.

Put simply, a patchbay is a single point where the inputs and outputs of the main pieces of equipment are located on one central panel. Patchbays are most commonly used to gain access to console line inputs, aux sends and returns, equipment inputs and outputs and mixer insert points, but can be adapted to access just about any line-level input or output. To connect and route audio within the patchbay the engineer uses short patch cables, which can be re-arranged to route audio signals in all kinds of ways.

While a typical DAW-based system no longer requires the large, complex patching systems of old, some form of patchbay can still be very useful where the project studio has more than a few pieces of outboard equipment – from compressors and reverb units to mixers – that get regular use.

Professional analogue patchbays generally use small Bantam jack plugs and sockets to conserve space.

Patchbays designed for the smaller studio tend to use TRS quarter inch jacks that carry both balanced and unbalanced signals. They are more convenient, as quarter inch jacks are also the standard connectors used for most guitars, synths, headphone amps and many outboard boxes, allowing them to be plugged directly into the front of the patchbay where necessary.

A typical patchbay follows the 19-inch rack-mountable 1U panel format, hosting two rows of either 16 or 24 sockets per row. Each socket on the top row is paired with the socket below it. Convention dictates that inputs go in on the bottom row. Outputs come out on top.

Although patchbays are relatively simple to set up, it is important to grasp the concept of **normalised connections** before you do so.

A mixer insert point is a good example of a normalised connection. The insert point features contacts within the socket that complete the signal path when nothing is plugged in. When an insert cable is plugged in however, the path is broken and rerouted through a piece of external hardware via the insert cable.

Mixer insert points that use a single **TRS jack** to carry both the insert send and return signal (common with smaller mixers) require a **Y cable** (right) to split the TRS jack into two mono jacks, one the send, the other the return. This type of connection is unbalanced. You can buy Y cables if you don't want to make your own.

A commonly adopted system in patchbay construction is to have each pair of sockets mounted on its own separate circuit board (PCB), one above the other. Another pair of sockets at the back carry the rear connections, which link to the various pieces of hardware you need to access. The simplest designs allow individual circuit boards to be removed, reversed and replaced so that either pair of sockets can be at the front.

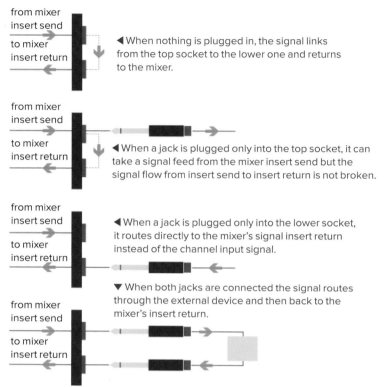

from mixer insert send
to mixer insert return

◄ When nothing is plugged in, the signal links from the top socket to the lower one and returns to the mixer.

from mixer insert send
to mixer insert return

◄ When a jack is plugged only into the top socket, it can take a signal feed from the mixer insert send but the signal flow from insert send to insert return is not broken.

from mixer insert send
to mixer insert return

◄ When a jack is plugged only into the lower socket, it routes directly to the mixer's signal insert return instead of the channel input signal.

▼ When both jacks are connected the signal routes through the external device and then back to the mixer's insert return.

from mixer insert send
to mixer insert return

▲ Fig 4: Semi-normalised patchbay operation.

The circuit board itself is designed so that one way round the sockets are normalised and the other way round they are not; the manual that comes with the patchbay will explain which way round is which. Other designs may use a switch on the circuit board. You may even have to solder a wire link to normalise a pair of connectors.

Most patchbays use a system of normalisation that, strictly speaking, should be called **semi-normalised**. In this arrangement there's a normalising contact only on the lower socket (Fig 4, above). This design has some practical advantages.

▲ Y cable that splits TRS jack into two mono jacks.

PATCHBAY WIRING

Wiring to and from the patchbay can be done using separate screened cables or multicored screen cables providing each balanced pair of cables in the multicore has its own screen. To avoid ground loops the screen connection needs only be connected to one of the two jack sockets at the back of the patchbay, although in most installations you shouldn't run into problems if both screens are connected.

Unless the patchbay contacts are kept clean (a spray of Caig DeOxit works wonders), patchbays can compromise the quality of audio signals because of contact resistance in the sockets and by interference pickup on the cabling. It is also easy to inadvertently introduce ground-loop hum, so it pays to plan your patchbay carefully and connect only those pieces of kit that you know you're going to have to reroute on a regular basis. If you have a compressor that you always use on the overall stereo mix, for example, then it makes sense to wire it directly to the mixer's stereo out insert points rather than via a patchbay.

In a typical DAW studio a patchbay may include the line inputs and outputs of the audio interface (which are usually on the rear panel of the interface), tie lines between the control room and studio, and any hardware outboard gear you wish to connect. Some audio interfaces also include insert points that can be brought out to a patchbay using normalised pairs of sockets.

When no plugs are inserted into the patchbay, the contact in the lower jack socket links the signal to the top one so the signal flow is maintained as it would be with a fully normalised pair of sockets.

However, if a plug is inserted only into the lower socket, the contacts open so no connection is made to the upper socket. The practical outcome is that you can plug a signal into the lower socket to feed it into the insert return of a mixer, essentially using it as a channel input that comes after the channel pre-amp.

If a jack is connected only to the upper socket, the normalising link isn't broken so the connected mixer channel works as normal but you can still take a feed from the insert send via this socket, which may be useful if you want to split the signal running through a mixer channel to go to two different places at the same time. A typical application would be to split a signal, process it in some way and then pan it to one side while panning the unprocessed sound passing through the mixer channel to the other. This was a common method of creating pseudo-stereo effects before plug-ins came along.

Where both patchbay sockets have jacks plugged in, the normalising contact is again broken so the signal is routed via whatever device you have on the other end of the jack leads. This could be a compressor, equaliser or effects unit.

This system of semi-normalisation is sometimes referred to as 'sniff and break' because connecting to only the top socket allows you to 'sniff' some of the channel signal without breaking the signal flow while connecting to the lower one 'breaks' the signal flow.

Caution / When connecting the inputs and outputs of outboard equipment (other then insert ins and outs) to pairs of patchbay sockets, **ensure that they are not set up to be normalised,** otherwise the input of the device will be connected to its own output when no jacks are plugged into the patchbay. This can cause equipment to oscillate and overheat. As a rule, normalisation is only used when a single piece of gear should default to being connected to another, such as a mixer insert send and return.

Caution 2 / **Avoid putting speaker-level signals, such as the outputs from power amplifiers, on a patchbay** as plugging them into something by accident can cause a lot of damage. When connecting side-chain inputs on external compressors or gates consult the relevant equipment manual to see how the side-chain socket is wired. There should be no problem if they're straightforward inputs selectable via a front panel switch, but if they're wired like an insert send/return so that they become active as soon as a plug is connected, you may have to plug directly into the equipment rear panel.

PATCHBAY LABELLING

Some patchbays come with their own labelling strips, but you can print your own on glossy photo paper and attach them using double-sided tape. Panel space is usually limited, so when dreaming up abbreviations make sure you pick ones you'll be able to decipher when you come back to a mix in a month's time!

Arrange the patchbay inputs and outputs as logically as possible so that, for example, all normalised connections are grouped together, possibly identified by a different colour label to remind you of the fact. ●

THE PROJECT STUDIO: THE BASICS...

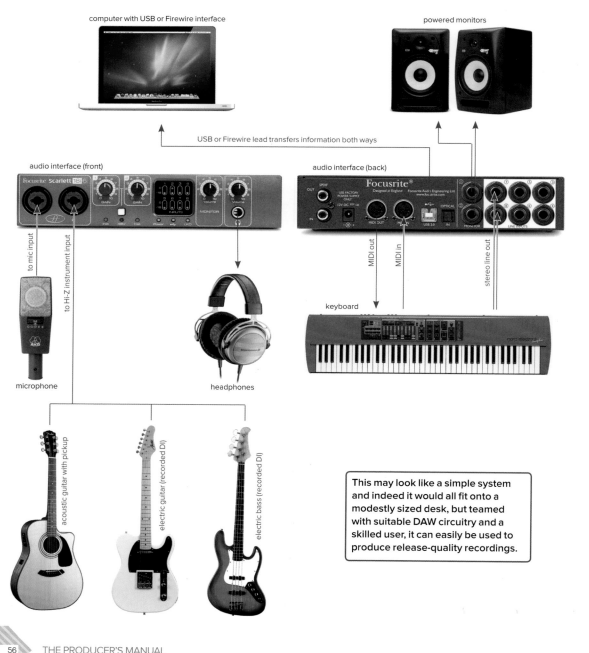

computer with USB or Firewire interface

powered monitors

USB or Firewire lead transfers information both ways

audio interface (front)

audio interface (back)

to mic input

to Hi-Z instrument input

MIDI out

MIDI in

stereo line out

microphone

headphones

keyboard

acoustic guitar with pickup

electric guitar (recorded DI)

electric bass (recorded DI)

This may look like a simple system and indeed it would all fit onto a modestly sized desk, but teamed with suitable DAW circuitry and a skilled user, it can easily be used to produce release-quality recordings.

... AND AREAS FOR INVESTMENT

❄ **Early upgrades**　　❄❄ **Realm of the pro**　　❄❄❄ **New car or...?**

❄ **DIY acoustic treatment:** If your room sounds bad then no amount of quality gear will enable you to get good recordings or mixes.

❄❄❄ **Fully treated room:** It may cost a lot but getting a team in to ensure the studio is professionally acoustically treated can be the most unglamorously wise money ever spent in the small studio.

❄ **Better speakers:** You don't have to spend a fortune on monitors, but if you started with computer desktop speakers or cheap hi-fi speakers then you should upgrade to some reasonably accurate studio monitors as quickly as possible. It's also worth buying at least one pair of accurate headphones.

❄❄ **Second set of studio monitors.**

❄ **Dedicated studio computer.**

❄❄ **As much monitor screen area as you can accommodate.** It makes DAW operation much easier. Two large screens are often more useful than one huge monitor.

❄ **Hardware monitor control device:** Some means of controlling active monitors from the desktop is essential. If your audio interface doesn't offer this, consider adding a monitor control device. It will normally allow you to switch between two or more pairs of monitors, drive headphones, switch the monitoring from stereo to mono and control the volume.

❄ **Comfy chair:** You will spend many hours in it. Don't scrimp!

❄❄ **Great audio interface:** As with mic pre-amps, the differences between audio interfaces may seem subtle but the better the A-to-D and D-to-A converter circuits, the smoother and more refined the sound of your mixes will be.

❄❄ **Quality mic pre-amp:** While the differences between mic pre-amps might seem subtle, once you have invested in a few serious mics it is worth teaming these with better pre-amps. There's a choice of pristine solid-state designs, warm valve models and faithful recreations of vintage classics. Some include EQ and compression.

❄ **Range of good plug-ins:** These days there's little to choose between the performance of the better plug-ins and dedicated hardware. Essential early upgrades would be at least one high-end reverb, EQ and compressor, probably in that order. You may also want to add to your armoury of software synths and drum instruments.

❄❄ **Hardware control surface:** Mixing entirely on a mouse can get tiring. A control surface makes life easier and improves workflow. These give you physical controls for operating the DAW transport as well as motorised faders and rotary controls for controlling channel levels, pans, effect sends, plug-in parameters and so on.

❄❄ **Range of high-end and workhorse mic/s:** Just as the quality of photographs is limited by the lens fitted to the camera, audio recordings can never be better than the mic/s used to make them. While you're at it, invest in a decent active DI box (or two).

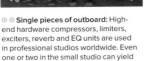

❄❄ **Single pieces of outboard:** High-end hardware compressors, limiters, exciters, reverb and EQ units are used in professional studios worldwide. Even one or two in the small studio can yield results that no software ever can.

❄❄❄ **Collectable outboard:** For those who win the jackpot (or get a number one!)

4
THE MICROPHONE

> THE ONE COMMON THING THAT ALL MICS DO IS RESPOND TO VIBRATIONS IN THE AIR (SOUND WAVES) THAT THEY CONVERT INTO ELECTRICAL ENERGY (THE AUDIO SIGNAL) TO BE AMPLIFIED.

GOOD VIBRATIONS

Although the human race shares just one design for the ear, trying to get an electro-mechanical device to do the same job has proved rather more difficult. Instead, we have a range of microphone types operating on different principles, each with its own strengths and weaknesses.

The one thing that all mics do, however, is respond to vibrations in the air (sound waves) that they convert into electrical energy (the audio signal) to be amplified.

Different mics convert these vibrations in different ways – but they all do so using a diaphragm, a very thin piece of material that vibrates when hit by sound waves.

This chapter looks at the common studio microphone types and their uses. It can be read alone or as reference alongside any of the chapters in **Section 3: Recording**.

DYNAMIC MICS

The simplest mic found in the studio is the dynamic model. There are two types of dynamic mics: **moving coil** and **ribbon** models.

The **moving coil dynamic mic** (Fig 1) is the most common and is used extensively in both the studio and live sound applications.

In this type of mic, a light circular diaphragm, usually made of a thin plastic film, responds to changes in air pressure caused by sound waves. The diaphragm is attached to a coil of very fine wire suspended in a magnetic field created by a permanent magnet – rather like a loudspeaker in reverse. As the coil follows the diaphragm backwards and forwards in the magnetic field, an electrical current is induced in the coil – the audio

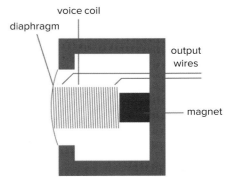

▲ Fig 1: Dynamic mic schematic.

signal. Although very small, this signal can be amplified using a pre-amp in the mixing console or audio interface.

PROS AND CONS

Moving coil dynamic mics have several advantages: they are **inexpensive**, can take a surprising amount of **mechanical abuse** and can be built to **tolerate very high sound pressure levels (SPLs)**. They also require **no power to operate**.

The main disadvantage is their **limited frequency response**. A typical moving coil dynamic mic can be made to work effectively up to around 16kHz. Above that its efficiency falls significantly, making it a poor choice for capturing the airy tops of a vocal or the sheen of an acoustic guitar.

This limited response is down to the mass of the coil attached to the diaphragm. The higher the frequency of the sound hitting the diaphragm, the faster it has to move back and forth, but the inertia of the diaphragm/voice coil assembly makes this progressively more difficult, causing the high end response to roll off. New materials and better magnetic alloys, such

◀ Shure SM57 dynamic mic.

as neodymium, have managed to squeeze a little more performance out of the moving coil mic, but in general they don't handle high frequencies as well as their capacitor cousins.

The other disadvantage of the moving coil mic is that it generates a **relatively small output signal**. If the sound source is quiet – like an acoustic guitar or harp – then a lot of amplification is required to make the signal usable. And the more amplification that is applied to a signal, the greater the level of background noise.

Because of these two drawbacks, moving coil mics are generally used with louder sound sources (that have little useful high-end content) and sound sources located very close to the mic. In the studio they are typically used for mic'ing drums and guitar amps.

On stage – where capturing the high end is less important than a mic's ability to withstand a certain amount of handling abuse – they're used for **vocals** and a range of **other instruments**.

RIBBON MICS

As with moving coil models, the ribbon mic's signal is generated by an electrical conductor moving in a magnetic field. But instead of doing the job with a diaphragm and voice coil, ribbon mics use an extremely thin, electrically-conductive ribbon – usually aluminium – suspended in a strong magnetic field (Fig 2). When sound moves the ribbon, a tiny electrical current is induced in the ribbon itself – the audio signal. Because the ribbon has such a low electrical impedance, a matching transformer inside the mic is required to match the impedance and output signal level to that of a normal mic pre-amp input.

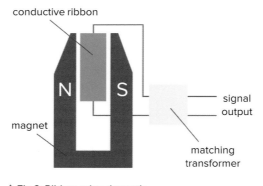

▲ **Fig 2: Ribbon mic schematic.**

A typical ribbon mic has a very low sensitivity and so needs a lot of amplification to get a workable signal level out of it.

Some models are built with pre-amps inside the mic, such as the sE Rupert Neve RNR1. Those without place high demands on the external pre-amp to which they are connected, which often needs to be run at near maximum gain. In practice this means that passive ribbon mics tend to be the most prone to electrical noise when amplified.

Passive ribbon mics do not require normal 48 volt phantom power. It is important to note that a ribbon mic should never by plugged or unplugged with the phantom power switched on as this can damage the ribbon. Instead it is good practice to connect ribbon mics to pre-amp inputs with the phantom power turned off. If the phantom power can only be switched globally, at least ensure it is switched off before you plug in or unplug a ribbon mic. Once the mic is safely plugged in, you can switch the phantom power back on; the mic will be perfectly happy as long as it is connected via a standard balanced mic cable.

ESSENTIALS: PASSIVE VS ACTIVE

Passive mics require no external power supply of any kind, while active mics generally use phantom power, although some can operate from batteries.

Valve models have their own dedicated external power supplies.

In the vast majority of ribbon mic designs, the ribbon is open to the air on both sides and so has a natural figure-of-eight response (page 66).

PROS AND CONS

Like the worst session singers, ribbon mics are **fragile** and **often expensive**. What's more, on paper the **frequency response** curve of the typical ribbon mic looks **no better than that of a typical moving coil dynamic model**, with many rolling away highs at an even lower frequency. You might therefore reasonably ask why we bother with these fragile, insensitive, potentially dull-sounding mics that rarely come cheap.

The fact is that despite its apparent limitations, the straightforward construction of the ribbon mic combined with the low mass of the ribbon gives it **a very natural sound**, while the limited high end of many models becomes a positive when trying to smooth out the sound of a strident **solo violin**, **harsh guitar amp**, **backing vocal parts** or the **cymbals over a drum kit**. They can even do great things with a laid-back **lead vocal**.

Some of the more modern ribbon designs have a frequency response extending up to 20kHz – although even these seem to sound smoother than most capacitor models with a similar response.

While the better known ribbon mics are fairly expensive, there are now many imported **lower-cost models** that are attractive to the home studio owner and which can achieve good results where a smoother tone is required.

▲ Coles 4038 studio ribbon mic.

Ribbon mics have a reputation for being physically fragile, and compared to other types of mic they are, although some of the modern designs are a little more robust than the models of old. Even so, few will survive being dropped and they should be protected from strong blasts of air (always use a pop shield).

It is also recommended that ribbon mics are stored upright to avoid the ribbon sagging and stretching, which would eventually affect the tonality of the mic.

Classic ribbon models come from companies such as Coles, Royer and AEA (with their accurate reissue of the RCA design). MXL, Golden Age and Shiny Box supply more affordable models. Mid-priced mics are offered by the likes of sE and Audio Technica.

Ribbon mics aren't suitable for every recording task, but it is definitely worth having one on hand for when their special tonal attributes fit the occasion.

CAPACITOR MICS

An electrical capacitor (some people use the term **condenser**) comprises a pair of conductive plates separated by an air gap or some other insulating material. The capacitor mic (Fig 3, overleaf) exploits a basic law of physics which holds that if you vary the distance between the plates of a capacitor while an electrical charge is applied, the voltage between the two plates also changes.

A typical capacitor mic capsule is built from two conductive plates, one fixed, the other a thin, metalised diaphragm (most often made from a type of plastic called mylar onto which is deposited a very thin coating of gold to make it electrically conductive)

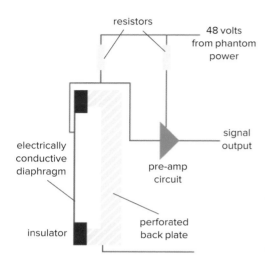

resistors

48 volts from phantom power

signal output

electrically conductive diaphragm

pre-amp circuit

insulator

perforated back plate

▲ Fig 3: Capacitor mic schematic.

that moves in response to sound. The two plates are mounted very close together, separated by a tiny air space. As the diaphragm vibrates in response to sound waves, its distance from the back-plate varies, changing the voltage across the two plates. This changing voltage corresponds to the changing audio signal.

To read this changing voltage without draining away the electrical charge requires a pre-amp with an extremely high input impedance, which is why capacitor mics always include active circuity, typically built around FETs (Field Effect Transistors) or valves.

In non-valve models the capsule's electrical charge, and the power for its on-board pre-amp, are invariably derived from a standard 48v phantom power source, usually located in the mixing console or mic pre-amp.

In valve models an external power supply provides the necessary capsule polarising voltage, as well as the high voltages and heater voltages required for the valve.

Although valve mics are more expensive to build and require more elaborate power supplies, the subtle overload characteristics of the valve produces a warm musical tonality that suits certain sound sources and often flatters vocals by making then sound a little larger than real life.

PROS AND CONS

Because the capacitor diaphragm can be made just a few microns thick, it has a very low mass, which enables it to follow the rapid changes in air pressure caused by high frequency sound. Most capacitor mics are therefore able to **cover the whole range of the audio spectrum**, easily capturing frequencies up to 20kHz. This makes them ideal for **vocals** and instruments that generate important high-end content like **acoustic guitars**, **flutes**, **harps** and so on.

And unlike dynamic mics, which are inherently quite insensitive, the on-board circuitry of a capacitor mic is able to deliver a healthy signal level at the mic's output – meaning **less noise**.

Capacitor mics can also be designed to have **any polar pattern** (page 64), with many models offering switchable or variable pattern shapes (achieved by using a pair of back-to-back capsules and then mixing their outputs in different ways).

Despite these strengths, capacitor mics can suffer from **temporary sensitivity loss** if used in a very humid environment. Although few producers conduct their sessions in the rainforest, a typical vocal booth or live room can get surprisingly sweaty. If you do find that a mic is starting to

▼ The Rode NTK capacitor mic.

lose its sensitivity, it should be taken out of service and left somewhere warm to dry out.

(The reason a capacitor mic loses sensitivity, incidentally, is that moisture has a relatively low electrical resistance compared with the FET pre-amp's very high input impedance so it effectively shorts out the capsule. Some companies, including Sennheiser, produce a range of 'RF' mics where the capsule is biased with high frequency alternating current. These are much less susceptible to moisture problems than conventional DC-biased capacitor mics and can save the day in situations where high humidity can't be avoided).

The other key downside of capacitor mics is their **cost** – although this is far less of an issue than it once was. Because a capacitor mic is more complicated – both electrically and mechanically – than a dynamic model, with many parts needing to be assembled by hand, good ones can be relatively expensive. In recent years, the far eastern market has geared up to produce lower cost models, and although some of the cheaper ones might not have such tight specifications as high-end European models, they can still produce excellent results.

BOUNDARY MICS

Although less common in the studio than the other mic types, you may occasionally come across boundary mics, sometimes referred to as Pressure Zone Mics (or PZMs).

Boundary mics work by exploiting the air pressure difference found at room boundaries – like walls, floors or ceilings.

When a sound wave reaches a solid boundary the air molecules can no longer move because the wall is in the way, so the sound energy is converted from air movement into a change in air pressure.

PHANTOM POWER

Phantom power is a standardised method of supplying DC electric power via a balanced XLR microphone cable to capacitor (or other) mics that contain active electronic circuitry. The term 'phantom' is explained by the fact that no additional wiring is needed to carry the power supply – it rides on the signal lines of a standard mic cable.

Although there are official 12, 24 and 48 volt variants of phantom power, the standard used in recording studios is invariably 48v. Many active direct inject (DI) boxes also use phantom powering as an alternative to batteries.

Phantom power works by applying the 48v power source to both signal lines of a balanced audio connector using the ground screen as the neutral (return) path (Pin 1 of the XLR connector). Capacitors in the mic then separate out the signal and the DC power.

Phantom power supplies are usually built into the equipment into which the mic or DI is connected, such as the mixing desk or mic pre-amp's mic input, with an option for turning it on or off, either per channel or globally. If the mixing desk or pre-amp doesn't offer phantom power, you can buy external phantom powering boxes that connect between the mic and its destination (above).

Dynamic mics do not require phantom power, and while using a balanced dynamic mic with a pre-amp where the phantom power is switched on will not cause any problems (providing a balanced XLR cable is used), the phantom power should still be switched off when a dynamic mic is being plugged and unplugged.

Non-active ribbon mics are particularly prone to damage if this advice is ignored. Though less of an issue, it is also good practice to turn off the phantom power when plugging and unplugging capacitor mics.

It is at these boundary points that boundary mics are placed.

A boundary mic's capsule is often mounted slightly above a small, flat plate, pointing towards it. The mic's plate is attached to the room boundary surface or other large sheet of material (Fig 4 and 5).

For a boundary mic to work effectively at low frequencies it needs to be placed at a large boundary, ideally where the wall dimensions are comparable with the wavelength of the lowest sound to be captured – usually a wall.

Where the wall is not the ideal place to locate the mic, it is possible to fix a boundary mic to a large wooden or perspex panel to enable it to be moved closer to the sound source. In practical terms the panel needs to be a minimum of one metre square and much larger when dealing with bass instruments.

If vibration is not a problem the boundary mic can be placed flat on the floor or attached to the ceiling. Importantly, because the boundary mic is mounted at the boundary rather than somewhere out in the room, reflections from the boundary can't reach it so it captures only direct sound and reflections from other walls.

Boundary mics fixed to the ceiling can be a good way to capture an **overall drum kit** sound where the ceiling is too low to use traditional overheads. A boundary mic can also be placed on the floor in front of a **kick drum** where it can be used instead of, or in addition to, a conventional close mic. I have also had good results wall-mounting a boundary mic for **acoustic guitar recording**, and placed beneath a **grand piano** lid (page 132).

▲ Fig 4: The mic is set flush with the boundary so that it responds to pressure changes at the boundary.

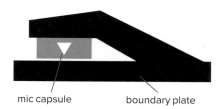

▲ Fig 5: In this version the capsule is set just above the boundary, facing it. Once again, it senses the air pressure changes at the boundary.

POLAR PATTERNS

The way a mic responds to sound arriving from different directions is illustrated by its 'polar pattern'. You'll often see a polar pattern graph supplied with a mic showing the shape of the pattern at two or three different frequencies.

Knowing how to use polar patterns to your advantage can help improve recordings and solve a range of spill-related problems when more than one instrument is being recorded.

Different mics have different sensitivities to sound arriving from different directions; some are equally sensitive to sounds arriving from every direction while others are less sensitive to sounds arriving from behind. Polar pattern types can be placed into three main groups:

▼ The Audio Technica U841A: omnidirectional condenser boundary mic.

MIC SPEC SHEETS:
THE TECHIE STUFF

The first time you see a mic specification sheet (right) can be daunting: so many figures, so little of it explained in laymans' terms. But actually, when broken down, spec sheets are easy enough to figure out, and a general understanding of the information can help you make more informed decisions about what mic might be right for a particular job — especially when investing in a new model for the studio.

Sensitivity: The sensitivity of a mic is simply a measure of how much electrical signal you get out of it for a given level of sound input. The higher the signal level, the more sensitive the mic is said to be. A mic that produces a relatively high signal requires less amplification, which in turn usually equates to less background noise.

As a rule capacitor mics are the most sensitive and ribbon models the least, with moving coil dynamic models somewhere in the middle. A typical capacitor mic might have a sensitivity quoted as: 'Sensitivity at 1kHz into 1kOhm: 22mV/Pa' — which is to say that when tested with a 1kHz signal the mic produces an output signal of 22mV for a sound level that causes a change in air pressure of one Pascal. If this all sounds overly technical, don't worry: it is sufficient to know that the more mV/Pa you

see on the spec sheet, the more sensitive a mic is.

Noise: Any noise generated by the mic is amplified by the mic pre-amp, so in situations where quiet or distant sounds are to be recorded — in the case of field recordings, for example — a mic's noise performance can be an important consideration.

It is usual to quote mic noise as an equivalent SPL, or Sound Pressure Level. You can think of this as the level of sound that would produce the same signal level as the noise at the output of a perfectly noiseless mic. This figure is usually termed the EIN figure (Equivalent Input Noise). An EIN figure below 20dB or so is quiet enough for general music recording

in a studio where the source is fairly close to the mic. Mics with EINs below 10dB are available where low noise operation is essential, such as when choosing ambience mics for an acoustic ensemble or for recording unusually quiet instruments.

In general, really quiet mics are more important in film and TV applications to capture things like whispered film dialogue and wildlife sounds.

Max SPL: A third important statistic quoted on mic spec sheets is the Max SPL, the maximum sound pressure level the mic can tolerate before the level of distortion becomes unacceptable. For vocal recording, a mic that can handle up to 120dB usually has more than enough level-handling capability. For close-mic'ing drums, guitar amps or brass instruments 135dB or more is safer.

Note that some mics come with a built-in pad or attenuator switch that reduces its sensitivity so that it can handle louder sounds. A mic rated at 135dB Max SPL should be able to handle 145dB SPL with its 10dB pad switched in.

The spec sheet will also include information on the mic's **polar pattern** (more than one where there are switchable options) and a **graph outlining its frequency response**.

> **1. Omnidirectional:** Captures sound evenly from all directions. Includes many capacitor mics.

> **2. Unidirectional, also known as cardioid:** Captures sound mainly from one direction. Includes many dynamic and capacitor models.

> **3. Bi-directional or figure-of-eight:** Captures sounds from two opposite directions but not from the sides. Includes almost all ribbon models and some capacitor models. Often available as a switchable option on a multi-pattern capacitor mic.

Understanding polar patterns is impossible without understanding the term '**on-axis**'. Sounds that arrive at the diaphragm where the mic diaphragm is pointing directly at the sound source are said to be on-axis (Fig 6). Sounds are 'off-axis' when the diaphragm is aiming in a different direction from the sound source. A mic is said to be '90 degrees off-axis' where it sits perpendicular to the sound source (Fig 7), and 180 degrees off-axis where it points directly away from the sound source (Fig 8).

OMNIDIRECTIONAL MICS
The omnidirectional ('omni') mic picks up sound evenly from all directions (Fig 9).

An omni mic is mechanically very simple, comprising a diaphragm fixed across the end of a sealed cavity. It responds directly to changes in air pressure, almost like an audio frequency barometer, and so is also known as a pressure mic. Because pressure changes occur regardless of direction, a theoretically perfect omni mic picks up sound equally well – regardless of which direction the sound comes from. It follows that the polar pattern of a perfect

omni mic shown in two dimensions is a circle with the mic at the centre, although in real life (which is three-dimensional) the pickup pattern is spherical.

Of course nothing is ever quite this perfect; placing any object, including a mic, in a sound field will affect the sound slightly, but the better omni models get very close.

Omni mics don't exhibit any proximity effect (page 68) so their tonal balance is essentially independent of distance from the source.

Although omni mics generate very natural results, in situations where a number of instruments are being played / recorded at the same time, either on stage or in the studio, the amount of spill picked up from other instruments by the various omni mics might be higher than ideal.

In such situations cardioid mics can be useful in reducing spill but with the caveat that the spill they do collect will tend to sound dull and coloured due to the off-axis response of a cardioid pattern mic at different frequencies.

FIGURE-OF-EIGHT MICS
Equally simple in concept is the figure-of-eight pattern mic (Fig 10), so called because a plot of its sensitivity looks like the number 8 turned on its side.

This is the natural response obtained when you have a single diaphragm that is open to the air on both sides (instead of just one). Sound approaching from 90 degrees off-axis reaches both sides of the diaphragm at the same time, resulting in no movement and no electrical output. However, sound approaching from the front or rear of the mic is picked up equally well.

▲ Fig 6: On-axis mic placement – diaphragm points directly at sound source.

▲ Fig 7: Off-axis mic placement – with diaphragm directed 90 degrees off-axis.

▲ Fig 8: Off-axis mic placement – with diaphragm pointing directly away from sound source.

ESSENTIALS: BAROMETER

To prevent an omni mic behaving as an actual barometer, a very small air vent is fitted to allow air to flow into or out of the cavity so that the internal air pressure matches that outside. The hole must be small enough to prevent this air flow from affecting audio frequency pressure changes.

CAPSULES AND POLAR PATTERNS

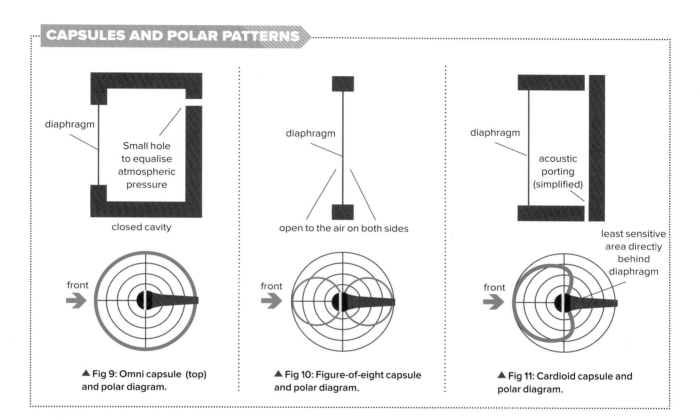

diaphragm

Small hole to equalise atmospheric pressure

closed cavity

front

▲ Fig 9: Omni capsule (top) and polar diagram.

diaphragm

open to the air on both sides

front

▲ Fig 10: Figure-of-eight capsule and polar diagram.

diaphragm

acoustic porting (simplified)

least sensitive area directly behind diaphragm

front

▲ Fig 11: Cardioid capsule and polar diagram.

As this type of mic works on the difference in pressure between the front and the rear of the diaphragm, it is often known as a pressure gradient mic. Note that the electrical polarity of the signal produced by sound approaching the rear of the diaphragm will be opposite to that of sound approaching the front of the diaphragm as it pushes the diaphragm in the opposite direction.

Figure-of-eight mics exhibit a strong **proximity bass boost effect** (page 68). With some ribbon mics that have a figure-of-eight response, the proximity effect can come into play even when the mic is a metre or so away from the source, getting progressively stronger as the distance decreases. The

practical outcome of this is that some low-cut filtering may be needed to restore the tonal balance for close-mic'ed sources.

One benefit of figure-of-eight mics is that they are totally 'deaf' to sound that arrives 90 degrees off-axis, a fact that can be exploited when trying to minimise spill simply by pointing the deaf axis towards the sound source that needs to be rejected.

CARDIOID MICS

Cardioid (literally meaning 'heart-shaped') describes the approximate shape of the cardioid mic's polar pattern (Fig 11), which is more sensitive to sounds arriving from directly in front. As the sound source moves off-axis, the mic's sensitivity to high frequencies falls away more rapidly than for lower frequencies, meaning that sounds arriving off-axis are both quieter and more dull-sounding than those that arrive on-axis. The rear of a typical cardioid mic is almost totally insensitive.

This kind of mic has the most complicated construction, as the designers have to find a way to allow mainly sounds approaching from the front to be picked up – while capturing less of sounds that come from elsewhere. A cardioid capsule is essentially a modified figure-of-eight mic with a specially designed sound path used to delay sound reaching the rear of the diaphragm.

A mic that is even more strongly directional is called a **super-cardioid** or **hyper-cardioid**. It has less sensitivity at the sides, though may be slightly more sensitive at the rear. This pattern produces a tighter focus but can pose problems with moving sound sources that keep drifting in and out of the mic's sensitive region.

Although engineers can exploit the polar pattern of a hyper-cardioid mic to some extent when recording, they are limited by the fact that hyper-cardioid mics still exhibit some sensitivity to sounds arriving directly from the rear, meaning careful use of acoustic screens may be beneficial. Their least sensitive area is usually around 45 degrees off the rear axis rather than directly behind, as would be the case with a regular cardioid pattern mic.

VARIABLE PATTERN MICS

Variable (or 'switchable') pattern mics offer a range of polar patterns and are therefore more flexible in the studio. Most are capacitor models, where two cardioid capsules are mounted back-to-back and

PROXIMITY EFFECT

Pressure gradient mics (cardioids and figure-of-eight) both exhibit a 'proximity effect' – a boosting of low frequencies when the sound source is close to the mic. The technical reasons for this are quite involved, but are related to the way that sounds arriving at the front and rear of the diaphragm combine. Vocalists with good mic technique can exploit this effect by varying their distance from the mic to control their tonality. Less experienced singers may move more randomly, causing unwanted changes in tone. In this case the best you can do is prevent the singer getting too close to the mic; a good way of doing this is by placing a pop screen between the mic and their mouth.

then their outputs mixed to produce the full range of polar patterns, from figure-of-eight to omni, with all shades of cardioid in between.

Popular capacitor mics with switchable response patterns include the AKG C12 VR, Neumann U87 and AKG C414 (right), as well as many of the more affordable Chinese, European and Australian models built for the project studio market.

EXPLOITING MIC PATTERNS

While many studio tasks can be handled by carefully placed cardioid mics, it is useful to know the strengths and limitations of all patterns.

Cardioid mics are used where unwanted off-axis sound, such as room reverberation or spill, needs to be minimised – when you are recording a **single instrument in a band** (and want to minimise spill from the other band members), for example, or for **semi-isolating multiple drums in a kit**.

Because off-axis sound picked up by cardioids tend to be coloured, the best results are usually obtained by using them in combination with acoustic screens to reduce the amount of off-axis spill reaching the sides and rear of the mic.

▼ The AKG C414 – note the range of polar patterns that can be selected.

The dull tonality of spill captured by cardioid mics can be a headache for engineers so they might opt to use omnidirectional mics instead. Inevitably this means more spill (remember omnis pick up off-axis sounds almost as well as on-axis sounds), but this spill sounds more natural. What's more, because omni mics don't suffer from a proximity effect or colour off-axis sounds, you can get them closer to a sound source (often as much as a third closer) than with other mic types without compromising the sound.

As long as you reduce the mic distance of an omni by around one third compared with the distance you'd normally use for a cardioid pattern mic, the overall spill situation isn't much worse with an omni then when using cardioids. And any instruments that do spill between mics will still sound a lot cleaner, so as long as you have enough separation to balance the various instrument against each other you'll probably and up with a more natural sound. Some engineers choose small diaphragm omni mics when **close mic-ing a drum kit** for this reason.

Omnis are also often used as **spaced pairs for stereo recording and as drum overheads** where the room acoustic suits the drum kit. **See Stereo mic'ing, below.**

Figure-of-eight pattern mics are used mainly for specialist applications such as **stereo mic'ing** or as **drum overheads** where the sound of a ribbon model is preferred. Where sound picked up from the rear of a mic might be a problem, acoustic screening can be used.

There are situations where the figure-of-eight's total deafness to sounds 90 degrees off-axis can be used to dramatically reduce spill in difficult situations, such as when recording **someone who sings and plays the acoustic guitar at the same time** (page 132). By screening off the area with acoustic panels or even simple duvets, careful mic positioning can achieve much better separation between the voice and guitar than with other mic patterns. In this scenario it is more important to have the mic's dead zone aimed at the sound source to be rejected than it is to have the instrument or voice being picked up absolutely on-axis.

MIC'ING TECHNIQUES

Knowing the characteristics of different mics and understanding how to exploit their polar patterns is important for getting the best from a recorded performance. Equally important is a knowledge of the different techniques engineers use to record various instruments in the studio.

Some techniques are straightforward enough – recording vocals for example, where a single capacitor mic is most often used (page 92). Other techniques are more complex, like those employed for recording drums (page 142).

For the most frequent studio tasks a range of common techniques have evolved over the years, detailed in the various **Recording** chapters. But there are other techniques to cover a wide range of recording demands that can be filed under 'theory' and called upon whenever the need arises.

STEREO MIC'ING

Stereo recording was developed in the early 1930s, where many major breakthroughs were down to Alan Blumlein, the engineer who established the technique for recording stereo using coincident mics.

To record stereo sound the engineer has two main options, each of which has a subset of variations:

> using **coincident (or 'XY') pairs**, where two mic capsules are mounted as close together as possible, or

> using two or more **identical spaced pairs**, where the two mics are mounted some distance apart.

These are both very different from faking stereo using a pan pot or taking a mono file and using any number of mixing techniques to generate a pseudo 'stereo' signal using delay, pitch shift, or clever filtering. Both of these 'real' methods have their specific advantages. The engineer should be familiar with both.

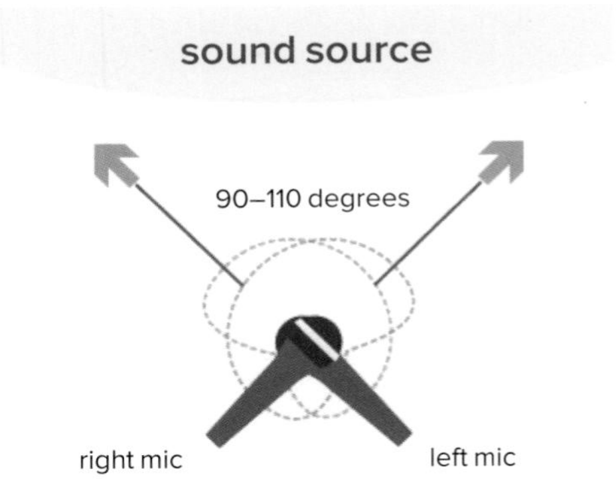

COINCIDENT (XY) MIC TECHNIQUES

The simplest coincident mic setup comprises two identical, cardioid pattern mics mounted in such a way that their capsules are as close together as possible (coincident means 'occupying the same area in space'), but with the mics angled apart so that one favours sound from the left of centre, the other sound from the right.

The outputs from the two mics are recorded onto separate audio tracks and panned left and right accordingly. As the mics are cardioid in pattern, the signal levels vary according to the angle between the mics and the sound source/s.

This doesn't quite replicate the way the human hearing system perceives sound – our ears are not coincident but rather spaced apart by the width of our head – but the technique works well enough and has

▲ Fig 12: Recording using an 'XY' coincident pair. In this case one cardioid mic is mounted directly above the other, the angle between them anywhere between 90–110 degrees.

the benefit that there are no significant time differences between sound arriving at the two mics, regardless of the direction of the sound source, which eliminates the problem of phase and comb filtering (page 74).

The usual way to set up coincident cardioids is to place one mic above the other so that the capsules are arranged on and above the other, angled apart by 90 degrees (Fig 12), although it is sometimes necessary to tweak the angle to get the best results – you can sometimes go as wide as 130 degrees. Various stereo mic mounting bars are available for holding the mics in the correct position; most fit on top of a standard mic stand.

A similar arrangement can be set up using figure-of-eight mics. Because a figure-of-eight mic has a more accurate off-axis response than a typical cardioid it is likely to capture a more natural sound, although the rear-facing sides of the mics will pick up more room ambience – unless acoustic screens are set up behind them.

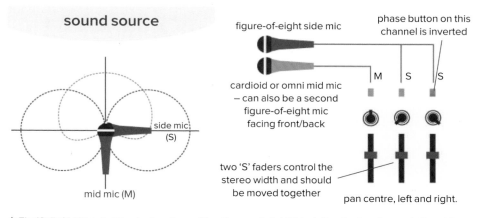

▲ Fig 13: (left) MS coincident mic setup, with a figure-of-eight (black lines) mic set up pointing sideways with a cardioid (blue) facing the sound source. (Right) Mixer set to decode an MS recording. Note the pan settings and the channel inversion.

A more complex approach, again developed by Alan Blumlein, is the Mid and Side, or Middle Side (M&S or MS), setup (Fig 13). Like the simple XY approach, it is coincident, the mics set up with their capsules placed as close together as possible. The difference is that instead of using two identical mics, the MS setup uses a figure-of-eight mic pointing sideways ('side') in conjunction with a cardioid, omni, or another figure-of-eight mic pointing towards the sound source ('mid').

In an MS setup using a cardioid mid mic, the resulting pickup pattern is similar to a pair of XY cardioids but without the off-axis tonal blurring in the centre of the sound stage that occurs with XY cardioids. Note that the positive side of the figure-of-eight mic should face left and be the same as the polarity of the M mic otherwise the stereo image will be reversed.

Simply taking the outputs from the two mics doesn't produce stereo; some signal manipulation, specifically a 'sum and difference matrix', is required to produce the final stereo signal (Fig 13, right).

To decode the MS signals into left/right stereo you need three mixer channels (that must be equipped with polarity invert buttons). The M mic is panned dead centre while a splitter cable is used to feed the S signal into a pair of adjacent channels. Switch in the polarity invert on the right channel and keep the two S channel faders together after setting the channel gain trims to identical values. Pan these two channels hard left and right.

You can ensure the gain trims and faders are set correctly by listening to just the S channels and then pressing the mixer's mono button. When the two channels are correctly balanced there will be virtually no output. With the two S channels balanced, switch back to stereo monitoring and bring up the M channel level.

Also check that the left/right stereo positioning is correct and if not, either swap

WALKTHROUGH

Setting up an MS co-incident pair

1 Set up coincident M/S mics with the figure-of-eight mic's diaphragm pointing sideways and cardioid, omni or forward-facing figure-of-eight mic aimed at the sound source.

2 Record to a stereo track in the DAW.

3 Insert an M/S decoder plug-in.

4 The width or spread control in the decoder plug-in changes the contribution of the side signal. When this is reduced right down you get a mono result.

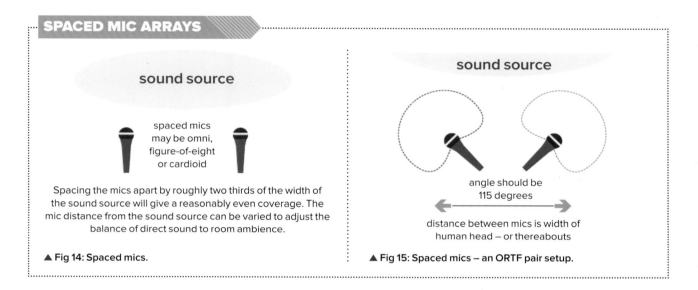

SPACED MIC ARRAYS

sound source

spaced mics
may be omni,
figure-of-eight
or cardioid

Spacing the mics apart by roughly two thirds of the width of
the sound source will give a reasonably even coverage. The
mic distance from the sound source can be varied to adjust the
balance of direct sound to room ambience.

▲ Fig 14: Spaced mics.

sound source

angle should be
115 degrees

distance between mics is width of
human head – or thereabouts

▲ Fig 15: Spaced mics – an ORTF pair setup.

the pan positions of the two S channels or press the polarity invert button on the channel carrying the M signal.

Now the stereo image can be adjusted from mono to stereo and beyond that to extra wide by varying the levels of the S faders, although if you bring up the S channels too far, the left and right images end up swapping over.

SPACED MIC TECHNIQUES

Spaced mic techniques, as the name suggests, depend on two mics being placed apart instead of together. They work with omni, cardioid and figure-of-eight mics, although both mics should be of the same type and well-matched. '**Matched**' in this context means two mics of the same model that have been specially selected to be as close to identical in performance as possible.

The inherent weakness of spaced techniques is the introduction of **phase cancellation effects** (page 74) when

summed to mono, with sound from either side of centre arriving at one mic before the other. But where mono compatibility is not a prerequisite, spaced mics can produce an enhanced sense of stereo width and, because there's no need to use directional mics, omnis can be used to produce a more natural result.

The simplest spaced setup comprises a matched pair of omnidirectional mics spaced apart by around half the width of the sound source you're trying to capture – sometimes a little less (Fig 14). It is a good technique for recording **small ensembles** or **choirs**, as well as (full) **drum kits** and **pianos**.

Where a recording sounds 'all left and right, with no middle', the mics are probably too widely spaced. Correct spacing ensures a fairly even coverage of all the sound source.

A variation of the spaced pair, sometimes known as an **ORTF pair** (after the broadcast service that developed it), uses a pair of cardioid mics spaced apart by around the width of a human head (specified as 17cm with an angle between the mics of 115 degrees) (Fig 15). Engineers often develop their own variation of the method, adjusting both the spacing and angle of the mics. The technique can generate good stereo results, although again, mono compatibility is compromised because of the physical spacing between the mics.

Only experience and your ears will tell you which of these techniques – or a range of other less common approaches – works best in any given situation. As a concluding generalisation:

❯ stereo pairs of mics are most likely to be used to record drum kits (overheads or room ambience), pianos, percussion ensembles and small choral groups.

❯ coincident mic setups have the best mono compatibility, with the M/S pair giving the most accurate result for sounds on-axis to the mid mic.

❯ spaced mics can create a greater sense of stereo width but suffer from mono compatibility problems.

AND FINALLY... PHASE

When setting up multiple mics, the constant headache to the engineer is phase cancellation. Understanding what it is will help you avoid – or at least minimise – it.

If you add two identical sine waves of the same frequency that start at the same time, their combined level is doubled (Fig 16). These waves are said to be 'in-phase' with each other. If you delay one of the sine waves so that its highest point coincides with the other wave's lowest point and

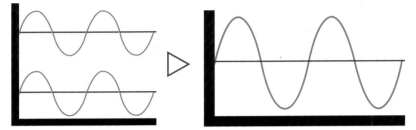

▲ Fig 16: Two sine waves in phase (left) and (right) the combined signal – note its increased level.

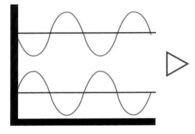

▲ Fig 17: The same two sine waves with the upper one shifted 180 degrees (left), and the mixed 'cancelled' signal (right).

then add them, they cancel each other out leaving you with no signal at all (Fig 17). This occurs at a phase shift of 180 degrees. Between these two extremes, you get various partial cancellations, resulting in level changes.

Things get a bit more complicated with real audio waveforms, which usually include a wider mix of frequencies.

The result is a complex filter, knows as a comb-filter (Fig 18), where some frequencies are emphasised and others suppressed. The frequency graph looks something like the teeth on a comb. As the delay time changes, so do the frequencies relating to the peaks and troughs in the comb.

We deliberately (ab)use the artefacts of comb-filter delays in music production when we employ phaser and flanger

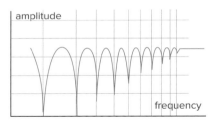

▲ Fig 18: When a signal is added to a slightly delayed version of itself, the result is a comb-filtering effect where some frequency components add out-of-phase and cancel while others add in-phase to form peaks.

THE DI BOX

Although not a type of mic, a DI box (page 45) plugs into a mic input. In the case of an active model it will probably also use phantom power to run.

The main purpose of a DI box is to allow a line level signal to be converted to mic level signal and then sent over long distances via a balanced mic cable.

Where a very high input impedance isn't required, the DI box can be built around a suitable audio transformer, which provides true electrical isolation between the input and output, avoiding ground loops and, in some situations, improving electrical safety.

Most models have a ground lift switch so that the signal ground path between the input and output can be broken if necessary to avoid ground loops.

Active DI boxes use active circuitry instead of, or in addition to, an audio transformer. They can be designed to have a high input impedance (usually around one megohm) so that electric guitars and basses can be plugged in directly. Those without transformers don't offer the same degree of electrical isolation as transformer-based types but still have ground lift switches for breaking ground loops. In the studio, a DI box might be used to connect an electric guitar to the audio interface where a software amp-modelling plug-in is used to shape the sound.

More advanced designs of DI box may offer a choice of input types such as line, instrument or even loudspeaker. The loudspeaker mode takes the signal from an external speaker jack, for example a bass amp, and then uses a network of resistors to reduce it to a safe level to feed into a mic pre-amp.

There will usually be a connection to pass on the signal to the speaker so that the amp can operate normally while a DI feed is being taken. This is not the same thing as a power soak (page 121): with valve amps a speaker still needs to be connected.

Under no circumstances should a loudspeaker output be fed into a DI box or other piece of audio equipment that isn't specifically designed to accept it as the receiving device could be irreparably damaged by the high voltages involved.

---

effects (page 303), but a similar, unwanted, effect can result when two mics pick up the same source but from different distances.

Sound travels at roughly 340mm per millisecond (page 80) so even a fairly small mic positioning difference can cause audible comb filtering to occur.

The usual studio solution is to adhere to the **'five to one' rule**, although with large multi-mic recordings — such as orchestral works — it is often necessary to apply delay to some of the mic tracks when mixing to line them up with the tracks from the mics set up at the greatest distance. To achieve this, the engineer measures the mic positions very accurately and keeps notes that can be referred to while mixing. It can also help to record the temperature in the room as the speed of sound changes very slightly with air temperature; tables of values are available to calculate the exact delay time.

Tip / Although mic pre-amps often have a button labelled 'phase invert', this is actually a polarity invert switch which isn't quite the same thing. It simply turns the signal upside down.

THE 'FIVE TO ONE' RULE

The simple five-to-one rule states that when multiple mics are set up in a situation where spill is inevitable, then you should aim to space the mics at least five times further apart than the distance between the mics and the source/s they're aimed at.

So where the first mic is picking up an acoustic guitar, and a second is picking up a mandolin, for example, if each mic is located around 40cm from each instrument then the two mics should be spaced at least 200cm apart. This reduces the level of spill and so minimises the tonal changes caused by comb filtering. The greater the mic spacing, the less serious any comb filtering effect will be. ●

MICS COMPARED:
AN OVERVIEW

	Dynamic mics		Capacitor mics
	Moving coil dynamic mics	Ribbon mics	
Operation	Thin, circular diaphragm with attached voice coil suspended in a magnetic field converts movement into an electrical signal	Thin metal ribbon suspended in a magnetic field converts movement into an electrical signal	Movement of a thin, conductive membrane close to a fixed back plate changes electrical capacitance to produce a signal that has to be amplified and impedance-matched inside the mic
Studio favourites	› Shure SM57 (right) › Electrovoice RE20 › Sennheiser MD421	› sE Rupert Neve RNR1 and Voodoo models › Coles 4038 › AEA R44 › Royer R121	› Neumann U87 and TLM103 › AKG C414 (right) › Audio Technica 4050 › Rode NTK › sE Gemini › ...but the list is almost endless. Vintage AGC12 and Neumann/Telefunken tube U47s are highly regarded.
Response shape	Cardioid	Figure-of-eight	Any polar pattern – some mics are switchable
Pros	› Relatively inexpensive › Rugged and hard to damage › Good for loud signals	› Very natural response › Can smooth harsh signals in a musical way	› Covers the whole frequency spectrum › More sensitive than dynamic models, so easier to use on quieter sound sources › Highly flexible range of polar patterns
Cons	› Limited frequency response – ineffective over 16kHz › Needs more ampification than capacitor models – meaning more noise when working with quieter or more distant sound sources	› Most models are more costly than moving coil dynamic models › Limited frequency response of conventional ribbon models, so may not suit all applications – although can also be a benefit › Fragile – care needed when handling and when recording loud signals that might produce air blasts › Passive models are less sensitive than dynamic or capacitor mic models and so require more pre-amp gain	› A good model is more expensive than a dynamic mic, although some very attractively priced capacitor mics are available › Some models are unreliable in humid environments, though they tend to recover if left to dry out
Commonly used for...	› Guitar amps – close mic'ed › Drums and percussion › Vocals (mainly live but some singers prefer to use them in the studio too)	› Drum overheads (reduces hat sizzle) › Overly harsh bowed string instruments › Electric guitar amps › Vocals (backing vocals and some lead vocal styles)	› Just about everything – large diaphragm models are normally used for studio vocals and small diaphragm models for instruments where accuracy is required
Notes	Versatile, requires no phantom power and can last for decades if looked after.	Take care during storage and don't switch on any phantom power in a system until the mic has been plugged in.	Non-valve models require phantom power. Valve models come with their own power sources.

TIPS FOR A BETTER MIX

Ensure you have the best possible recordings to work with.
Correcting performance errors using editing techniques invariably takes longer than re-recording the part – and it rarely sounds as good. The better the performance, the easier the mixing job will be.

COMMON MIX MISTAKES AND HOW TO AVOID THEM

Poor tuning and timing.
Scrutinise the original recording to make sure everything is in time and tune. Defective parts are best fixed by recalling the musicians and overdubbing. Where this is not possible, take as long as you need to fix errors. Solo monophonic lines – from guitars to vocals – can be corrected with Melodyne (or similar). For chordal guitar parts try Melodyne DNA. You stand a better chance of correcting polyphonic parts if you have a clean, DI'd recording alongside the take/s with distortion. Ensuring everyone checks their tuning using a good electronic tuner prior to each take saves a lot of headaches.

5
STUDIO ACOUSTICS

HAVE YOU EVER MADE A GREAT SOUNDING DEMO IN YOUR STUDIO AND THEN PLAYED IT BACK ELSEWHERE TO FIND THAT IT SOUNDS NOT ONLY DIFFERENT, BUT MUCH WORSE?

JARGON BUSTER

An anechoic chamber is a room custom-made to absorb all sound reflections and is normally used for equipment testing purposes. Speaking inside them yields an unnaturally 'dead' sound; nowhere in nature sounds so non-reflective.

The absorbers lining the entire room (including beneath the wire mesh floor) are typically made from wedges of mineral wool, often over a metre deep.

The anechoic chamber at Orfield Laboratories Inc, Minnesota, is the 'Quietest Place on Earth' according to the Guinness Book of World Records.

WHY ACOUSTICS MATTER

While many of us are happy to spend our hard-earned cash on new mics, audio interfaces, plug-ins and speakers in the pursuit of a better sounding mix, we often give rather less thought to the more mundane, but arguably more important, business of treating the room we mix in.

When you mix do you find that some frequencies — usually in the bass area — leap out at you while others appear quieter than they should? And have you ever made a great sounding demo in your studio and then played it back elsewhere to find that it sounds not only different, but much worse?

These type of problems are common if you mix in an untreated room, when you can end up using unnecessary EQ to get what you imagine to be an acceptable sound, only for the track to sound wrong when played elsewhere.

Why does this happen? Take two different spaces. Space A is an untreated studio, which has a room layout that emphasises the bass and reduces the upper-mids. Space B is a friend's neutral-sounding living room. You mix in space A, your studio, where you end up using EQ to reduce the bass frequencies that the room itself is emphasising, while also increasing the upper-mids your room has dulled. The result is a mix that might sound great in your studio, but which when taken to space B — the neutral-sounding living room — sounds bass-light and overly forward in the upper-mids. Your friend is understandably unimpressed and the flawed mix is said not to 'translate' well.

The fact is that getting studio acoustics right is neither a luxury nor an afterthought; it is a pre-condition of a solid mix. An appropriate room acoustic is also key to a good recording: in my experience around 90 per cent of the quality of a recording is determined before the sound even hits the microphone.

Acoustic treatment does more to improve both the quality of recordings and accuracy of mixes than even the most expensive mics, plug-ins or outboard. What's more, treatment need not be costly — especially if you take a DIY approach and build your own kit.

While the approach described in this chapter won't give you the same tightly-controlled acoustic environment you'd expect in a professionally-designed studio, you may be surprised at how much better your mixes end up sounding after applying even very basic acoustic treatment.

WHAT YOU HEAR IN THE STUDIO

When you listen to a pair of speakers in the studio what you actually hear is a mix of direct sound from the speakers plus reflections from all hard surfaces in the room, including the walls, ceiling, desk and equipment racks. This is to be expected — we live in a reflective world, and without reflections everything sounds unnaturally dead, like in an anechoic chamber (a specially designed test chamber that absorbs all sound to avoid any reflections — Jargon Buster, left).

In the real world we don't mix music in anechoic chambers, nor would we want to: people who have tried mixing in very dead studios say that find them oppressive. Besides, you'd probably end up with a final mix that would only properly translate to the handful of worldwide music listeners with access to their own anechoic chamber.

SOUND WAVES: THE PHYSICS

Where sound reflects from a solid surface it causes a pattern of constructive and destructive interference as it combines with the incident sound. At lower frequencies related to the room dimensions, the peaks and troughs in the waves 'stand' in fixed positions in the room.

Standing waves are undesirable in the studio as they can cause large peaks and troughs in the frequency response – especially at low frequencies – that can seriously hinder making informed mixing decisions. These standing waves are responsible for the resonant room modes (page 85).

WAVELENGTHS

Sounds travels at roughly 340 metres per second (m/s). If it were possible to see sound as sine waves (pure tones of a single frequency) in space, you would see a 1kHz tone repeating every 340 divided by 1000 m/s = 0.34 metres. A 50Hz bass tone, on the other hand, repeats every 340/50 = 6.8 metres. This distance between cycles is known as the wavelength. You can work it out by dividing the speed of sound by the specific frequency. As this example shows, high frequencies have short wavelengths, whereas low frequencies have wavelengths of many metres. A basic awareness of how sound travels is useful for understanding the different approaches to soundproofing and explains why some approaches are more likely to work where others fail.

The typical studio, then, is still somewhat reflective. But these reflections need to be kept under control to allow your monitors and ears to do their jobs properly. At middle and high frequencies excessive room reflections compromise both the clarity and stereo imaging of the speakers while at low frequencies reflected sound builds into resonant peaks that can make some bass notes appear significantly louder than others.

A carpeted room with soft furnishings will always sound more dry than one with a hard floor. Although this might suggest that carpeting the walls will produce a better listening environment, this is not the case. In the ideal studio, reflections are controlled in such a way as to allow all frequencies to decay at the same rate (a reverb decay time of around 0.3–0.5 seconds). The problem with carpet is that it is too thin to effectively absorb anything other than high frequencies, so carpeting the walls produces a short reverb decay time at high frequencies but does nothing to tame the mids and lows. The outcome is an even worse spectral balance than before you applied the carpets, with a sound that is both boxy and dull.

TOOLS OF THE TRADE

In the quest for the perfect room there are two main tools in the acoustic treatment armoury: diffusors and absorbers, both of which deal with a different acoustic problem.

> **Diffusors** scatter sound energy over a wide angle rather than bouncing it back like a mirror. They randomise hard reflections that might otherwise confuse stereo imaging and cause flutter echo.

> **Absorbers** absorb sound energy, reducing reflections and reverberation in the room. They are used to reduce a room's reverb time at different frequencies.

DIFFUSERS

The simplest type of diffusor is an irregular solid surface, often made from different sized wooden blocks fixed to a flat panel or from moulded plastic. By breaking up hard reflections and scattering them, diffusors help create a more even, musical sound without reducing the room's reverb time significantly. This explains why diffusion is often used to sweeten the sound of larger live rooms, as well as control rooms.

THE GREAT EGG BOX MYTH

At one time it was believed that putting egg cartons on the walls of a studio would improve soundproofing and introduce useful diffusion. In reality egg boxes are too light to do anything useful on the soundproofing front and their profile is too shallow to produce much scattering other than at very high frequencies.
So bin those egg boxes (and the myth) – there are far better solutions available nowadays.

DIFFUSION: DIY VS PRO

▲ Shelving unit containing books and records (left) is often all you need to break up strong reflections at the rear of the room. On the right is a purpose-made wooden diffuser on the back wall of a pro studio.

Large commercial diffusors typically comprise a series of rectangular wooden chambers of differing depths, where the depth and spacing is calculated to give optimum diffusion. However, a shelving unit partly filled with randomly positioned items – books, CDs and DVDs for example – also scatters sound well at mid and high frequencies.

You can glue different sized wooden blocks to a backing board for a cheap, practical alternative (left). The heights of the irregular features in diffusors need to be a quarter wavelength or more of the sound being scattered for them to work. In practice this means surface height variations of 100mm or greater are required to have any real effect at mid and high frequencies. 100mm is most effective at approximately 1kHz and above.

▲ DIY diffusor: Wood blocks of different heights are fixed to a solid backing board. The higher (blue) blocks should be around 300mm high, with all blocks made from 100mm square timber.

Diffusors are often used in larger rooms or on the rear walls of mid-sized spaces, and in the vast majority of studios they are used alongside absorbers. Diffusors tend to be less effective in very small rooms as there isn't space for adequate scattering to take place.

ABSORBERS

Absorbers are panels of porous materials, such as mineral wool, glass fibre or open-cell foam, that dampen sound reflections. They do this by allowing sound waves to pass through them and back out, but in the process friction converts some of the sound energy to heat — meaning less sound is reflected out than goes in (Fig 1).

With absorbers, size matters (right). For a porous absorber to be effective, it needs to have a thickness comparable to a quarter wavelength of the sound being absorbed, which means that at 1kHz, where the wavelength is approximately 340mm, the material needs to be 85mm thick. A porous panel this thick absorbs frequencies of 1kHz and above very efficiently, but it can also do useful work lower down the audio spectrum. The reason for this is that not all sound arrives at right-angles to wall-mounted absorbers and the more oblique the angle of approach, the greater the

thickness of material the sound wave has to pass through. The outcome is that in real-life situations porous absorbers are effective to a lower frequency than their thickness might suggest.

Tip / Spacing an absorber away from the wall improves its ability to absorb lower frequencies (Fig 2). A 50mm absorbing panel spaced 50mm from the wall is almost as effective as a 100mm thick panel fixed directly to the wall. Use offcuts of foam to make spacer blocks and glue these to the back of the main absorption panel to create these cheap artificially thicker panels.

DIY ABSORBERS

You can make your own mid/high frequency absorbers by putting 30 or 50mm mineral wool cavity wall insulation slabs into 100mm deep wooden frames where the mineral wool is flush with the front of the frame so as to leave an air space behind (Fig 3). These

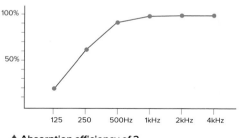

▲ Absorption efficiency of 2 inch thick mineral wool fixed directly to the wall at different frequencies.

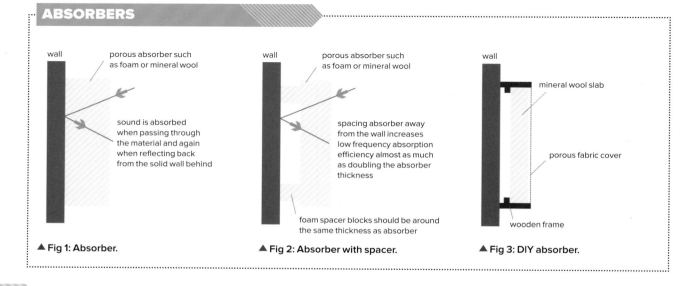

▲ Fig 1: Absorber. ▲ Fig 2: Absorber with spacer. ▲ Fig 3: DIY absorber.

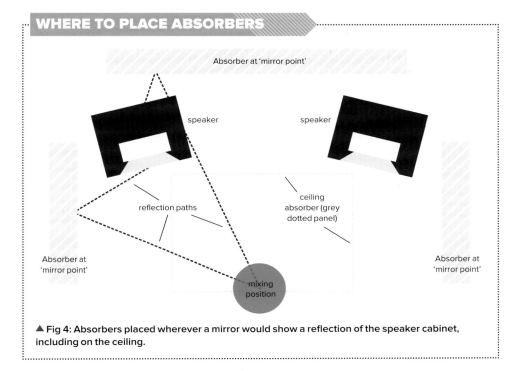

WHERE TO PLACE ABSORBERS

Absorber at 'mirror point'

speaker   speaker

reflection paths

ceiling
absorber (grey
dotted panel)

Absorber at
'mirror point'

Absorber at
'mirror point'

mixing
position

▲ Fig 4: Absorbers placed wherever a mirror would show a reflection of the speaker cabinet, including on the ceiling.

will be at least as effective as an equivalent thickness of acoustic foam, and a lot cheaper. Cover the whole thing with porous fabric, such as cotton or a polyester bed sheet, staple it around the back of the frame and hang it on the wall just like a painting. Wear gloves and a dust mask when handling mineral wool or glass fibre as the fibres can cause irritation to the skin and lungs. **Always cover DIY traps with material** to prevent fibres from escaping into the air.

Tip / If you don't want to damage walls by gluing foam directly onto them, simply glue an old CD to the back of the foam panel and then hang this onto a screw or picture nail on the wall.

WHERE TO PLACE ABSORBERS
You don't need to cover the entire surface of a room with sound absorbing panels:

doing so results in a dark and oppressive sound (remember, high frequency sound is more easily absorbed than low, so by adding more absorption to the studio the overall reverberation will become more bassy in tone). Instead aim for a coverage of around 20 per cent: you'll hear a big difference.

But which 20 per cent? When deciding where to place absorbers you need to keep in mind at all times the single overriding aim: to reduce the effect of room reflections **from the perspective of the mixing position** – not the perspective of the bed in the corner, or the cupboard by the door (Fig 4).

While large commercial studios may be able to get a consistent sound in the areas where clients sit, in smaller project studios the acoustics of the wider room only matter in as much as they impact on the sound in your mixing position.

Fortunately there is a tried-and-tested method to help decide where absorbers should go. Get a friend/significant other to move around the front of the room holding a mirror held flat against the wall while you sit in your usual mixing position. Wherever you see a reflection of one of your monitors in the mirror you need to place an absorber to prevent a reflection bouncing directly back at you.

In most rectangular rooms these mirror points are found on the side walls between the mixing position and the speakers, and also behind and between the speakers. Look up and you'll find one on the ceiling too. Don't worry about the floor – we're so used to hearing floor reflections that our ears tune them out.

Where the rear of the room is also reflective, hanging absorbers there may also help, although you may find that diffusers are a better bet: a sofa with shelves above it containing books, CDs and DVDs is often all you need to break up strong reflections.

To make your own combined absorber and diffusor for use on a rear wall, first build a large mid/high mineral wool absorber as illustrated on page 82 and then fit vertical split-log fence posts on top with a 20mm gap between each (Fig 5). The curved wooden surfaces provide some useful HF scattering, especially in the horizontal plane, while the mineral wool absorbs some of the mid and high frequency energy. The same kind of wooden posts can also be used to add reflection and diffusion to studio walls that have been carpeted in error.

FLUTTER ECHOES

A side benefit of absorbing mid and high frequencies at the mirror points is that it helps dampen so-called flutter echoes, which occur when sound bounces back and forth between parallel walls or between a hard floor and a ceiling. In smaller rooms the spacing of these echoes is so close that it forms a musical pitch or ringing sound. You hear the effects of flutter echo when clapping your hands while standing between two buildings or in an empty, rectangular room.

Professional studio designers use non-parallel walls to reduce flutter echo, but in the type of rectangular room most of us work in absorbers at the mirror points will prevent flutter echo from being a problem at the listening position, even if it remains audible elsewhere in the room. Diffusors also help reduce flutter echo. (Note that flutter echoes are different from **standing waves**: flutter echoes affect mid and high frequencies while standing waves are most problematic at low frequencies.)

BASS PROBLEMS

A typical absorber that is 100mm thick or a 50mm absorber spaced 50mm from the wall gives useful absorption down to around 250Hz. Below that its efficiency decreases rapidly. For lower frequencies a different approach is needed.

Taming bass starts with the model of speakers. A common mistake made in home studios is choosing monitors that are too powerful for the room. A good rule of thumb when choosing speakers is not to put more low bass energy into your room than it can deal with. If you use large monitors or a system with a sub in a small room with marginal acoustic treatment then the low bass region is likely to be very inaccurate. A better strategy is to pick smaller speakers with a more modest bass response.

If the speakers you own have too much bass extension for the room check any rear panel controls (page 88) to see whether you can reduce the bass output. As long as you get used to the sound of your monitoring system with some commercial recordings and don't try to EQ any

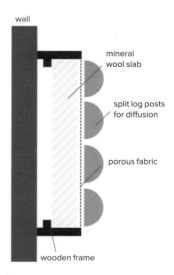

▲ Fig 5: Home-made absorber / diffusion hybrid – note the split wooden posts, available from good garden centres.

> **THE MORE BASS ENERGY THAT IS ABSORBED OR ALLOWED TO LEAK INTO THE WIDER STRUCTURE OF THE ROOM YOU MIX IN, THE TIGHTER AND BETTER CONTROLLED THE BASS IN YOUR STUDIO WILL SOUND.**

frequencies lower than the monitors can reproduce you should be able to get good results even with quite small monitors.

Fortunately, for all their faults, the kind of residential space the home producer typically mixes in does a reasonable job of controlling bass energy – albeit inadvertently.

While bass frequencies are efficiently reflected by thick walls, more lightweight walls, such as those made from plasterboard on a wooden frame as found in many modern houses, allow a significant amount of bass to pass through them. They also vibrate in response to bass frequencies, absorbing energy as they do so. Doors and windows vibrate too, damping energy through absorption and leakage – although excessive vibration can lead to a lack of focus or tightness at the bass end. The more bass energy that is absorbed or allowed to leak out via the wider structure of the room you mix in, the tighter and better controlled the bass in your studio will sound.

The reason most bass problems occur in the first place is that at frequencies where the distance between the walls is a multiple of the half wavelength of the bass note, the reflected sound bounces back and adds to the direct sound causing an increase in level at that frequency (creating the **standing wave** on page 80).

It's not just standing waves we need to be wary of though. At other frequencies the reflected sound may be out of phase (page 74) with the direct sound and so will cause a reduction in level. We call the resonant peaks related to room dimensions **room modes**; the more solid the walls, the stronger they are. Other modes exist

caused by less direct reflection paths. These 'tangential' and 'oblique modes' tend to be less severe in their effect than the primary modes related to room width, depth and height.

Cube-shaped rooms are the most difficult to work in as all room modes occur at the same frequencies, creating very strong peaks. To make matters worse there's invariably a dead spot around the centre of the room where the bass level dips alarmingly. In smaller home studios this is often where the engineer is forced to place the mixing seat, and from my own experience no amount of practical bass trapping ever completely fixes the problem. The best sounding rooms are ones where the room modes are evenly distributed, which usually means fairly large rooms where the principle dimensions are not equal or exact multiples of each other.

Tip / A good way to check for bass problems without resorting to specialised test equipment is to program a musical sequence to play a chromatic (semitone) scale over the lowest octaves and to use a sine wave as the tone. Ensure all notes play at the same velocity and then listen for unduly loud or quiet notes as the sequence plays back. Expect the level to gradually fall off as the pitch decreases – this is quite normal. What you're looking for are individual notes that stick out as being too loud or too quiet. If you find one (or more) it's a sign that you need to add more bass trapping and/or move the speakers slightly.

BASS TRAPPING
Using solid chunks of porous material to absorb bass is problematic as the wavelength of sound at 50Hz is around seven metres, so a quarter wavelength

deep trap would require an absorber almost two metres thick — a thickness few home studios can accommodate.

However, as mentioned above, not all sound arrives at an absorber head-on — some of it approaches at an angle — so filling the corners of the room, from floor to ceiling, with large acoustic foam blocks or wedges can help.

At between 30–40mm these absorbers have a limited effect on bass frequencies hitting them dead on, but reflections coming at steeper angles pass through a far greater thickness of foam. There are many commercial bass traps based on this design, either with plain or decorative surfaces. Where space is an issue, corner traps can also be fixed along the wall/ceiling joins.

Some commercial bass traps combine heavy, limp membranes (often mineral-loaded vinyl sheeting) with porous absorbers. These can be very effective but tend to be more costly than simple foam or mineral wool absorbers. It is important to understand that bass traps are not designed to reduce the amount of low-end you hear in a room, but to even out level fluctuations at different frequencies.

Finally, it's worth saying that it's almost impossible to install too much bass trapping, so if you do have bass problems fit as much in as you can.

Tip / If you're handy at DIY you can build your own corner traps using 600 x 1200mm sheets of high density mineral wool slab (30 or 50mm cavity wall insulation slab is good for this) fixed diagonally across the room corners and then stuffing the space behind with insulation-grade mineral wool.

POSITIONING THE SUB

A good way of finding the best position for the subwoofer is to temporarily set it up on the floor where you normally sit. Play a record or test disc with a busy bass line (or program a chromatic test sequence) and then listen from a position low down and close to the front wall. As you alter your position you should notice that the levels of the different bass notes become more or less even. Once you've found the best spot, place the sub there. This is normally off-centre and somewhere along the front wall. Avoid placing the sub under a table or desk with closed-in sides as this creates a resonant chamber that will cause bumps and dips in the bass response.

STUDIO LAYOUT

While the inherent structure of the room, some bass trapping and the right choice of monitors will all help control bass, there are some important considerations relating to the layout of the studio that will make a difference too. At the very least you should:

❯ Point the speakers down the length of the studio. In smaller rectangular rooms — less than around four metres wide — the bass end is invariably better behaved when the speakers face down the length of the room rather than across it.

❯ Avoid a layout that has you sitting mid-way between the front and rear walls, especially in very small rooms.

❯ Avoid siting speakers too close to walls or corners. Placing them in these areas results in complex reflections that cause an overall increase in perceived bass (of up to 6dB near walls and a whopping 12dB at corners!), but it will be very uneven, with some notes much louder than others.

> THE GOLDEN RULE WHEN POSITIONING SPEAKERS IS TO FORM A ROUGHLY EQUILATERAL TRIANGLE WITH THE SPEAKERS AT THE LEFT AND RIGHT CORNERS AND YOU IN FRONT.

❯ Ensure that the speaker-to-side-wall and speaker-to-front-wall distances are different.

❯ Ensure that the speakers aren't positioned exactly mid-way between floor and ceiling.

Moving a speaker closer to or further away from a wall by a few centimentres can change the evenness (or otherwise) of the bass response by a surprising amount, so it is worth experimenting with their positions to see what gives the most even result at lower frequencies.

Tip / The modal peaks and troughs are least severe around a third of the room's length from the end of the room (specifically 38 per cent), so if you can, place your monitoring seat there.

SPEAKER POSITION

The golden rule when positioning speakers is to form a roughly equilateral triangle with the speakers at the left and right corners and you in front (Fig 6). The tweeters should be pointed directly at your head in both the horizontal and vertical planes. You can afford to widen or narrow the speaker spacing slightly if it helps iron out bass problems.

❯ Make sure both the monitoring layout and acoustic treatment is set out **as symmetrically as possible**. This will produce the most balanced stereo image.

❯ It was once fashionable to set up small monitor speakers on their sides, but unless your speakers are specifically designed to be used this way **they will work better upright**, producing a wider sweet spot and a more even frequency response.

SETTING UP STUDIO SPEAKERS

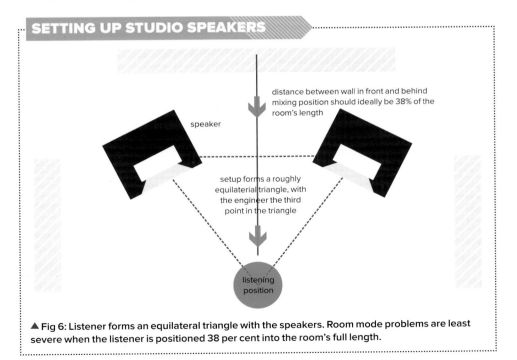

distance between wall in front and behind mixing position should ideally be 38% of the room's length

speaker

setup forms a roughly equilateral triangle, with the engineer the third point in the triangle

listening position

▲ Fig 6: Listener forms an equilateral triangle with the speakers. Room mode problems are least severe when the listener is positioned 38 per cent into the room's full length.

❯ **Avoid placing speakers low down** at the back of a deep desk as you'll hear strong reflections from the desk's surface, which will colour the sound and compromise the stereo imaging and clarity of the mix.

❯ Where desk mounting is unavoidable, you get a much tighter sound if you use **isolating speaker platforms** (below) rather than standing the monitors directly on the desk's surface. A typical isolating speaker mount comprises a slab of dense acoustic foam, sometimes with a metal or ceramic plate on top; if you can't afford a ready-made one, you can make one that's almost as good. Most commercial isolation stands can be angled up or down to ensure the tweeters point towards the listener's head.

❯ **Solid speaker support** is important, as any vibrations generated by the loudspeaker drivers that cause the cabinets to move will compromise the sound and result in a less well-defined bass end. If you use separate speaker stands, consider the hollow metal type that can be filled with sand to increase their mass and damp resonances. I also use **non-slip matting** under the speakers to hold them in place.

THE LIVE ROOM

If you're lucky enough to have both a mixing room and a separate live room for recording acoustic instruments then

SPACE SWITCHES

Some active monitors have switches on the rear panel labelled 'full space', 'half space' and 'quarter space'. These are designed to modify the bass response of the speaker to compensate for proximity to walls and corners. Full space is optimised for speakers set up away from walls or corners while half space is used when speakers are close to one wall. Quarter space settings are used when there is no option other than to mount the speakers close to corners. Where a speaker is mounted very close to the wall the reflected sound can reinforce the bass end by up to 6dB. The half space setting switches in low-cut filters to cancel the effect.

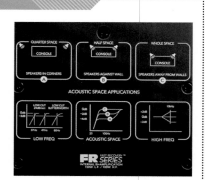

▲ Rear of the popular Mackie HR824 studio monitors: note the A, B and C settings for different spaces. The switches are below this panel.

much of the advice for acoustic treatment covered so far in this chapter will apply to the live room too. As with the mixing room, your overriding aim is a reasonably neutral sounding space with a shortish reverb time that decays evenly across the frequency spectrum.

Many commercial studios have the luxury of several rooms — some more live than others — and some of these rooms have gone down in production folklore as yielding particularly musical ambiences, such as the country house hallway where John Bonham recorded his drum parts for Led Zeppelin. Sadly back in the real world, domestic rooms and garage conversions tend to be too small to add any useful musical ambience, meaning you're usually better off treating them to get as dry a signal as possible, to which you can add high-quality artificial space at the mix stage using a suitable reverb unit or plug-in.

❯ To **damp excessive reverb** use the same mid/high and bass trapping techniques as described for the mixing room.

VOCAL BOOTHS

Purpose-built vocal booths are used in some studios but unless they are fairly large and very well designed they are best avoided in the home studio: they are easy to get wrong and it's easy to colour the sound in the wrong way.

If you do want to give it a go, the booth should be around 1.5 metres square or larger with 100mm or deeper absorbers around the upper half of the walls and over at least half the ceiling.

> Set up **acoustic screens** to further dampen reflections. Hang duvets around the recording area or build plywood panels faced with acoustic foam to reduce mid and high frequency reflections.

> When recording vocals, acoustic guitars or other acoustic instruments, set up a **Reflexion Filter** or similar behind the microphone to reduce reflected sound (page 94).

> If you plan to record acoustic instruments as well as vocals, having a section of **hard floor** can be beneficial. Hard floors reflects some sound back at the mic, adding life to the signal. You can always put a rug down temporarily when you want a drier sound.

> **Avoid – as much as you can – recording bass guitars and bass synths via mics in smaller live rooms**. The long waveforms they output, and the subsequent problems these can cause (some notes end up much louder than others) are almost impossible to control in domestic spaces. It's usually safer to record bass signals using DI methods and then use amp modelling software to shape the sound at the mixing stage as required (page 124).

Tip / You can build your own acoustic screen using acoustic foam glued to one side of a plywood or MDF sheet fitted with simple feet to keep it upright (Fig 7). The foam side can be used to create a less live environment. Reverse the screen for a livelier, more reflective sound.

These screens can also be used as separators between musicians playing at

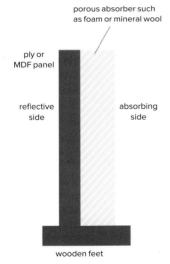

porous absorber such as foam or mineral wool

ply or MDF panel

reflective side

absorbing side

wooden feet

▲ Fig 7: DIY acoustic screen.

the same time as a means of reducing spill (page 161). Hang blankets over them if you need absorption on both sides.

ELECTRONIC ROOM ACOUSTIC COMPENSATION

Various products, such as the KRK Ergo System (above), are available that measure a room's response and then apply corrective EQ.

They do this using your own monitor loudspeakers and a flat-response measurement mic. A complex EQ profile is created to flatten the response. This EQ profile is then permanently applied to the output of the DAW so that – in theory at least – what you hear at your normal listening position is what you would hear in a neutral-sounding room.

I'm a little wary of these kinds of products. Although they can certainly help identify and dip EQ hot-spots, they shouldn't really be used to boost any bass frequencies that are lacking as you can find your monitors running out of headroom fast. A second problem is that this type of system can't cure flutter echoes or poor stereo imaging.

My own view is that you should get your room working as well as you can by fitting absorbers and choosing suitable monitors before considering compensation.

ACOUSTICS IS NOT SOUNDPROOFING!

It is important to appreciate the difference between acoustic treatment and soundproofing as they are two very different things. Fitting acoustic foam tiles to the walls to improve the listening environment won't keep sound in or out of the studio, and conversely, filling wall cavities with insulation material or adding extra layers of plasterboard to a drywall partition to improve sound isolation won't change the acoustics of the room to any significant extent. In short, don't think that investing in absorption to help your mixing will stop the neighbours (or significant other) moaning about the sounds coming from your studio.

Soundproofing is far too big a topic to cover here in any depth – and there are some good books out there that discuss it in detail – but if you do want to keep sound in (or out) of your studio here are some key things to consider:

> What prevents sound getting out also prevents it getting in.

> In most domestic spaces the weakest links are the doors and windows. Commercial double glazing is reasonably effective – especially more modern types that have a large air gap between the glass panes.

> Windows should be well sealed when closed: with no gaps or unwanted airflow.

> Internal doors are more problematic because unless they are heavy and seal completely on all four sides when closed they tend to leak a significant amount of sound. While commercial UPVC doors have very effective seals, they are often cosmetically unacceptable for use as internal doors; a heavy fire door with good seals may be more suitable.

> Double doors are far more effective than single doors, so fitting two doors, one flush with the outside of the door frame and another flush with the inside of the door frame, will deliver a big improvement. The larger the gap between the two doors, the better.

> Sound travels through solid structures in the form of vibrations, so place amps and other noise-making devices on foam isolation pads rather than directly on the floor.

Making a room airtight also creates its own problems – how do you ensure an ongoing supply of fresh air, for example?

A pragmatic solution is to open the doors between takes and fit a commercial air conditioner to keep the temperature down if equipment heat becomes a problem.

WHICH MINERAL WOOL?

For mid and high-frequency absorption, most acousticians recommend Owens-Corning 703 insulation (3lbs per cubic foot) **mineral wool**. This is rigid enough to keep its shape but still quite flexible. The denser 6lbs per cubic foot Owens-Corning 705 variety (right) is more often used for building bass traps (in conjunction with other materials) but it also makes an acceptable mid-high absorber, especially when used behind acoustic foam, where its rigidity makes it easy to work with.

The brand is unimportant – it's the density that matters. As long as the density (weight per cubic foot or per cubic metre) is correct, there should be no significant performance difference between glass fibre and mineral fibre. As a rule, these grades of mineral wool absorb more sound energy than an equivalent thickness of acoustic foam because of their higher density. These materials satisfy most fire regulation requirements, although you have to choose your frame material and covering with care if building them for use in a commercial environment as these too need to meet the appropriate fire regulations.

Acoustic foam is usually less dense than mineral wool, which makes it a little less efficient at absorbing lower frequencies. Furthermore, any surface shaping will reduce the average thickness. Foam is however, light, easy to fix and there's no problem with loose, irritating fibres as there can be with mineral wool or glass fibre. In my own studio I've used acoustic foam to cover mineral wool that itself has an air gap behind it and I've found the results to be both effective and aesthetically acceptable. ●

SECTION THREE
RECORDING

- Recording Vocals
- Recording Electric Guitar & Bass
- Recording Acoustic Instruments
- Recording Drums
- Recording Bands

6
RECORDING
VOCALS

> TO GET A GOOD VOCAL SOUND YOU NEED TO STOP AS MUCH UNWANTED NOISE AS YOU CAN FROM REACHING THE MIC'S CAPSULE .

SINGING IN THE RAIN

Despite what people say about singing in the bath or shower, finding a domestic room that sounds good for recording vocals without further treatment is rare. A room with carpets and soft furnishings is a useful place to start – although you can make significant improvements on this very easily (see Studio Acoustics, Chapter 5).

NOT JUST THE VOICE

Many musicians struggle to record vocals and tend to worry most about those aspects of the job that are often the least important – usually because they get hung up on the choice of mic or pre-amp when they should be paying attention to the real source of the problem: the singer's performance and the acoustic space in which it is recorded. Once you get these basics right, then you can think about the incremental benefits that better mics and pre-amps bring.

Stick a mic in front of a singer and what does it 'hear'? It hears the singer, of course, but it also hears reflections from the walls and other hard objects in the room, as well as unwanted sounds from outside – such as passing cars and next door's dog. While the human hearing system is adept at ignoring unwanted sounds, a studio mic picks up everything.

This means that to get a good vocal sound you need to stop as much unwanted noise as you can from reaching the mic's capsule and address any room acoustic concerns so that the mic only hears the vocal and not sounds bouncing from the walls and ceiling (see **Studio Acoustics, Chapter 5**).

While a pro studio will have an area that is properly treated for recording vocals, the home producer often needs to improvise in order to avoid recording a significant amount of room reverb alongside the vocals. Any compression used on the vocal during the mix raises the volume of this unwanted, often boxy-sounding reverb – particularly at the ends of phrases – yielding a signal that is at best less than ideal and at worst unusable.

A much better approach when recording vocals for most styles of modern music is to capture the recorded vocal as dry as possible, with as little room sound as you can manage. This results in a far cleaner signal that leaves much more flexibility for processing the vocals during the mixing stage. (Trying to hide bad-sounding room reverb by adding more digital reverb really doesn't work.)

Treating the room you record in and reducing the amount of external noise that hits the mic will both help to improve a vocal recording. But you also need to reduce the risk of unwanted vocal artefacts being captured during the recording itself – like blasts of air from the singer's mouth battering the mic's sensitive diaphragm resulting in audible popping on plosive B, P and occasional M sounds. Often these are so loud that they cause clipping, which means you can't even fix them using low-cut EQ.

CAPTURING THE RIGHT SIGNAL

Most vocals are recorded using a cardioid-pattern or uni-directional mic, which is most sensitive at the front (see **The Microphone, Chapter 4)**. This kind of design naturally excludes sounds coming from directions other than the front, but it isn't a complete solution. Unfortunately, although less sensitive at the sides and rear, the mic will still pick up some sound from these areas. And because the high frequency response of a typical cardioid drops off faster than its response to low frequencies the further you move away from the mic's main axis, by the time you get close to the sides and rear, the sound being picked up is often dull and coloured.

To combat this problem, in recent years manufacturers have started producing curved screens that fit around the back of the mic to reduce the amount of sound reaching the rear and sides of the capsule. These can really help clean up the sound of a recording, significantly reducing the amount of muddy, boxy sounding room reverb recorded alongside the vocal.

The best known device is probably the sE Reflexion Filter (right), which was the first commercially available screen of its type, but there are alternatives, and if you can't justify the expense you can improvise using folded blankets, sleeping bags, duvets or pieces of furniture foam. If you are using a Reflexion Filter or similar, set the mic up so that it is roughly level with the open side of the screen; pushing it too far inside can colour the sound (page 98).

While an acoustic screen will certainly improve a vocal recording by limiting the amount of reflected sound reaching the rear and sides of the mic, it doesn't offer a complete solution, because when you sing in a room, sound bounces off every surface, including from the wall behind the singer. Some of this invariably finds its way into the front of the mic where it is most sensitive. Hanging a folded duvet or

sheet of acoustic foam behind the singer's head and shoulders reduces the amount of unwanted reflected sound reaching the front of the mic; a simple duvet hung across the corner of a typical domestic room should produce a good result.

When selecting a duvet, pick heavy, polyester-filled ones – the filling won't settle to one end as it does with feather types. You can clip the duvet onto a cheap lighting T-bar stand using plastic woodworking clips if you don't want to screw hooks into the walls. If the ceiling is low, a sheet of acoustic foam suspended above the singer's head will bring an additional improvement.

Using these basic DIY treatments in conjunction with a Reflexion Filter or similar behind the mic will deliver results at home that rival those you'd expect to get in a professional studio's vocal booth.

WHEN WET IS BEST

Although 95 per cent of the time it is best to record vocals dry, some styles of music do sound best recorded in man-made spaces.

If you specifically need the sound of a church choir or somebody singing in a panelled library, for example, then by all means take your laptop and a couple of mics to that space.

A good starting point is to record two tracks for each vocal part, one using a close-up vocal mic (or stereo pair) and one using a more distant omni (or figure-of-eight side on the singer/s) room mic to pick up the room ambience. The two signals can be blended to give the right balance of dry vocal and ambience later.

Of course, you can fake the sound of the space using any number of quality convolution reverb plug-ins, which are based on the measured acoustic properties of actual buildings and spaces. Nevertheless, the real thing will always sound somehow – well, more real!

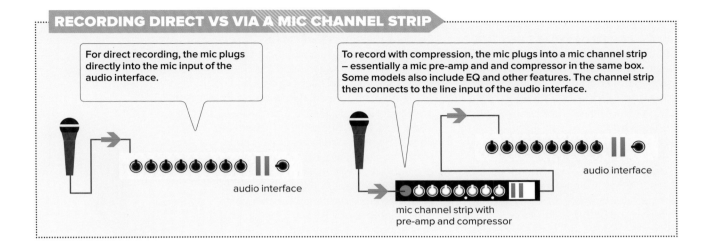

RECORDING DIRECT VS VIA A MIC CHANNEL STRIP

For direct recording, the mic plugs directly into the mic input of the audio interface.

audio interface

To record with compression, the mic plugs into a mic channel strip – essentially a mic pre-amp and and compressor in the same box. Some models also include EQ and other features. The channel strip then connects to the line input of the audio interface.

audio interface

mic channel strip with pre-amp and compressor

PRO TIPS

Tony Visconti once said that one of the biggest differences between British and US engineers was that British engineers weren't afraid to record (or 'print') their effects and signal processing direct to tape, whereas US engineers tended to record unprocessed audio to keep their options open until the mix. My own view? Keep it unprocessed unless you're confident enough to print.

Tip / Before investing in an acoustic screen make sure you have a solid, weighted mic stand rather than a cheap/light one. Stand-mounted filters are heavy and you don't want to risk damaging it (or the mic!) if the stand falls over.

THE RECORDING CHAIN

Many professionals have favourite equalisers and compressors that they like to use directly after the mic pre-amp to give them a specific sound.

The danger of inserting hardware into the recording chain for the less experienced engineer is that once the rest of the track has been recorded, the processing used on the vocals may turn out not to be quite what you need. And once recorded it may be very difficult – or even impossible – to undo.

Overall, with so many excellent and affordable processing plug-ins now available to the project studio owner, I tend to think that it is safer to record the vocals

'flat' – directly into the audio interface – and then make any necessary adjustments at the mixing stage. You can always print the vocals through any high-end outboard during mixdown anyway.

THE MICROPHONE

Although some rock and rap singers like the raw tone of a live **dynamic** mic, by far the most common choice in the studio for vocals is the large diaphragm **capacitor** model (**Chapter 4, The Microphone**). These are mainly side-address mics, in which the singer sings into the side, not the end.

The capacitor mic has the ability to capture high frequencies more accurately than dynamic models and many are also designed to produce a flattering, slightly larger-than-life sound that helps vocals stand out in a mix.

With the exception of valve mics, which have their own power supplies, capacitor mics need 48 volt phantom power to operate, but most mixers, separate pre-amps and audio interfaces with mic inputs can provide this. Mics must be connected using balanced (3-pin) XLR cables to make use of phantom power (page 63). Cardioid pattern mics are the usual choice for vocal recording as they are most sensitive to sounds arriving from the front.

Different models of mic have different tonalities, emphasising different parts of the audio spectrum, so it is useful to test a range – both when considering what to invest in and before recording a new singer to find the right model for their specific voice. If a singer has a thin or harsh-sounding tone, for example, you might choose a warmer-sounding mic, whereas for warm voices that lack definition, a brighter-sounding mic may deliver the missing higher-end sheen.

As a rule, valve mics have a slightly smoother-sounding high end combined with a flattering warmth at the lower end of the vocal range.

Now that most entry-level mics are built in China, there's plenty of choice at affordable prices and the quality of even the cheaper models can be extremely high.

Capacitor mics can be quite sensitive to vibrations that travel from the floor via the mic stand, so a **shock mount** is recommended.

RIBBON MICS FOR VOCALS

As outlined in Chapter 4, The Microphone, **ribbon mics** can look like the capacitor's poor relation: they are less sensitive than other mic types and their high end response rolls off at a relatively low frequency, making the top end sound smoother than in real life.

However, ribbon mics can sound very flattering on both instruments and voices – especially in situations where the high end needs to be made to sound smooth and creamy. Ribbon mics were favoured by many old-school jazz singers and crooners and still have applications in some areas of pop music. If you need to record **backing vocals** that sit naturally behind the main vocal, for example, the tonal smoothness of a ribbon mic will help achieve that. Even some of the newer models with their more extended high-frequency capability still deliver the smooth tonality for which the best ribbon mics are prized.

If you're using a ribbon mic for recording vocals then it's more important than usual to employ a rear acoustic screen as virtually all ribbon mics have figure-of-eight pickup patterns. A good pop shield is essential too, as much to protect the mic from potentially damaging air blasts as to reduce the impact of plosive consonants. Note that figure-of-eight mics have a strong **proximity bass boost** (page 106), so don't let the singer get too close to one.

Tip / Don't judge a mic solely on price. In Sound On Sound's shootout of 14 mics ranging from £60 to over £5,000, the listening panel all chose the same £80 mic as sounding the best for one particular singer. It wasn't ideal for everyone of course, but it does show that identifying the right mic for the singer is more about listening than reading spec sheets.

SHOCK MOUNTS

Studio mics tend to be mounted in shock mount cradles to reduce the level of floor vibrations passing through the stand and into the mic. These vibrations can add unwanted content – particularly in the (often subsonic) low-end – to a recording.

KIT LIST

Although not right for every singer, the **Neumann U87** (below) can be relied upon to deliver a slightly flatteringly bright, punchy, and modern sound on most vocals across a range of musical styles.

The **Neumann Tube U47** delivers a warm, full, rounded tone. An original will cost you a fortune and require regular servicing. Some of the modern clones are arguably just as good.

Although designed as a stage mic, **Shure's SM58** (right) has been used by more than a handful of rock singers in the studio where its upper-mid presence helps vocals cut through a busy mix.

The **RCA44** ribbon mic was found in big studios in the '30s, '40s and '50s. Used on both voices and instruments, it exhibits the classic smooth high-end of a ribbon model. Today AEA make a replica using the original materials.

Killing the acoustics

Before setting up a vocal mic, reduce the effect of room reflections by placing a screen behind the mic and hanging blankets or a duvet behind the singer – a white duvet in the above example. A commercially available curved screen provides the tidiest solution for shielding the rear of the mic but you can improvise using foam or more blankets.

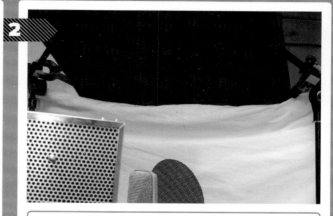

Where the ceiling is low, consider hanging a foam sheet or another blanket above the singer and the mic to reduce ceiling reflections.

Use a side-address, large diaphragm, cardioid pattern capacitor mic for most vocal recording with a pop screen between the mic and the singer's mouth. A shock mount will reduce the effect of floor vibrations. It can also help to get the singer to remove their shoes if they tap their feet as they sing.

Mics are available with different tonal characters, from bright and crisp to warm and rounded. Try to pick one that works both for the singer and the style of music being worked on. Many engineers set up two or three mics and then make a short test recording to see which sounds best with the individual singer.

Using a shock mount alone doesn't guarantee adequate isolation. Vibrations also travel along the mic cable itself. To minimise these make a loop of cable behind the mic and clip this to the mic stand using the plastic clip that came with the stand.

It's worth noting that many of the cheaper shock mounts that come bundled with far eastern mics don't offer adequate isolation. For a shock mount to be truly effective the resonant frequency of the structure should be well below the audio range; this isn't always the case.

UK company Rycote probably offer the most effective shock mounts on the market today, using a framework of resilient lyre-shaped springs moulded from a nearly indestructible plastic rather than simple elastic. If you have to work over a wooden

floor (wood transfers vibrations more effectively than concrete), it may be worth upgrading to one of these. Their Universal mount (right) is adjustable and fits most side-address capacitor mics.

POP MUSIC

Plosive Ps and Bs ruin good recordings. Fortunately they are easily tamed: all you need is a pop shield fitted in front of the mic. Don't be tempted to use slip-on foam shields as they do little to prevent popping and usually dull the high end. Instead, buy a mesh shield or make your own from stocking material stretched over a hoop or wire frame.

Commercial pop shields usually come with a flexible arm for fixing them to the mic stand with mesh made of nylon or

▲ A Rycote 'Universal' shock mount: considerably more robust than the ones that get bundled with cheaper capacitor mics.

KEEPING YOUR DISTANCE

The shock mount reduces the level of floor vibrations passing through the stand and into the mic. It is worth investing in a good one – particularly if you record above a wooden floor.

Singer should be around 200–250mm from the pop shield. Moving closer will give a more intimate, bass-heavy sound.

50-100mm   250mm

Acoustic screen behind mic secured to solid, weighted mic stand.

Pop shield is placed between 50–100mm directly in front of the mic.

Fully enclosed headphones work best for vocal monitoring as they help stop the backing mix spilling into the mic.

perforated metal. The metal mesh type causes virtually no tonal change while stocking material filters can reduce the high end very slightly. The latest incarnation of the pop shield is a plastic screen fitted into a tough plastic mount that can be clamped directly to the side of most shock mounts. This has virtually no effect on the sound and is less prone to sagging than the more common 'gooseneck'-attached screens.

The distance between the singer's lips and mic should be around 200–250mm, with the pop filter between 50–100mm from the mic. An experienced singer will vary their distance from the mic during performance, both to keep the level even and to exploit the proximity bass boost exhibited by all cardioid pattern mics when used very close to the sound source (page 106).

Obviously the better the vocal level is controlled at source the less work you'll have to do when mixing, but don't worry too much if the level does vary – there are many ways of dealing with that when you start mixing (see Vocal Production, Chapter 14).

SIBILANCE

Mics specifically designed to flatter the high end can exaggerate sibilance on Ss and Ts, especially if the singer already has problems controlling these sounds.

Furthermore, when the vocal has been compressed and equalised to help it sit in the mix, any recorded sibilance tends to become more obvious.

Where possible, tackle sibilance at source – which can be as simple as trying a different mic or turning it a little so the singer sings slightly off-axis.

▲ The classic 'pencil in front of the mic' trick – can save the day with particularly sibilant vocalists.

Another simple trick is to fix a pencil vertically up the front of a side-address mic using elastic bands (left). This shields the centre of the diaphragm and reduces sibilance to a useful degree without compromising the overall vocal sound. Any remaining sibilance can be dealt with while mixing using a dedicated de-esser plug-in or hardware box (page 212).

Another potential problem, often exacerbated by sibilance, is that of S and T sounds occurring at slightly different times when recording **layered backings** or **harmony vocals**. Although software like Melodyne and Logic's Flex Time make it easy to move and stretch or shorten individual vocal phrases, the simplest and most natural-sounding solution is to ask the vocalist or vocalists singing harmony parts to deliberately soften or even omit hard endings from words – specifically those ending in S or T sounds (Another one bite' the du' (or duss) instead of Another one bites the dust). It may sound odd when you're recording, but it can make life much easier when you begin mixing.

The same trick can also be used when **double-tracking** the lead vocal – assuming you plan to use the double track as a supporting track rather than at the same volume. Whether this is necessary or not will depend on the accuracy with which the double-track is performed: some singers deliver almost exactly the same performance every time while others vary their phrasing considerably with each take.

Tip / Getting a vocalist to sing into an off-axis mic, where this offers a tonal benefit, can be tricky. One way of stopping them drifting back on-axis is to set up a (silent) dummy mic alongside the live one and get the singer to sing into that so that the live mic picks up the slightly off-axis signal. Alternatively, turn the mic slightly in its mount and then place the pop shield in front of the part of the mic you want the singer to use. Most singers will align their performance to the pop shield.

SIGNAL LEVEL
The highest quality recording is achieved when each piece of equipment in the recording chain is running at its optimum signal level (not low enough to be noisy but not high enough to risk distortion – see page 34). This starts with the mic pre-amp. As the singer runs through the song to warm up, adjust the pre-amp gain so that its meters show a healthy signal level.

In the case of analogue circuitry this usually means getting the level meters to peak at or close to the top of their scale. You can afford to leave a little headroom in case the singer suddenly gets louder than they did during the warm-up – but don't leave more than you have to.

If you're recording digitally at 24-bits straight into the audio interface you have more room to manoeuvre. Adjust the mic gain so that you are left with around 12–15dB of headroom on the loudest

USING AN EXTERNAL PRE-AMP

Although the majority of home producers route the mic straight into their audio interface, it is sometimes possible to achieve better results by running an external pre-amp into the line input of the audio interface in situations where a lot of mic gain is needed.

While most basic interface pre-amps deliver acceptable results at low and medium gain settings, on some models you may hear low-level digital interference being added to the recorded signal when working towards the top of the gain range – a possible reason for investing in a mic pre-amp.

In most cases though, the choice of pre-amp makes much less subjective difference than the choice of mic, and the pre-amps built into all but the cheapest hardware recorders and audio interfaces are usually perfectly adequate for use at low to medium gain settings.

When you get more discriminating, a separate pre-amp may be a good investment, but don't expect a dramatic improvement in quality unless you spend a lot of money: the duvets you hang round the singer often make more difference than the choice of mic and pre-amp combined.

signal peaks (the signal only needs to peak around half way up the meter). Note that with computer systems the recording level has to be controlled at source (i.e. on the audio interface); the faders on screen control how loud the signal **plays back** but they can't be used to turn down the actual recording level.

If you're using a separate pre-amp set its gain as above, to leave 12–15dB of headroom, then feed its output into the line input of your recording system. Set the line

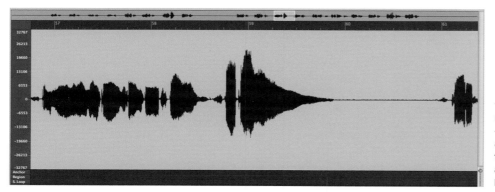

◀ How a healthy vocal recording might look – note the amount of available headroom, with the signal peaking at around -12dB during the loudest passages.

input gain on the audio interface to its unity gain position (the setting where the output signal remains the same level as the input). If the unity gain point isn't marked then set the gain control to half way and adjust the pre-amp's output level until you see around 12dB of headroom on the recording system meters. Attending to 'gain structure' in this way achieves the lowest distortion and best signal-to-noise ratio (page 35).

HEADPHONES

Fully enclosed headphones work best for vocal monitoring as they help stop the backing mix spilling into the vocal mic. Where you need to record two or more singers at the same time, use a multi-output headphone amp where each output has its own level control. In my studio I site this in the studio area so that the musicians can set their own overall monitor level rather than constantly complaining to me that their 'phones mix is too loud or too quiet!

Tip / Some singers prefer to work with one phone on and one phone off, in which case you should ensure that the unused phone is pressed against the side of their head to prevent sound leakage. Another option is to make up a custom headphone extension lead where one earphone is permanently disconnected, or with a switch in the cable to turn one side on or off.

PREPARING TO RECORD: SETTING UP THE MONITOR MIX

When you've selected the right mic and the singer is ready to start recording, it's time to set up the monitor mix. This is simply the backing mix that the singer will hear in their headphones, plus as much of their own voice as they need to hear. It is this mix that they will sing along to while recording.

It is important to understand the difference between the **control room** (or engineer's) **mix** and the **monitor mix** (sometimes also called a 'cue' or 'foldback' mix). The former is the one that you as producer and engineer hear in the control room or at the mixing desk. The latter is the mix that is fed to the singer (or other musician/s) through their headphones, and that they perform to during recording.

While it is possible for a performer to work hearing the same mix as the engineer, different players and singers usually like to hear a different balance. For example, drummers and bass players need to hear more of each other, while a vocalist might want to hear less of the drums and more of the instruments playing the chordal parts.

The simplest way to balance the monitor mix for a single singer is to adjust the control room mix to give them the balance they are after and then send a headphone feed from the main audio output so that they hear the same mix as you during recording. You can always revert back to the original mix settings when the vocal take is complete. Start with the balance as it would be if you were about to mix the song, then ask the singer what elements they'd like to hear more of and which they'd like to hear less of. Usually they like to hear more from the pitched instruments and a little less from the drums and bass.

Where multiple performers (like a full band) need to hear different monitor mixes the setup needs to be more elaborate and you will need a recording system or audio interface with multiple outputs – at least four and ideally eight (page 103). In this instance you set up the various monitor mixes using different pre-fade sends in your DAW's mixer and then route each pre-fade send to a different physical output on the audio interface.

Several commercial, multi-channel headphone amps have the facility to feed different signal inputs to each headphone output, in which case you need to connect these individual inputs to the corresponding outputs on the audio interface used to carry the monitor mixes. Generally mono is fine for performance monitoring.

If you find yourself needing multiple monitor mixes on a regular basis then you might consider buying a dedicated personal monitor system such as those made by Hear Technologies (right) or Behringer. The general concept is much as described above, except that each performer has a miniature mixer clipped to their mic stand where they can balance the different monitor mix elements for themselves (rhythm section, chordal parts, vocals and so on) rather than relying on the engineer to do it for them.

REVERB IN THE CANS

Some singers like to hear reverb in the headphones, while others like to hear their voice dry. Ask them what they prefer and take the time necessary to get the overall level, balance of voice and backing, and amount of reverb right.

To set up this temporary reverb use a post-fade aux send on the vocal track or install a temporary reverb plug-in in the vocal track insert point. To ensure latency doesn't become a problem, bypass all plug-ins in the mix that introduce noticeable delays and ensure the monitor-mix reverb is as processing-light as possible: synthetic reverb plug-ins introduce less delay than some convolution types. This reverb is not

▲ **Hear Technologies' Hear Back Personal Monitor System** – offers outputs for up to eight mini mixers.

designed to be recorded, of course – it's just there to help the singer feel comfortable and it can also help with tuning, giving a longer tail for the singer to focus on.

A second option is to use Direct source monitoring (below), where your hardware interface or mic pre-amp supports it (see Walkthrough, page 43).

It may also help to turn off some lights and ask anyone not required for the session to leave the room if the singer is shy. (On the flip side, some singers are natural performers who work better when they have an audience – ask what works best for them.)

MONITORING DELAY

All computer recording systems introduce a small time delay between a sound being fed in and it coming out of the monitor output (See Latency, page 42). To ensure this isn't long enough for the singer to notice, turn off any plug-ins that introduce long delays (these are usually the more expensive, non-native ones) and set an audio buffer size of 128 samples or less.

An alternative approach, which avoids delays altogether is to use an audio interface or mic pre-amp that has the ability to set up **direct source** **monitoring** by mixing the live vocal mic sound with the backing track as it plays back from the computer.

When using **direct monitoring**, turn down or mute the playback slider of the track being recorded in your DAW (to avoid the dry vocal being heard along with the delayed version) and if you need to add some comfort monitor reverb feed a reverb plug-in from a pre-fade aux send on the vocal track in your music software. Even if the reverb suffers a bit of delay it won't be noticeable, as long as the original dry vocal is not delayed.

Setting up separate monitor mixes

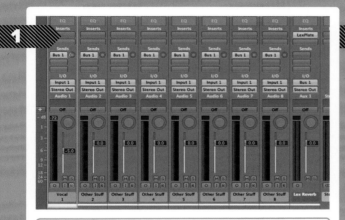

1

If the performer/s need to hear reverb in their headphones then set up a post-fade send to feed a reverb plug-in in the usual way. Temporarily bypass any plug-ins that might introduce excessive latency. In this example Bus 1 houses the reverb.

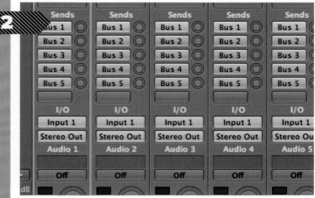

2

Set up as many pre-fade aux sends on the DAW mixer channels (and the reverb return) as you need headphone mixes for the different performers.

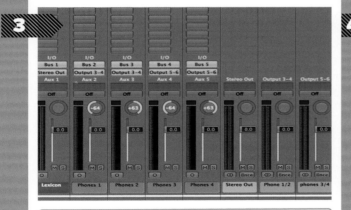

3

Route the pre-fade buses to different outputs on the audio interface and use these to feed separate headphone amps.

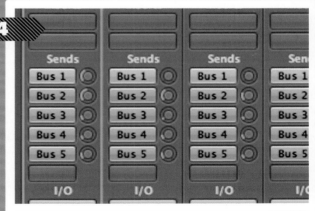

4

Adjust the relative levels of the pre-fade sends to set the correct monitor cue mix for each performer.

THE RECORDING

Your aim during the recording is to get the best possible performance from the singer. This requires a mix of talent and hard work on their part and encouragement and experience on yours. Although the producer should always aim for the elusive 'perfect take', the vast majority of vocals on commercial tracks are '**comped**' or compiled from the best parts of several different takes (page 263). It's always worth remembering that a near-perfectly pitched vocal delivered with feeling can be fine-tuned to sound wonderful while truly bad singing can never be rescued using technology – no matter what the ads tell you!

There's no hard and fast rule as to how long it should take to get a good take or how many times the singer should attempt to improve on what they've done. I usually find that once I've heard a singer run through the song a few times I can tell how good they are and how far it is safe to push them. If they don't nail most of a line in half a dozen takes they're probably not going to improve on it that day.

If just one phrase is giving the singer trouble you can set a loop to start a few bars before the trouble point and then record several versions of just that phrase. (It often helps for the singer to hear their own vocals in the previous line, in which case extend the loop backwards by a bar or so and then drop in to record the troubled phrase). Sometimes the phrase may need to be broken down into even shorter sections and, in extreme cases, a part may need to be rewritten on the spot to keep the notes within the singer's range.

Where a specific line or word lies outside a singer's range try getting them to sing as close to the desired note as possible and then when the recording is finished use Melodyne or another graphical pitch editor to force the problem notes into their intended pitches. It's something that should be avoided on lead vocals as far as possible as it seldom sounds entirely natural, but it can be a useful emergency trick when you've exhausted other avenues. (You can get away with a lot more manipulation when working on backing vocals and harmonies.) See **Pitch Correction 101, Chapter 13**.

Tip / On rare occasions it may be necessary to change the key of an entire song if too many notes fall outside a singer's range. If you need to do so quickly and haven't got time to retune each of the track's constituent audio files, simply bounce down the full mix, import it into a new project and pitch the whole audio file up (or down) as required. The drums won't sound great but you'll be able to get on with the recording quickly and return to the original project to perform full retuning or part replacement later. (It's worth saying that if you do end up in this situation you are very likely to need to re-record some parts later: even the best pitch shifting software will struggle to transpose all tracks without introducing unwanted side-effects.)

ORDER OF THE DAY

The order in which you record the different elements of the song is entirely up to you and the singer. Where possible I prefer the singer to try for a complete take of the whole song as it captures a better sense of performance. Where this isn't going to work, you might try these common alternatives:

❯ Verse by verse and choruses last: As it sounds. Start by recording verse 1, then move onto verses 2, 3 and so on before recording the choruses. The advantage of

> ❝ THE VAST MAJORITY OF VOCALS ON COMMERCIAL TRACKS ARE COMPED FROM THE BEST PARTS OF SEVERAL DIFFERENT TAKES.

TECHNIQUE: DOUBLE TRACKS

Setting up to record a double track or harmony is exactly the same as setting up the initial cue mix except that you may need to adjust the level of the lead vocal and the amount the singer can hear of themselves.

They may also prefer to hear the lead vocal with a different amount of reverb.

this approach is that you'll be recording the all-important choruses when the singer's voice is warm and relaxed, and when they are comfortable with the feel of the song. I always prefer to record each chorus separately rather than copying and pasting the same one.

❯ Chorus first, then the verses:
The opposite approach is useful when a song places greater import on the verses – like some folk tracks. Nail the chorus, then move onto the verses when the singer's in the zone.

❯ Verses, chorus, then verse 1 again:
An amalgam of both approaches allows you to return to verse 1 when the singer is fully warmed up. Because the singer may not be warmed up early in the session, or if they are faced with an unfamiliar track for the first time, verse 1 – often the most important verse – can be the hardest to get right (by verse 3 they'll be happy with their tone and the wider feel of the track). Sometimes returning to verse 1 when they've cracked the rest, even if it's just for one final take, can deliver good results.

As a general rule **double tracks** are recorded immediately after the track they're doubling, so verse 1's doubles are recorded after the lead verse 1 take and so on. This helps the singer remember the phrasing they used for the first pass. **Harmonies** are usually recorded when all the main lead lines are complete, although when they play a pivotal role in a song you may want to record them verse by verse too (verse 1 lead, then verse 1 double track if applicable, then verse 1 harmony before moving onto verse 2).

To ensure that double tracks, triple tracks (if applicable) and harmonies are sung to

the right lines, it is important to set up an accurate comp of the lead line/s before you start to add overdubs. It doesn't have to be 100 per cent perfect in terms of trimming and crossfades at this point, but it does need to be good enough to serve as a solid, and representative, **anchor** against which the double tracks and harmonies can be sung: you can do the more fiddly editing tweaks when the singer has left.

The most important thing when making this 'anchor' comp is not tuning, but the rhythm. This should be spot on, otherwise the singer will build up wrongly-timed harmonies above the wrongly-timed anchor, generating hours of additional work for you when it comes to the editing stage (page 264).

Bridges may be recorded after the verses, and before or after the chorus, depending on their importance to the song.

Tip / It is perfectly normal to have short breaks during a vocal recording, but you need to ensure that when the singer resumes singing that their tone doesn't change. This is partly a technical concern (if they change their position in relation to the mic significantly then the tone of the recording will change too), but it is also a factor of delivery; if they were belting out verse 1 and then in verse 2 (after a short break) they ease back on the pressure you can end up with disjointed vocals across verses. To avoid these issues ensure the singer maintains a consistent position before the mic and give them the tail end of previous verses in their headphones so that they can tonally carry on where they left off. When you're checking the recording you should do the same – auditioning each newly-recorded verse in the context of the one that went before.

BIGGER BACKING VOCALS

If you have a group of backing singers who are happy to perform together you can either stand them around a single mic or a stereo pair (page 69), arranging them so that the loudest singer is furthest from the mic so as to achieve a reasonable level balance between them.

Alternatively, you can give each singer their own mic. If you decide to work this way, try to ensure that each singer is standing at least 1.5 metres from their nearest neighbour to avoid phase problems caused by spill into adjacent mics.

As a rule though, the simplest mic techniques tend to sound the most natural so I'd be inclined to stick with a simple stereo pair. Many of the live recordings made at Nashville's Grand Ole Opry are done with the whole band around just one mic, with distances adjusted to balance their levels.

When recording backing vocals each singer will need headphones and, ideally, a means of adjusting their own headphone monitor level. It may not be necessary to give each singer a separate headphone mix – although this would be expected in pro studios.

For a thicker sound, get the singers to double-track what they've already done by repeating the line on a new track. Where backing singers are performing different harmonies you may be able to get them to swap parts with each other to add more tonal variety to the sound.

In the days of analogue tape it was common practice to speed up or slow down the tape very slightly when layering backing vocals so that the voices would have different timbres when returned to normal speed. You can do something similar using the varispeed option offered in some DAWs. In Melodyne you can also use the formant control to subtly (or not so subtly) alter the timbre of a take; your ears will soon tell you when you've gone too far and turned singers into cartoon characters.

A related technique is to detune the headphone mix by a few cents using a pitch shifter plug-in. Record one backing vocal with, for example, a -6 cents shift and

TECHNIQUE: GROUPS

When recording a group of singers, start with the same mic setup as you use for a solo singer -- or a stereo pair if appropriate.

The key differences are you will want to site the singers further from the mic, and it is not normally necessary to use a pop shield (the singers will be far enough from the mic to avoid causing pops).

In a suitably dead room you might also choose to place a group of singers all the way round an omni mic.

PROXIMITY BASS BOOST

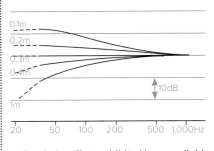

▲ Proximity effect exhibited by a cardioid mic that has a built-in low cut filter.

All pressure-gradient mics (including cardioid and figure-of-eight mics) exhibit a bass 'proximity effect', which simply means that the closer a sound source moves to the mic, the more the low end of a signal is boosted, as though bass EQ has been applied (page 67).

The effect gets significant at distances of less than 100mm or so, as shown in the graph on the left, which indicates how much more low-end is recorded when the singer is just 100mm from the mic.

This is not a fault of mic design, simply a matter of physics, and it can pose problems for inexperienced singers who randomly change their distance from the mic resulting in unwanted tonal changes.

An experienced singer, however, can use this proximity effect to their advantage, leaning into the mic to make a phrase sound more intimate or increasing their mic distance and/or turning slightly off-axis to deliver louder phrases.

▲ Jazz recording held at Capitol Records Studio, California, shows two singers in front of a single capacitor mic — note that the pop shield has been turned aside. (Photo by Jesse Grant/WireImage).

another with a +7 cents shift. The singers will pitch to what they hear so you'll end up with one part very slightly flat and the other very slightly sharp. This can produce a rich sound without the side effects sometimes heard when you try to pitch-shift vocals at the mixing stage. Note that it is preferable to set slightly different sharp and flat pitch shift amounts to help randomise beating effects that are often heard when two identical sounds are slightly out-of-tune with each other.

Yet another ploy used with larger vocal ensembles is to have the singers record multiple layers in a stereo pair of mics but change their positions before the mic for each take. They might do three takes standing first to the left, then in the centre, then to the right of the mic array. When mixed this produces a natural-sounding soundstage spreading the singers evenly from left to right. Changing the mic type and mic distance can also introduce tonal variety.

Tip / Not all of us are lucky enough to work with groups of backing singers. When you need to build big block harmonies using a single singer you can use the above techniques as starting points. You might try pitching the harmonies up and down very slightly, for example, or asking the vocalist to change their position in relation to the mic for each take. Asking them to adapt a slightly different singing style (breathy, warm, big etc) for each take can also help build a big-sounding vocal section.

Tip / Another simple trick is to change the model of the singer's mic for different takes to generate different kinds of tones. This alternative recording can be used as a low-in-the-mix double or triple track. ●

GETTING THE BEST FROM SINGERS
(AND OTHER PERFORMERS)

If only recording a great vocal was as simple as dealing with room acoustics and putting a suitable mic in front of the singer. The truth is these are the easy bits. The real work is about coaxing a great performance from the singer – a process that can push even the seasoned producer's bedside manner to the limit.

Getting the best from a vocalist demands that the producer adopt a number of roles, from diplomat to amateur psychologist – even downright liar, as demonstrated in an anecdote recounted to me by an engineer friend of mine. He had an opera singer in to record, and when she saw him setting up the mic she said: "Young man, I've never needed a microphone in my life and I don't intend to start using one now!" Instead of entering into an argument about the futility of her trying to sing directly at the tape recorder, he simply said "OK"

and moved the mic to one side, ostensibly putting it away, and hit the record button. It wasn't the ideal mic position but he captured a great performance and she went away happy in the belief that she hadn't used a mic.

Whatever you need to be – diplomat, psychologist, tactician, friend, purveyor of mistruths – there are a few general considerations that will help you get the most from a singer, both before and during the recording:

BEFORE RECORDING

❯ Give the singer time to do any vocal **warm-up exercises**. Many find their voice works best if they **avoid milk and cheese** before the session.

❯ Take care to get a **headphone monitor mix** the singer is happy with. Not only will it help

▼ Do whatever you need to do (within reason!) to get the best performance from the vocalist: if they need scented candles then accommodate them as best you can.

them perform better; it will communicate to them that you care about doing a good job.

> Make sure your recording system is set up so that you can do **multiple takes** without long pauses between them. Nothing wears down a performer more than having to wait around when they're ready to sing.

> Ask the singer to **remove noisy jewellery** or watches that might get picked up on the recording. I once recorded someone whose digital watch made no noticeable sound but its tick still managed to get onto the mic signal as the watch circuitry was radiating electromagnetic interference.

> If a singer likes to tap their feet while singing, get them to **remove their shoes** to avoid the mic picking up bassy vibrations.

> Make sure there is **plenty of water** at hand – although it's best not to have it too cold as that can cause singing problems.

> Make sure the singer is **both physically and mentally comfortable**. Be sensitive to their needs/quirks: if they can't perform without a scented candle in the recording room then so be it. Accommodating reasonable requests may be all that's needed to help relax a singer and coax an even better performance from them.

> Some singers like to have their **vocal coach** sit in on sessions. Their input can really help (on the flip side, an overly aggressive manager sitting in on a vocal session can be truly unhelpful).

DURING RECORDING

> Never tell a singer they've done a bad take as it may undermine their confidence. **Gentle constructive criticism** is OK ("That's

good, but how about you try this?"), but in the main, be encouraging. Saying "How about you ease off the pressure?" rather than "You sound like you have an anger management problem" will make for a more successful session.

> No matter how good the singer, **always get them to record several complete takes** on separate tracks so you can pick the best lines and phrases later to compile the ultimate take. Having several takes will also get you out of trouble if a lorry drives by on one of them and gets picked up on the recording.

> **Record everything.** Sometimes those throwaway warm-up lines can't be bettered.

> I find it helps to have a **printed copy of the lyrics** so that I can mark particularly good sections or sections that definitely need replacing using coloured marker pens.

> Pay specific attention to **line ends**. These are often the shakiest parts of individual takes, coming when the singer has least breath.

> When you have a take that you know will work OK, ask the singer to do **another – just for fun** ("Awesome: how about we do one more for the road?"): they may deliver something even better when the pressure's off.

> Don't push a singer who is obviously tiring. **Take a break**, have a cup of tea (without milk!), then try again.

> Keep **alcohol** out of the studio. And **drugs**. Legal aspects aside, any form of stimulant may make the performer think they're singing well when in fact they're delivering a less precise (or awful!) performance. I'm sure there are exceptions, but they are rare.

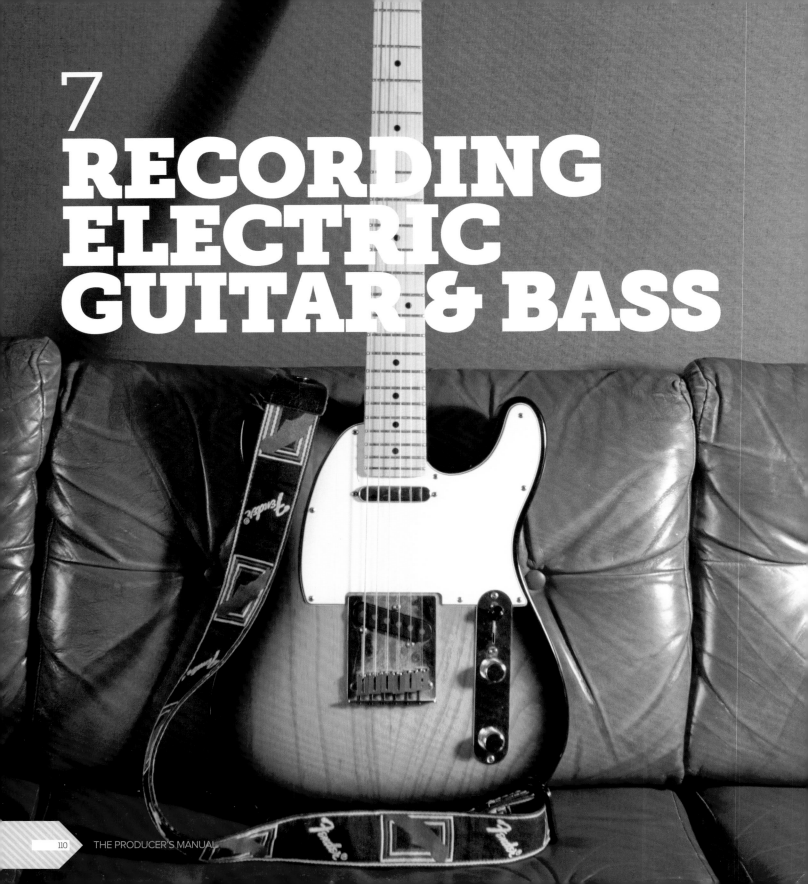

7
RECORDING ELECTRIC GUITAR & BASS

A traditional valve amp uses all-valve circuitry and an audio output transformer. Valves distort in a unique way when driven past their normal operating level producing their distinctive sound. The transformers also contribute to the tone. Some models include a specialised circuit around the output transformer to add brightness, usually called a presence control.

Solid state amps (below) employ a range of (analogue) circuitry tricks to emulate the distortion created by an overdriven valve. These include FETs (Field Effect Transistors), which can sound very valve-like when driven hard, or complex circuits involving integrated circuit chips and diodes. Solid state amps are cheaper to build and tend to be lighter to carry than their valve cousins.

Modelling uses digital rather than analogue technology to emulate the way a 'real world' circuit behaves. This can be done by analysing the behaviour of individual circuitry building blocks, or in some cases by emulating all the individual electrical components in a circuit. When applied to a guitar amp, the modelled signal is usually amplified using a solid state amp.

A MILLION TONES

The almost limitless number of combinations of guitar, amp, effects and – most importantly – playing styles means that there are as many different guitar sounds as there are players. And more importantly for our purposes, there are as many ways of recording guitar as there are studio engineers.

The up-side of this wealth of options is the sheer number of tones that can be generated and recorded: from delicate chorused shades through warm bluesy workouts to raw rock grinds and metal shreds. Part of the skill of being an engineer or producer is knowing which of the possible recording methods is likely to be most suitable for any given project.

The first decision when recording electric guitar is whether to use a mic or not. A certain breed of purist will argue that mic'ing an amp yields the best results, and they may be right; it is the traditional method that has shaped countless genre-defining sounds and is still the preferred choice of many engineers and players.

But sometimes mic'ing is not an option: in situations where excessive sound levels or spill into other mics might be a problem, for example. Fortunately, advances in guitar amp modelling hardware and software over the past few years have opened up a whole new world of great-sounding alternatives to traditional mic'ing that now seriously challenge the more traditional recording methods.

What are the options then?

> **DI (or Direct Inject) recording:** in which the signal from the guitar goes direct to the DAW's soundcard or audio interface.

Unless the interface has a dedicated instrument input, a **DI box** (page 45) is inserted into the signal chain between the guitar and audio interface to correctly match the signal level and pickup impedance. DI recording is commonly used in combination with amp modelling plug-ins to shape the unprocessed tone into the sound the guitarist is after. However, a range of perfectly useful clean sounds can be achieved by simply DI'ing the guitar (without amp modelling) and adding compression and a touch of reverb or delay. This was reportedly how David Gilmour recorded the main guitar part in Pink Floyd's 'Another Brick in the Wall'.

> **DI recording via a 'direct-connect' hardware modelling pre-amp** like the Line 6 POD: in which the signal from the guitar goes into the modelling pre-amp to be amplified and effected, and then into the DAW's soundcard or audio interface to be recorded. The up-side of this approach is that no computing power is needed to create the sound (as it is if you use a plug-in amp model). The down-side is that, as with mic'ing an amp, you're pretty much stuck with the basic sound you start with.

> **Mic'ing the guitar amp:** the 'traditional' approach, where the guitar is fed into an amp and then the amp is mic'ed, using one or more mics to capture the amplified sound. Low-volume adaptations of this mic'ing technique include placing the speaker and mic in a **sealed cabinet** or **offloading power** onto **dummy loads** to generate the same amp sound at a considerably lower volume.

> **A combination of these:** it's not uncommon, for example, to mic a guitar amp in the traditional way but also run a DI signal from a DI box used as a signal splitter

to generate a second unprocessed signal that you can record to its own track and then process differently, or feed to an amp and re-mic if the mic'ed amp sound turns out not to work in the context of the later mix.

RECORDING DI

The simplest way of recording electric guitar is by plugging the guitar output directly into the computer system's soundcard or interface input.

For the best results, the guitar signal needs to be fed into a **high impedance input**, around 10 to 20 times higher than a typical line input. If the interface has an **instrument input**, this will work fine as it will be specifically designed to match guitars and basses. If not you'll get the best results using an **active DI box** with a high input impedance that will match the guitar signal to the mic input of the audio interface (most active DI boxes are designed to feed into mic inputs rather than line inputs). Guitars seem happiest used with equipment that has an input impedance of between 500kOhms and two megohms.

You can still get a semi-usable sound if you record directly into the interface's **line input**, although the lower input impedance causes the guitar to lose some top end. This less lively tone may be fine in the context of a mix – particularly if you use plug-ins to create more overdriven tones. However, a high impedance instrument input stage is always preferable.

You can ignore this impedance adjustment with guitars and basses that have **active pickup systems** (usually powered by batteries in the guitar): these work fine plugged directly into a normal line input. Similarly, a guitar pedal connected between the guitar and a line input

THE GENESIS OF A SOUND

The sound of the electric guitar has been evolving for around three quarters of a century, and while the original premise of the electric guitar was nothing more than the amplification of an acoustic guitar to let it play at higher volumes, the limitations of both the amps and speakers of the time soon pushed performers towards experimentation and creative abuse – specifically, driving their amps to deliberate distortion to increase sustain.

This would have sounded awful but for the fact that those early amps used 10- or 12-inch speakers without tweeters (page 19). Their limited upper-frequency response rolled off steeply above 3–4kHz, suppressing the unpleasant-sounding higher harmonics created by distortion and producing the overdriven blues tone that has passed into western musical tradition.

It's a classic case of limited technology spawning a new tonal genre, one that we may never have stumbled upon had those old amps been full-bandwith and powerful enough not to distort. And it's why today's guitar amps still use limited bandwidth speakers – even though

Photo: Roland Godefroy

we now have the technology to amplify the entire audio spectrum.

From this early blues sound evolved the almost vocal tones of **BB King**, the rock and roll edge exploited by **Chuck Berry** (above), the more obviously overdriven rock sound that flourished in the '60s and '70s as exemplified by bands such as The Yardbirds, Free, Cream, Led Zeppelin and The Who, and of course today's high energy metal sounds with pounding low end, biting tops and scooped mids.

will also match the impedance for you, although only pedals with an electronic bypass (not a hard-wired bypass) will do the same when bypassed. Most Boss pedals are fine for this purpose; if you use one make sure that it has a good battery fitted, set it to Bypass and use it between the guitar and the audio interface.

The guitarist may be tempted to insert their favourite distortion pedal or stomp box into the DI recording chain. This is fine, although it's worth noting that you won't get a good overdrive sound this way unless you follow it with some kind of speaker emulation filter to remove the fizzy upper harmonics. This can be done using either hardware or a plug-in.

Remember that in the real, non-virtual world, guitar **amplification is always followed by a speaker**, which performs an important role in shaping the sound. In practice, the speakers roll away the highs steeply above 3–4kHz to create the warm, mid-heavy tone we associate with the electric guitar (see The genesis of a sound, left). If you bypass the speaker or speaker emulation you can end up with unpleasantly raspy bright tones. Of course it is (just) possible you may have a valid artistic reason for wanting your guitar to sound like a wasp in a paper cup, in which case... go ahead!

if you want to DI without using software amp modelling, there are several analogue speaker simulator boxes around, such as the Palmer Junction Box and the Hughes and Kettner Red Box (left), which can be inserted in the signal chain after any stomp boxes but before the recording input.

However, in my experience many players prefer to use a combination of software amp/speaker modelling with their favourite analogue stomp-box pedals as this offers far more tonal flexibility than a simple analogue speaker emulator.

MODELLING PRE-AMPS
A neat alternative that mitigates the need for a DI device, amp or mic is a hardware modelling pre-amp like Line 6's POD (right), that offers plenty of classic tones from which to choose — from squeaky clean, via gently overdriven blues to out-and-out rock mayhem.

Although analogue boxes designed to deliver a fully-produced sound direct to the recorder without the need for an amp have been around for a while (like the Tom Sholtz Rockman and Sansamp from Tech 21), the concept of a guitar recording pre-amp only really gained momentum when Line 6 unveiled its first POD.

The POD is a guitar pre-amp that can be DI'd directly into a recorder and which uses digital modelling technology to emulate not only specific models of guitar amps, but also their speakers, typical mics that might be placed in front of their speakers, and a host of effects such as delay, reverb, chorus, flanging, overdrive and so on. They also deal with any impedance matching issues too. In other words, you get everything you need to produce a finished guitar sound in one box.

The attraction of the modelling approach is obvious: you can play at relatively low levels and get big-sounding results in the knowledge that the sound you hear over the studio monitors while playing will be the same sound you'll hear in the final mix. You also get a wide choice of amp types and a whole rack of effects to play with.

Of course, there are down sides. When the first POD came out it wasn't long before some traditional guitarists started complaining that the new modelled amps didn't sound like the real thing and didn't offer the same tactile playing experience.

It was true. But technology has developed significantly since then, with more realistic results being delivered at every new product launch. Nowadays there are several different manufacturers producing modelling recording pre-amps for guitar, most of which have stereo outputs allowing additional effects to be inserted in stereo.

Other than setting record levels and choosing the sound you want, there's little more to say about the pre-amp modelling approach to guitar recording – it's as easy as it gets, although if you're recording via a hardware unit it can be useful also to record a clean feed (see Walkthrough, right) at the same time in case you overdo the modelled overdrive and/or effects.

Once the hardware models had a firm grip on the market it wasn't long before their **plug-in** counterparts followed, designed to be placed on tracks in the user's DAW. The raw tone is DI'd using one of the methods already discussed.

When using the modelling approach it is important to remember that what you hear over the monitors will never have the same effect as the trouser-flapping reality of standing in front of a large stack cranked to 11. But this is partly intentional: the models are designed to sound the way you'd expect the guitar to sound on a commercial record – and that is how hardware and software models should be judged.

MODEL BEHAVIOUR

When creating algorithms for speaker emulation plug-ins, software designers have to factor in a wide range of variables – some of which come closer to the sound of the real thing than others.

Open-backed guitar cabinets tend to have different low-frequency characteristics from sealed box speakers, for example, primarily because the air in a sealed box acts like a spring to prevent the speaker cones travelling too far. This produces a tighter bass end than the open box, which has a more relaxed sound with more thump in the bass end. There's also a big difference in sound between a small combo and a 4x12 cabinet – even when played at the same level and fed from the same amp.

When designers take the digital modelling route they have to replicate all these different factors, which is why it is so difficult to get modelling exactly right.

My own view is that amp models don't need to be entirely accurate as long as they sound musical and deliver an acceptable playing experience.

At the time of writing the main players in the software amp-modelling market include Line 6 with PODFarm, Waves with GTR, AVID with Eleven, Native Instruments' Guitar Rig, IK Multimedia's Amplitube and Softube's Vintage Amp Room. Amp modelling is also included in Logic Pro and Garage Band as standard. Each plug-in has its own character, but all are capable of delivering excellent results, and most follow a similar paradigm, where the effects, amps, speakers and mic position/s are adjustable separately.

Tip / A common approach when using a hardware pre-amp model is to use the pre-amp to get the basic guitar sound (without added effects) and then add any necessary processing and effects such as compression, reverb, chorus or delay using DAW plug-ins, allowing you to adjust their settings in the context of the full mix. These plug-ins can be left active during recording if the player needs to hear the effects while playing as they won't actually be recorded (although be ever-wary of **latency** – page 42).

MY VIEW: MODELLING

The best advice I can give about recording electric guitar via an amp or hardware modelling device is to aim to get as close to the sound you want to hear at the recording stage; the amount of rescuing that can be done when mixing is less than many players imagine.

If in doubt err on the side of less – less distortion and less compression. Both are easily added when you start the mixdown.

Guitars using the DI method

1 Record the mic'ed amp on one track while simultaneously recording a clean DI feed from the guitar onto a second track.

2 Use an amp modelling plug-in to shape the tone of the DI'd track.

3 Balance and pan the two tracks to taste.

4 If necessary EQ the mic'ed amp track and maybe add some compression to the DI'd version – especially if you're after a cleaner sound for that track. Using compression instead of overdrive adds the necessary sustain without adding dirt. When the settings are right you may want to send the two tracks to the same guitar group bus.

Tip / Audio editing is made considerably more difficult if a track is recorded with echo or delay, as you have the effect tails to worry about when joining or removing sections. Non-delay effects such as chorus, overdrive or wah can be recorded without making editing any more difficult. Remember that almost all effects can be added after you've recorded the raw guitar track. That said, whatever gets the best performance from the player is the right way to go — regardless of the headaches it might give you when you come to mix.

TRADITIONAL MIC'ING TECHNIQUES

While DI approaches can be boiled down to setting the record level and tweaking settings to get the best sound over the studio monitors, recording using mics is more of an art form.

At its most basic the traditional mic'ing approach is as simple as choosing a mic and placing it somewhere near the amp. In practice there are many variables that affect the recorded sound, including the type and position of the mic used, the room acoustics, the height of the amp above the floor, and the combination of mics and their positions when two mics are used at the same time.

THE RIGHT MIC

Different mics sound very different when placed in front of the same guitar amp. Experiment with whatever you have as you never know what will produce the best sound — it will sometimes be the cheap dynamic model you've got in the back of the drawer. You don't need a mic with ultra low noise or high sensitivity, but at the very least it must be able to withstand fairly high sound pressure levels (SPLs, page 65).

Dynamic models are the most common choice among engineers, but there are other good alternatives. Popular dynamic guitar mics include the Shure SM57, Sennheiser MD421 and occasionally the Electrovoice RE20, although in recent years there has been an increased interest in using ribbon mics. Established brands include Coles, RCA/AEA and Royer, although there are now many cheaper ribbon mic alternatives of eastern origin that sound good on guitar amps.

The ribbon's tendency to smooth out highs stops the guitar sound from getting too gritty, although you may need to roll off a little low end to stop the bass end getting overblown — especially when working close to the grille: ribbons, being figure-of-eight pattern mics, exhibit a pretty fierce proximity bass boost effect (page 106).

Capacitor mics often sound too edgy on guitar amps, although some models deliver extremely good results, not least the modestly-priced Audio Technica 4050. When Alan Parsons was heading Abbey Road Studios his view was that capacitor mics had a more open sound with a more appropriate low end than dynamic models, although he preferred to site them further from the amp.

MIC POSITION

The textbook method of recording the guitar amp is to position a dynamic mic close to the grille but not quite touching it (Fig 1, right). Aiming the mic at the centre of the speaker gives a bright, hard-hitting tone, which becomes warmer and less brash as you move the mic out towards the edge of the cone (Fig 2, top). I often find I get a better sound by moving the mic away from the grille by a few inches.

KIT LIST

The **Shure SM57**: Essential studio workhorse and first port of call for many studio engineers (cheap as well!). Great for all kinds of guitar recording, often used right against the grille. The high mid-range peak delivers aggression without high-end fizz.

The **Audio Technica 4050**: High quality condenser mic that can tolerate higher SPLs and that works well on a number of sources — including guitar amps.

The **Royer 121** ribbon mic: Modern classic that delivers big and seriously warm guitar tones. Specifically designed to accept high SPL levels.

MIC'ING THE AMP: EASY OPTIONS

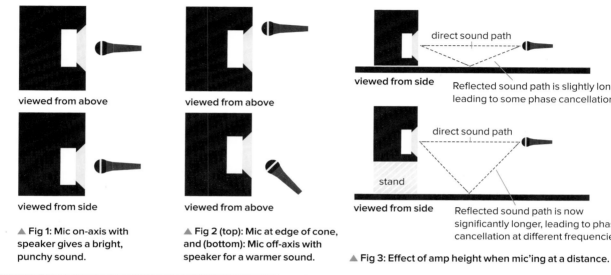

viewed from above

viewed from side

▲ **Fig 1: Mic on-axis with speaker gives a bright, punchy sound.**

viewed from above

viewed from above

▲ **Fig 2 (top): Mic at edge of cone, and (bottom): Mic off-axis with speaker for a warmer sound.**

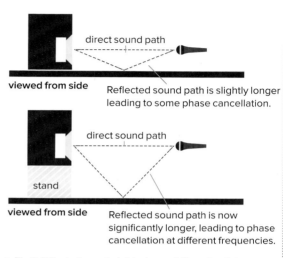

direct sound path

viewed from side

Reflected sound path is slightly longer leading to some phase cancellation.

direct sound path

stand

viewed from side

Reflected sound path is now significantly longer, leading to phase cancellation at different frequencies.

▲ **Fig 3: Effect of amp height when mic'ing at a distance.**

If a particular mic sounds too bright you can try keeping it in the same place but angling it so that it is a little off-axis to the speaker (Fig 2, bottom): most cardioid pattern mics sound more mellow when used off-axis. The larger the mic's diaphragm, the more the tonality changes as you move off-axis, making it a particularly good technique to explore with large diaphragm capacitor mics.

Where the cabinet has multiple speakers, check whether one sounds better than the others. If it does then mic that one. If you can't get the sound you need from the amp without turning it up excessively loud, then consider a power soak (see Low-noise options, page 120).

Of course, you don't have to close-mic the amp. Different tones are generated using distant mic'ing, invariably taking in more room sound which – if the room sounds good – can add a whole new flavour to the recorded sound.

▲ **Mic on-axis with speaker – see Fig 1.**

▲ **Mic at edge of speaker cone – see Fig 2 (top).**

It is important to note that when mic'ing an amp from a distance the height of the amp above the floor will change the length of the reflected sound path, giving rise to phase cancellation at different frequencies (Fig 3). The height and mic distance can be adjusted to use this phase cancellation to change the sound – rather like a mechanical EQ. To audition the results put on headphones and listen to the changes as you reposition the mic and amp.

USING TWO MICS

Although you can generate a range of great tones using a single mic, introducing a second opens up many new sonic doors. Common techniques include:

❯ **Blending the tight, mid-range tones of a dynamic mic placed close to the grille with a more distant room sound from a condenser placed further from the amp** (Fig 4, right). The close mic generates warmth and toppy definition, while the distant mic gives the guitar sound ambience and depth. The distance of the second mic from the amp can be anything from half a metre to much further back if the room sounds good enough.

❯ **Setting up two different types of close mic at the same distance from the speaker** (to avoid phase cancellation problems) and mixing their outputs to get the sound you want (Fig 5, right). In an interview with Andy Jackson at around the time David Gilmour recorded 'On an Island', Andy told me he'd had great success using this method combining an SM57 with a ribbon mic.

❯ **Using different mics on two speakers** in a 4 x 12 cabinet or a two speaker combo and then processing each signal in a slightly different way when mixing can help achieve a more dense sound (Fig. 6,

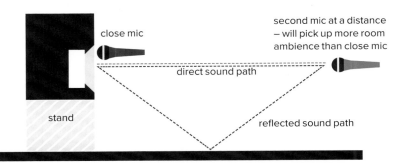

Fig 4: Use of a close and distant mic combination on a single amp. The second mic is often a condenser model. Note that as in Fig 3, the final sound depends on both the height of the amp from the floor and the distance between the two mics.

right). Many of the classic AC/DC guitar sounds were made using this technique and Andy Summers' amp was mic'ed this way for many of the classic Police tracks, where his amp featured chorus on one speaker and no effect on the other. This arrangement really fools the ears: when the two signals combine, the impression is of a three-dimensional chorus sound with no sense of which speaker is processed and which isn't.

Tip / Capacitor mics come into their own in multi-mic setups when used alongside dynamic models, with many engineers opting for a 'dynamic up close, large diaphragm capacitor out in the room' approach. However, some capacitor mics

Tony Visconti has said he sometimes searches out reflective areas for his more distant mics and has been known to aim a second room mic at the control room window to pick up reflections from there.

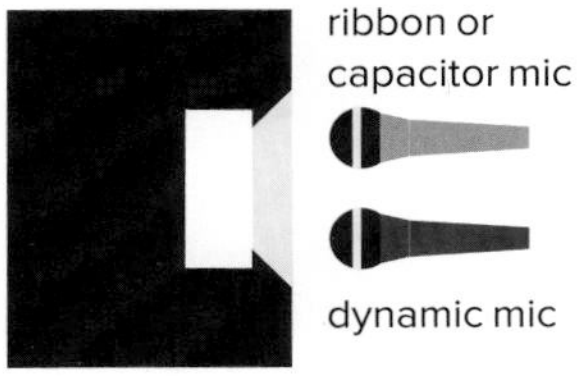

▲ **Fig 5: Combining the outputs from two different mics, each the same distance from the grille, can produce tonalities not achievable using a single mic.**

▲ **Fig 6: Where the cabinet has more than one speaker, you can record two of the speakers using different mics and then blend the two outputs.**

deliver an equally good guitar sound when used on their own. It really is all down to what works in the given situation.

ON REFLECTION

It is easy to think that because a guitar amp is loud you don't have to worry about sound reflections from elsewhere in the room. But this is not the case: the louder the amp, the louder the reflections, and while you may not hear the reflections if you work with the mic right up against the grille, as you move the mic back, the room reflections will make a progressively greater contribution.

If you have a Reflexion Filter or similar you can reduce these reflections by placing the screen behind the mic in the same way you would when recording vocals (page 94). If you don't have a screen you can improvise using blankets, duvets or slabs of acoustic foam. The need to use screens is often more acute with ribbon mics; their figure-of-eight patterns pick up as much sound from behind as from in front.

But depending on the room, reflections are not always bad news. In live rooms that have a good sonic character, distant mics can be pushed ever further away from the amp to capture more room sound.

In smaller rooms with a less obvious room sound, try using a figure-of-eight mic towards the back of the room, side-on, so that its dead axis faces the guitar speaker. This will reject most direct sound from the speaker so the mic picks up only reflected sound. Some experimentation is required to find the best position, which will probably be to one side of the room's centre so that each side of the mic receives a different pattern of reflections. If this technique is used in the exact centre of a perfectly symmetrical, unfurnished room with the amp also placed centrally along one wall, the sound picked up by both sides of the mic may be so similar that much of it will cancel out.

Tip / Even unlikely setups can yield good distant-mic results. A while ago I was recording an electric guitar part and forgot to reset the input selection in my DAW software, so while I thought I was recording via the mic stuck in front of the speaker, in reality the guitar was being picked up by a vocal mic a couple of metres away. The result was a raw, raunchy tone that worked better in the song than if I'd close-mic'ed the amp. The moral of the tale? Happy accidents do occasionally happen!

PHASE ISSUES

If you use a close mic alongside a more distant one and combine the results you can expect phase cancellation (page 74) depending on the difference between the mic positions. This will colour the sound, but that's all part of the creative process and you can adjust the mic positions to change the tonality in a way that EQ alone may not be able to manage.

Alternatively, you can leave the mic positions set and then use the DAW's track delay feature to move the distant mic in the

TUNING

It is imperative that guitars are correctly set up, that the intonation is spot on and that the strings are not so old that they've lost their tone and/or pitch. This may sound obvious, but I've had clients turn up with unplayable instruments and I've had to spend the first hour of the session being a guitar tech.

If a guitar is correctly maintained it can be tuned using a good quality

electronic tuner and all the chords will be in tune too (as far as the equal temperament scale permits!). If it is badly set up, the open strings might be in tune but chords can sound out of tune – especially further up the neck. Some players always sound out of tune: they press down too hard on the strings causing fretted notes to sound sharp. All you can do is offer advice on playing technique or suggest that the player uses heavier strings.

virtual world. Adding a delay of 1ms is roughly equivalent to moving the mic one foot (roughly 300mm) further away. Using a negative delay of the same amount brings the mic closer by the same amount – at least as far as phase cancellation is concerned.

You get a different result if you place the amp on a chair or stand rather than on the floor; with the amp raised, the more distant mic will capture both the direct sound and a reflection from the floor, which will arrive slightly later (Fig 3, page 117). The more the amp is lifted from the floor, the greater the path length difference between the direct sound and reflected sound.

Using the relative phase between two mics as a form of EQ can be extremely useful when mixing to create a guitar tone that cuts through the mix without becoming too loud.

ADVANCED MIC TECHNIQUES

Tip / To separate two guitar parts in a mix you can get a spacious but uncluttered result by panning the close mic of the first guitar to one side of the mix and the distant mic to the other. Pan the second guitar in the opposite way and you get a result that is something close to how the guitars might sound played live with the two amps at opposite sides of the stage.

Tip / Where the speaker cabinet has an open back, see how it sounds mic'ed from the back – it invariably generates a less bright tone (Fig 7). If you mic both the front and rear of the cabinet simultaneously you'll need to phase invert one of the mic inputs. Varying the distance/s will reintroduce some phase cancellation effects that can be used to fine-tune the sound.

Tip / Because guitar amps interact with the room in which they are recorded – even when close mic'ed – you can get very different results by moving the position of the amp, if only be a few centimetres.

Tip / To help keep a flabby low-end under control, keep the amp away from room corners and walls and lift it above the floor. To further reduce floor reflections, try tilting the amp up slightly to direct the sound away from the floor. Lay acoustic foam or blankets on the floor between the amp and mic to minimise the effect of floor reflections if these are causing tonality problems.

Tip / Many producers split the guitar signal to feed two or more different amps, which are recorded onto separate tracks to be mixed later (page 123). You can buy dedicated **splitters**, although a passive splitter made by wiring three jack sockets together in parallel does the same job on the cheap if the leads are kept short. Changing the balance between different amps during different parts of the song will give the track additional dynamics.

Tip / Equally, the same amp can be recorded with several different mics and recorded onto separate tracks. This allows the engineer more scope when getting the final guitar sound to sit correctly in the mix. I find this approach a touch excessive for routine sessions, but it can be a worthwhile exercise to find out which of your mics works best on a particular guitar amp.

LOW NOISE OPTIONS
What do you do when you want to use traditional mic'ing techniques but your equipment / neighbours mean high-volume recording is not an option? if you've absolutely decided that the DI and modelled amp options are not for you, and

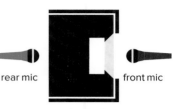

rear mic   front mic

open-backed amp

▲ Fig 7: The rear mic picks up a less toppy sound but must be phase inverted to bring it into phase with the front mic. Blending in the rear mic can add warmth to a thin sound.

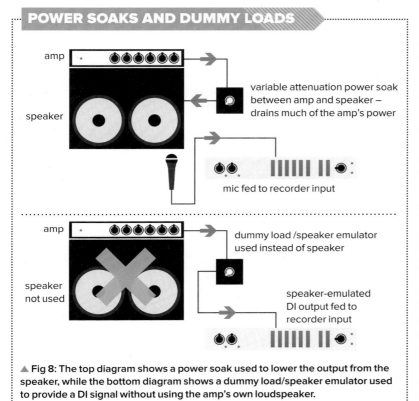

amp

speaker

variable attenuation power soak between amp and speaker – drains much of the amp's power

mic fed to recorder input

amp

speaker not used

dummy load /speaker emulator used instead of speaker

speaker-emulated DI output fed to recorder input

▲ Fig 8: The top diagram shows a power soak used to lower the output from the speaker, while the bottom diagram shows a dummy load/speaker emulator used to provide a DI signal without using the amp's own loudspeaker.

and loudspeaker, and passes on only a relatively small amount of power, the excess being dissipated as heat via inductive and resistive components (Fig 8, top). The amp is mic'ed in the normal way, but even though it is working hard to deliver the tone that only a tube amp driven hard can make, the amount of power reaching the speaker may only be a few watts — meaning you get a fully-cranked tone without excessive volume.

Another approach is to dispense with the speaker entirely — although **never try running the output of a valve amp directly into the soundcard or audio interface as you risk wrecking both**!

For this to work, the amp still has to be run into a load of the correct impedance, which requires the use of a speaker DI unit incorporating a **dummy load** in place of the speaker to soak up most of the power (Fig 8, bottom). A mic or line level feed using only a small fraction of the amp's output is then derived from within the power soak device.

One of the best hardware examples of this type of device is the excellent Sequis Motherload, which connects to the speaker output of amps rated up to around 100 watts and produces a speaker-emulated feed that can be plugged straight into the input of the recording system. In other words, you get a dummy load and a speaker emulator in one unit.

If the DI/load device doesn't include speaker emulation, then the signal you get is only the sound of the amp without the warmed tones of the speaker. The same is true of DI boxes that have a speaker input connection and a Thru connection to feed a separate dummy load (such as the EMO Dual Direct Injection box).

that only the sound of a mic'ed amp will do, then you need to look at other options.

The most obvious approach is to **mic a low-powered amp of only a few watts**, which is how many of the classic Led Zeppelin tracks were recorded. This requires little in the way of explanation: a smaller amp can be overdriven at a much lower sound level. Mic as you would a larger amp.

But there are also techniques for operating a high-powered guitar amp at lower volumes — most of them involving a device known as a **power soak**. A power soak connects between the amp

To create the sound of a mic'ed speaker in these instances you need to introduce some electronic filtering into the signal chain to replicate the resonances and high-frequency cut of a typical guitar speaker cabinet. This can be done using hardware or software. My preference is software: some of the speaker emulation plug-ins are exceptionally accurate and you get a choice of speaker types and models.

Warning / **It is important to reiterate that both power soaks and dummy loads present an electronic load to the amp that fools the amp into thinking a speaker is connected. Running a valve amp with no load connected can burn out the output transformer.** (Solid state amps are usually safe to operate with no speaker load, incidentally, although most recording guitarists favour the sound of valve amps.)

A final low-noise option is provided by small **sound isolation enclosures** with built-in speakers and mic positioning points that allow the player to use their favourite amp at a relatively high level with barely a whisper escaping into the studio (Fig 9).

These work well from a practical point of view, although you're restricted to the sound produced by the type of speaker fitted to the isolation cabinet, which may sound rather different from the one the guitar player normally uses. You can, however, try different types of mic and mic position/s to tailor the end result.

GUITAR NOISE

While most studio equipment has got quieter over the years, guitars generally haven't. The basic single-coil pickups used on instruments such as Telecasters and Stratocasters produce a bright sound, while

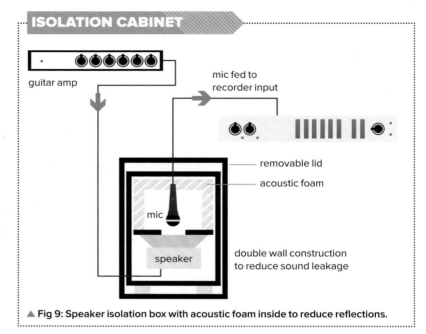

ISOLATION CABINET

guitar amp

mic fed to recorder input

removable lid

acoustic foam

mic

speaker

double wall construction to reduce sound leakage

▲ Fig 9: Speaker isolation box with acoustic foam inside to reduce reflections.

guitars with humbucking pickups usually produce a thicker, more solid sound. Humbuckers have two coils wired in opposite ways so that any induced interference cancels out: the use of these two coils also produces their signature sound.

To reduce the noise from instruments fitted with single coil pickups, several companies produce specialist stacked humbuckers, the best known from Kinman, Dimarzio, Seymore Duncan and Fender. Some of these get very close to the sound of a true single coil pickup. There's also a system made by the US company Suhr, which produces a Strat backplate with a noise sensing coil built into it. This follows the same humbucker principle of sensing the noise, then adding it out-of-phase with the guitar signal to cancel out the noise component.

All these solutions involve modifying the instrument; where this isn't an option it pays to be aware of the specific sources of noise so you can avoid them.

Hum is often induced into guitar pickups from devices with built-in power transformers, which is why the hum level increases as the guitar get closer to the amp. The orientation of the guitar pickups relative to the transformer affects how the magnetic field of the transformer interacts with the pickup coil which means you can usually find a null position where the hum is at a minimum.

Lighting dimmers and CRT computer screens cause **buzz**, as does proximity to laptop computers, so any dimmer-controlled lighting should be turned to full brightness or switched off before recording.

Hiss is another problem. It is essentially the contribution of circuit noise amplified by the gain required to create overdrive effects. It is possible to hide the noise when the guitar isn't playing by using a gate or expander. Many guitar amps and multi-effects units now have these built in.

Gates and **expanders** should be inserted into the signal chain before delay or reverb effects, otherwise the tail of the delay or reverb can be cut obviously short as the gate closes.

When using an overdrive pedal the gate can be placed directly after it so that both the pedal hiss and pickup hum are silenced when the guitar is not playing. The gate release time should be adjusted so as to fade out the tails of notes gracefully but without being so slow as to leave noise exposed.

> WHILE MOST STUDIO EQUIPMENT HAS GOT QUIETER OVER THE YEARS, GUITARS GENERALLY HAVEN'T.

SPLITTING SIGNALS

What sounds like a great guitar sound when you're running through a song may not always be right for the final mix when the other parts are in place.

You can give yourself more flexibility by feeding the output of the guitar amp via an active DI box. The DI box splits the signal, allowing you to take a clean feed from the guitar to record onto an adjacent track (the second output goes to the speaker cabinet which can be recorded as usual).

By splitting the signal in this way you end up with two recordings on their own tracks: one a dry and uneffected signal and one the distorted signal recorded

from the speaker. You may never need the dry track, but if the original recording can't be massaged to fit the track you're working on, you can always process the dry sound using amp modelling plug-ins and then either use it to replace the original recording or mix it in with the original recording.

RE-AMPING
A second option if you have a dry DI'd guitar track to work with is 're-amping' (right), where you feed the unprocessed guitar track in the DAW out into a guitar amp, then re-record it using mics just as you would with a live player. Pedals can be included in the signal chain, just as

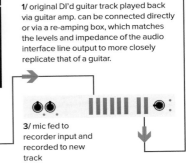

1/ original DI'd guitar track played back via guitar amp. can be connected directly or via a re-amping box, which matches the levels and impedance of the audio interface line output to more closely replicate that of a guitar.

2/ guitar amp and speaker

3/ mic fed to recorder input and recorded to new track

when playing live. When re-amping, it is necessary to adjust the track playback level so that it matches the output you'd get from a guitar pickup. If this is something you feel you might do on a regular

basis you can buy dedicated re-amping boxes from companies such as Radial that make the output from your recording device match both the level and impedance of a typical guitar.

THE BIG GUITAR SOUND
Chapter 16, Electric Guitar Production devotes 13 pages to a range of popular — and more esoteric — techniques that are used when mixing guitars. As will become apparent when you read through them, many depend on the guitarist adopting a range of playing styles during the recording itself and so have to be considered at the recording stage.

Various producers have experimented with different tunings and recording strategies to create impressively big guitar sounds. What are their secrets?

The first secret weapon is used where heavily distorted guitar chords end up sounding too indistinct in a mix. The trick is to **record the guitar part in two layers**. On the first pass the guitarist only plays the top three strings of the chord and on the second only the bottom three. When the two parts are summed they sound more powerful but also less muddled than a six-string distorted power chord played in one go (page 227).

A second technique, which I first noticed on the Canned Heat record 'On the Road Again', is to **tune all six strings to the same note**, in this case E. The bottom E string remains the same, the top E remains the same, but the middle four strings are tuned to the nearest E note. In other words, the B string goes up to top E, the G and D strings settle on middle E and the A string tunes to lower E.

This simple technique produces a powerful droning sound and was resurrected during the glam rock era to add power to simple chord sequences. You can expand this technique by layering the unison guitar with conventionally tuned guitar chords, playing

all six string with a barre to match the unison note of the specially-tuned guitar to the root note of the chord being played on the standard tuned guitar.

It is also commonplace to create dense-sounding guitar parts by playing the same part twice and recording it on two different tracks. You can do it three or more times if it produces the result you need. This technique is known as **double-tracking**, and is also often used on vocals (page 228). Although there are plug-ins that are designed to fake it, nothing ever sounds quite as rich as the real thing.

As with vocal double-tracking, the effectiveness depends on the performer's ability to play the part in pretty much the exact same way every time, although if you have the patience you can use your DAW's editing functions to move individual notes and phrases into line to fix timing discrepancies. ●

RECORDING ELECTRIC BASS

A whole chapter on recording electric guitar and then only one box on bass? It's not because we don't love bass! It's just that the techniques for recording bass are almost identical to those for recording guitar.

By far the most common mothod of recording bass is to take a DI feed either from the instrument or from the amplifier. Many bass amps have a DI output built in.

However, some players still prefer to mic the bass. The technique here is similar to that for recording the guitar except that it is normal to use a single mic to avoid phase effects diluting the low end. The mic is also set up a few inches away from the speaker grille rather than up-close.

Dynamic or capacitor models can be used, although a good bass response and a high SPL handling capability are required.

Avoid mic'ing bass amps in small rooms if possible as standing wave effects (page 80) can cause the levels of different notes to vary considerably. Moving the position of the speaker relative to the walls can improve the situation, but in some smaller rooms DI'ing may be the only practical option.

TIPS FOR A BETTER MIX

The vocal is the most important element in most mixes.
Spend time on its production, and don't let it slip back in the mix. When you listen to the song from the next room, the vocal should always be the part you focus on.

COMMON MIX MISTAKES AND HOW TO AVOID THEM

Too much compression.
A vocal might be compressed on its original track, then on the vocal bus, then on the mix bus and then at the mastering stage. Although the compression at each stage may be mild, the cumulative effect can be to squeeze the life from the sound. Where multiple parts are given a similar treatment, the overall mix can lose dynamic energy too. If you simply need to keep a lid on levels then automating the volume first and applying modest compression afterwards is often a kinder way to go.

8
RECORDING ACOUSTIC INSTRUMENTS

WHAT THE LISTENER HEARS IS A COMPLEX BLEND OF SONIC VIBRATIONS THAT COME FROM THE MANY PARTS OF THE INSTRUMENT AS WELL AS REVERBERANT REFLECTIONS FROM THE WALLS AND OTHER HARD SURFACES.

ACOUSTIC GUITAR

After vocals, the acoustic guitar is the instrument most likely to be recorded in a home studio using a microphone. Many of the principles used for recording acoustic guitar can be used on other acoustic instruments too – from trumpets to double bass – so a good understanding of the techniques serves well in a host of studio situations.

WHAT THE MIC NEEDS TO HEAR

To record the acoustic guitar well you need to appreciate that, in common with most other acoustic instruments, what the listener hears is a complex blend of sonic vibrations that come from the many parts of the instrument as well as reverberant reflections from the walls and other hard surfaces. As a consequence, a mic placed too close to any single part of the instrument will pick up sound mainly from that area, and the resulting recording will not provide a true sonic picture of how the instrument really sounds.

That's one reason why under-saddle piezo bridge transducers don't sound the same as the guitar sounds acoustically; they only pick up the bridge vibrations – although with a little EQ and some other processing they can produce an acceptable sound for some styles of music.

It is worth looking at the pros and cons of recording using pickups – the easiest method of recording acoustic guitar – before moving onto more traditional (and more effective) mic techniques.

RECORDING USING PICKUPS

A typical acoustic guitar pickup system has a pre-amp and sometimes basic EQ built into the instrument. This means recording it can be as simple as plugging the guitar into the soundcard or audio interface's line input.

Used alone, pickups rarely yield realistic or particularly useable results. To improve the sound, a number of companies use digital modelling to recreate the subtle resonances that are lost when a piezo bridge pickup is used, the most well-known probably being the Fishman Aura system (below left). These usually come as external pedal-style processors.

The Fishman Aura (or similar system) works by modelling the difference between what a mic hears and what the bridge transducer picks up. When creating the modelling algorithm the designers record a number of different types of guitar, both via well placed mics and again via their in-built pickups. The difference between the two signals is then analysed and a 'correction' profile – essentially a complex EQ curve – is generated. This profile is then used by the Fishman hardware to process the pickup signal to make it sound closer to the result you'd get when mic'ing the instrument.

Because different guitars and mics generate different sounds, any number of profiles can be made available. These are usually offered as a choice of presets. On some devices new profiles can be downloaded from the internet.

This approach certainly improves the authenticity of the sound and diminishes the 'quacky' attack of a typical piezo pickup. It also has the advantage of avoiding much of the spill suffered by mics when several instruments are playing in the same room.

It is possible to go some way towards replicating what these modelling processors do by using a Fingerprint or Match EQ plug-in. These analyse two pieces of audio, then create an EQ curve to make the spectrum of one sound match that of another. If you record some guitar strumming using both its built-in pickup and a good mic, you can use the mic'ed version as a reference to make the DI'd pickup sound match the mic'ed sound more closely.

If you are prepared to spend a little time experimenting with the settings, you can generally get a DI sound that functions reasonably well in the context of a mix, but I'd still recommend recording using a mic where the acoustic guitar part plays an exposed part or delivers a solo performance.

THE IMPORTANCE OF ENVIRONMENT

However close you get to an authentic sound using pickups, you invariably get a better one by mic'ing the guitar.

If you choose this route then the first thing to bear in mind is that it's not just the guitar you'll be recording – it's the acoustic environment in which the guitar plays too. This means that recording in a sympathetic acoustic environment is as important as the quality of the guitar, mic and player.

Acoustic guitars usually sound and record best when played above a hard floor which reflects some of the sound back to the mic to produce a more vibrant, lively tonality. The floor can be wood, tiled or concrete. If your studio is carpeted you can easily create a reflective area by placing a sheet of hard material, such as hardboard, MDF or plywood, on the floor at the low-level mirror point between mic and guitar. An adjacent hard wall can also help liven up the sound, but do experiment to find out which area of your room works best (when you've found it you can position guitarists there whenever you have a session).

While nearby hard surfaces do help improve the sound, avoid allowing too much room reverberation into the mic unless you have a very flattering room. Some improvised duvet screens behind and to the sides of the mic will help reduce room colouration, as can curved sound-absorbing screens of the type used behind vocal mics (page 94). These really help when placed behind omni mics (or figure-of-eight mics such as ribbons), as they reduce the level of room reflections reaching the rear and sides of the mic, but they are also useful on cardioids too.

Remember that reducing the contribution of (unflattering) room reflections in a signal gives you much more space to add your own choice of artificial ambience later.

THE RIGHT MIC FOR THE JOB

Unlike the electric guitar, which has little very high frequency content, the acoustic guitar covers most of the audible frequency range. The mic that deals best with high frequency information is the capacitor model, although some of the better dynamics give good results too. Don't ignore ribbon mics either; some may handle the job well — especially new generation models with an extended high-end response.

Whichever mic you choose, you may need to resort to low-cut EQ to control the bottom end and you may also need to boost the highs to get the guitar to sit in a busy mix without getting lost. The treatment for a solo acoustic guitar and one that plays a supporting role in a pop mix is very different.

TECHNIQUE: OMNI MICS

While it is tempting to use cardioid pattern mics for just about everything in the small studio, a small-diaphragm, omni pattern mic may be more forgiving of placement, as its off-axis response is essentially even, whereas the signal of a cardioid pattern mic quickly starts to dull as you move off-axis.

Although small diaphragm mics are the first choice for acoustic instruments where you're after tonal accuracy, many engineers like the results they get from large diaphragm models. Most home studio operators are also likely to invest in a decent large diaphragm vocal mic before a smaller diaphragm model, so there's no reason not to try that out.

Other factors that impact on the choice of mic include the type of guitar being recorded, the type of strings (different mics respond differently to steel and nylon strung guitars) and the player's picking style. There are no set rules; try all the mics you have available and see which one works best for the song.

MIC POSITION

Those new to recording often aim the mic at the part of the instrument that produces most sound. In the case of the acoustic guitar this is the sound hole. In reality the sound hole emits a lot of low frequency energy and if you point a mic at it you can expect to be rewarded with a boomy, dull sound. A better position is one that picks up sound from all over the guitar body – as the whole top vibrates when the instrument is played.

A common technique is to aim the mic towards the point where the guitar neck joins the body (Fig 1, overleaf). This can produce good results, picking up nice string harmonic detail. Start with a mic distance of between 250–400mm from the guitar body. This is close enough to exclude much of the unwanted room ambience but far enough away to collect sound from the whole guitar body.

Aiming the mic either side of the bridge work wells on some guitars too. If you

find that a different placement gives better results that's fine: I've got good recordings mic'ing the guitar body from above, from underneath and even from over the player's shoulder. Experimentation is good and flexibility is key. The easiest way of finding the best tone is to put on a high quality set of headphones, ask the guitarist to run through the song, and then monitor the results in realtime through the headphones as you adjust the mic position.

The sound you're after in most cases is one that is both warm and lively without being harsh or boomy. When you find the best place for the mic the sound will seem to come into focus and you'll just know it's right. In this position the recorded sound should work well with little or no EQ, although if you're using the guitar in a pop mix you may have to remove some low end. Smaller plucked string instruments, such as mandolins, tend to be more forgiving of close-mic'ing as they produce much less low end than a guitar.

Tip / A few companies produce lightweight guitar mic'ing systems that can be clamped to the guitar body. The main benefit of these is that the relative position of the mic and guitar remains constant, regardless of how much the player moves. Care needs to be taken to position them so that they are not in the performer's way. It is also worth using smaller mics to avoid physically unbalancing the instrument and making playing awkward.

STEREO RECORDING

Some engineers record acoustic guitar in stereo. Spaced stereo techniques can deliver good results but they also give rise to potential phase problems (page 74). This is because no matter how careful you are when placing the mics to get them

▲ Fig 1: Mic aimed towards the point where the guitar neck joins the body. Start with a mic distance of between 250–400mm from the guitar body.

the same distance from the guitar, the distances will vary as the player moves the instrument, causing tonal changes when the track is played back in mono.

The classic approach when recording guitar in stereo is to use a **coincident pair** (page 70). This eliminates the possibility of serious phase problems as both mics are positioned in almost the same place. You can either use a pair of coincident cardioids or an MS (middle and side) stereo pair. While a **spaced pair** (page 73) might work well on an artistic level, the player has to keep very still to avoid phase problems, which can be overly restrictive.

Some engineers use **two mics in a non-traditional configuration** to create the impression of stereo by choosing mic positions so that each mic picks up a different aspect of the instrument. You might mic the body as described for mono recording, for example, and then use a second mic aimed midway up the neck to pick up a thinner, brighter sound. Panning the two signals apart introduces a sense of

stereo width to the guitar part, even though the source material is not a true, accurate stereo recording. You don't need to use the same types of mic for this.

A third option is to mic the guitar in mono and mix in a second signal generated by the guitar's DI output (if it has one). Again, pan the mic signal to one side and the DI output to the other to create a sense of width.

Ultimately, although knowledge of two-mic techniques is useful to have, the phase complexities introduced often render the recorded audio less useable than results from the simpler mono method. Above and beyond this, the instrument is small enough — at least from the audience's perspective — to essentially be a mono point source of sound. Any impression of stereo comes from the room reflections, which can easily be introduced while mixing using stereo reverb.

Suffice to say that over the years I've tried many options but always come back to the same setup: a single high quality mic placed in the best position possible.

> **OVER THE YEARS I'VE TRIED MANY OPTIONS BUT ALWAYS COME BACK TO THE SAME SETUP: A SINGLE HIGH QUALITY MIC PLACED IN THE BEST POSITION POSSIBLE.**

THE RULE-OF-THUMB MIC PLACEMENT TECHNIQUE

> THIS RULE-OF-THUMB APPROACH WORKS ON A SURPRISINGLY WIDE RANGE OF INSTRUMENTS, FROM GRAND PIANO TO THE KAZOO, BUT ALWAYS REMEMBER THAT IT IS ONLY A STARTING POINT.

width of the sound-producing part of the instrument

mic distance same as width of the sound-producing part of the instrument

Although specific instruments often have specific mic techniques developed for them – the drum kit for example – you can get good recordings from many acoustic instruments by following the simple two-stage technique outlined below.

I refer to this 'rule-of-thumb' method frequently during this book as it is a useful starting point for mic'ing most acoustic instruments, delivering near fail-safe results when you're faced with an unfamiliar situation.

> **Step 1:** Examine the instrument and listen to hear where the majority of the sound is produced. Most of an acoustic guitar's sound comes from the body, for example, while a wind instrument such as a flute produces sound from the open end, the finger holes and the player's mouth. Rarely does an instrument's sound come from a single place.

> **Step 2:** Take the longest dimension of the sound-producing part of the instrument and use that as your initial mic distance. You'll probably get a useable result straight away.

The thinking behind this technique is that the mic and extremes of the instrument form an equilateral triangle so the mic picks up more or less all of the instrument at a similar level. The further you get from the instrument, the more the sonic contribution of its different parts are picked up equally. This 'three-way'

geometry is a good compromise between evenness of sound capture and exclusion of excessive room colouration.

The rule-of-thumb approach works well on a surprisingly wide range of instruments, from alto sax to zither, but always remember that it is only a starting point and you'll still need to fine-tune the mic position to find the magical sweet spot.

If all else fails, try placing the mic close to the player's ear: if the instrument sounds good to the player then it should sound good to a mic in a similar position.

When applying the rule of thumb to **spaced stereo** mics, make the distance between the mics roughly the same as the distance between the mics and the sound source. Adjust this spacing according to the results you get. If you get a hole in the centre of the stereo image try moving the mics closer together.

If you're using a **coincident** mic technique, place the mics in the same spot as you would for a single mono mic.

I must stress again that however useful this rule-of-thumb technique is, it should only be used as a starting point.

A little fine tuning of the mic positions almost always improves the situation – keep the headphones on and tweak until you're happy with the results.

GRAND PIANO

The majority of today's pop records that feature piano parts are made using sampled pianos – either in the form of plug-in instruments or hardware keyboards based on sampled sounds – rather than a real instrument. This approach is convenient, avoids spill problems, doesn't require expensive mics and gives consistent results regardless of the acoustics of the room in which the instrument is played. You also avoid having to pay for a piano tuner!

Nevertheless, for solo piano performances or tracks where the piano is the main instrument, it may be more appropriate to record the real thing.

Few home studios have space for a grand piano, although it is often possible to take a mobile setup to a school or concert hall where there is a resident grand piano to record there.

THE RIGHT MIC FOR THE JOB

Capacitor models are the obvious first choice for piano recording as they have the widest frequency response, but I've also had good results using ribbon mics – especially some of the newer generation models that have an extended high end response, such as the sE RN1R .

Some engineers fix **boundary mics** under the piano's open lid (page 64). This approach has its benefits; boundary mics don't suffer from phase difference problems caused by receiving the direct and reflected sound at different times by virtue of them being positioned at the reflective boundary itself. They need to be fixed to a large, flat surface to pick up low frequencies effectively.

▲ Fig 2: When recording an acoustic guitarist who sings at the same time, set up a single mic for the guitar as normal and then use a figure-of-eight pattern mic to record the vocal. The figure-of-eight mic should be set up so that it is as deaf as possible to the signal coming from the guitar (page 69).

As a rule **dynamic mics** don't deliver an accurate piano sound, but they can be useful if the piano part needs to sit in the background as they tend to blur the transient detail of the sound to some extent: apparently some of The Beatles' tracks that feature piano were mic'ed using dynamic models for this very reason.

FURTHER CONSIDERATIONS

The grand piano is a large instrument, so sound will arrive at the mic over a wide range of angles. An omni or figure-of-eight pattern mic has, by virtue of its simpler design geometry, a better off-axis response than a cardioid pattern mic and so should deliver a more accurate sound.

Fig 3 (left): Recording with a spaced stereo pair, and (right): mics placed above the strings for a more forward sound.

That said, some great sounding piano recordings have been made using cardioid pattern mics, and where these are set up as a coincident stereo pair (page 70) the coverage angle becomes wider than using a single mic to record in mono.

Another point to remember is that the larger the mic's diaphragm, the more coloured the off-axis response is likely to be, although I've heard perfectly good-sounding piano recordings made using a pair of AKG C414 large diaphragm mics.

Both cardioid pattern and figure-of-eight pattern mics also exhibit a significant degree of proximity effect bass-boost when used close-up, so where a mic is placed inside the piano lid an omni mic is probably the safest choice to avoid excessive bass build-up.

Finally, things can get pretty loud inside a piano, so if you're planning to record up-close and personal then mics with high SPL handling capabilities (page 65) are essential. You may also

need a model with a pad switch to prevent the pre-amp from being overloaded on louder notes.

So far then, the laws of physics seem to favour small diaphragm, omni pattern, capacitor mics with reasonably high SPL handling abilities — but remember this is also about art, and hard logic doesn't always win out. Try whatever mics you have available as you might stumble on something unexpected that gives good results.

MIC PLACEMENT

Where you place the mics depends on the result you're trying to achieve. It is common to record the piano in stereo, and for omni or figure-of-eight mics, that usually means a **spaced pair** (unless you use one of each to form an **MS pair**, page 71).

For a piano recital in a room that is acoustically sympathetic to the instrument, you can afford to place the mics some distance away from the piano so that both the piano sound and the room ambience is picked up.

You can vary the amount of room acoustic picked up by varying the mic distance, which might be as little as 1.5 metres or as much as four or five metres from the piano, with greater distances more appropriate where you're after the kind of sound the audience would hear.

The usual arrangement is to place the mics to the side of the piano facing towards the propped open lid (Fig 3, left). The lid acts as a reflector that throws the sound towards the audience. There is no point mic'ing the tail end of the piano or the side behind the lid as they omit little high frequency detail.

Set the two mic heights to around half way up the piano lid and space them apart by between one and three metres depending on their distance from the piano. The further away they are, the wider the spacing can be.

Note that the low end response may change as you vary the mic distance due to phase cancellation. Some low frequencies will radiate directly from the piano to the mics, while some will reflect from the floor causing them to arrive slightly later. The way these two paths combine causes some frequencies to be exaggerated and others to be suppressed; you will need to adjust the mic distance to get the best-sounding low end.

Where the piano needs to sit further forwards in the mix try placing mics above the strings – just beneath the open piano lid (Fig 3, page 133).

The most common approach here is to use a spaced pair of omni mics and position them 300mm or so above the bass and treble string group. Adjust the spacing so that there's an even coverage of notes across the keyboard.

It is possible to combine the close and distant mics techniques, mixing the signal from two pairs of mics to produce the desired result, but – as ever – beware phase issues.

Note that in this double setup the more distant mics can be a coincident stereo pair of cardioids, figure-of-eights or an MS pair. Coincident arrays always offer better mono compatibility than spaced mics.

Tip / A neat trick used to reduce spill where other instruments are playing at the same time is to place the mics inside the piano. Make a trial recording to ensure the notes are in balance then drape blankets over the open lid to reduce the amount of sound getting in or out. This will have some effect on the tone but it rarely causes serious problems in pop work.

TECHNIQUE: PIANO NOISE

The piano is a complex piece of machinery with many moving parts, and sometimes these moving parts make more noise than you might want – especially the pedals.

Getting the player to wear soft shoes or slippers can help reduce noise, as can wrapping material around metal pedals – gaffa tape and elastic bands can both come in useful.

If you're recording a piano on location, take a box of tools with you, including candle wax for lubricating wood parts, WD40 for metal parts, elastic bands to reduce the play in mechanisms and gaffa tape for just about everything.

As every seasoned engineer knows, black gaffa tape is like The Force – it has a dark side and a light side and it holds the universe together!

STEREO SPREAD AND PIANOS

A piano played in a concert hall produces little or no perceived stereo spread between lower and higher notes as a significant part of the sound is created by the resonance of the soundboard and the ambience of the acoustic environment. Recording using a stereo pair some distance from the instrument will create a sense of space but there will be little or no sense of higher notes being at one side and lower notes at the other. By contrast, putting mics inside the grand piano or using a stereo pair close to an upright piano with panels removed will provide some stereo separation between the strings with convention stating that high notes are panned right and lower notes to the left, just as a player would hear them. Avoid panning the mics too widely though – it can create the impression of an unfeasibly wide piano.

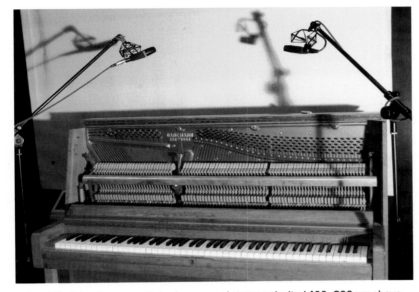

▲ Fig 4: Upright piano recorded using an omni stereo pair sited 400–800mm above the keyboard. Mics are placed 600–800mm apart.

THE UPRIGHT PIANO

The humble upright piano lacks the depth of tone — and visual appeal — of a grand, but it works well in certain musical styles and has the benefit of fitting into much smaller spaces.

Whenever I mic an upright piano the first thing I do is remove the lid and front cover above the keyboard to allow the bright sound of the strings to radiate upwards and towards the player.

The simplest way of recording the upright is with a pair of omni mics, their distance from the piano and height adjusted to get the tone you're after. Placing the mics too close together will favour some strings over others so try to space them around 400–800mm from the piano and around 600–800mm apart (Fig 4).

If you want the mics to capture something close to what the player hears, place the mics either side of their shoulders. The brightest sounds radiate upwards, so moving the mic over and above the piano will give a livelier tone.

You'll get a slightly different tone using a coincident cardioid pair, where the mic distance ideally needs to be around the same as the width of the piano to provide even coverage. Start with the mics 800mm or so higher than the top of the piano and fine-tune from there. The proximity of walls and ceilings will affect the sound; change the mic positions accordingly.

If the piano is set up in an acoustically sympathetic room then you can emulate the grand piano ambient mic technique by leaving the cover in place and propping the lid open at around 45 degrees so that it throws the sound out towards the player. Set the mic heights at halfway up the lid and adjust their distance behind the player to get the right balance of piano and room ambience. Check for even coverage across the keyboard and adjust the mic positions to compensate if there are problems.

STRINGS

While it is unlikely you'll ever need to record a full string section in the project studio, it isn't unusual for a project to include one or two bowed instruments such as violins, violas or cellos. A composition that uses sampled strings can also be given a far greater degree of realism by adding real stringed instruments — however few — to the mix. Occasionally you may also find yourself recording larger string sections on location, so it pays to be prepared.

As with the piano and guitar, understanding how the sound radiates from a bowed instrument will give you a better understanding of where to place the mic/s.

The basic mechanism isn't that different from the acoustic guitar, except that instead of plucking the strings, the player bows them to produce long, sustained notes that have a rich, harmonic complexity. The string vibrates and in turn causes the wooden body of the instrument to resonate.

Like the acoustic guitar, the resonant volume of the sound 'box' is fixed, meaning the tonality changes as the pitch of the note changes, exciting different resonant modes in the instrument body. The radiating sound energy pattern also changes with pitch, although the main axis of radiation is perpendicular to the sound board or top of the instrument body. As a rule the broad 'beam' of sound narrows more at high frequencies.

Bass instruments tend to have large bodies because of the longer wavelengths involved, while the violin – which produces relatively high pitches – has a fairly small body.

Although the sound of a bowed instrument is harmonically complex, the amount of high frequency musical energy above 10kHz is small – even with the violin. The larger stringed instruments roll off highs at a progressively lower frequency. In fact, most high energy is generated not by the strings, but by bowing noise.

In the classical world strings are usually heard in a lively-sounding room or hall and at a distance from the player, so the sound has time to blend with the acoustic reflections to produce what we have come to accept as the 'right' string sound.

In ethnic and folk music, meanwhile, a stringed instrument is normally heard in smaller spaces or even outdoors, which tends to produce a more strident sound as there's less in the way of natural reflections to smooth it.

THE RIGHT MIC FOR THE JOB

When recording a solo stringed instrument the choice of mic depends on the natural sound of the instrument and the musical style you're aiming for.

Capacitor mics capture an articulate and detailed sound, but avoid those with built-in presence peaks designed to flatter vocals as these make some instruments, particularly violas and violins, sound too strident.

Large diaphragm mics tend to have a naturally warmer colouration than small diaphragm models so may sound more musical, although you can also get good results from **small diaphragm** models.

Where you're after a sweeter string sound a **ribbon mic** will help suppress the higher, more aggressive harmonics and bow noise.

Omni mics (or figure-of-eights in the case of ribbons) produce the most natural sound due to their good off-axis response, but the final choice depends on whether the room reflections picked up benefit the sound or compromise it.

Bowed strings rarely get louder than around 80dB so no decent mic should have problems handling the levels.

MIC PLACEMENT

The mic should be aimed at the sound board or top of the instrument, which in the case of a violin held normally means positioning the mic on a tall stand above the player, directed down towards the violin (Fig 5).

Screens can be used to reduce room reflections, but as with the acoustic guitar, a reflective floor and possibly one nearby reflective wall will help breathe life into the sound. A mic distance of between 600mm–1m works well for most stringed instruments mic'ed individually, but as always, put on those headphones and search for the sweet spot.

In theory you can bring a violin mic a little closer in, but this tends to produce a more aggressive tone and unless the player stands or sits very still, both the tone and level is likely to change.

SECTIONS AND ORCHESTRAS

A common technique for multi-mic'ing an orchestra or large group of strings is to set up a single mic above each couple of rows of violins and violas, with a further mic for each pair of cellos and double basses. Additional mics placed some distance from the ensemble are commonly used to help 'glue' the sound together, in a similar way to drum overheads. Although the various strings invariably spill into each others' mics there should be enough separation to allow some balancing to be done at the mixing stage.

Where other instruments in the orchestra are overly loud (a problem not uncommon with more amateur orchestras), it can be difficult to keep them out of the string mics. The usual solution is to place the string mics closer to the string players and

▲ Fig 5: Mic angled down at the board at a height of around 600–800mm above the instrument.

arrange for greater physical separation between players. This may end up compromising the string sound – as well as favouring the player nearest the repositioned mics – so take some time to ensure the new balance is right. A professional orchestra will usually strike a more natural acoustic balance.

In some ways mic'ing an orchestra is not unlike mic'ing a drum kit (Chapter 9) where a main stereo pair out front captures the overall sound of the orchestra, with closer spot mics covering individual sections. The various signals are then balanced during mixing to fine-tune the combined sound.

Depending on the natural balance of the sound picked up by the stereo mics, you might choose to use this as the main sound and then bring in the close mics to balance it. Alternatively, where the natural balance isn't so good, you may rely more on the close mics and use less of the stereo out-front mic in the mix.

The same technique can be used on a smaller scale for string quartets – one mic favouring each individual player plus a stereo pair out front to capture the ensemble sound. The minimum mic distance can be worked out using my rule-of-thumb mic distance formula (page 131): don't place a mic much closer than the length of the instrument's body.

Tip / Figure-of-eight pattern mics can get you out of trouble when the offending spill comes from a single source, such as a loud sax player. By aiming the dead 90 degrees axis of the figure-of-eight mic at the sound you want to reject, you'll get better separation than when using cardioid or omni pattern mics. Of course the rejection won't be perfect: reflected sound will still enter the mic from angles where the mic is more sensitive.

BRASS AND WIND INSTRUMENTS

Brass instruments, and their woodwind relatives, are loud (a trumpet can produce levels of over 130dB half a metre from the bell) so they need to be recorded using a mic with high SPL-handling capabilities. In direct contrast to the flute family, which generate a purer tune, brass instruments have rich harmonic structures.

In pop and jazz circles the saxophone remains popular, and although it is made from brass, the use of a vibrating reed to produce the sound means it technically belongs to the woodwind family. Nevertheless, it is mic'ed in a way similar to brass instruments.

A typical brass instrument has a flared bell to produce the maximum sound level from the player's efforts. High frequency harmonics are strongest directly in front of the bell, with lower frequencies radiating over a wider angle as the frequency falls. In this respect it has something in common with a guitar amp's loudspeaker.

THE RIGHT MIC FOR THE JOB

A **large-diaphragm capacitor** mic often gives the most predictable results, although those with exaggerated presence peaks can give unpleasantly aggressive results.

Certain **dynamic** mics – such as the Electrovoice RE20 and Sennheiser 421 – work well, as can some of the newer ribbon models.

If you go down the **ribbon** route take care not to expose the mic to more SPL than it is designed to handle. It can also be helpful to put a **pop shield** in front of ribbon mics to prevent wind blasts from the instrument damaging the ribbon.

MIC PLACEMENT

While close-mic'ing the bell might be practical in a live situation, it doesn't produce a particularly accurate or representative sound – although it can occasionally be suitable for some rock and pop work.

To get a representative tone, position the mic a little off-axis around a metre or slightly more from the bell. Shorter mic distances produce a brighter sound; moving further away yields a more natural sound.

PRO TIP

I attended a mic test session with Courtney Pine playing sax where we tested a number of different mics. He favoured the sound of the sE RN1R ribbon, which has an unusually wide response for a ribbon model.

The mic is normally aimed from above, pointing between the bell and the mouthpiece of the instrument.

When working at greater mic distances, the room ambience will play a greater part in the recorded signal; the more distant the mic, the better the room needs to sound.

Sometimes mechanical noise from the keys can be a problem, but this is an inherent part of the sound of the instrument. It is affected by the player's technique as well as the quality of the instrument.

Tip / Some pop records are made with a close mic on the sax, favouring the tones from the bell. This delivers a more penetrating – but less accurate – sound than mic'ing from 500mm or so away.

Tip / As with the acoustic guitar, you can sometimes get good results in a smaller space by playing the instrument facing a reflective wall or window and with a reflective rather than carpeted floor. The mic is set up as before but now also picks up strong early reflections from the adjacent reflective surfaces, creating a more lively sound.

Tip / The further the mic is moved away from the axis of the instrument, the less pronounced the high frequencies will be. This allows the engineer to use the mic as an effective EQ.

THE BRASS SECTION

A pop brass section typically comprises four or more instruments and produces a lot of sound. Recording a section can be done in one of two ways.

❯ One option is to **record the section together with a different mic for each instrument.** Substantial acoustic screens are set up to shield the players from each other to keep spill under control. This approach allows you greater flexibility when mixing to change the level (and treatment) of each instrument.

Circular perspex screens are available to fit behind mics which reduce spill but still allow the players to maintain eye contact.

Where a good degree of separation isn't possible it is probably safest to **overdub** the brass parts, recording each instrument onto different tracks.

❯ The second option, which generally results in a more homogenous sound, is achieved by **mic'ing the whole section from around a couple of metres away**, either using a single mic or a stereo pair at around head height or slightly higher. Balancing the instruments is then done on the studio floor, by moving individual players closer to or further from the mic/s until you get the balance you want (keep checking the headphones!).

Bigger sections can be recorded in a similar way as long as you have enough space to move the players around to achieve a natural balance.

That said, you get more freedom when mixing if each section (trumpets, sax, trombone and so on) is covered by its own stereo pair of mics.

DOUBLE BASS

Acoustic double bass can be a challenge to record. Double basses don't produce a particularly high volume of sound, yet you need to avoid getting the mic too close to them if you're after a natural result. The problem is exacerbated when the bass

MOVING TARGETS

What do you do when faced with an instrument that can't be kept still, such as the piano accordion or similar squeezebox? The bellows action keeps the instrument in constant motion and means the instrument also changes its width from moment to moment. Any attempt to close mic the instrument will be a compromise, yet positioning the mic several metres away to simulate what the audience might hear isn't often practical either as you end up with too much room ambience.

My solution is generally to set up two mics, not necessarily because I want to capture the instrument in stereo, but because the way these instruments are constructed means the bass register comes out of mainly one side while the treble notes come out of the other.

In this instance, set up two mics, either omnis or cardioids, around 1.2m apart and about 500mm in front of the instrument. If the room is reasonably dead or you can put up screens you may be able to increase the distance further without compromising the sound.

The accordion generates a lot of harmonics so a pair of capacitor mics is the obvious choice, but at a push you can try any two mics that are identical, or at least that have similar specifications and frequency characteristics.

When you come to mix you may still hear some level fluctuations as the bellows move, but these are easily evened out with gentle compression.

The two sides of the instrument should be panned apart, but ideally not too widely or you can end up creating the illusion of an accordion as wide as the stage.

---

is recorded alongside other instruments where spill becomes an additional concern.

Fortunately many pop and rockabilly bands that feature double bass aren't after a natural sound, in which case it can be recorded using a pickup, a contact mic or even a conventional mic wrapped in a sock or foam and stuffed under the tailpiece. These techniques can be mixed with conventional acoustic mic'ing for the best of both worlds, though take care to get both signals in phase. Where a pickup is used, ensure that the cable doesn't rattle against the body of the instrument – this is an easy way to ruin a good double bass recording.

The double bass, like the bass guitar, can generate fundamental frequencies down to around the 40Hz mark so a mic with a decent low-frequency response is essential. A **large diaphragm capacitor** mic is well suited to the task; the Neumann U87 or AKG C414 are both good choices, although there are many more affordable

capacitor mics that also do the job. You might also try a **small diaphragm model** like the Neumann KM184 or more affordable Rode NT55.

In theory the mic should be placed at least the length of the instrument's body away from the bass, but in many situations that is too far away to be practical from a spill perspective, in which case try a spacing of between 250–400mm.

Place the mic higher than the bridge, aimed down towards the strings, but move the mic while monitoring the headphones to find the sweet spot. Every instrument is different and you'll find that the front of the body vibrates in different ways depending on its quality and construction.

As with the acoustic guitar, getting too close to the holes (F holes in this case) may produce too much low end, but you can move the mic in their direction if you feel the tonality isn't deep enough.

Cardioid and figure-of-eight mics exhibit a proximity bass boost at these closer distances that can help balance the low end. If there's too much bottom, increase the mic distance from the instrument, move the mic further from the F holes or engage the mic's (or pre-amp's) low-cut switch.

Tip / It's best to record double bass on a solid floor; wooden stages or lightweight floors can resonate and compromise the recording.

PERCUSSION

With percussion instruments, such as hand drums, marimbas, balophones, bells and so on, you can either mic individual instruments or, where several instruments are played together in an ensemble, treat the whole group of instruments as a single entity and use a stereo pair to capture the sound as a whole.

TECHNIQUE: PERCUSSION

To inject some ambient life into a percussive performance, try moving the instrument/s above a hard floor, and possibly close to one reflective wall. This will produce a more lively sound than if the instrument was sited on a carpeted surface away from any walls.

When you mic as an **ensemble**, the balance you capture is the natural balance between instruments. Mic'ing **individual instruments** gives you the opportunity to balance them afterwards.

When mic'ing percussion as an ensemble, you can get an initial mic distance by using my usual rule of thumb mic placement technique ('mic distance equals width of ensemble'). The two mics should be spaced apart by around the same amount. As with brass ensembles, adjust player positions to alter the balance of the sound being recorded.

When recording hand drums using individual mics you can afford to get the mic/s as close as 200–300mm to the drum. For wider instruments, such as tuned percussion – like congas and bongos, or groups of instruments – putting the mics

▲ Fig 6: Congas recorded with a single mic located 650mm above them and angled down towards the drum heads.

around 600mm–1m above the instruments tends to work well in most cases (Fig 6). These mic placements also work well for small percussion instruments such as shakers, tambourines and latin percussion.

Percussion covers a wide frequency range so a **capacitor mic** is the most usual choice, although both **large** and **small diaphragm** models can produce good results. Where the room ambience isn't flattering, try placing acoustic screens around the instrument/s and mic/s to lessen the impact of room reflections.

Tip / Avoid placing mics too close to a tambourine as the natural movement of the instrument will cause level variations. ●

9
RECORDING DRUMS

>
> **THE KEY FACTORS IN GETTING A GREAT DRUM SOUND ARE A WELL-TUNED DRUM KIT AND A GOOD DRUMMER.**

NO TYPICAL DRUM KIT

There is no single 'typical' drum recording setup. With some musical styles you can get a fabulous drum sound using no more than a single well-placed microphone. Other sessions require mics on every drum, mics above the kit, mics in front of the kit and mics at the back of the room.

Fortunately there **is** such thing as a typical drum kit, which comprises a kick drum (two in some cases), a snare drum, two or more tom-toms, a hi-hat and a selection of crash and ride cymbals. The resulting sound is loud, covers pretty much all of the audio spectrum, and inevitably features very steep transients.

The simplest approach to drum recording is to adopt my universal 'rule-of-thumb' mic position trick (page 131). Using this, you treat the full kit as a single instrument, measuring its longest dimension (usually the width of the full kit) then placing a suitable mic at that distance in front of the kit.

For a stereo recording use the same technique but place a stereo mic array (page 70) in front of the kit instead of a single mic. In both cases, can you can adjust the height of the mic(s) to balance the contribution of the kick drum to some extent, but other than that you get the sound of the kit as heard in the room.

Most pop and rock productions use more elaborate multi-mic techniques, outlined in detail over the coming pages.

Before getting to these it's important to note that the key factors in getting a great drum sound are a well-tuned drum kit and a good drummer. There are countless stories of top session drummers going into studios, tuning the studio's house kit,

doing the session and sounding great. Later in the day another band comes in, uses the same kit tuned exactly as it was with the same mic setup, yet they get a bad sound because the drummer doesn't have the right technique for hitting the drums. Of course you can't always work with top drummers, but there are several things you can do to ensure the kit sounds its best.

PREPPING THE KIT

> **Heads:** Where the kit belongs to the studio start by checking you've got the right heads for the recording. This applies to heads for all the kit, of course, but to the snare in particular. Plain heads sound brightest, ones with a central black dot or black ring are slightly damped and those made from dual layers of material with a thin film of oil between them are the most damped-sounding. Remo pinstripes are a popular general-purpose choice as they ring long enough for most musical styles but are easy to damp down using patches of Moongel (a sticky synthetic plastic material designed for drum damping – left) or similar.

In the old days we used pads of cloth or tissue and gaffa tape to damp individual drums if there was excessive ring, but Moongel has largely taken over as the damping material of choice. It has the benefit of being both effective and reusable. Most drum stores stock it.

As with guitar strings, a drummer should aim to come into the studio with a set of new heads that have been used for a day or two so they've had a chance to settle in. This might sound like an expensive luxury, but compared to the other costs associated with recording, it's a small investment for a much better sound. Where the kit belongs to the studio, the heads should be changed whenever they show signs of wear or tonal degradation.

> **Kick drum:** For pop and rock music I prefer to use a kick drum front head with a hole in it large enough to allow a mic to be positioned just inside the shell. For damping, a folded blanket still seems to give as good a result as any commercial alternative such as foam rings. If the drummer turns up with a kick drum fitted with two heads and no hole then you either have to mic it as is or consider removing the front head altogether. The latter gives a drier sound more suited to classic rock.

> **Cymbals:** Cymbals sound very different depending on their size, make and weight. Once chosen there's little you can do to modify their sound.

BASIC TUNING

Tuning a drum kit well takes time, but it is time well spent: good recordings become great when attention is paid to the details.

The basic method of tuning a drum head is similar for every drum in the kit, but before you start tuning, the head must be pushed firmly into place and centred so that it sits evenly on the rim of the shell.

While the old head is off, it is worth checking the edge of the shell for damage: it should provide a smooth bearing surface for the edge of the head.

Once the head has been pushed into place and its alignment checked, the rim can be fitted. Check that it fits properly over the head hoop. Next, replace all the tuning lugs and screw them in until finger tight, ensuring that the head and rim alignment is not disturbed.

DRUM TUNING

A drum is a mechanically simple device with two resonant mechanisms. The volume and shape of the drum shell with fitted heads forms a resonant cavity, rather like the sound box of a guitar. The drum heads also resonate, their pitch varying according to tension like a guitar string; the higher the tension, the higher the pitch.

For the drum to 'speak' correctly, the heads need to be tuned in the region of the drum shell's natural resonant frequency so that the vibration of the head is reinforced by the resonance of the shell. There's a certain amount of tuning leeway, but tuning the head much too low or high in comparison with the shell resonance will produce a noticeably inferior resulting tone. Whether the drums are tuned to specific musical intervals or just to what feels right is a matter of taste.

Push the centre of the head with the flat of your hand and then re-tighten if any of the lugs have gone slack. Now the drum is ready to tune.

Most books on drumming suggest tuning by adjusting the opposite lugs and then working around the drum making small adjustments at a time to keep the tension even. More experienced drummers take a more direct approach and simply tighten the lugs until any wrinkles have gone, at which point the drum is almost in tune.

The key to a good sound is getting an even tension – it's why you see drummers tapping around the edges of the head checking that the pitch is the same in all areas. If one area seems a little flat, the nearest lug can be tightened slightly to correct it. (It helps to push down on the centre of the head with a finger or thumb while doing this test as it makes the pitch easier to hear.)

TUNING THE TOMS

With the toms, start by tuning the lower head to the same pitch as the batter head. You can then experiment by dropping its

TECHNIQUE: TENSION

A newly fitted head needs to be stretched before it is fully tensioned, which most drummers do by simply pushing down on it with their hands after it is loosely fitted.

You can apply further tension using the tuning lugs to remove wrinkles before getting down to more precise tuning.

When removing and replacing heads, check for any loose nut boxes on the drums, as these are usually fixed via bolts from the inside of the shell and so can't be accessed when both heads are fitted.

pitch very slightly to reduce ringing and add more punch to the sound. If the bottom head is removed the sound changes to become more percussive and sometimes louder as well. The resonant Q of the drum is also reduced so it can be tuned over a wider range without sounding wrong.

Note that toms can only be tuned over a limited range to exploit the shell resonance. If the heads are tuned too low, the sound lacks volume and sustain; if the pitch is too high it loses body and sounds thin. You'll know the right tone when you hear it as the drum will 'speak' correctly, delivering a solid, punchy sound.

Tip / One trick employed by some drummers after tuning their smaller toms is to detune one or two adjacent lugs on the batter head slightly to deliberately unbalance the head tuning. The result is that the pitch of the drum drops slightly after it has been hit. This is exaggerated if the lower head is tuned lower than the batter head. Some drummers like to tune the different toms to specific musical intervals — often musical thirds. Others simply aim for a good spread of pitches.

TUNING THE SNARE

Snare drums can be trickier to tune because of the snare wires stretched over the lower head.

The usual approach is to tune the snare head (the one on the bottom) fractionally higher in pitch than the batter head (the one you hit). You can test this with the snare tension switched off by damping one head while tapping the other to establish its pitch. Different types of snare drum shell impart different amounts of ring to the sound, with metal shells the most lively. Check the snare itself for bent or broken wires and replace if necessary.

In addition to tuning the drum, the snare tension also needs to be correct. A loose snare will rattle while an over-tight one will sound tubby or choked. The right tension adds a nice snap to the sound.

Careful tuning of the snare drum can reduce the amount of snare buzz when other drums are hit, but it is a rare kit that doesn't suffer from this problem to some extent. A bass guitar played in the same room will also cause snare rattles. Although getting the snare tension right will keep buzz to a minimum, you may have to gate the snare drum mic during recording or when mixing to keep things clean. Ironically, many sampled drum kits include small amounts of snare rattle and sympathetic vibration to keep things sounding authentic.

Tip / It is common for inexperienced drummers (and engineers) to over-damp drum kits in the studio. Be careful of going too far: when heard in isolation the drum kit often sounds wetter than when mixed with other instruments. Use small patches of Moon Gel on the toms and snare as needed, but try to keep the sound fairly lively.

TUNING THE KICK

I've had drummers turn up with a whole duvet or large pillow stuffed into their bass drum — something that completely kills the tone. A small folded blanket laid in the bottom of the drum, just resting against the lower edge of the batter head, is usually all that's needed.

As with other drums, there is a tuning range over which the kick drum speaks properly. This is often achieved by tensioning out any wrinkles then tuning up slightly until the sound takes on the required depth of tone. If the head is too slack you'll hear more thwack than thump. Conversely, when pitched too high you get too much ring and probably not enough of the beater impact sound.

If the front head has a small hole or no hole at all then it can be tuned a little higher than the batter head to add punch and weight to the sound. If it has a very large hole cut in it – as was common when recording '70s rock music – it will have less effect on the overall sound. In either case, the front head may need damping to stop it ringing on after each beat.

The type of beater can affect the tone dramatically, with hard plastic beaters giving the most attack and felt the least. Cork beaters offer a sound that's somewhere in-between. Commercial pads are available to stick to the batter head to increase the amount of click for styles that demand it.

FINAL PREPARATIONS

Before setting up for a session, see if the drummer is planning to hit all the drums and cymbals during the song. If not, remove unused drums and cymbals: this will help reduce unwanted resonances and rattles, as well as giving you more space to rig the mics.

As far as kit location goes, if you're lucky enough to work in a large space, try carrying the snare drum around the room while hitting it with a stick to see if there are any magic spots that sound better than simply siting the kit in the most convenient place.

When the individual drums are tuned, check the kit for rattles and pedal squeaks, the latter being easily fixable with a squirt of WD40. I usually keep a pack of Blu Tak on hand too for damping any rattling hardware that can't be tightened using a screwdriver or spanner.

RECORDING THE KIT: THE SIMPLE OPTION

As stated in the introduction, you can get a perfectly acceptable kit recording from a single mic or a stereo pair if the kit is located in a good-sounding room and the overall sound suits the kind of music you're producing.

The obvious down-side of a single/paired mic approach to drum recording is that there's very little you can do to re-balance the drums once recorded, but there are two practical factors that can help shape the balance before the sound hits the mic/s.

Firstly, the sound from crash and ride cymbals radiates mainly upwards and downwards, so if the cymbals are too loud, you can tame them slightly by **setting the mic/s at the same height as the cymbals** so they 'see' them edge-on. The amount of difference this makes is limited by the amount of reflected sound, and if the room sounds good for drums it is probably pretty lively. Note that hi-hats tend to radiate more sound horizontally because of the way the two cymbals interact.

Secondly, you can influence the amount of kick drum picked up by **varying the mic height from the floor**. With the mic raised 300mm or so above the floor (about half way up the kick drum), the kick will make a greater contribution than if the mic is at cymbal height or above.

Moving the mic/s closer to the kit will reduce the room's contribution, while moving them further away will generate a more ambient sound.

Because the drum kit needs a mic that can handle high frequencies and sharp transients, a **capacitor mic** is the usual

BEFORE SETTING UP FOR A SESSION, SEE IF THE DRUMMER IS PLANNING TO HIT ALL THE DRUMS AND CYMBALS DURING THE SONG. IF NOT, REMOVE UNUSED DRUMS AND CYMBALS: THIS WILL HELP REDUCE UNWANTED RESONANCES AND RATTLES, AS WELL AS GIVING YOU MORE SPACE TO RIG THE MICS.

▶ Mic'ing a drum kit the simple way: Using a spaced stereo pair to capture the whole drum sound. These are typically set up 2–2.5m high in a small studio and around 1–2m in front of the kit.

choice, although for a smoother, more vintage drum sound, a **good ribbon mic** can also work well, giving a warm, solid sound that's less splashy at the high-end.

For **jazz kits** where you're after a natural sound rather than a highly-produced pop sound, a single capacitor mic in front of the kick, level with the hi-hat and aimed at the snare, can produce lovely results. If you have a multi-pattern capacitor mic, try both omni and cardioid patterns to see which suits the room best.

RECORDING THE KIT: MULTI-MIC OPTIONS

While the single mic or stereo pair approach works well for jazz kits in a nice room, the more normal approach in pop and rock production is to use multiple mics, with most of the mics positioned much closer to the drums. The aim here is not the natural

sound of the single mic approach, but enough separation to process each drum individually, and an overall sound that can be balanced with far greater flexibility.

The number of mics employed can be as few as four (stereo overheads plus close mics on the kick and snare) to as many as the job requires (a creative engineer might hook up as many as 15 or 20 mics to capture the kit and wider room). More mics can be added as you increase the size of your studio mic collection.

The initial step up from using a single stereo pair is to move those two mics above the kit to act as **overheads** and then place separate **close mics** on the **kick** and **snare**. Small diaphragm capacitor mics are commonly used as overheads; ribbons are also popular because of their smoother sound. Some engineers prefer the sound of large diaphragm capacitor mics too, such as the AKG C414.

In the early days of pop recording, the overhead mics were seen as the way to capture the cymbal sounds, that were added to the individual close-mic'ed drums. Engineers today tend to use the overhead mics to capture the whole drum kit as a single stereo instrument. Individual drums are then balanced using the close mics.

How high you place the overheads depends on the height of the room you're in, but you should aim for a metre or so above the cymbals with the two mics around 1–1.5m apart (top photo, page 150).

Where more distant **room mics** are also used, the overheads provide the 'full kit' sound with less room ambience than is picked up by the room mics. Overheads can pick up significant reflections from the ceiling – an area you will need to treat (Acoustics for drums, below).

Using this basic four mic setup you can usually capture a well-balanced drum sound. The weak links in the chain are the cymbals and toms, where the engineer must rely on the overheads.

A more complex, and more flexible, modern drum mix comprises **overheads**, **room mics**, **individual drum close mics** (including for **toms**) and often a separate **hi-hat mic**.

While using separate mics on **crash** and **ride** cymbals is unusual, some engineers use a capacitor mic on the hi-hat, positioned a little way above the cymbals and around 100–150mm away so that they can bring the hi-hats up in level if required. For practical purposes this mic is usually set up on the opposite side to the snare where it is not in the drummer's way. Although nice to have as an option, the hi-hat is usually picked up so strongly in the overheads that the dedicated hi-hat mic often remains unused.

When multi-mic'ing the drum kit you can sometimes afford to bring the overhead

ACOUSTICS FOR DRUMS

Purpose-built drum rooms are often clad with stone or other reflective materials and are frequently isolated from the rest of the studio to afford a degree of isolation between the drums and other instruments.

Few home producers have the luxury of such spaces, but you can still get a very good sound in the small studio. One option is to record drums on location (in a nice sounding room) to a click track along with a couple of guide guitar and vocal parts if you have access to a suitable venue. A more pragmatic approach is to deliberately exclude as much (poor sounding) room ambience as possible and then reintroduce a more appropriate

ambience when mixing using a suitable reverb sound.

You can improvise effective screens using piles of cardboard boxes or chairs covered with duvets, or by leaning mattresses against walls. As well as taming the acoustics, you can use such screens to improve the isolation between the drum kit and other instruments playing in the same room. (If you do so, however, you still need to leave a line of sight between the players – page 161.)

One often neglected area is the ceiling. In my experience it is the overhead mics above a multi-mic'ed drum kit in smaller

rooms that suffer the most from spill and room reflections as they're furthest from the kit. Companies such as sE make small instrument-specific Reflexion Filters that sit behind mics. Auralex also make little foam panels cut to slip over mic bodies. Either of these will help but I'd recommend using them in conjunction with a couple of sheets of four inch acoustic foam suspended just above the overhead mics to screen them from the ceiling. Nearby walls can be treated in the same way. Close mics above the drums pose less of a problem as their proximity to the drums means that the direct sound they capture far outweighs any reflected sound.

The **Shure SM57**: Useful on snares.

The **AKG D112** dynamic mic: popular for drums. Its frequency response is designed specifically for the kick. It's also pretty rugged.

Large diaphragm capacitor mics like the AKG C414 are popular choices for overheads.

mics closer to the cymbals to make balancing the cymbal levels a little easier. In a professional drum room or large studio, the engineer would probably also put one or more additional stereo pairs in front of the kit at different distances and use these to add **room ambience**. In the smaller studio this is rarely practical; additional ambience can be introduced using reverb.

As a rule I record all drums clean, with no EQ or other processing, taking care to leave enough headroom to avoid clipping. If you like the squashed analogue tape drum sound there are effective ways to fake that during the mixing stage using compression and/or analogue simulation plug-ins (Drum Production, Chapter 16).

Above and beyond these typical setups, engineers have adopted all kinds of more creative approaches, employing a wide range of mics and mic techniques, to get their own unique drum sound. Some of the most popular – and esoteric – are outlined at the end of this chapter.

With the number of drums, mics and wider variables involved, it's easy to understand why recording drums brings some engineers out in a rash. But starting with a basic setup and adding to it as budget allows (and your experience grows) is a good way of building an understanding of the kinds of sounds that are possible.

MIC'ING THE SNARE AND KICK

The usual position for the **snare close mic** is pointing over the drum rim angled towards the centre of the head – in a place where the drummer won't hit it! I usually place it close to the hi-hat side of the snare aimed away from the hi-hat, which not only rejects much of the hat sound, but also stops the closing hats blasting air onto the mic.

A spacing of around 40–50mm above the drum and about the same distance in from the rim usually works fine. **Moving-coil** mics are commonly used for this, although some **capacitor** models are also suitable. Shure SM57s and Sennheiser MD421s work well, although the MD421 is on the bulky side and harder to place.

While omnis pick up more spill, the quality of the spill is far better than with cardioid mics as an omni mic is as accurate off-axis as on-axis.

Many of the big name mic manufacturers make dedicated drum mic sets where the snare and tom mics clip to the drum rims. These have the benefit of being considerably easier to set up. This is the type used in most of the photographs overleaf.

Kick drums are often recorded in pro studios using Neumann FET47s. At the more realistic end of the price spectrum, the AKG D112 dynamic mic is popular. It has a frequency response designed specifically for the kick, with peaks that coincide with both the click and thump components of the sound. Being dynamic, it is also pretty rugged. Other mic manufacturers produce their own kick drum mics, also with carefully tailored response curves.

Where you place the kick mic depends on whether or not there is a hole in the front head and whether that hole is large enough to allow you some leeway with positioning.

My preferred starting position is with the mic just inside the drum shell, aimed back at the batter head and around mid-way between the centre and edge of the shell. If you put the mic in line with the beater, the sound loses depth and usually sounds too 'knocky'. You hear more beater click when you mic close to the batter head and more depth of tone as you move the mic further away. As with any mic positioning task, try experimenting with the mic position to see what difference it makes; you'll often find a position that improves on your first attempt, even if only slightly.

If the front skin has been removed entirely, use Blu Tak to secure any loose fittings. Stories abound of '70s rock bands spending three days in the studio trying to get a good kick drum sound (some urban and dance producers today claim to spend considerably longer!), but half an hour is usually enough.

MIC'ING THE TOMS

If more definition is needed from the toms then these may be close-mic'ed in much the same way as the snare drum, with mics placed to give the maximum possible distance from adjacent drums while kept out of the drummer's line of fire.

With single-headed toms there is also the option of placing mics inside the toms, which gives more isolation, although the sound becomes more resonant with less stick attack. Nevertheless, this can work well when combined with the overheads. As with mic'ing snare drums from underneath, you may need to use the polarity invert button to get the signal back into phase with other mics. Try both positions to see which sounds best.

Note / The more mics you have around the kit, the more **spill** you get. This can be controlled to some extent by judicious (and forensic) audio editing; it is common practice, for example, to use manual editing techniques on tom tracks to silence anything that isn't a tom hit (page 244).

Overheads sited a metre or more above the highest cymbal/s and at least 1–1.5m apart.

Kick drum mic'ed with a close mic aimed into the hole in the front head augmented by a second capacitor mic 600mm or so in front of the drum.

IF ALL ELSE FAILS...

Where the studio space simply isn't conducive to a good drum sound, you'll need to think of a creative solution.

I've had great success in the past setting up an electronic drum kit (such as a Roland V-Drum kit) and using its MIDI output to trigger a good sampled kit, such as one from BFD, Toontrack or Steven Slate. To complement the sampled drums I set up

real cymbals and hi-hats with a stereo mic pair above to record them. Having real cymbals alongside the sampled drums gives the recording more life and natural variation than using sampled cymbals. Providing the drummer is good, you can get a very convincing fully 'live' sound; few people will ever be able to tell the difference between your halfway house and the real thing. And because the kick, snare and toms are all captured as MIDI data, you've also got the freedom to **change the drum sounds** and drum balance when you start mixing.

You may also be able to **replace / mix in new drum sounds** at the mixing stage where acoustic drums have been recorded with reasonable separation using individual close mics (page 239). Several companies make dedicated drum replacement software.

Pro Tip / If you know in advance that some drum replacement may be necessary, it may be worth fitting each drum in the kit with contact mic-style pickups and recording the outputs from these onto separate tracks. The sound will probably be pretty bad but the separation should be good enough to allow reliable triggering when replacing the recorded sounds with samples.

TRICKS OF THE PROS

Looking back over the producer and engineer interviews we've done in Sound On Sound over the years, there are a few techniques used by the pros that come up time and again:

❯ **Tuning:** It is common for drum kits to be tuned to fit particular songs; rarely is the same kit mic'ed in the same way for an entire album. There are even examples of drummers tuning their toms to notes in the key of the song – although this is rare

PHASE CONSIDERATIONS

As soon as you put multiple mics on a single sound source, such as a drum kit, you run the risk of phase cancellations affecting the overall tonality.

Phase cancellation arises due to the slight time delays introduced when a sound arrives at different mics placed at different distances from the same source.

To reduce the risk of phase problems when multi-mic'ing drums, the overhead mics should be arranged so that both are the same distance from the snare. This ensures that the pivotal snare won't suffer if heard in mono.

It is also worth trying the phase invert button when introducing the kick drum to the overheads to see if that gives more or less low end. The setting that gives the most low end is the right one.

Some engineers mic the underside of the snare as well as the top. This is useful if you can't get enough snap using the top mic alone. To get the underside signal in phase with that from the top head its polarity must be inverted (when you hit the top drum head it moves down, away from the mic, while the bottom head moves in sympathy towards the mic beneath it); do so using the phase switch on the mic pre-amp or a phase-invert plug-in.

and not always desirable as it can force the drum pitch away from its natural resonant frequency (page 144).

❯ **Snare:** Engineers are divided over whether or not mic'ing the underside of the snare is worth doing. Some mic the side of the snare shell instead and mix that in. Where a snare head mic is used, it is common to reduce lingering rattles – something that is easy to do using plug-in gates when mixing. I'm reluctant to gate while tracking; an inappropriate gate setting can ruin what might otherwise be a brilliant, unrepeatable performance.

❯ **Kick:** If there's no hole in the kick drum front head and you mic from the front, you get more spill from the rest of the kit and a less defined beater click. Some engineers address this problem by mic'ing from a greater distance – up to one metre away – which helps preserve a more natural sound. Others mic just the rear of the head or both the front and rear together. If you mic both sides, test the phase buttons to

There's little agreement on how to create a big drum sound among the pros.

Many engineers and producers like to place the drums in large, lively-sounding rooms while engineer John Leckie has been known to prefer the sound of small, acoustically dead spaces as the resulting sound is easier to place within a busy mix.

Leckie also stresses the importance of choosing an appropriate snare drum sound for the song as it is the one element of the drum kit that sounds very prominent when a song is played on the radio.

see how the sounds best combine with each other and the rest of the kit.

> **Bigger kicks:** For a bigger kick sound it is not uncommon to feed the kick mic to a sub-bass PA speaker located close to the kit so that some of the PA signal is picked up in the other kit mics. Some engineers combine the outputs from both internal and more distant kick mics, often using a dynamic model inside and a capacitor or ribbon model outside (lower photo, page 150). Both Eddie Kramer and Toni Visconti have employed this technique.

> **PA energy:** A similar PA trick used for increasing the energy of the snare and kick is to set up a full-range PA system out in the room at some distance from the kit and feed it with a suitable mix of the kick and snare mics. The amplified sound is picked up by the overheads and room ambience mics along with the natural sound of the kit to give greater emphasis to the kick and snare. This approach was reportedly used to beef up the snare sound on the Rolling Stones' 'Start Me Up'.

> **Multiple kick mics:** Some engineers use up to three mics on the kick drum alone. A typical setup is a dynamic mic just inside the drum shell, a large diaphragm capacitor mic a metre or so in front of the drum and a third mic around the back aimed at the batter head (which can either be quite close to the head or as far away as behind the drummer's stool). The rear mic usually requires its phase flipping to keep it in phase with the front mics.

> **Tunnelled kicks:** At the more experimental end of the spectrum, producer Butch Vig has talked about creating a 'tunnel' for the kick drum – in his case made from headless kick drum shells placed in line and covered in blankets – although it is worth experimenting with a plastic bin with the bottom cut out pointing at the kick when working in the home studio. The close mic is placed in the drum shell as normal with a more distant mic set up in the tunnel where it captures a more resonant sound that is fairly effectively screened from external kit spill. Mix the signals to taste.

> **Gated verb:** Although dated when used in an obvious way, no chapter on drum recording would be complete without mentioning the classic Phil Collins gated sound used on tracks such as 'In The Air Tonight'. The technique relies on a good-sounding live room with ambience mics set up some way from the kit which are fed through a gate triggered by the close kit mics. Whenever a drum is hit, the gate opens and a burst of room ambience is heard before being abruptly extinguished by the gate, which has a hold time adjusted to control the length of the ambience burst followed by a fast release. This technique is still used in a more subtle way today during rock recordings to add power to the drum sound. The effect can be convincingly faked when mixing using reverb plug-ins, many of which can create a similar effect without the need for a separate gate.

> **Full drum bang:** In extreme cases, where the full drum kit just doesn't cut the sonic mustard, entire drum tracks have occasionally been played back over a PA set up in a concrete stairwell and the result re-recorded. This massive new ambient drum sound is then mixed in with the original to create a larger-than-life amalgam. Today we'd probably use replacement sampled drums – we don't all have access to a concrete stairwell – but the results are earthily organic and can bring something special to a lacklustre original recording. ●

IN EXTREME CASES, WHERE THE FULL DRUM KIT JUST DOESN'T CUT THE SONIC MUSTARD, ENTIRE DRUM TRACKS HAVE KNOWN TO BE PLAYED BACK OVER A PA SET UP IN A CONCRETE STAIRWELL AND THE RESULT RE-RECORDED.

10
RECORDING BANDS

> THE BEST
> PERFORMANCES
> INVARIABLY HAPPEN
> WHEN AS MANY
> BAND MEMBERS
> ARE PLAYING
> TOGETHER
> AS POSSIBLE.

THE OPTIONS

Faced with a band in the studio that want to record a new track, there are three main approaches to choose from:

❯ **1: Fully live** – Where all the main parts are recorded at the same time. This is often the best approach when recording bands, although it may not always be practical. Some parts – typically vocals, vocal layers and solos – may be overdubbed after the initial recording. This can be thought of as the 'all-at-once' approach.

❯ **2: Fully layered** – Where all parts are programmed and/or recorded as separate overdubs. Ideal for solo songwriters/ producers and common practice among urban and dance producers. This is less successful for traditional band recordings.

❯ **3: A mix of the two** – A part live, part layered amalgam necessitated either by the limitations of the studio, the nature of the material or the instrumentation of the track. In practice, most band recordings are done on a sliding scale somewhere between the 'fully live' and 'fully layered' approaches.

The producer needs to master all three approaches to suit different projects and clients, and understand the technical and artistic ramifications of each. The singer/songwriter, for example, may require a layered approach, recording their guitar first, then vocals, and then supporting instrumentation as a series of different overdubs.

But for bands, the first option (or as close to it as you can get) invariably generates the best results, capturing both the feel of the band and the raw energy of a live show.

The experienced producer knows that performance is everything – that performance is when the magic happens, and that a performance is immeasurably better when the band plays together, with overdubs limited to those parts that aren't essential for the feel of the track's foundation. The best performances invariably happen when as many band members are playing together as possible.

All-at-once recording makes life trickier for the producer of course, demanding a host of imaginative ways of taming spill, reducing drum resonance and controlling phase, but since when did the producer either seek, or get, an easy ride? One of the first lessons you learn is that you need to make the technology adapt to the artist, not the artist to the technology.

ALL-AT-ONCE RECORDING: THE DRAWBACKS

The main – and overriding – concern when recording multiple instruments in the same space is **spill**.

Spill can come from any source, but the usual suspects, particularly when recording rock and indie bands, are the drum kit and electric guitars spilling into the vocal mic/s and drum overheads. A related problem is **buzzing** caused by the snare drum resonating in tune to bass frequencies coming from the bass and guitar amps.

Not all spill is bad of course – sometimes it can be helpful in gluing a performance together (page 306). But when using cardioid pattern mics in a less than optimal sounding acoustic environment, spill is rarely useful and so is best minimised.

One way to tame spill is to **cut the volume** of those elements that are excessively loud; if the guitarists can get their signature sound at a lower level or by using a power soak (page 121) then that's often a good option for the smaller studio.

Taken to its logical conclusion, the 'less volume' approach results in the **silent session** (page 160), a scenario that relies on plug-in amp simulators to generate the kind of sound the guitarist would normally expect from their amp. This is fed to the players' headphones for monitoring. Sometimes an electronic drumkit is played too.

The second most effective spill tamer is **space**. Those lucky enough to have it – either in the form of multiple rooms or a big enough live space to allow for good separation between instruments and mics – have a far greater chance of being able to isolate individual sound sources and record a band using the all-at-once approach.

Sadly, few of us have access to as much space as we'd like and even high-end studios often make do with less than they need. In these instances the engineer must make the best use of the space and kit they have to reduce as much spill as they can.

In practice this means **exploiting mic polar patterns** (page 68) to reject unwanted sound and tame spill, setting up **acoustic screens to isolate instruments** (page 89) from each other as best as possible, and thinking carefully – and occasionally creatively – about **how the instruments, mics and screens are arranged**.

Getting these fundamentals right can go a long way to generating a solid mix with a good degree of separation between parts.

HOW MANY PASSES?

Recording a band using an all-at-once approach doesn't mean you need to nail it in one glowing take. If you're recording to an anchor click track (or percussive loop) then you would typically record two or three passes of the same song so that you have enough material to copy and paste into one optimal version or to patch up an otherwise brilliant take with a couple of fluffs in it.

Nailing a solid rhythm part is usually the priority: it is the drum track and bassline that locks the groove, providing a rhythmic foundation for all that sits above.

Sometimes it may be necessary to edit the drum part, using sections from other takes to build a single comped drum track and then check that this works in the context of the other instruments before moving on to overdubs. If any parts still need to be re-recorded then they can be played against the comped drum track, either as full tracks or as punch-in sections.

Be warned that taking individual drum parts from alternate takes can cause problems if there's audible instrumental spill on the parts as you'll be able to hear the ghosts of the other instruments playing in the background. For this reason you should endeavour to take sections from the same locations of the various takes rather than simply looking for a section where the rhythm is the same.

TO CLICK (OR NOT)

An early decision you face when recording a full band is whether or not to record to a click. It is a decision that hinges both on the style of the music you're working on and the drummer's ability to play to a click without losing the natural feel of the song.

I dislike basic clicks; when the drummer plays to a simple on-the-beat click their own playing invariably masks the click. In other words, the only time they get to fully hear it is when they've drifted out of time – which is already too late.

A more effective method is to program a simple percussion rhythm, or use a percussive loop (shaker, tambourine, bongos etc) that follows the groove of the song, and let the drummer play along to that. It feels more natural than a click and invariably generates better results.

Where a song includes **tempo changes** — a chorus pushed up by one or two bpm for example — then the guide rhythm track or click will need a specific length count-in so that everyone starts at the right place and hits the tempo change at the correct point in the song. Planning tempo changes involves some pre-recording bar counting. It helps to get somebody in the band to strum the chords or play a guide keyboard part as you work through the song structure before recording to make sure the tempo changes fall in the right place.

WHO PLAYS?

Even if you choose an all-at-once approach, it doesn't follow that all parts you record have to be final takes. Indeed sometimes that's not an option. Unless you have a well-isolated vocal booth or a large enough room to space the players apart, the vocal mic will almost always pick up too much spill from other instruments, which can only be solved by replacing the vocal later.

In other words, the vocal you record during the initial performance may only be useful as a guide.

If you know the vocal is only going to be a guide then you can record it perfectly adequately using a hand-held dynamic mic (knowing you'll be moving onto a more suitable studio mic later). But remember to keep the singer away from the drum overhead mics; the less guide vocal spill you capture on the drum tracks the better.

If spill in a particularly small room is a problem you might also consider asking the vocalist to lower the volume of their performance a little if the part is only going to be a guide. Improvised screens can also help reduce spill.

There are rare exceptions where the original vocal can be used in the final track, such as when the singer has a particularly powerful voice and/or the room is big enough to allow you to create enough separation. In such a case, following the usual guidelines for recording a vocal — using a pop-shield, fitting a Reflexion Filter or other acoustic screen behind the mic and so on — will both improve the quality of the take and help isolate the signal.

In reality though, keeping a loud drum kit and a couple of screaming guitars out of the vocal mic in the same room is a tall order and overdubbing is often required. Other parts that are regular candidates for overdubbing include:

> **Acoustic guitars:** Where an acoustic guitar plays a pivotal role in the track it will almost always need to be overdubbed — volume-wise it simply can't compete with guitar amps and drums. If the DI sound from the acoustic guitar is acceptable in the context of the overall mix then you can use that, of course. A DI version can also be used for any initial takes to help cement the performance and provide a guide when re-recording it using a mic later.

> **Acoustic keyboards:** Although electronic keyboard parts can be DI'd, unless you have a really big studio or an isolation booth acoustic pianos usually need to be recorded separately.

> **Guitar solos:** Solos are almost always overdubbed — usually for the logistical reason that a guitarist can only play one part at once (and also because they only seem satisfied after playing mulitple versions!)

> **Backing and supporting vocals:** Where you need to build complex vocal

arrangements, overdubbing the various double-tracks and harmonies allows you to add as many parts as you need and won't affect the overall feel of the song in any detrimental way.

BASS

Loud low-frequency sounds are major contributors to both bleed and drum rattle. Fortunately the damage a live bass can do is minimised by the fact that in most modern recordings it is common to **DI the bass guitar** (page 124).

In cases where an amped sound is required, there are plenty of excellent bass amp emulation plug-ins that can provide it (page 291). The bass player can still use an amp for monitoring purposes – using either a DI box or the amp's own DI output, where fitted – to provide the recording feed. This arrangement allows the bass amp to be run at a lower volume to help reduce spill and snare rattles.

A cleaner option again is to omit the amp altogether so that the bass is only audible via the headphone monitoring system. This is the best option for avoiding rattle and spill, although a good musical performance should take priority over all other considerations, so go with whichever arrangement makes the players happy.

DRUMS

The drums should be set up and mic'ed in whatever way you feel is most suitable given the room acoustics and available space. Where excessive snare rattle is a problem, one option is to record the drum kit with the snare lever flipped off and a contact mic fitted to the drum head so that you can record it to a separate track and then apply one of the drum replacement techniques outlined in Chapter 16. A side-

benefit of working with the snare off is that it reduces the level of bright snare spill affecting other instruments' mics .

Sometimes damping the snare, retuning it or putting tape over the ends of the snare will help reduce rattle, but in my experience these measures tend to compromise the tone to an unacceptable degree and rarely reduce the rattle enough to be worthwhile.

There's also the option of using an electronic kit, ideally with real cymbals (page 150) – a potentially useful approach in the smaller studio. Capturing the MIDI data recorded from the electronic kit allows you to use a choice of world-class drum samples covering just about any genre while the real ride and hi-hat cymbals add a sense of reality to the performance. There will still be some spill in the cymbal mics, but cymbals are pretty loud so it shouldn't be excessive and it can be further reduced using low-cut filters.

Tip / Where individual drums are close mic'ed, the close mics rarely pick up too much spill (the drum signal is so loud), but the drum overheads are further from the kit and so tend to pick up more. To give the overheads a little more isolation, position them slightly closer to the kit than you normally would and then use foam collars or mini Instrument Reflexion Filters behind them to reduce the amount of outside sound reaching them. Cardioid mics can help reduce off-axis spill – but such spill as they do pick up may sound dull and coloured. Sometimes omni mics give better results – even though the level of spill is greater, at least it sounds clean.

ELECTRIC GUITARS

First up, electric guitar amps don't have to be turned up as loud as the guitarist might

> **ELECTRIC GUITAR AMPS DON'T HAVE TO BE TURNED UP AS LOUD AS THE GUITARIST MIGHT WANT! INDEED MANY GUITARS OFTEN SOUND BEST RECORDED USING RELATIVELY LOW-POWERED VALVE AMPS.**

want! Indeed many guitars sound best recorded using relatively low-powered valve amps, although I've found that the Vox VT-series hybrid amps and some of the Line 6 models also record well at a moderate volumes. Much depends on the sound you're after.

Where a **close mic** is used, the amount of spill reaching the amp mic is usually low enough not to cause problems. Acoustic screens can be set up behind the amp mic to reduce the amount of amp spill reaching the drum and vocal mics. Even a duvet hanging over a chair or clothes drying frame will improve separation. On occasions I've simply draped a duvet or two directly over the amp and mic.

Where the studio adjoins a house, or where there are spare rooms adjoining the studio, it might be possible to run cables to adjacent rooms or to closets so that the **guitar amps can be physically separated** from the main recording area (and each other). The players and the drum kit can be arranged so that everyone has eye contact, while the guitar amps can be run as loud as the guitarist wants to get the right sound.

Multiple rooms can be exploited in other ways too: how about putting the bass and guitar players (recording via DI) in the same room as the drummer, with the vocalist and (DI'd) keyboard player in the control room? You end up with a spill-less drum and vocal recording, with DI'd bass and guitars. As long as eye contact is maintained between as many players as possible, the energy and feel of a live recording can often be retained.

For some styles of music, the guitar sound that can be obtained from a **software amp-modelling plug-in** works perfectly well for

the final mix, in which case the guitar can simply be DI'd into the audio interface via an instrument input or a separate active DI box connected to a mic input (page 112).

If the guitar player doesn't like the sound of amp modelling, the clean guitar DI track (once edited and comped if necessary) can be fed back through a guitar amp and mic'ed conventionally, then recorded back to a new track (page 123). **Re-mic'ing** in this way can be a lifesaver in the smaller studio, allowing the engineer to experiment with multiple mics in a situation where there's no spill (or time restraints!) to worry about.

Solos and doubled or overlaid melodic lines are usually added as **overdubs**. Because spill isn't a problem with the overdubs you have a choice of DI'ing or amp mic'ing — whatever works best for the part.

Tip / To reduce the amount of guitar spill hitting the drum overheads, and to lower the amount of snare buzz, try rotating the guitar amps away from the drums. This works particularly well with closed-backed models.

Tip / Take advantage of all furniture you have at your disposal: sofas, mattresses, even duvet-draped tables placed over amps can help reduce spill and improve isolation. Don't think this is unprofessional — many classic recordings have been made using improvised screens.

Tip / Remember that you can tame spill in two key locations: at source (i.e. reducing the spill from a guitar amp by using acoustic screens behind the amp mic), or at destination (i.e. by placing screens between the guitar amps and drum overheads to reduce the amount of guitar signal reaching them).

THE SILENT BAND

Where an electronic drum kit is available and the electronic cymbals and hi-hats work well for the song (triggering fresh samples if necessary), there's absolutely no reason why you can't DI every part – from drums to guitar – so that the only sound in the room, other than the tapping of sticks on drum pads and the scrape of plectra on strings, is the vocalist. In this 'silent band' scenario, all monitoring is done via headphones. The vocal part can either be used as a guide or the first take of the real thing as spill should be minimal.

For the band to record using the silent method, the studio needs to have a multi-output headphone amp with individual level controls on the various outputs (page 103). Where your audio interface has multiple outputs, you can use these to set up multiple headphone mixes with different balances. Most serious multi-channel headphone amps have the option to route individual outputs to each headphone amp if you don't want them all fed from the same stereo source.

A clear benefit of this 'everybody DI'd' approach is that you get to capture the feel of people playing together, while the complete absence of spill means that parts can be replaced or patched up later without worrying about hearing a ghost of the old version in the spill recorded on other instrument mics.

The silent band method can also be used when you are recording quieter acoustic instruments that play a key role in the song, like an acoustic guitar, as part of a louder band. Because spill from the drums and amps into the sensitive acoustic guitar mic invariably swamps the quiet acoustic signal, capturing the acoustic guitar via a mic in a conventional all-at-once recording is all but impossible. The only options are to overdub the guitar later (losing the live feel) or use a DI pickup system, which almost always gives a less satisfactory sound than mic'ing. Using the silent band approach allows you to record the acoustic guitar using traditional mic'ing techniques (page 127) without worrying about spill.

> **THERE'S ABSOLUTELY NO REASON WHY YOU CAN'T DI EVERY PART – FROM DRUMS TO GUITAR – SO THAT THE ONLY SOUND IN THE ROOM, OTHER THAN THE TAPPING OF STICKS ON DRUM PADS AND THE SCRAPE OF PLECTRA ON STRINGS, IS THE VOCALIST.**

CASE STUDY: AMP SEPARATION

In the Studio SOS column in Sound On Sound, staff visit readers' studios to help them improve their recordings and mixes. In one session, we had the brief of controlling the amount of guitar spill reaching the drum overheads (which made the drum tracks almost unuseable).

The band's home studio was in a wooden outbuilding with mattresses stacked against the walls. They had wisely bought power soaks so that their high-powered amps and 4x12 cabs could be run at a lower level while still delivering the sought-after metal 'thrashed' sound.

Even so, the small space they were recording in meant all amps were facing towards the centre of the room so attempts to get a good drum sound were thwarted by the still fairly high level of guitars bleeding into the overhead drum mics only a couple of metres away.

To improve the situation we suggested rotating the speakers through 180 degrees to face the mattress-lined walls, leaving just enough space to get a close mic between the speakers and mattresses. As the speaker cabinets had fully enclosed backs, this reduced the

amount of guitar sound leaking into the room by a useful amount – especially at higher frequencies – and enabled us to get enough separation to achieve a decent drum sound.

Some low-cut EQ was required on the drum overheads to further reduce the effect of the guitar spill, but it served to demonstrate that even in the smallest spaces a bit of lateral thinking can turn a seemingly impossible situation into a workable one.

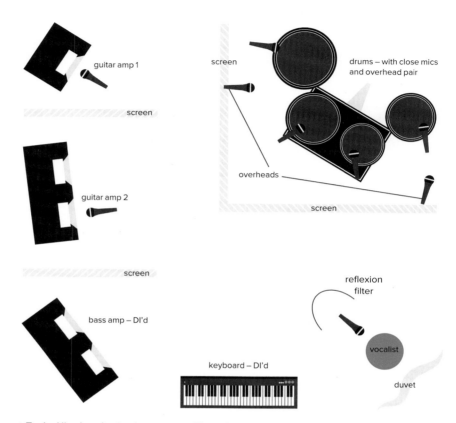

guitar amp 1

screen

guitar amp 2

screen

bass amp – DI'd

keyboard – DI'd

screen

drums – with close mics and overhead pair

overheads

screen

reflexion filter

vocalist

duvet

▲ Typical live band setup in one room: The guitar players can wander away from their amps and out into the room to maintain eye contact.

Of course the silent approach won't suit everyone; some guitar players need to hear a real amp in a real room and not all drummers like playing electronic kits — even the good ones with mesh heads that feel like real drum heads. But it's a useful approach to have in your armoury.

ACOUSTIC BANDS

Recording an acoustic band using an 'all-at-once' approach isn't necessarily difficult, as long as the instruments have a reasonably natural balance — ideally not a ukelele and a drum kit for example! A good method is to get the various players to sit in a circle facing inwards so they have good eye contact. The 'five-to-one' rule (page 75) should be followed where possible to reduce comb filtering. Where the acoustics of the room suit the sound of the performance, consider using omni mics rather than cardioids.

Although using cardioid mics minimises spill, the down-side is that what spill there is can be coloured to such an extent that the recording becomes oppressively dull. Omnis pick up more spill, but this spill is uncoloured and can work in the producer's favour — generating a more natural and gelled composite sound.

Separation can be increased by the clever use of acoustic screens. Reflexion filters behind the individual mics can help, as can screens located between adjacent performers to reduce spill without compromising eye contact.

In some situations a stereo pair of mics over the ensemble can be used as an additional blending element.

Where some of the players also sing, figure-of-eight mics can be used to separate voice and instrument. In this case, aim the figure-of-eight mic's null (90 degrees off axis) at the signal you want to reject.

For example, the null of the vocal mic can be aimed at the instrument being played while the null of the instrument mic is aimed at the singer's mouth (page 132).

Because figure-of-eight mics are as sensitive at the rear as at the front, acoustic screens should be set up to control the level of any spill at the rear.

CONCLUSION

When recording a band, it isn't always necessary to record all parts at the same time, but it is desirable to have the rhythm section and at least one chordal instrument, such as a guitar or keyboard, playing together along with a guide vocal to lay down the track's fundamentals and capture the rhythmic feel of the piece. Other elements — from vocals to strings and keyboards — can be overdubbed later.

Always remember the cardinal, overriding goal: a musical performance with feel. To capture that, you will generally want as many band members playing together as you can. As long as this initial recording has the right vibe, other

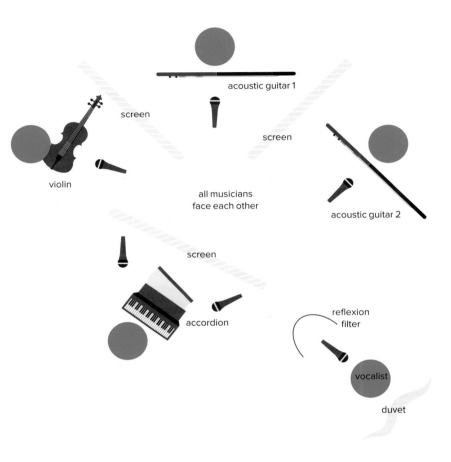

▲ Typical acoustic band setup in one room. Screens would normally be just low enough to permit eye contact between the players. Pro screens are often fitted with perspex windows for this purpose.

parts can be overdubbed without the recording sounding as though it has been built up a layer at a time.

The various DI options we have available to us today allow us to record something close to the 'silent band' without incurring spill penalties. There's no reason not to combine any of the techniques discussed here if doing so produces the desired end result. ●

SECTION FOUR
MIXING

- Compression & Dynamics
- Reverb & Ambience 101
- Pitch Correction 101
- Vocal Production
- Electric Guitar Production
- Drum Production
- Pre-Mix Housekeeping
- The Arrangement
- The Mixdown
- Mastering

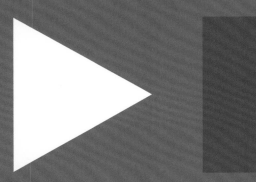

11
COMPRESSION & DYNAMICS 101

UNDERSTANDING HOW COMPRESSION WORKS AND WHEN TO DEPLOY IT CAN SIGNIFICANTLY IMPROVE THE CLARITY AND PUNCH OF A MIX.

A MISUSED ESSENTIAL

Alongside EQ (page 32) and reverb (page 181), the compressor is one of the three key tools in the producer's armoury. Yet it is also one of the most misused. Understanding how it works and when to deploy it can significantly improve the clarity and punch of a mix, adding bulk and body to individual sounds and giving them added definition. Compression is also used in a number of advanced production techniques that can take a mix to the next level.

HOW DOES A COMPRESSOR WORK?

Compressors reduce the dynamic range of a signal (page 101), changing the relationship between its loudest and quietest parts. You can visualise it as the electronic equivalent of an engineer with a volume fader and incredibly fast reactions. The key controls are:

Threshold: The level (measured in dB) at which the compressor starts doing its job. Signal below the threshold remains untouched. That which exceeds it is compressed or reduced in level.

Ratio: The amount of gain reduction applied to signals above the threshold level. At a ratio of 1:1 there is no compression. At a ratio of 3:1, a 3dB increase in input level is required to generate a 1dB increase in output whenever the signal level rises above the threshold. In other words, the ratio figure tells you how many dBs of input level increase is needed to result in a 1dB output level increase for above-threshold signals.

Attack: How quickly the compressor responds when the input signal exceeds the threshold, usually measured in milliseconds (ms). High values preserve early transients by delaying the onset of compression slightly. It can be useful to think of the attack time as **reaction time**.

Release: Length of time the compressor takes to return to 0dB worth of gain reduction after the signal has dropped back below the threshold. It can be useful to think of the release time as **recovery time**.

Make-up gain: Compression lowers the volume of the signal by reducing the level of the peaks. The level needs to be 'made up' again to bring the peaks back up to their original level. The result of this operation is that the peaks remain at the same level as before but quieter sounds are made louder.

Tip / When evaluating the effects of compression, adjust the make-up gain so that the subjective level is the same with the compressor switched in or bypassed. If you don't do this it's easy to fall into the trap of thinking what sounds loudest sounds best.

COMPRESSION IN THE MIX

The compressor is used for two purposes, which are intrinsically linked:

> **altering the shape or envelope of a sound**, and

> **reducing the dynamic range of a signal** — useful when an audio track has significant volume fluctuations that you want to even out.

The effect of the compressor on a sound's shape is most obvious where the source sound is transient in nature, such as a drum hit. A standard compressor set up to process a snare drum, for example, will produce very different results depending on the attack and release times. Altering these settings and listening to the results is the best way to gain an understanding of how a compressor affects a sound.

Fast attack, fast release: If you set the fastest possible attack and release times the compressor will react extremely quickly when the input signal exceeds the threshold level. This means the attack transient of the snare drum is pulled down in level almost immediately . As soon as the hit is over, the fast release time restores the gain to normal in a matter of milliseconds so that any decay in the snare sound is brought back up to its unprocessed level. Once you add some make-up gain to get the peak level the same as it was before compression, the result is that **the drum sound loses some impact at the start but the ring or sustain of the drum is increased** (see waveforms, right). At higher compression ratios, the result is similar to that produced by a limiter — a typical limiter has very fast attack and release times.

Fast attack, longer release: If you increase the release time but leave the attack at its fastest, both **the initial transient of the drum sound and any decay or ring is reduced by roughly the same amount**. This is useful where you need to make the level of the hits more consistent without changing the character of the sound too much. The important point here is not to set the release time too long as the compressor's gain needs to return to normal before the next hit comes along. You can judge this by watching the gain reduction meter and using your ears.

Slower attack, moderate release:
To **accentuate the attack of a drum hit** the compressor attack time should be decreased so that it takes a little longer

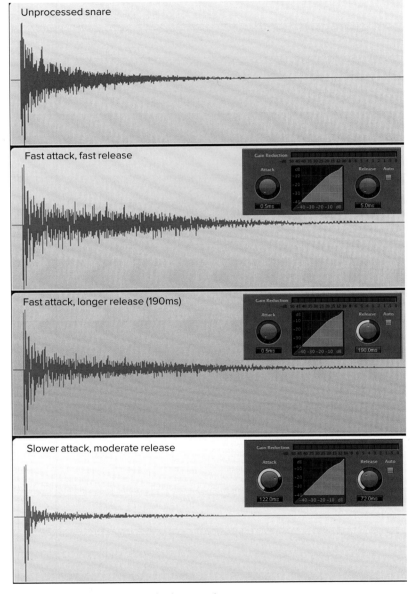

▲ **Waveforms showing how a single snare drum hit is affected by different compression settings, with compressor screengrabs inset.**

THE TRANSIENT DESIGNER

The problem with using a compressor to shape the sound of drum hits is that the compression process changes as the level of the incoming hits changes – loud hits receive more gain reduction and quieter ones less. This is not a problem when you only need to even out the levels, but in some situations you may want to change the shape of the sound without affecting the relative levels of the different hits (in the case of a busy, widely dynamic jazz drum solo, for example).

That's where a transient designer comes in – a processor developed by SPL that has inspired more than a few competitors to develop similar products.

SPL Transient Designer

Available both as hardware and a plug-in, the genius of the transient designer is that it has no threshold setting; it constantly calculates it based on the input signal. This allows it to apply the same processing (almost) regardless of the input signal level.

The SPL Transient Designer only has two controls, attack and sustain. Upping the attack can turn an ordinary-sounding kick drum into a hard-hitting beast, while easing back on it can yield a softer, 'bouncing basketball'-type sound.

To adjust the subjective damping of a drum kit or alter the attack of recorded drums that vary in level, a transient designer is the best tool for the job.

---

to react when a transient comes along. By setting the attack time to 10–20ms, the initial drum transient passes through the compressor unchanged before the compressor pulls the signal down. Kick drums may need an attack setting as high as 60ms to avoid pulling down the level of the first cycle or two of the waveform where most of the low frequency energy resides.

The overall outcome of a slower attack time and a moderate release time is that the initial hit of the drum ends up louder relative to the decaying part of the sound. It is a useful setting for adding definition to drum hits or tightening up under-damped drums, but reduce the attack too much and the drum sound will lose weight.

AUTO ATTACK AND RELEASE

Some compressors include an 'Auto' setting that controls the release time. On some models both attack and release are affected.

The Auto setting monitors the input signal level and attack characteristics then modifies the compressor's timing settings on-the-fly to optimise performance, usually to produce the least obtrusive processing.

You still need to adjust the threshold and ratio to get the required amount of gain reduction but the Auto setting looks after the release timing (or both attack and release on models that control both).

Auto settings can be especially useful when dealing with complex material where the attack and decay characteristics are constantly changing, such as a slap bass line or acoustic guitar part, or on vocals and submixed groups where you want to create a more even level without altering the character of the sound.

Note / Most modern compressors have a built-in 'hold' time to delay the release phase by around 50ms (the length of a single 20Hz cycle of audio). Without this you would hear distortion when setting the compressor to its fastest attack and release times as it would respond quickly enough to affect individual cycles of low frequency waveforms, changing their shape and harmonic structure. If you hear such distortion it suggests your compressor doesn't have a built-in hold time; remedy this by increasing the release time until the distortion disappears.

PEAK AND RMS SENSING

Many plug-in compressors include a switch for choosing between Peak and RMS (Average) sensing. This determines the way the compressor interprets the incoming signal levels. When set to **Peak** the compressor monitors the absolute peak level of the input – regardless of its duration – so even a short rim click will register its maximum level and be processed accordingly.

However, the human hearing system doesn't perceive loudness based on peak levels alone; the length of the event also influences perceived loudness, with longer duration events appearing louder than short ones (page 302), even though their peak levels may be exactly the same. The **RMS** or **Average** setting takes this into account and applies gain reduction more in line with what humans perceive the loudness to be rather than on what the peak level actually is.

As a general rule the Peak setting is best for short-duration percussive sounds such as drum hits while RMS/Average is more applicable to vocals and other non-percussive sounds.

WHEN TWO COMPRESSORS ARE BETTER THAN ONE

Sometimes no single compression setting works on a signal – gentle compression with a lower threshold may add density and even out the overall sound but the louder peaks still jump out at you. Bass guitar and vocal lines are particularly susceptible to these kinds of problems.

Mix automation can be used to reduce the level of offending peaks, but it's also worth experimenting with two compressors in series. In the case of a vocal you might

use the first compressor to add gentle density to the signal, and the second, with a higher ratio and a faster attack, to tread more heavily on any peaks that were left untouched by the first.

In some cases you might even follow this second compressor with a limiter, to place a final brick wall ceiling on the maximum signal peaks. Care must be taken not to limit too heavily though if a natural sound is to be retained.

Tip / Engineers and producers that use a chain of compressors to process a signal – either on individual tracks or during mastering – take great care when choosing the processors, with each picked to do a specific job (tame transients, accentuate hits etc) or bestow a certain sonic colour.

USING (AND ABUSING) THE SIDE-CHAIN

The side-chain of a compressor is the part of the circuit that 'listens' to the input signal, following the level of the audio before passing it on to the variable-gain amplifier.

Where the compressor has a side-chain insert point, you can insert an equaliser to influence the way the compressor behaves. Because the EQ is only in the side-chain and not in the main signal path, it affects the way the compressor behaves but doesn't change the tonality of the sound being processed.

If you were, for example, to apply low end boost to the side-chain signal, the compressor would react more strongly to bass sounds than bright ones. Alternatively, applying a strong EQ boost in the 4–8kHz range where vocal sibilance can be a problem will cause the compressor to react more assertively when those

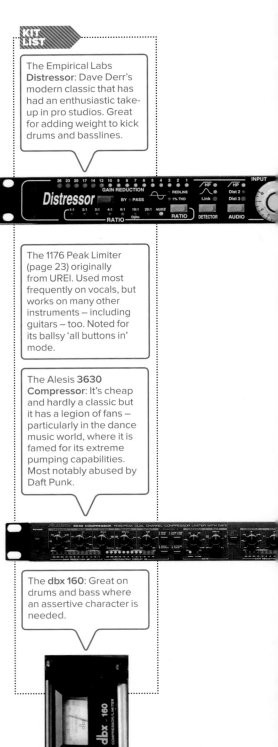

KIT LIST

The Empirical Labs **Distressor**: Dave Derr's modern classic that has had an enthusiastic take-up in pro studios. Great for adding weight to kick drums and basslines.

The 1176 Peak Limiter (page 23) originally from UREI. Used most frequently on vocals, but works on many other instruments – including guitars – too. Noted for its ballsy 'all buttons in' mode.

The Alesis **3630** Compressor: It's cheap and hardly a classic but it has a legion of fans – particularly in the dance music world, where it is famed for its extreme pumping capabilities. Most notably abused by Daft Punk.

The dbx **160**: Great on drums and bass where an assertive character is needed.

When two are better than one

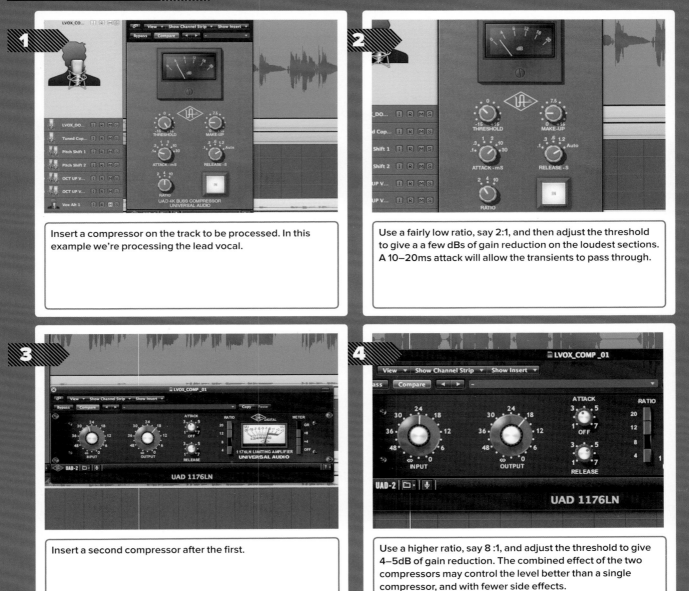

1 Insert a compressor on the track to be processed. In this example we're processing the lead vocal.

2 Use a fairly low ratio, say 2:1, and then adjust the threshold to give a a few dBs of gain reduction on the loudest sections. A 10–20ms attack will allow the transients to pass through.

3 Insert a second compressor after the first.

4 Use a higher ratio, say 8:1, and adjust the threshold to give 4–5dB of gain reduction. The combined effect of the two compressors may control the level better than a single compressor, and with fewer side effects.

frequencies are present. This latter arrangement is the basis of a simple single-band de-esser. However, there are better ways of de-essing, such as using a multi-band compressor so that only the offending sibilant region is processed (see opposite).

A more common use of the side-chain insert point – one that has been taken to (occasionally wild) extremes by Parisian house and nu-rave producers – is to feed it with an on-the-beat kick drum to compress a bassline. At subtle levels the technique can be used to dip the level of the bass when the kick hits – useful when the two parts inhabit the same sonic space.

Side-chain driven compression is also occasionally used by dance producers across whole mixes – again, with the side-chain fed from the kick track – to create the now classic 'pumping' sound.

MULTI-BAND COMPRESSION

The multi-band compressor was developed to get around some of the inherent limitations of the conventional single full-band type.

In a full-band compressor the entire signal is subjected to gain reduction whenever a loud event exceeds the threshold, regardless of where in the audio spectrum that event occurs. What this means in practice is that if a poor, innocent low-level hi-hat happens to be playing at the same time as a loud kick drum, everything dips in level, including the hi-hat, which risks getting knocked way back in the mix by the kick.

This is a particular problem when a compressor is used across the master bus, or on a group bus, where the compressor reacts by pulling back the volume of the

whole mix when a loud event – usually a kick drum – hits. Not only do parts start losing definition, but the mix can soon start audibly 'pumping' against the kick.

The multi-band compressor solves the problem by splitting the audio into two or more frequency bands and giving each band its own set of compressor controls, allowing different parts of the spectrum to be compressed more than others. High level, low frequency sounds such as bass guitars or kick drums can be allowed to trigger significant amounts of gain reduction in the low frequency band, for example, while moderate level higher frequencies – where the vocals sit – remain unaffected in the higher bands.

The fact that you can set different attack and release times for the different frequency bands also allows more forensic adjustment

▲ Logic's native multi-band compressor: Note the four bands, each with the usual compression settings, plus the ability to expand a signal as well. The large blue blocks at the top show the gain reduction in each frequency band.

TECHNIQUE: MASTERING

Multi-band compression is usually only used during mastering to rectify specific mixing problems. A good full-band compressor is generally used to master the whole mix.

than giving everything a blanket treatment.

Multi-band compressors can seem daunting; compression is hard enough to understand without multiplying the confusion by three or four! But while setting up four sets of compressor controls across four frequency bands might seem like hard work, you'll often find that you only need to process one or two of the bands to get the result you need; the others can be left alone.

There are many applications for multi-band compressors. Common uses are across the **whole mix** or **group buses**. But they are also useful for balancing the tonality of individual instruments. I've used them to improve **acoustic guitar** recordings which have been made with the mic focusing too much on the sound hole, for example, which invariably leads to an excessive level of low-end boominess and muddiness. By tuning one of the bands to the sound-hole resonance the boominess can be brought under control without affecting the rest of the sound.

Similarly, the hard edge of a **piezo bridge transducer**, which can be quite obtrusive in the 3–6kHz range, can be tamed by dedicating a tightly-compressed band to that part of the sound.

Tip / Most multi-band compressors have a solo facility to allow you to hear what each band is doing in isolation. Use it to help you fine-tune both the compressor settings and the upper and lower frequency limits of each band.

Tip / Some multi-band compressor plug-ins allow the ratio control to be set to a negative value so that the band acts as an **expander** rather than a compressor. An expander is used to suppress rather than enhance low level sounds. Using

one it is possible to partially clean up noisy electric guitar tracks by setting the various thresholds so that the highest band closes first, then the next one down and so on as the input level falls. This gradually trims away the highs as the guitar sound decays, thus disguising any hiss. It can sound much smoother than using a simple gate to achieve the same result.

Tip / The ability of a multi-band compressor to adjust the level of each band separately means it can be used in much the same way as EQ; increasing the level of the high frequency band slightly while leaving the lows unchanged will brighten the sound, for example. The more bands the compressor has, the more surgical this EQ process can be. This kind of treatment can be used to massage off-the-shelf samples and loops into sonic shape where the original character isn't quite what you want.

MULTI-BAND PROCESSING
The simplest application of multi-band compression is perhaps the split-band de-esser.

Here a crossover circuit is used to split the audio signal into two bands at around the 4kHz point. Frequencies below 4kHz are passed through with no change while those above are subjected to gain reduction whenever a loud sibilant sound is detected. A variable threshold combined with side-chain EQ is used to detect the offending sibilants.

The results aren't usually that great; the sound is temporarily dulled whenever a sibilant sound triggers the de-esser leading to a tonal imbalance that can make vocals sound somewhat lispy at higher gain reduction settings.

MY VIEW

Their undoubted power aside, I have to say that I tend to think of multi-band compressors as salvage tools. While they can solve a problem where more conventional processors fail, they should only really be brought out when the material being mixed needs forensic – rather than general – tweaking.

A more transparent-sounding approach is to attenuate (reduce) only those frequencies that lie in the sibilant range, leaving the lows and extreme highs unchanged. This can be achieved by splitting the audio into three bands and tuning the middle band to the offending sibilants and compressing only that band. Various plug-ins adopt this approach.

The most elegant solution to de-essing that I've come across comes from the German company SPL. Its de-esser applies similar level-independent techniques to the ones used in its Transient Designer (page 167) to detect sibilants, regardless of their loudness. The system attenuates only the narrow frequency range containing sibilants, not by conventional multi-band compression but by separating out the sibilant sounds and then adding them back to the original sound with an inverted polarity so that they cancel them out. While it might sound complicated, the user interface comprises just one knob to adjust the depth of de-essing and a button to select male or female vocals.

PARALLEL COMPRESSION

The technique of mixing a dry or lightly compressed signal with a heavily compressed version of itself is known as parallel or 'New York'-style compression. By mixing the 'parallel' signals together you can get the benefit of a highly compressed sound without sacrificing the all-important dynamics.

Employing parallel compression can push a good mix into the premier league, but its

DYNAMIC EQ

A dynamic EQ is best viewed as a cross between a conventional multi-band equaliser and a multi-band compressor. Where conventional EQ has a gain control for each band that you set and then leave alone, a dynamic EQ links the gain of each EQ band to a side-chain so that it can be set to vary according to the level and spectrum of the material being processed.

The operation is almost identical to that of a multi-band compressor except that rather than having simple crossover points to split the various sections of the audio spectrum, the multi-band EQ has all the controls you'd expect to find in a parametric equaliser, ensuring far more control over the exact frequency range being treated. For example, if there's a very narrow frequency spike causing problems, you can tune one band to that frequency, then set the dynamic

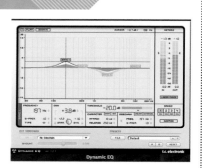

controls to compress it whenever it exceeds a certain level.

Using dynamic EQ, you can suppress the less attractive sounding frequency peaks that some singers generate when pushing themselves hard or singing at the upper extremes of their range (with some singers these narrow peaks of energy can be high enough to upset the subjective balance of a song).

use should come with a large 'USE WITH CAUTION' warning; it can either be the magic ingredient in a monster mix or it can render a production aggressive and tiring. It is also far too tempting to use it on more tracks than either deserve or need it.

The concept of parallel compression is simple enough. Rather than processing an audio track through a compressor placed on its insert point, you feed the 'parallel' compressor using an aux send and then mix its output back in with the unprocessed signal as you might do with reverb or delay.

◀ SPL's De-Esser: Attenuates only the narrow frequency range containing sibilants.

PRO TIP

Mix engineer Michael Brauer (Rolling Stones, KT Tunstall, James Morrison and Coldplay) revealed to Sound On Sound that in the past he has routed lead vocals in parallel to no fewer than five different compressors at once, mixing the outputs to create a single, final sound. (Setting this up is easy – see page 175 – the skill is in choosing the compressors, the settings and the relative level of each).

Why would you want to use compression as a parallel process when it already works perfectly well connected 'in-line' with a signal, though? To answer this we have to back up and review what a basic compressor does.

A compressor has a threshold level below which no processing takes place and above which gain reduction is applied. This means **only the loudest parts of a signal are processed**, which are subsequently reduced in volume.

When you use parallel compression you introduce a highly compressed signal into the mix. So compressed is this signal that it's not just the peaks that are affected – it's **the whole signal**, which becomes denser, all dynamics pulled back so that quieter sections are given almost as much prominence as loud parts.

On its own this hyper-compressed signal is all but useless. But when it is mixed in with the original dry (uncompressed) sound, the combined signal remains highly dynamic (the peaks are not compressed) while the lower level signals of the compressed sound are allowed to make a greater contribution. In this respect, you can get the best of both worlds: a signal with a larger-than-life character that retains its dynamics and transients.

Another way to think of parallel compression is that while a conventional compressor works from the top (peaks) down, parallel compression works from the bottom (low level sounds) up.

The results you achieve using parallel compression depend very much on the character of the compressor/s you use. I like to pick one of the 'bad boys' for the job

as the more pumping and attitude that can be coaxed out of the compressor, the more impressive the end result. The Empirical Labs or UBK Fatso can give good results, as can the dbx 160.

For something truly dirty try the SSL free Listen Mic Compressor plug-in. This models the talkback mic compressor from a vintage SSL SL 4000E mixing console. There's only one knob that goes from Less to More but this seriously nasty little compressor pumps like a devil! It has limited low end, but for sheer filth and attitude, not to mention value-for-no-money, it has to be tried to be appreciated. It works well on drums and guitar but can also be applied to rap vocals or death metal buses to add attitude and an extra slice of death.

Used with care, parallel compression can add weight and density to **drums, bass sounds, vocals** and even **whole mixes**. But – as I said at the outset – this is a powerful technique, and like all power, it should be used wisely!

Tip / You are not limited to using compressors on the bus when using parallel techniques. You can apply moderate conventional in-line compression to the original track at the same time.

Tip / Parallel compression rewards experimentation. I'd strongly suggest setting some time aside to try the different compressors in your armoury to see which work best. Because you're blending flavours, some compressors will work much better than others.

Tip / Placing EQ after the parallel compressor allows you to emphasise certain parts of the audio spectrum without affecting the compressor's operation.

Parallel compression

1

Set up post-fade sends on the tracks and buses that need parallel compression. In this example we are using sends on the drum mix bus, the main vocal and the bass bus.

2

Insert a suitably assertive compressor on the aux return bus. The very basic Logic Silver compressor works well on some material.

3

Adjust the compressor to produce heavy gain reduction using a high ratio and low threshold setting, then fine-tune the attack and release times so that the gain pumping works with the song rhythm, not against it. Here gain reduction is peaking at -15dB.

4

Bring up the parallel compressor bus fader until the desired weight has been added to the tracks being processed. A good starting point is around 15–20dB below the original track levels.

Advanced parallel: 4-part vocals

1

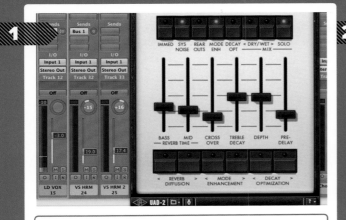

Producer Michael Brauer's multi-part parallel compression technique on vocals is easy to set up — it just demands a lot of processing power. First, place the lead vocal on an audio track. Leave it uncompressed so it retains its dynamics. Here it is treated to a gentle splash of reverb.

2

Route four post-fade sends to four different aux buses. These will become the four parallel compression channels.

3

On each of the four channels insert a compressor. Choosing the right compressors is important here: picking at random is not what this technique is about. Instead you're after different models that do something specific to the compressed voice. Audition each solo'd and then in the context of the combined signal to see the effect it has.

4

In this example a Fatso is hit hard — with added warmth — while a UA 1176 is inserted in All Buttons In mode. An SSL X-Comp and an LA-2A complete the picture. Take time adjusting the relative balance of all the signals; even small changes can have a significant impact on the resulting sound.

Tip / Responding to the increasing popularity of parallel compression, some plug-in compressors now offer a wet/dry mix control, which means you can use them in a channel insert point and achieve parallel results without setting up sends.

Tip / Parallel compression across a whole mix is one of the worst kept secrets around. Just route the mix to the main master bus via a stereo bus and then arrange a send from that bus to a compressor. Route the output of the compressor to the master mix bus and mix as desired to give it the parallel treatment. I've used this technique very successfully to master dance tracks that came in sounding lightweight.

Tip / If you have recorded vocal (or guitar) double tracks, try using very heavy compression on one of them and then blend it with the second unprocessed (or lightly compressed) track. This gives an effect similar to conventional parallel compression, this time using two different but still very similar original recordings. Route both tracks to the same group and then compress conventionally to gel the final signal if required.

PARALLEL DISTORTION
Parallel processing techniques are not limited to compression.

The original **Aphex Aural Exciter** exploited parallel distortion in a novel and creative way, although if the tale told to me by Aphex founder Marvin Caesar is correct, the whole thing was a happy accident thanks to a wrongly-assembled valve amplifier kit!

The Aural Exciter essentially splits the signal into dry and processed paths and then remixes them at the output. The processed signal is first high-pass filtered via a user-adjustable filter, then it is compressed and distorted before being added back to the dry signal at a relatively low level. The resulting signal has a sense of enhanced brightness and definition. This is one example where adding distortion can actually make something sound cleaner.

I first heard the Aural Exciter on the backing vocals for the Trevor Horn-produced 'Video Killed the Radio Star'. The sound was an instant hit and we all rushed out to buy Aural Exciters but it soon became apparent that you had to use them sparingly to avoid the sound becoming harsh and abrasive. What's more, it was easy to get used to the increased brightness, so unless you kept checking the bypassed sound the temptation was to keep adding more as the day went on. When you listened to the mix the next day it felt like someone was massaging razor blades into your ears.

Over the past couple of decades a long line of similar hardware and software based on the original Exciter have entered the marketplace.

Used in moderation the Aural Exciter (or similar) creates a seductive sense of intimacy and clarity, helping to position individual tracks towards the front of a mix. But, as with parallel compression, it should be used sparingly.

While many people still believe you can use EQ to achieve the same results, this isn't always the case, as EQ can only emphasise those frequencies present in the original sound. By contrast, the distortion process used in the Aural Exciter can synthesise new high-frequency harmonics based on the existing mid-range content. Furthermore, the

PRO TIP

You can set up a form of 'parallel recording' when tracking instruments or vocals by sending part of the signal to the DAW dry and a second split signal in via a compressor.

You end up with two different audio tracks from the same recording, one dry, one compressed. These can then be mixed to taste later. Of course this only makes sense if you have a hardware unit you like the sound of – it's just as easy to set up suitable plug-ins after recording.

compression used as part of the process adds more processed signal at lower levels than at high levels, which also helps improve intelligibility.

If you do choose to use it, keep switching the effect off and make sure you're only adding enough to create the desired effect – too much generally sounds horrible.

Tip / Distortion can also be used to increase the perceived level of bass. The Waves MaxxBass plug-in exploits this psychoacoustic effect by reducing the level of deep bass and adding distortion components an octave or so above so that you still perceive a healthy level of bass, even on smaller speakers.

DIY EXCITEMENT

You don't need an Aural Exciter to use parallel distortion. Using a distortion plug-in as a send effect in your DAW can help add life and density to a whole host of sounds, especially bass, drums and sometimes vocals.

Raw distortion generally sounds nasty, especially heavy distortion; the high-frequency harmonics produce a fizzy, grating sound that is distinctly unmusical. To demonstrate this plug a guitar into a distortion pedal (or plug-in) and feed the result though your studio monitoring system for an instant 'wasp trapped in paper cup' sound. The reason distorted guitars (usually) sound better than this is that the loudspeakers used in a typical guitar amps can't reproduce the high frequencies, resulting in an altogether rounder, smoother sound (page 19).

This has an impact on how you set up parallel distortion. While a nasty, gritty top end on the parallel track might work well

for adding attack to a lacklustre snare sound, if you're going to use it on any other signal you'll probably have to filter out some of the high end first.

Although you can use EQ to filter out the unwanted high end my own preference is to use a guitar amp and speaker modelling plug-in (just as you would with an electric guitar) as you get a choice of speaker flavours and amp tonalities. Most also come with an assortment of modelled distortion devices, from edgy fuzz boxes to smooth 'tube' overdrives.

In most cases the reason for adding parallel distortion is to add density and harmonic complexity without adding so much that the listener perceives that any distortion is actually being used. Like with parallel compression, a signal that has been treated with parallel distortion has a far narrower dynamic range than the untreated signal because of the way the waveform peaks are squashed.

A modest amount of added distortion may have little effect on the transient peaks of the signal to which it is added, but as the dry sound decays, the distorted sound makes more of a contribution and so helps beef up the overall density. Unlike parallel compression, though, parallel distortion also adds harmonic complexity, so a dry bass guitar that has, for example, too much low end and not enough content in the 150–300Hz region (essential for making it audible on smaller speaker systems), can be made to stand out more as the newly-generated harmonics help fill the gaps.

The same technique can be used on drums too, particularly where the toms and kick need a little mid-range enrichment to help them cut through the mix. ●

TOOLS OF THE TRADE

Even if you're not a guitar player, you'll find that at least one guitar amp modelling plug-in is an invaluable mixing asset, useful for processing drums, bass, synths and even vocals across a whole range of musical styles.

DIY parallel distortion

1

Set up a post-fade send on the track you wish to treat and route it to a bus. Here a guitar track is the candidate for the parallel treatment.

2

Use this send to feed a distortion plug-in inserted on the bus. Alter the tone setting to dampen the highs.

3

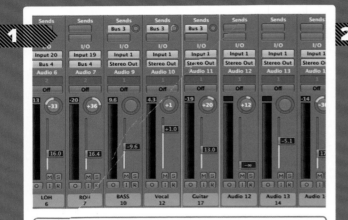

EQ the output of the distortion plug-in if necessary. High-cut filtering the distortion will add warmth whereas low-cut filtering will add bite and brightness.

4

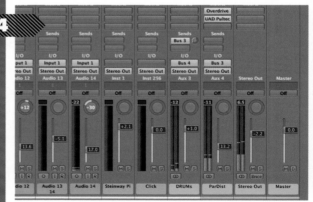

Adjust the amount of distortion and any subsequent EQ while balancing the distortion return signal with the dry guitar sound and the rest of the mix.

TIPS FOR A BETTER MIX

Do what is necessary for the song, not the egos of the performers.
If the track sounds better with parts removed, then remove them.

COMMON MIX MISTAKES AND HOW TO AVOID THEM

Too much reverb.
Excessive reverb can ruin a solid mix. Contemporary styles are generally mixed fairly dry. The reverb that is used, is used subtly. Sometimes reverb is best judged by its absence: you notice when it's not there, but not when it is.

12
REVERB &
AMBIENCE
101

WHAT IS REVERB?

Reverberation – reverb for short – is a natural phenomenon caused when sound reflects from surfaces, often in complex ways. The shapes of large buildings like cathedrals often result in long, impressive reverb patterns, but every natural environment includes some level of reflected sound – even if only from the ground, as in open fields and deserts.

There is some academic discussion about what is simply reflected sound and what is reverb. For our purposes I'll define reverb as the effect created when sound bounces back and forth between two or more reflective surfaces. We all know what reverb sounds like; just clap your hands in a church or concert hall to hear it. But what is actually going on, and what determines the length and character of the reverberant sound? The answers are important; a basic understanding of how reverb works in nature is key to getting it right in the mix, whatever kind of music you produce.

WHY WE NEED REVERB

Most studio recordings are made in relatively dry-sounding, controlled environments, often using close-mic techniques. This is particularly true in the home studio where, without the luxury of nice-sounding live rooms, we generally aim to record as dry a signal as possible to leave us space to process it further in the mix.

All this effort to tame natural reverb means we end up with artificially dead sounding recordings that sound unreal and uncomfortably dry – which in turn means we need to add reverb back into mixes to give them a sense of space and dimension.

Reverb also helps glue the various tracks in a mix together by making them sound as though they belong in the same acoustic space – even when we are mixing samples and overdubs that were DI'd or recorded in different studios.

There are various complex psychological explanations as to why music sounds better when mixed with reverb. I think it is enough to accept that most listeners prefer the sound of vocals and acoustic instruments with a little reverb on than with none at all. It is probably also a cultural thing: we're used to the sound of music played or sung indoors where wall reflections form part of the listening experience. Cultures with an outdoor music tradition probably think differently and may regard reverb as sounding rather odd.

Recording engineers realised the importance of reverb early on. Their solution was to build **echo rooms** to add reverb to their mixes. An echo room is a large reflective room, often with hard objects (concrete sewer pipes were popular) placed within it to add further reflections. Sound was fed into the room via a loudspeaker and picked up elsewhere in the room with a mic. This 'wet' signal was then added back into the mix to provide the reverberation.

Echo rooms took up a lot of space and it wasn't long before alternatives were sought. This gave rise to the design of early plate and spring reverbs.

A **reverb plate** is a thin steel plate suspended in a frame and driven to vibration by means of a transducer not unlike a loudspeaker coil. Contact mics attached to the plate pick up the vibrations, which are then amplified and fed back to the mixing console. Remote-controlled mechanical dampers were used to reduce

A BASIC UNDERSTANDING OF HOW REVERB WORKS IN NATURE IS KEY TO GETTING IT RIGHT IN THE MIX, WHATEVER KIND OF MUSIC YOU PRODUCE.

the decay time while tape recorders were often wired up to add pre-delay. While the plate doesn't produce strong early reflections like a real space, it does produce a dense and musical decay.

The cheaper **spring reverb** (right) uses a loosely coiled spring instead of a plate to generate its vibrations. Although spring reverbs tend to produce unpleasant twangy sounds when fed with transients such as drums, they fare better on vocals and other non-percussive sounds. And they can sound great on guitars: indeed, spring reverbs are still used in guitar amps to bestow their characteristically bright, washy, lo-fi ambience to the right guitar sound.

Although real spring and plate reverbs have become virtually obsolete other than these spring units found in some guitar amps, many digital reverbs include emulations of both, with plate reverbs used on anything from vocals to strings. I often think the success of the plate sound is down to the fact that it adds the required wet sound without suggesting any specific space.

REVERB IN NATURE

As with much of our interpretation of sound, our instinctive assessment of reverb has an evolutionary basis. Knowing the size of the space we're in is important – particularly at night or in the dark, when we have to rely on our ears rather than our eyes.

We are so used to hearing reverb as part of the natural world that we are able to make assumptions about the size and character of a space just by listening to reflections – however brief they are. The analysis isn't conscious: our brains are

▲ Folded Line spring reverb device: Note the folded coil spring clearly visible inside.

able to visualise the type of environment simply based on the reverberant sound that follows, for example, a handclap.

If you stand on a hard concrete surface away from any buildings and clap your hands you hear two sounds: the **direct sound** of the clap and then a single **reflection** from the floor (Fig 1, right). You may not realise it though; the reflected sound arrives at your ears so quickly (typically less than 10ms after the clap) that the brain is unable to separate it from the direct sound of the clap. However, the perceived timbre or tonality of the clap sound does appear to change as the direct and reflected sounds combine, and the same clap will sound different in a grassy field or above a tarmac road.

The situation becomes considerably more complex in an enclosed space such as a concert hall. Here the same handclap not only bounces back from the floor, but also at different times from the walls and ceiling. These **early reflections** then go on to hit other walls to be re-reflected. It is this re-reflection process that creates the effect we call **reverb**.

In a very large reflective room such as a cathedral, then, we hear a mixture of:

Reverb decay times in famous musical halls (at 1kHz):

Vienna
Grote Musicvereeinsaal
2.0 sec

New York
Carnegie Hall
1.6 sec

Jerusalem
Binyanei Ha'oomah
1.75 sec

Paris
Notre Dame Cathedral
8.5 sec

India
Taj Mahal
28 sec

> the **direct sound** travelling directly from the source to our ears;

> followed by the **early reflections (ERs)** as the sound bounces back from the nearest solid walls and ceiling/s;

> then almost immediately afterwards, the complexity of reflections and re-reflections merges into what we think of as **reverb**, which die away over a period of several seconds as the reflecting sound energy is absorbed.

Our brains are able to make use of the ERs to tell us something about the nature of the space. A long delay between the initial sound and the first of the ERs, for example, suggests you're a long way from the nearest wall/ceiling. If the reflections sound bright we can infer that the environment

incorporates hard surfaces such as stone. If the reflections sound less bright we might be in a concert hall with a mix of hard surfaces and soft furnishings.

The time the reverb takes to die away also tells us something about the space; large, empty rooms with hard surfaces, for example, tend to produce long reverb times (like the Taj Mahal, with its highly reflective marble walls generating a whopping 28 seconds of reverb tail – see Fact File, left).

SYNTHETIC REVERB
Synthetic reverb (sometimes known as **algorithmic reverb**) is the easiest type of reverb effect to understand. It attempts to emulate what happens in nature and provides a great deal of control over various parameters to allow you to shape the space

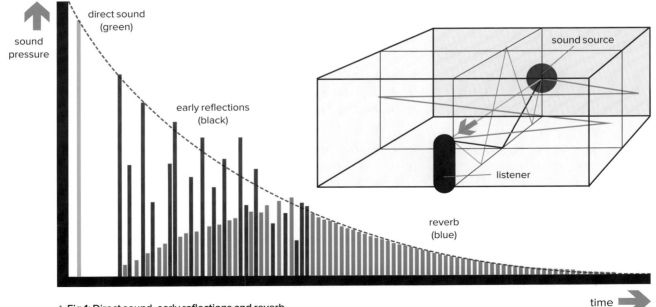

▲ Fig 1: Direct sound, early reflections and reverb.

in a number of ways, as well as offering simulations of halls, rooms, unnatural spaces and earlier mechanical reverb devices. Synthetic reverbs can be made to sound as natural or unnatural as the producer wishes.

PRE-DELAY

Other than reflections from the floor, no reverb is heard until the source sound has reached the nearest wall and bounced back to the listener. This initial delay between the direct sound and ensuing reflections provides one of the most powerful auditory clues to room size: the longer the delay between sound and first audible reflection, the larger the space. This can be simulated in an algorithmic reverb by placing a digital delay between the original sound and the reverb generator. This is known as pre-delay.

Pre-delay sets the time between the original sound and the first reflection. Values of up to 120ms are most common.

EARLY REFLECTIONS

The early reflections follow the initial pre-delayed signal.

Because the pattern and spacing of ERs provide auditory clues about a room's geometry, software engineers usually provide different sets of ERs that are typical of **various types of natural space** (room, hall etc).

The **size** parameter scales the spacing between individual reflections, making them closer together to decrease the apparent room size, or spacing them further apart to simulate a larger room. Better reverb algorithms also add some **diffusion** or **blurring** to these ERs, as well as some **EQ** to simulate the way real surfaces reflect sound. Intimate ambience effects

REVERB TONALITY

When a sound is generated in a room, it moves out from its source in the form of spherical wavefronts travelling at around 340 metres per second (m/s) like ripples in a 3D pond.

When these waves encounter an obstruction some of their energy is absorbed and some is reflected back into the room. Surfaces rarely reflect equally at all frequencies. Instead reflections are equalised by the type of wall surface and its physical properties. A marble surface, for example, reflects both high and low frequencies quite efficiently, whereas a wood panelled room reflects the low end more efficiently than the high end (effectively dampening the high end). Additional high frequency loss is caused by friction within the air itself – which can be significant in very large spaces.

These variables need to be duplicated within reverb software for the result to sound realistic, and reverb algorithms frequently allow the decay time of high frequencies to be made longer or shorter than low frequencies. High frequency damping allows the high frequency decay time to be shortened independently of the low frequency decay time to simulate the way high frequencies die away more quickly in a real space.

In the studio, engineers often roll away low frequency reverb content that would otherwise make the low end of a track messy or badly-defined. It's not unusual for reverbs placed on buses to have their lows cut aggressively, freeing the bottom end of the mix for kick, bassline and other instruments that extend into the low-end.

are created by using just ERs – with little or no late reverb tail added – a common technique in modern pop production.

While a single source of sound, such as a hand clap, creates a specific pattern of ERs because of its distance from the walls and ceiling, multiple musicians in an ensemble placed in slightly different positions will each create a different set of ER patterns.

An excessively strong ER pattern therefore creates the illusion that the sound source is in a single location, which may be appropriate for a single performer – in the case of a lead vocal, for example – but is less realistic when applied to ensembles such as choirs and orchestras. In such cases ERs may need to be mixed lower than the longer reverb tail to maintain a natural sound. Doctor David Greisinger,

TERMS OF THE TRADE

The decay period or reverb time is defined as the time it takes for the level of the reverberation to decay by 60dB. This figure is also referred to as the 'RT60' value.

who developed the early Lexicon reverb algorithms, understood this fact and developed a less obtrusive way of simulating the early build-up of reverb that added the necessary colouration and auditory clues of space and size without making the individual repeats too obvious. How he did it remains a trade secret to this day.

DECAY

The other key control in digital reverb units is the all-important decay time. The decay control adjusts how long the dense reverb tail takes to decay by 60dB. The reverb tail is less important than the ERs at creating the illusion of room character (other than longer tails being associated with larger spaces), but its tonality and the rate at which different frequencies decay can reinforce the illusion that the space comprises hard or softer surfaces. In this way the tail is used alongside the ERs to complete the sonic picture.

Because the initial reflections lose energy, both in the air and each time they re-reflect against the further surfaces they encounter, the decay character of reverb in a typical room tends to be roughly exponential.

However, in complex buildings, such as cathedrals (which can be thought of as several separate but acoustically-coupled spaces), the reverb decay might take on a less regular shape as these separate spaces interact. The reverb may start to decay exponentially, for example, then level out for a while, then decay again.

Most basic reverb units produce a nominally exponential decay, which is fine for simulating a simple room. More sophisticated models attempt to emulate the decay shapes produced by more complex types of building, such as our hypothetical cathedral.

In modern music production, most useful reverb treatments have a decay time below 1.5 seconds.

DENSITY AND DIFFUSION

Another important set of parameters are Diffusion and Density.

Density controls the number of reflections in the reverb tail (which can be several thousand per second) while **Diffusion** sets the rate at which the density of the tail builds after the initial sound.

As a rule, lower values of density and diffusion create coarser, more grainy-sounding reverb treatments. While these might sound unnatural on percussion, they can sound very musical on other sounds, particularly vocals.

MODULATION

Modulation adds a gentle chorus-like pitch and time shift to the reflections in the reverb tail to make the sound more complex and help avoid resonances.

Another Lexicon innovation, these so-called 'Spin and Wander' parameters help randomise the reverb tail to avoid metallic resonances as well as making the reverb texture more lush. They have become an important element in synthetic reverb.

Such an effect would not occur in nature unless the sound source was continually moving within the room, but it works well in a musical context.

Tip / As a general rule no significant modulation should be added to reverbs used on instruments that produce precise, unwavering pitches such as pianos if the end result is to sound natural.

KIT LIST

Early digital reverbs, such as the Lexicon 224 and EMT250, didn't have the processing power available today so the reverbs were less dense than might have been considered ideal at the time. However, their sounds graced countless hit records and have become part of our musical heritage – a big reason for their continued popularity, either in their original forms or as plug-ins.

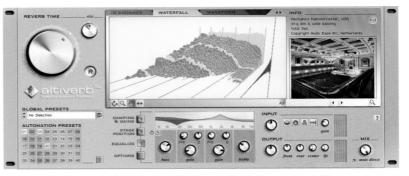

▲ Altiverb, from Audio Ease – one of the best multi-platform convolution reverbs.

CONVOLUTION REVERB

While all early digital reverb units were algorithmic, using networks of filters and delays to fake real-life reverb, a more realistic way of recreating the sound of real spaces is offered by a process known as convolution.

Using convolution it is possible to record the actual reverb characteristics of a real space and then apply it to your own mixes. It allows producers to add the reverb characters of places like Westminster Cathedral, or the Grand Canyon, or even classic live studio rooms.

The theory of convolution is straightforward. If you take a single sample of digital audio (like a very short click) and then play it into a room via a very accurate speaker system, you can record the resulting reverberation as an impulse response (or IR). These IRs can then be applied to any signal in the producer's DAW.

To apply this impulse response to a section of digital audio it is necessary to multiply every single sample of the recording by the impulse response – easy enough but very hungry on computing power, especially with longer reverb times. However, this is exactly what a convolution plug-in does, its job made significantly easier thanks to today's fast processors.

Some software convolution reverb systems come with a utility program for creating your own IRs using an accurate monitor speaker (or pair for capturing true stereo IRs) to play a frequency sweep while a pair of flat response microphones pick up the result in stereo. You can also use these programs to capture IRs from existing hardware reverb processors by sending the sweep signal through them and then recording the results.

Most convolution reverbs come with such a large library of spaces and hardware IRs, however, that it's only the real die-hards who go out and record their own.

It's worth noting that convolution isn't entirely successful at recording IRs from other hardware reverb units as some of these include pitch modulation which can't be captured by convolution – although the results are often still quite useable.

Tip / Straightforward convolution may be used to capture the character of many devices (not just reverb units) providing these systems are linear, by which I mean they must not include time modulation (such as chorus or vibrato), or non-linear level changes such as distortion, compression, limiting or expansion. I've heard convincing IRs made from tape echo units for example (although they can't capture the tape distortion), as well as equalisers and even guitar speaker cabinets.

CONVOLUTION LIMITATIONS

When convolution reverbs first appeared it felt to some like the tide might have turned on the algorithmic reverbs of old;

> **THERE'S A LIMIT TO HOW MUCH CONVOLUTION REVERB CAN BE ADJUSTED BEFORE IT STARTS TO SOUND UNNATURAL.**

the landscape had changed overnight and suddenly the sounds of expensive spaces – both real and imagined – could be downloaded by even the thriftiest studio owner.

Yet these new reverbs didn't make the much-loved Lexicons redundant. Nor did they render irrelevant the many artificial plug-ins that had served producers so well for so long. Why? Partly because of their inability to faithfully capture non-linear characteristics, as outlined above, but mainly because once you have an IR loaded into a convolution reverb processor, such as Logic's Space Designer or Audio Ease's Altiverb, there's a limit to how much it can be adjusted before it starts to sound unnatural.

It is possible to shorten the decay time, change the shape of the decay envelope and change the EQ; with some plug-ins you can also stretch or compress the IR to make the room seem larger or smaller. But there's only a limited range of adjustment if you want the sound to keep its natural tonality. Just as a sampled voice sounds unnatural when transposed too far from its original pitch, the reverberant characteristics of a room also start to sound unnatural if the length of the IR is changed too much.

The trade-off, then, is that while convolution makes it easier to capture the sound of real spaces, such as studio drum rooms, churches, concert halls, car parks, forests and train stations, there's less adjustment available than you have with an algorithmic reverb.

Furthermore, the slightly unnatural sound of an algorithmic reverb sometimes suits music better than an absolutely realistic IR reverb.

My own preference is to use convolution reverb where the recording style merits the recreation of a real space, such as an orchestra or choir that you want to place in a concert hall. Similarly, you might want to treat your drums with an IR made in a famous great-sounding studio drum room.

I'd also consider using a convolution reverb IR based on a hardware reverb plate or other artificial reverb processor for use in a pop mix – in most pop productions you don't necessarily want a reverb to conjure up any specific style of space, you just want to use it as a blending agent and to add some dimension and sparkle to the vocals. But where an IR doesn't offer the level of tweakability you need then a high quality synthetic plate may be better.

Ultimately it is down to your artistic judgement which kind of reverb is best for a specific project.

STEREO REVERB

Both convolution and synthetic reverbs can be used to process a mono signal to produce a stereo output, or to process a true stereo signal.

In both cases the dry part of the signal is normally kept in stereo, although for mono-in, stereo out processing the reverb engine is usually fed from a mono sum of the left and right inputs.

Feeding a reverb engine with a mono source in this way is perfectly OK as in real life the original sound source is often small enough to be considered a mono source – it's the way the sound reflects and arrives back at the two ears that creates the sense of stereo space.

For true stereo reverb each input is processed slightly differently but the difference is usually subtle. Most algorithmic reverbs create the illusion of stereo by varying the left and right ER patterns very slightly and introducing small differences in the network of filters and delays that creates the late reverb.

True stereo convolution reverb is captured by setting up a pair of loudspeakers (for the necessary test signals) in the space to be captured with two mics arranged as a stereo array to capture the reverb. For mono-in, stereo-out convolution reverb, the setup is a single speaker for the test signal and stereo mics to pick up the reverb.

REVERB IN THE MIX

Reverb can be applied to any sound that needs to be given a sense of space in the mix and is most often associated with percussion and vocals. The amount of reverb you use depends on the style of music, and fashions are constantly changing. In the 1970s and '80s reverb took centre stage – particularly on vocals and snare drums. Today's vocal treatments tend to be considerably more subtle, often using ambient treatments (in combination with simple delays). Dance tracks are often mixed dry, brash and up-front, with occasional reverb spins used as spot effects rather than as more traditional glue tools to bring mix elements together.

That said, it is still commonplace to find at least two reverb types used on a typical pop record. The engineer might set up a short ambience effect on one aux send and a longer plate on another, for example, the two signals mixed as required for the different instruments and voices.

REVERB ON VOCALS

Vocals almost always sound better with reverb on them than they do dry as we're most used to hearing singing in a reflective room, but you may not need to add as much reverb as you think to create the necessary sense of space. Modern vocals are typically mixed surprisingly dry – there's often so little ambience added that the only time you realise what effect it's having in the mix is when you mute the reverb return.

Ballad-style songs typically require a longer decay time, but it is rare to need a reverb decay time of longer than 1.2s. A more subtle approach is to use a modest amount of plate reverb combined with a very low level of repeating delay (300–700ms

REVERB DUCKING

Where the style of song dictates a long and prominent reverb, consider feeding the reverb output through a gate or compressor set up to operate as a level ducker, where the vocal track feeds the ducker side-chain. The ducker is then adjusted to pull down the level of the reverb by two or three dBs when the vocalist is singing.

When the singer pauses between phrases the reverb level will swell back to its full level giving a more dramatic sound, the reverb neatly tucking away when the vocalist is singing. The ducker attack and release times should be set so that the reverb level changes aren't too abrupt. Fine-tune these by ear.

depending on the style and tempo of the music), although an ER ambience treatment can also work well for a more intimate sound.

Long reverbs tend to push a sound back in the mix. Bear this in mind when treating vocals as the lead vocal is usually placed up-front. Where longer reverbs are more artistically appropriate, adding a pre-delay of 30–60ms helps keep the reverb from pushing the sound too far back.

Also remember that when adding higher levels of reverb, the longer the reverb decay, the more likely it is that intelligibility will be sacrificed (page 301). Experiment with the ER balance for the best results.

Modern pop vocals – including urban and dance vocals – are typically given a deceptively dry treatment, often made up of ERs and carefully timed pre-delay. Longer tails, if used at all, are judiciously EQd and tucked well back in the mix.

Tip / Be aware that the combined effect of vocal compression and bright reverb might sound exciting but it can also emphasise sibilance (page 213). One way around this is to use a de-esser plug-in before the reverb on the bus to pull down the levels of S and T sounds before they hit the reverb.

> VOCALS ALWAYS SOUND BETTER WITH REVERB THAN THEY DO DRY AS WE'RE MOST USED TO HEARING SINGING IN A REFLECTIVE ROOM, BUT YOU MAY NOT NEED TO ADD AS MUCH REVERB AS YOU THINK TO CREATE THE NECESSARY SENSE OF SPACE.

REVERB ON DRUMS

Close mic'ing results in a relatively dry drum sound and in large studio drum rooms with live acoustics the engineer usually relies on the overheads or room mics to provide the necessary ambience. In smaller studios that have little or no useful natural reverb it is usual to add artificial reverb to the overheads, and some of the close mics, to achieve the required degree of liveliness.

The close mics can be made to sound bigger in the mix by adding an ER ambience; this has the effect of lengthening the drum hits and adding transient detail. The overheads can then be treated with an appropriate drum room-type reverb to add liveliness without too much in the way of reverb tail (convolution reverbs modelled on specific live rooms can work well here).

INDIVIDUAL DRUMS

❭ **Kick drums** tend to be mixed fairly dry, although it can sometimes be appropriate to treat them with a short ambience or gated reverb to give them more presence. Excessive reverb on the kick drum muddies the mix and is best avoided. For most styles you can afford to leave the kick drum's close mic 100 per cent dry as any reverb added to the overheads will also add ambience to the kick.

❭ **Snares** often benefit from added reverb, although there is no typical snare reverb — so much depends on the style of the track. If you're recreating a Phil Spector wall of sound, try a longish reverb with pre-delay and strong ERs to create a larger-than-life effect. Bright plates or ambience treatments often work well. In modern productions it may be enough to add no more than a touch of half-second plate to take away the dryness that comes from close mic'ing. Plates have a fast attack and a bright, dense

tonality but it may help to roll off some of the low end to prevent the sound from becoming muddy. Remember that you get plenty of snare in the overheads, so whatever treatment you add to these will also affect the snare.

❭ **Toms** don't need masses of reverb as they can be damped to have a long or short decay time as required, although a little ambience can give them a sense of space and definition. More obvious reverb tends to be used in classic rock styles. As a general rule, the busier the drum part or the faster the song tempo, the less reverb you'll need. Gated reverb can also be used on toms and snares; the current fashion is to mix it low so that it is felt rather than obviously heard. The overheads treatment will also affect the toms.

❭ **Hi-hats** respond well to short, bright ambience treatments, although don't overdo it: you only need to make the hats sound lively — too much reverb will make them sound messy. Often the reverb you add to the overheads will be enough to bring the hats to life.

❭ The **overhead mics**, and in a live studio space the **room mics**, glue the drum kit together. They also provide the room ambience sound. In a small, dry studio you can add any required room ambience sound to the overheads, where small bright reverbs, such as tiled rooms or plates, can work well. Many reverb units and plug-ins offer a range of drum room and ambience settings. Try them and make a note of which ones work well for your style of music.

❭ **Percussion**, such as bongos and congas, respond well to short ambience treatments. These inject life without clouding the sound.

Note / It is important when adding artificial reverb to mic'ed drums that the original recording be made as dry as possible. Adding artificial reverb to a kit recorded in a bad-sounding room rarely manages to disguise the sound of the room.

GUITARS

Electric guitars work well with spring reverb or spring emulations as that's the sound most guitar players grow up with. Examples of where a long spring reverb can work well crop up in many minor-key blues pieces such as Peter Green's 'Black Magic Woman' and Gary Moore's 'Still Got The Blues'.

For some styles you may want to try longer reverb treatments or combinations of reverb and delay – or just delays. Who can forget the up-front, tempo-sync'd delay treatments used by The Edge on so many classic U2 tracks? Then there are those guitar solos where you'd swear you were hearing reverb but in fact the effect is created entirely by delays. David Gilmour favours delays over reverb to create his signature sound.

For **steel-strung acoustic guitars** a short plate reverb or ambience setting can make the sound more lively. For strummed parts that play a more rhythmical part in the mix you can often get away with very little reverb.

A **solo guitar** piece, on the other hand, may benefit from a more obvious reverb treatment, where plate, concert hall and even outdoor space settings can be useful – there's a forest IR that I've turned to time and again on sparse guitar-led tracks.

Tip / As a general rule you can afford to use more prominent reverb and delay treatments where a mix has plenty of space to play with. If the mix is already busy, adding lots of delay and reverb to the guitars can make it sound messy. If you need reverbs in a busy mix, try adding pre-delay to create a little more space around them.

KEYBOARDS

Percussive keyboard sounds, such as pianos or vibes, can be treated as you would their acoustic equivalents. Note that many contemporary keyboards and soft synths have effects built in. These may need turning down.

The kind of treatment you pick depends on the effect you're after, which in the case of a piano could be anything from a concert hall setting to evoke a more classical vibe to a subtle ambience or small room treatment to capture the intimacy of a small club. Vintage analogue synths rarely have effects built in, so you'll have to add your own. It's worth

AS A GENERAL RULE YOU CAN AFFORD TO USE MORE PROMINENT REVERB AND DELAY TREATMENTS WHERE A MIX HAS PLENTY OF SPACE TO PLAY WITH.

REVERB AND PERSPECTIVE

Reverb units create an illusion of stereo width but they also dilute the sense of stereo placement of the original dry sound. That's because regardless of where the original sound is panned, the reverb comes equally from both sides. Some engineers get around this by feeding pivotal instruments into their own mono reverb and then panning the reverb to the same place as the dry sound. This is not a natural way for reverb to behave, but mixing is art more than science, so if it sounds good and does what you need it to do then it's fair game.

Reverb can also be used to create the illusion of depth by making some sounds appear to be further away than others.

If you sit close to a performer in a real performance space, you hear a greater proportion of direct-to-reverberant sound than you would if you were sitting at the back of the hall. ERs also appear stronger close to the sound source: at the back of a hall ERs build up more slowly, creating a reverb envelope with a noticeably slower attack time.

What this means is that in the studio you can make a sound seem more distant by:
› adding more reverb to it,
› reducing ER levels on it, and
› cutting a little top-end from the dry sound.

And to bring a sound forward you should:
› keep the dry sound reasonably bright,
› use a pre-delay to separate the reverb from the dry sound,
› mix in some ERs, and
› reduce the level of the reverb tail.

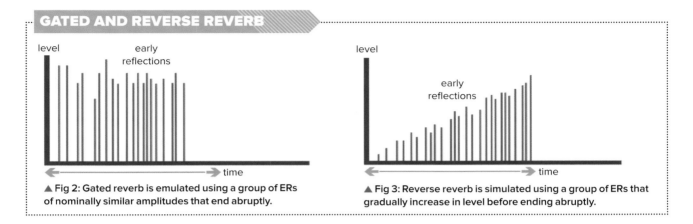

▲ Fig 2: Gated reverb is emulated using a group of ERs of nominally similar amplitudes that end abruptly.

▲ Fig 3: Reverse reverb is simulated using a group of ERs that gradually increase in level before ending abruptly.

sounding one note of caution: already dense pad sounds, whether digital or analogue, can become very messy if treated with more than a minimal splash of reverb.

REVERB EFFECTS

There are many unnatural effects that can be created using reverb, the most common being **gated reverb** (Fig 2). This effect was used extensively on early Phil Collins records, where the drums were played in a live, reverberant room and then the room mics were gated so that the room reverb cut off abruptly when it fell below a certain volume rather than being allowed to decay naturally.

The same effect can be recreated digitally by generating a burst of ERs with no subsequent reverb tail. While this big gated drum sound is somewhat dated, the effect is still regularly used in a more subtle way to beef up drum tracks.

Another popular classic trick is **reverse reverb** (Fig 3), originally generated by turning over an analogue multitrack tape so that it played in reverse, then recording the reverb from this reversed part onto a spare track. Turning the tape the right way

round again made the reverb occur before the sound that created it.

Today we can do this in a DAW by reversing an audio track, adding reverb, bouncing the result to a new file then re-reversing it to put it the right way round again (Reverse reverb walkthrough, page 193). While this isn't an effect to use on every mix it can be useful as an occasional spot effect, to create unique vocals, or to build unusual atmospheres in soundtrack work.

ADVANCED REVERB TECHNIQUES

Tip / If you need to add reverb to a full track that has been mixed too dry to give it more life and space, try placing a high-pass filter before the reverb input to tame anything below 150–200Hz to stop the resulting sound from becoming too muddy. A subtle ambience effect can liven up a mix or live recording that was initially too dry, and it's not unheard of for mastering engineers to run a final mix through a high quality reverb to give it a last sonic gloss.

Tip / Don't be afraid to try lo-fi or primitive reverb units; in the right contexts some of these can sound more artistically appropriate than expensive, highly-realistic algorithms. This is particularly true for gritty rock, dance music that embraces pseudo 8-bit sounds (electro, dubstep, breaks and so on) and many breeds of lo-fi chillout.

Tip / Try feeding the reverb input via a chorus or flange plug-in placed directly before the reverb. This will add movement and complexity to the reverb sound without affecting the dry part of the sound and works particularly well with long new age-style reverb treatments.

Tip / Automation of the reverb send/return to create spot effects has become something of a fine art in Berlin-born minimal and tech-house productions. Reverb builds are created across individual parts or even across the full mix by gradually increasing the amount of signal sent to the reverb so that the track gets wetter and wetter until the reverb is suddenly cut and the track kicks back in 100 per cent dry.

Tip / Another trick is to employ spot spins, created by sending occasional drum, synth or percussive hits to a long hall reverb bus for occasional wet splashes. These same wet splashes can be copied and reversed to provide useful lead-ins after a breakdown.

Tip / A typical pop, rock or dance mix has most of the sound energy concentrated at the bass end of the spectrum, so avoid making this pivotal area sound cluttered by low-cut filtering the reverb return at between 150–200Hz. Also avoid adding all but the most subtle of ambience treatments to bass instruments and kick drums unless there's a strong artistic reason for doing so.

Tip / Reverb normally plays a supporting role but you can convert it into an extreme, centre-stage effect using additional processing. For one guitar part I'd recorded I wanted to create the effect of a keyboard pad playing above it, so I used a pitch shifter before a fairly long reverb to pitch the sound up by one octave, then placed a rotary speaker plug-in after the reverb to give it an electric organ character. You could also place a compressor before the reverb to keep the effect level high. The result of this experiment sounded a little odd in isolation, but mixed under the guitar part gave the impression of a synth pad. You could also try distorting the reverb feed using an overdrive plug-in and chopping the reverb output in a rhythmic way using a square-wave tremolo effects sync'd to the song tempo.

Tip / When you have a mix sounding as you think it should, try reducing the overall reverb level/s to see if you can achieve the desired result with less. This can help deliver a cleaner mix. Also listen to the way the reverb affects individual instruments as this will sound different when the whole mix is playing to how it does when individual tracks are solo'd. Reference your mix against commercial mixes in a similar style to see if the reverb treatments you've used give comparable results. Home demos often suffer from excessive reverb when the truth is that the spaces in a piece of music are just as important as the sounds.

Tip / You can get interesting effects by using 100 per cent wet reverb treatments. Either insert the reverb on a track and change the ratio to wet, or send a track to a bus using a pre-fade send (with fader dropped to 0). The result is that you only hear the reverb and not the original sound. This can be useful during intros or breakdowns, or for experimental sound design. ●

PRO TIP

Because our hearing systems have evolved as survival mechanisms, we're naturally highly attuned to changes in our acoustic environment; things that remain constant tend to get tuned out by our brains.

One way to exploit this to maintain interest during a song is to change the reverb character throughout it, using a different type of reverb as a spot effect during a breakdown, for example, or using a different vocal treatment in the chorus.

Of course this theory doesn't just apply to reverb; slight changes in a drum pattern hold the interest of the listener way more effectively than the same loop repeated indefinitely.

Reverse reverb

1

Copy the part to be processed onto a new track and then reverse it in the DAW's waveform editor. Note that you may have to convert the copied region to a new audio file before doing this, otherwise the original part will also be reversed.

2

Insert a reverb plug-in on the reversed track set to 100 per cent wet. Adjust the reverb decay time to taste and then bounce the processed track as a new file.

3

Reverse the processed track so that it now plays the correct way round again, but this time with the reverb tail coming before rather than after the sounds on the track. Move it in time so that it works with the original dry file.

4

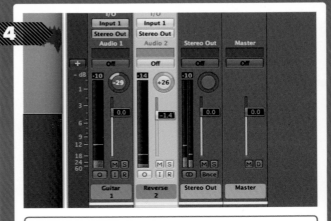

Balance the level of the reverse reverb track with the dry track. Try panning the two tracks apart to create a sense of movement.

13
PITCH CORRECTION 101

> NOWADAYS YOU'LL STRUGGLE TO FIND A STUDIO THAT DOESN'T HAVE A PITCH CORRECTION PLUG-IN OF SOME DESCRIPTION THAT GETS HEAVY USE.

A MODERN PHENOMENON

Arguably no single aspect of modern music production has changed so completely and so swiftly as pitch correction.

Two decades ago it was barely used and in the main was limited to what could be achieved using tape varispeed or early pitch shifters such as the Eventide Harmonizer (page 27). One decade ago correction was a little easier — but it was still time-consuming, awkward, and the results were not always useful. Nowadays you'll struggle to find a studio that doesn't have a pitch correction plug-in of some description that gets heavy use. And rare indeed are those vocal-led pop tracks that don't employ it to a greater or lesser extent.

Those looking at the industry from the outside often consider pitch correction to be cheating in some way. Technically they may be right, but a recording isn't the same thing as a live performance; a recording may be listened to thousands of times across many decades; a minor slip that would go unnoticed on stage is open to scrutiny for all time once recorded.

For this reason, and where the genre demands perfection, the engineer and producer is duty-bound to help the artist achieve that goal, or as close to it as possible, by whatever means available.

It should be noted, of course, that not all music needs to be so polished. Sometimes a raw, unpolished edge can help convey sincerity, for example in traditional blues music, and a few rough edges never harmed Bob Dylan or Shane MacGowan either. Part of the producer's job is to decide whether applying pitch correction will improve the end product or not.

BACKGROUND

The first recordings were of complete performances (in one perilous take!). The genesis of multitrack tape, and the ability to punch in, allowed engineers to replace individual words or phrases in vocal tracks to patch up mistakes. At last dodgy performances could be repaired once and for all.

When punching-in first came to the public's attention several high-profile artists were derided when it was learned they'd had to attempt a particularly difficult note half a dozen times before they got it right. Nowadays comping a vocal from the best parts of several takes is so routine we think nothing of it.

Even with the ability to punch in, in the all-analogue world there was still little that could be done to fix pitching problems once a performance was on tape other than re-record it. The only real option was to use varispeed to slow down the tape during recording for short sections where the singer struggled with a particularly high note. Replaying the tape at the normal speed returns the recorded note back to the correct pitch, although the tonal quality of the voice tends to change noticeably if the speed change is enough to alter the pitch by more than a semitone.

The first piece of kit that allowed the kind of re-tuning we take for granted today came from Eventide. Their 1974 digital H910 (and later H949) Harmonizer could change the pitch of a sound without changing its length. It gave wealthy studio owners a host of new strategies for fixing vocal pitching problems. A favourite method, once MIDI control was also available, was to use a physical control to adjust the amount of pitch shift via MIDI so that if, for example, a singer had hit one note a little sharp, the control could be adjusted just for the duration of that note to flatten it slightly. The corrected note could then be recorded onto a spare tape track; if it sounded OK it could be copied back into the original track in place of the iffy word.

These and similar strategies were commonly used – although rarely in the home studio – until a major US trade show at the tail end of the '90s where the previously unknown Antares Audio Technologies introduced the pro audio world to a box that could fix pitching problems in real time. It was the first incarnation of Auto-Tune. The rest is history.

Auto-Tune's algorithms were developed by Andy Hildebrand, an engineer whose main expertise was in the area of seismology – the analysis of vibrations in the earth. The concept was – and remains – both simple and brilliant. It works by following the fundamental pitch of the audio input, which has to be a single voice (or monophonic instrument) to enable it to be tracked accurately. This 'tracked' pitch is compared with the notes in a user-specified musical scale. Pitch shifting algorithms are then used to adjust the pitch of the sung notes to match the nearest note in the musical scale.

If such a system is used to exactly correct notes so that they never deviate from the scale, all human inflection is stripped from the performance and you end up with a somewhat vocoder-like (but not vocoder-derived) effect – the now infamous sound first heard on Cher's 'I Believe'.

The effect has since been exploited by a generation of R&B producers, including T-Pain who took his one-time love affair with the sound full circle by publicly renouncing

▲ **The Antares ATR-1a: Hardware genesis of a studio legend.**

it in the lead single of his The Blueprint 3 album, D.O.A. (Death of Auto-Tune).

But this kind of creative abuse is only part of the story. Used sparingly, Auto-Tune is capable of delivering subtle and transparent results. Its **speed** control determines how quickly an off-pitch note is corrected. Adjusting it to slow down the correction process allows natural vibrato, scoops and slides between notes to come through. Then, as soon as the singer settles on a note, it is gently nudged into pitch.

More advanced users program in automation to change the level of effect in accordance with the demands of the tuning across the whole vocal part, for example, by slowing down the pitch correction speed to minimum when no correction is needed. Better still, the effect can be left bypassed and then automated to come on only when it's needed – for the odd duff note or drifting phrase.

Tip / Problems can arise with Auto-Tune if you're processing a vocal line that includes a significant level of **spill**. Spill can confuse or stall the pitch tracking process and – even where the pitch correction still works OK – the pitch of the background spill can be heard rising and falling as Auto-Tune does its thing. It's another good reason to keep original recordings free of spill. Use a gate to kill the spill if the track is dirty.

TECHNIQUE BEYOND VOCALS

Non-fretted string instruments such as bowed basses, violins, violas, cello and fretless bass can all benefit from the Auto-Tune process, providing the correction speed is adjusted so that Auto-Tune doesn't attempt to iron out all natural playing inflections. A number of guitarists, including Joe Satriani, have also employed the process on solos as an effect.

The real-time process can only (currently) track and correct monophonic sources so whenever multiple notes are detected, the correction process is bypassed. However, there are occasions when multiple notes fool the pitch tracking into assuming the wrong note has been played so if at all possible, exclude (or bypass) Auto-Tune during any double notes or chords.

WALKTHROUGH Using Auto-Tune on lead vocals

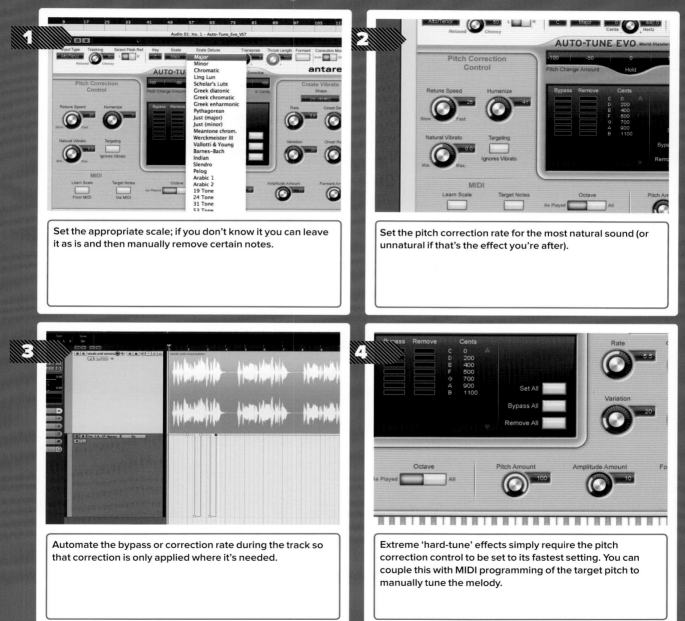

Set the appropriate scale; if you don't know it you can leave it as is and then manually remove certain notes.

Set the pitch correction rate for the most natural sound (or unnatural if that's the effect you're after).

Automate the bypass or correction rate during the track so that correction is only applied where it's needed.

Extreme 'hard-tune' effects simply require the pitch correction control to be set to its fastest setting. You can couple this with MIDI programming of the target pitch to manually tune the melody.

Tip / Where the song changes key or flips to a different musical scale in the chorus, divide the vocal part accordingly and place the different parts on different tracks so that each can be treated with a pitch correction plug-in set to the appropriate scale. If not all notes in a musical scale are sung, it is possible to set up a 'User Scale' comprising only those notes that are needed. Doing this further reduces the risk of a badly-pitched note being moved to the wrong note.

BRING ON THE CLONES

Auto-Tune was such a success that other companies soon followed with their own version of the concept. Logic users get a pitch corrector bundled, but there are also perfectly capable alternatives from the likes of Bias, TC Electronic and Waves. Most use a similar paradigm, with a screen showing a section of keyboard for selecting the scale notes and a correction speed fader with some also offering formant correction to help reduce the Micky Mouse effect heard when a voice is increased in pitch using conventional pitch-shifting methods. All of them work pretty well.

But the whole landscape changed again when another previously unknown company, Celemony, headed by Peter Neubäcker, showed up at a trade show and unveiled Melodyne.

While Auto-Tune is fast to use and works in real time, it has limitations — most notably artefacts when a note is corrected too quickly or pushed to the wrong scale note. It also corrects at a set rate, which might not deal with all the singer's problems without also stripping away some of the wanted inflections (although this can be automated if you have the patience). Melodyne, by contrast, gives producers a tool to deal with audio offline, and it can do some pretty magical things.

In Melodyne (below), sung (or played) notes are displayed on a piano roll-style grid not unlike the edit page of a MIDI sequencer. Amber blobs show the average pitch of each note. Inside each blob is a solid line showing the exact pitch along with any slurs and vibrato. Tools are available not only for correcting the average pitch of each note, but also for levelling out

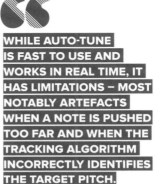

> WHILE AUTO-TUNE IS FAST TO USE AND WORKS IN REAL TIME, IT HAS LIMITATIONS — MOST NOTABLY ARTEFACTS WHEN A NOTE IS PUSHED TOO FAR AND WHEN THE TRACKING ALGORITHM INCORRECTLY IDENTIFIES THE TARGET PITCH.

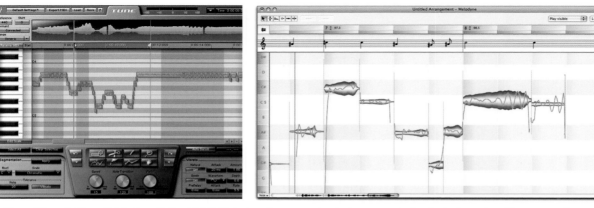

▲ Waves' Tune (left) and Melodyne Editor (right). Melodyne has earned an industry reputation for its forensic offline processing abilities.

WHICH CORRECTION TO USE?

Auto-Tune's automatic approach tends to work best where the vocal performance is almost perfect and where the note scoops and vibrato applied by the performer are fine left as they are. Small pitch errors on sustained notes are then nudged to the nearest scale note. The result is pretty natural as long as the correction speed control isn't set too fast. It can also work well on backing vocals or select parts in stacked harmonies to gently ease them into tune.

Melodyne or other graphical pitch editors (including the graphical mode in Auto-Tune) take longer to apply, but where the vocal needs more drastic touching-up on certain problem notes or phrases, it can do a better job as it allows very detailed editing of common faults such as pitch drooping at the ends of words or phrases.

Melodyne is also the tool of choice for editing timing problems when aligning harmonies or double tracks.

pitch droops and even increasing or decreasing the depth of natural vibrato. Note lengths can be changed, as can the starting positions of individual phrases (and syllables within phrases).

In short, everything about a performance can be altered, either subtly, to refine the material, or not so subtly to deliver the kind of abuse that Auto-Tune excels in. Even more than that, in multi-track mode notes can be dragged to completely new pitches to create complex harmonies and block chorus parts.

Among vocal producers, Auto-Tune's automatic mode has generally became regarded as the quick fix tool while Melodyne is the more forensic option. Fixing a vocal using Melodyne can be time consuming and requires a level of operator skill, but it offers a depth of precision and finesse as yet unmatched by other pitch fix software (See Which correction to use?).

AFTER MELODYNE
Melodyne's success invariably led to competing companies playing catch up, just as everyone did when Auto-Tune first

put in an appearance, with Antares soon adding graphical editing to Auto-Tune. But in the meantime Celemony had been busy doing the impossible with Melodyne DNA or Direct Note Access – a new take on the original Melodyne concept that brought (almost) all the editing power of the original, but this time to polyphonic recordings.

When it was first demonstrated at a press launch at the Frankfurt music show I was as entranced as everyone else when Peter Neubäcker set to work on a complex, polyphonic acoustic guitar performance, separated it into its individual notes and then adjusted individual notes within the chords. It's the only time I've ever seen a new product get a spontaneous round of applause from the music press.

It took a further year to get the software into production and it still has some limitations – the processing can produce audible side-effects with some material, particularly complex ensembles – but if you have to work on a piano recording or other polyphonic piece and can't get the original player to come and replay a faulty part you now at least have a chance of correcting it. (In this respect it can also be used to modify samples, when by definition you don't have access to the original musicians.)

LIMITATIONS
The theory goes that pitch correction allows anyone to record professional, polished vocals. But this is an obvious misconception; there's a lot more to a great vocal than simply staying in tune. A good singer controls expression, vocal timbre, vibrato, phrasing and a host of other essential elements of performance almost without thinking about them. Even with the finest pitch-shift algorithms, the best we can do is take an indifferent singer and get

Editing the vocal lead in Melodyne

1

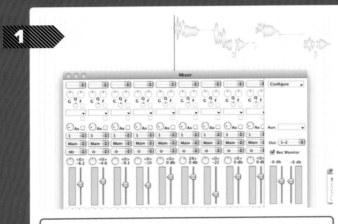

Melodyne offers a range of powerful tools that can be used to micro-edit the lead vocal. To get started import a backing track and the lead vocal line onto two tracks. Set the bpm in the Transport bar (this aligns the tracks you've imported with the grid to make life easier) and tweak the mixer fader levels to taste.

2

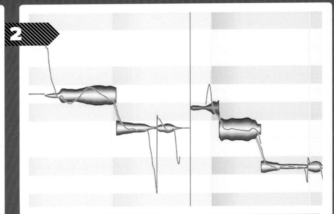

Double-click the vocal line to open it in the Edit window. Then select the Pitch tool. This reveals a single pitch line threading through the various notes, with a hyper-detailed visual representation of the various rises, falls and any vibrato. To move a note simply click on it and drag it up or down. Holding down Alt allows for smaller movements.

3

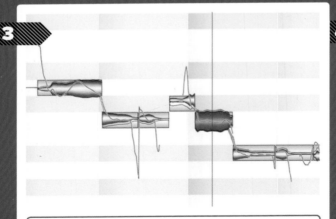

Using the Move Notes tool allows you to move individual notes in time – useful if a singer is a little too far behind the beat, for example. Be careful of going too far with any processing – the more you process, the further you get from the original artefact-free recording.

4

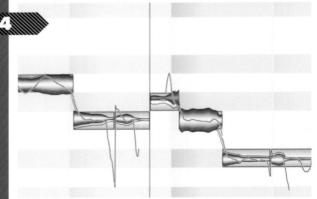

The Pitch Modulation tool allows you to alter the amount of pitch waver there is within an individual note. Reducing the amount of modulation pulls a note closer to an artifically exact '0 per cent deviation' – the kind of effect you get with Auto-Tune when it is pushed to its limit.

Artificial harmonies in Melodyne

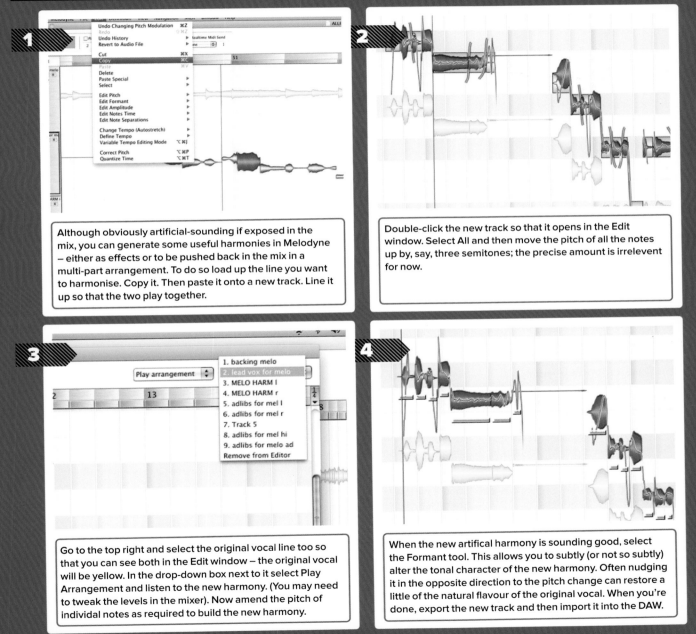

1

Although obviously artificial-sounding if exposed in the mix, you can generate some useful harmonies in Melodyne – either as effects or to be pushed back in the mix in a multi-part arrangement. To do so load up the line you want to harmonise. Copy it. Then paste it onto a new track. Line it up so that the two play together.

2

Double-click the new track so that it opens in the Edit window. Select All and then move the pitch of all the notes up by, say, three semitones; the precise amount is irrelevent for now.

3

Go to the top right and select the original vocal line too so that you can see both in the Edit window – the original vocal will be yellow. In the drop-down box next to it select Play Arrangement and listen to the new harmony. (You may need to tweak the levels in the mixer). Now amend the pitch of individual notes as required to build the new harmony.

4

When the new artifical harmony is sounding good, select the Formant tool. This allows you to subtly (or not so subtly) alter the tonal character of the new harmony. Often nudging it in the opposite direction to the pitch change can restore a little of the natural flavour of the original vocal. When you're done, export the new track and then import it into the DAW.

their pitching to sound adequate. Making the performance itself perfect is a whole different matter — and best looked after by a vocal coach! Furthermore, the more automatic approach taken by Auto-Tune and its imitators only works effectively when the singer's pitching is reasonably good in the first place: if the singer is tone deaf, the sung notes may be nowhere close to their intended pitches and the software may force them to the wrong note altogether.

Over and above that, any re-tuning inevitably alters the original performance, introducing artefacts which, however well concealed, do subtly change the sound. On intimate, exposed vocal lines the effect should be used sparingly.

PRODUCTION TRICKS

It seems to be the way of the world that whatever a tool is designed for, somebody finds a new application for it that the designer never considered. That's what happened when Auto-Tune was used to create the now familiar vocoder-like, robotic vocal effect.

Setting the pitch correction speed to its fastest setting gives you the robotic effect straight away, but if you want to have more control over it you'll need a plug-in that allows the target pitch to be controlled not by a fixed user scale but by incoming MIDI notes, either directly from a keyboard or from a MIDI data track in the sequencer. The advantage of MIDI control is that you are in precise control of where the notes change and there's also no danger of a wrong note popping out because the singer was more than a half semitone off-key.

Have fun with this by all means but as an effect in its own right it is getting a bit old

MY VIEW: PITCH CORRECTION

My view on pitch-correction is that software fix solutions can be hugely effective for adding a gloss of perfection to an already strong performance or for tweaking the odd difficult note, but we're as far away from having a talent plug-in as we ever will be.

Pitch correction can score highly where a singer is able to deliver a more emotive performance by really going for it — at the expense of some pitching precision.

But overall, if you can coax a better performance out of a singer while recording rather than accepting second best and then trying to bend it into shape with software tools afterwards, you'll end up with a much better result.

TO TUNE OR NOT: THE ETHICS OF CORRECTION

Over the past decade or so, pitch correction plug-ins have become essential tools in the producer's armoury and their legacy a new, more polished vocal sound that spans the terrain of modern music. Where the sound of the '60s was defined by multitrack tape, the '70s by generous reverb and the '80s by sample-based reworkings, the sound of the noughties can easily be considered the sound of artificial pitch enhancement, both obvious and subliminal.

Of course the quest for tuning perfection has had its critics. Country singers including Loretta Lynn, Allison Moorer, Dolly Parton, Garth Brooks and Reba McEntire have all reportedly refused to use Auto-Tune. Even in the pop world, critics have emerged, with R&B legend T-Pain — one of the highest profile advocates of its use (and indeed the only man to release an Auto-Tune App) — penning the lyrics 'D.O.A. (Death of Auto-Tune)' on his The Blueprint 3 album.

The question of whether to use correction (or how much to use) holds a wider philosophical slant. In a culture that values artificial perfection — in terms of physical attributes and often personal morality — should music fall into line too? Or is part of the inherent power of music its ability to reveal imperfections, reflected in performances that may be full of soul, but also (potentially) some way short of perfection?

Is not part of the vocal beauty of a Dylan or a MacGowan the meandering, wavering journey that lies just off — or some way off — the note? Do we as listeners respond better to the kinks and cadences of the human than the glistening unreal of the machine?

It's a question for the philosophers to debate. For the producer, the question is what kind of effect you want to achieve. Whether it's 100 per cent perfect, or 10 per cent fixed, or 100 per cent natural, in Auto-Tune and Melodyne — and the newcomers — we have powerful tools to do the jobs we need them to do.

Beyond that it's a matter of taste; of the demands of the genre you're working in; and of your own personal choice. Ultimately music is an art form, and in art pretty much anything goes. If you can apply Auto-Tune to next-door's dog and get a hit single out of it, who's to say you're wrong to do so?

> **YOU KNOW SOMETHING'S HAD ITS DAY WHEN SIMON COWELL BANS ITS USE ON ONE OF HIS SHOWS.**

hat (you know something's had its day when Simon Cowell bans its use on one of his shows). However, if you can think of a new way to use it, then you might have a hit on your hands. Here are a few suggestions:

Single-note artefacts: **Set the pitch correction scale to just one note** and the correction speed to fast. Feed in a signal that varies considerably in pitch. The result is a sound that jumps wildly between octaves accompanied by interesting timbral changes caused by the large amounts of pitch shift taking place. The more radically you process the input signal, the more the processing artefacts are likely to show up. In some cases these technical imperfections can make for interesting effects in their own right. Rhythmic material can work particularly well with this effect. Bouncing down the effected material gives you further flexibility: you can re-import the audio file and then add additional processing and/or edits to create all manner of glitched sounds and toned percussive hits.

Artificial double-track: **Copy a vocal track onto a new track and apply Auto-Tune (or similar) to the copy**. It will adjust the pitch and rate at which one note slurs to the next to some extent — even if the original performance was very well sung. Play it alongside the original unprocessed track and you get something that sounds like a cross between double tracking (where the same thing is sung twice) and a mild chorus/flange effect as the two slightly differently pitched sounds interact. Add a few tens of ms of delay to the processed track and the illusion of double tracking gets even closer. While this can sound a bit artificial on a lead vocal line, it can be useful as a special effect or to add density and texture to backing vocals and

harmonies. Try panning the processed and unprocessed tracks to opposite sides.

Eastern vibes: **Apply Auto-Tune to a guitar solo that includes bends and vibrato**. With the correction speed set as you might for vocal processing none of the natural playing nuances are lost, but as soon as the player bends up to a note and sustains it, the pitch is nudged into alignment with the chosen scale making the playing seem tighter and better controlled. Speed up the correction process, however, and all those slow bends turn into more rapid pitch slurs giving something of an eastern feel to the melody.

Tip / In large, multi-part choruses try using Auto-Tune on half of the constituent harmony tracks to pull them further into tune, while leaving some untreated for a natural / tuned hybrid. You can add further bulk and variation to the chorus block by altering the speed of re-tune on each of the Auto-Tuned lines — from fairly extreme to relaxed. If the extremely treated tracks are pushed well back in the mix you should hear few, if any, side effects.

Tip / Use Auto-Tune on MIDI-generated synth parts to force them into new scales. The bigger the difference between the input and output notes, the more digital side effects will be introduced, which can yield highly useable lo-fi lead sounds. Add to the effect by sending a second version of the same synth to a different instance of Auto-Tune programmed to play a harmony.

Tip / Instances of Auto-Tune can be added in series. Sometimes using two on a single track with both set to their fastest correction speeds can deliver even more extreme-sounding results. ●

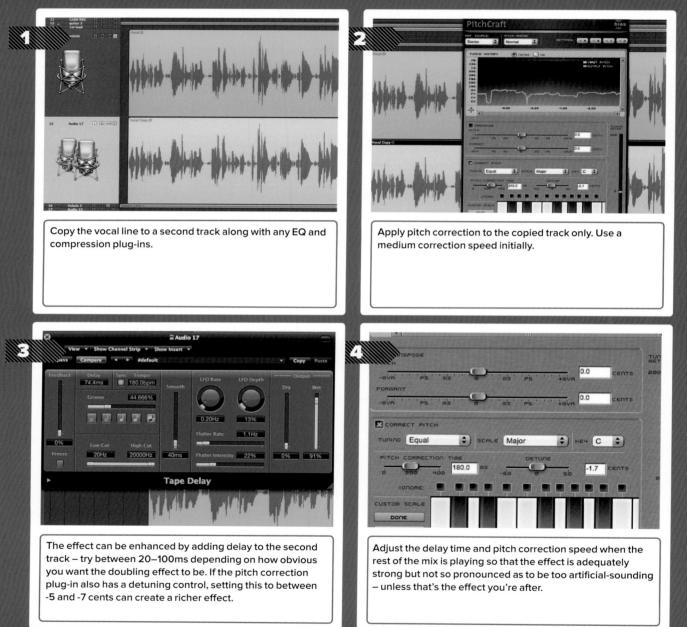

1 Copy the vocal line to a second track along with any EQ and compression plug-ins.

2 Apply pitch correction to the copied track only. Use a medium correction speed initially.

3 The effect can be enhanced by adding delay to the second track – try between 20–100ms depending on how obvious you want the doubling effect to be. If the pitch correction plug-in also has a detuning control, setting this to between -5 and -7 cents can create a richer effect.

4 Adjust the delay time and pitch correction speed when the rest of the mix is playing so that the effect is adequately strong but not so pronounced as to be too artificial-sounding – unless that's the effect you're after.

TIPS FOR A BETTER MIX

Everything in the mix must be there for a reason.
Don't use plug-ins and processors just because they are available. A track that is well recorded and arranged rarely needs as much processing as you might at first think.

COMMON MIX MISTAKES AND HOW TO AVOID THEM

Too much distortion.
Distortion adds harmonic complexity, and harmonic complexity causes sounds to occupy more of the audio spectrum. Use only as much distortion as you need to create the appropriate texture for the track. Overdo it and you quickly run out of space in the mix. You can always follow milder distortion with compression if it's more sustain you're after.

14
VOCAL PRODUCTION

"

NO AMOUNT OF TECHNOLOGY CAN ASSURE A SPINE-TINGLINGLY BRILLIANT PERFORMANCE.

ALL ABOUT THE PERFORMANCE

In the majority of mainstream musical genres – with the possible exception of some breeds of dance – the vocal is the most important element in the mix. The time spent on its production usually reflects this.

Indeed so central is the lead vocal track, and its supporting harmonies, doubles, spins and ad-libs, that some of today's producers go to extraordinary lengths to massage a good-sounding vocal into a great one, forensically tweaking both tuning and timing, and painstakingly aligning multiple harmonic layers in the quest for the perfect vocal arrangement.

But arrangement is not the same as performance. And perfection is not the same as soul. And the fact is that while the technological advances of the past decade have given producers unprecedented control over the vocals they treat – down to the finest timing adjustment and the slightest pitch drift – no amount of technology can ever assure a spine-tinglingly brilliant performance.

You should always ask yourself if the vocals you've captured are the best the vocalist can deliver: a great vocal is one that communicates an emotion and resonates with the listener – this is more important by far than perfect pitching and timing.

PRELIMINARY EDITS

A good vocal starts with a strong performance, often with a series of takes that the engineer comps down to the final master take (page 263). It doesn't have to happen this way, though: Bob Dylan is notorious in engineering circles for refusing to repeat anything.

When this final master comp is made, you may or may not choose to do some offline re-tuning and re-phrasing using a program like Melodyne (page 264). Many vocal producers do, and some do it with more vigour and detail than others. How much you do (if any) depends on the source material and the quality of the final comp/s you're working with.

An alternative method of pulling the pitch into tune – more time-efficient if the vocal is already pitched pretty accurately – is to use a gentle application of Auto-Tune or equivalent real-time pitch correction plug-in to pull drifting phrases gently into tune (page 197).

If you choose the Auto-Tune route, once the correct musical **scale** has been set, the most important control is the one that adjusts the **speed** of pitch correction. Set this too fast and you get the familiar vocoder-like effect. Set it too slow and any out-of-tune parts sneak through before the plug-in has time to react. The middle way is found by automating the correction speed to its slowest speed where little or no correction is required and then speeding it up briefly for those sections that need fixing. Use your ears to ensure that you don't set the speed so fast that the result sounds unnatural; I seldom set the speed faster than around half way.

In the early stages of the mixdown you may also choose to programme in a few coarse fader automation moves (page 290) to keep the vocal more or less balanced with the rest of the mix and to give you a general idea of how the track is coming together.

Now it is time to apply a variety of production techniques to fit the vocal into the wider mix.

While vocal treatment often involves level automation, compression, EQ, delay, reverb and any number of other effects, there's no single way to apply these processes. Every voice is different, and every performance will require a different treatment in its unique musical context.

How much processing you apply will depend both on practical matters, such as the singer's mic technique, and artistic considerations relating to the song and the genre of music. But there are common issues that will need addressing in almost every case, including dynamics, tonality and ambient treatment.

DYNAMIC PROCESSING

A great vocal conveys emotion, and emotion has its highs and lows, in terms of both impact and volume.

Polished mic technique will mean that a good singer eases towards the mic during quieter sections and away for louder phrases, taking advantage of the mic's proximity bass effect (page 106) to add warmth and intimacy (less experienced singers can be kept back from the mic using a carefully placed pop shield).

But however good the singer's technique, even the best vocalist will vary their volume in accordance with the way the song develops, and a vocal with no dynamic range can sound sterile indeed. In terms of dynamics, the challenge for the producer is to **keep the lead vocal sounding well-balanced** within the context of the musical backing **without squashing the life from it**. Getting the right balance is also dictated by the demand to retain the all-important **intelligiblity** of the vocal lead (page 301).

Producers use a range of techniques to control the level of vocals, including:

❯ **volume automation** (the modern day equivalent of riding the channel fader),

❯ **compression** (and occasional **limiting**),

❯ or **a mix of both**.

The first thing to say is that vocal compression isn't mandatory — few opera singers would require it for example. Too many producers reach for the compressor when dealing with vocals without considering whether it is really necessary. It is only the right tool when there's a reason to use it. Where only level control is necessary, carefully programmed automation may be enough to maintain a good vocal balance throughout the song.

In most modern pop songs, however, where the levels in the backing track tend to be tightly controlled to produce a very limited dynamic range, and where adding a natural vocal to a more-or-less level backing invariably means that some words will come over too strongly while others get lost, some degree of compression is usually inevitable.

This is not only because a compressor helps to reduce level differences but it also adds **density** to the vocal track, making it sound more solid and helping it stay at the front of the mix. In other words, the compressor is not just a **problem solver** (taming peaks and raising the overall signal level); it also **adds character** to the vocal — in the form of a more confident, more present signal. In this respect the compressor is part processor, part effect.

PRO TIPS: COMPRESSION

Engineer **John Leckie** says he likes the sound of an 1176 set to a low ratio on vocals. **Tony Visconti** is also a fan of compression on vocals, both when recording and again when mixing, and will often let the compressors look after the gain levelling rather than doing much in the way of level automation.

By contrast, **Alan Parsons** is on record as saying that he dislikes compression and even on vocals he may only use a limiter to take care of excessive peaks while using level automation or manual gain riding to keep the level even.

This 'effect' varies widely depending on the model of compressor and the settings used. Different models and makes produce different subjective results. VCA compressors tend to produce the most transparent gain reduction while compressors based on tubes, field-effect transistors (FETs) and optical circuits often add character and colouration to the sound. The same applies to their digital emulations. (See **Compression and Dynamics 101, Chapter 11**).

What is true of them all, however, is that the more even the vocal level can be made prior to compression, the less work the compressor has to do purely to control levels, which is why automation or a plug-in like Waves' Vocal Rider (left) can be useful inserted before a compressor where you're looking for a more transparent result.

Of course some musical genres cry out for a heavily compressed sound — in which case you can let the compressor handle most of the gain levelling and only use level automation to fix up any sections that the compressor can't handle.

A good initial compression setting for most vocals is a fairly **fast attack time** to help bring any loud opening syllables under control quickly. Around 10–25ms will allow the starts of F, S and T sounds to come through clearly before the compressor pulls back the gain, helping maintain intelligibility while at the same time evening out the volume of the words.

Where possible I try to use an **auto release** time on vocals (page 167). This allows the compressor to constantly change its release time to suit the material rather than the operator having to find a 'one size fits all' setting. Where no auto option if available, or where you don't like the results, a **fixed release time** of 150–350ms usually works pretty well. With more aggressive pop, rock and urban vocals a faster release time may be more appropriate; audible gain pumping can add to the impact and sense of energy.

VOCAL RIDER PLUG-INS

Waves was the first company to come up with a new approach to gain control in the form of its Vocal Rider plug-in.

The Vocal Rider (left) uses a side-chain much like that of a compressor, but instead of applying the gain reduction directly, it uses it to automate its own level fader to iron out excess level changes. The interface is simple: the user sets a nominal target level as well as the upper and lower limits of gain adjustment.

Unlike a conventional compressor, the Vocal Rider also detects the spaces between vocal phrases to avoid adding unnecessary gain boost at these points.

And because the fader data can be written as automation, the user can make further edits in the same way as with conventional fader automation.

In my experience this type of processor works really well in establishing an initial automated level, but it helps to low-cut filter the vocal first, otherwise inaudible low frequencies (such as wind blasts that get through the pop shield) can trigger gain reduction when you don't need any.

An **RMS setting** usually produces a more natural result than Peak if you have the option, as you're looking to control the subjective loudness, not deal with peak events (page 168).

The **amount** of compression used will vary enormously depending both on the musical style and on the singer's mic technique. A well-controlled performance of an intimate ballad might work well using a 2:1–3:1 ratio with threshold adjusted to give around 3–5dB of gain reduction on the loudest peaks. By contrast, heavy rock or dance styles might benefit from a more obvious compression setting. Start with a higher ratio (5:1 or above) and up to 10dB, sometimes more, of gain reduction. With a high-end compressor you may be able to get away with even higher values without choking the life out of a sound.

If a vocal needs more compression but you feel like you're overdoing it when you increase the ratio and/or gain reduction, try easing back on the values and **adding a second compressor in series** to catch any volume peaks that the first misses.

The second compressor can be set more aggressively than the first, with a higher ratio and more gain reduction on the peaks – you can often go as high as 10dB. Alternatively, use level fader automation or a Vocal Rider in combination with the compressor. This will allow you to use less severe compressor settings.

Some engineers use a **limiter** instead of the second compressor where a more assertive level of control is needed. This is a good solution where the singer has difficulty controlling their level in certain pitch ranges, where select notes seem to jump out of the mix.

WHEN TOO MUCH IS GOOD

Although excessive compression is usually best avoided due to the risk of making the vocal sound unnaturally squashed (while also bringing up unwanted noises and breaths), these same artefacts are enthusiastically exploited in some musical genres.

The technique is featured heavily in the first two Daft Punk albums, where the inexpensive Alesis 3630 compressor was pushed hard to create the pumping, breathing vocal tones that have since become commonplace in many dance, pop and urban productions.

Useless trivia / The Alesis 3630 (below) was named after the address of the Alesis company headquarters at the time: 3630 Holridge Avenue, Los Angeles.

On occasion you may need to go even further. It has been known to follow two compressors with a limiter to provide a three-stage gain control. Here the first compressor evens the sound in a fairly gentle way. The second compressor reduces the level of any over-loud peaks missed by the first. By adding a final stage of limiting any really wild peaks are prevented from going any higher – although these should be relatively few after the compression stages. When using cascading compressors the idea is to make the gain control sound more transparent – not beat a signal into submission.

Always listen carefully to the treated vocal to check you're not ging too far. A/B regularly between the compressed and the dry sound. Appropriate compression helps to place a vocal comfortably and confidently in the mix. But go too far and you risk stripping all life and dynamics from the performance. To ensure any A/B comparisons are fair, the volume of the compressed signal should be similar to that of the uncompressed one, otherwise you can be fooled into thinking that whatever sounds loudest sounds best.

Hard-hitting vocals

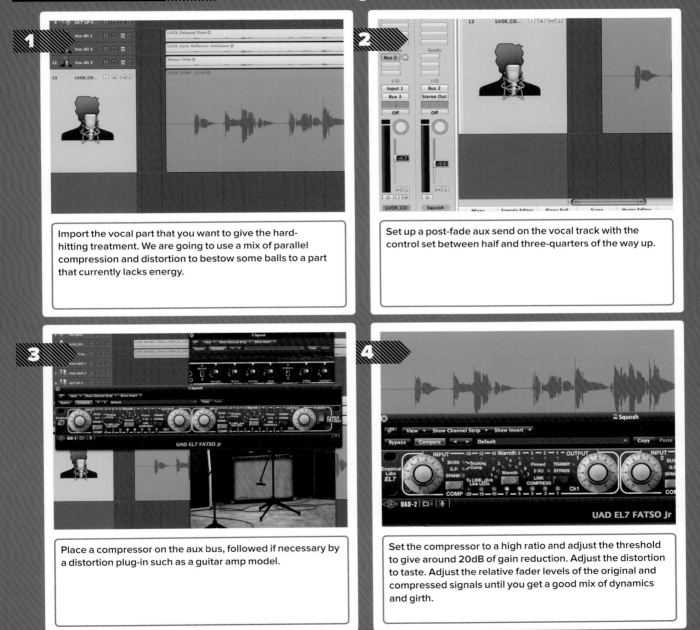

1 Import the vocal part that you want to give the hard-hitting treatment. We are going to use a mix of parallel compression and distortion to bestow some balls to a part that currently lacks energy.

2 Set up a post-fade aux send on the vocal track with the control set between half and three-quarters of the way up.

3 Place a compressor on the aux bus, followed if necessary by a distortion plug-in such as a guitar amp model.

4 Set the compressor to a high ratio and adjust the threshold to give around 20dB of gain reduction. Adjust the distortion to taste. Adjust the relative fader levels of the original and compressed signals until you get a good mix of dynamics and girth.

Tip / When adding a lot of compression, any spill or noise between words or phrases is also brought up in level. If you apply 10dB of gain reduction and then adjust the compressor's make-up gain to get the maximum level back to where it was before, for example, the noise and spill between phrases will be raised by 10dB. To get around this, you can either gate the vocal before adding compression, use fades to trim the various phrases, or use level automation to dip the level in the spaces between phrases. The last is probably the most natural sounding solution.

PARALLEL COMPRESSION

The hard-hitting vocal tones popularised in urban production circles, and increasingly used in pop mixes, are often created using parallel compression (page 172) on the lead, and often backing, vocals.

To set it up, compress the vocal(s) as you normally world, then feed some of the signal to an aux bus which contains a second aggressive-sounding compressor. Increase the feed going to the bus until you get the right blend of energy and punch.

High ratios and large amounts of gain reduction are the order of the day on the parallel compressor, where you should audition all of your least polite models.

Where an even tougher vocal sound is required, try adding a distortion or overdrive plug-in directly after the parallel compressor (page 211). The distortion plug-in doesn't have to be pushed hard — just enough to generate additional harmonic content in the signal (although more outrageous settings sometimes work too). While the raw distorted tone might sound awful on its own, mixing in just a little with

the clean vocal can add serious weight and attitude. This technique can be used to beef up vocals in a range of genres, from rock and metal to hip hop and dance.

AUTOMATION

Assuming you've not gone down the route of serious excess, even a compression treatment that pulls back 10–12dB of gain may not deliver a vocal part in which every word is clear. In such cases some post-compression automation is required.

Note that level automation is most effective when applied **after** compression, as any changes you make to the compressor/s will affect the overall vocal level and dynamics.

In situations where the vocal needs levelling **before** compression (if there are significant level changes caused by poor vocal technique to deal with for example), the vocal will need routing via a bus with automation programmed on the vocal track and the compressor located on the bus insert point.

Another option is to use a vocal rider-stlye plug-in to manage the level changes automatically prior to compression. This should be placed before the compressor.

It's not just fader levels that benefit from automation. **EQ automation** can also be used to enhance a performance. You might raise the highs to add more emphasis on certain syllables, for example, or pull back strident overtones on specific words.

Here the usual EQ rules apply: boosts sound more natural when they are wide and gentle, while cuts can be narrower and deeper. Automating vocal EQ in this way can be extremely effective, but it requires a gentle touch and a good ear.

MY VIEW: AUTOMATION

How forensic you get when programming automation will depend on the original vocal performance, your compression settings (if any) and the style of the music.

It's easy to get obsessed with automation, fine-tuning the vitality from a vocal.

While an exposed singer/songwriter performance with sparse instrumentation might present a strong case for fine tuning, you have to remember that before the days of digital recording few studios even had basic fader automation so the amount of forensic tweaking that was possible was almost non-existent. All the fader moves were done manually during the mix.

Did those old classic records sound any worse for it? I'll leave that for you to decide. Probably the best maxim when deciding how much is too much, is the one used in all fields of engineering that states: 'If it ain't broke, don't fix it'.

DE-ESSING

Every book on recording includes a section on vocal de-essing. I've covered it before, both in **Recording Vocals, Chapter 6** and **Compression & Dynamics 101, Chapter 11**.

Chapter 6 outlines common techniques to mitigate (or eliminate!) sibilance at source. It's worth re-reading, mainly because most sibilance problems come about when the wrong mic or wrong mic position (or a mix of both) are used. If the original signal has even a small amount of excess sibilance then it will sound a whole lot worse after any compression and top-end EQ has been added.

The reason for re-iterating the importance of the recording is that it is hard to make post-recording de-essing sound entirely natural if the initial level of sibilance is high.

If you do need to de-ess, you can either use a **dynamic EQ** set to attenuate only the sibilance range in which the sibilants exceed the threshold level (page 172), or a **dedicated de-esser** plug-in. Whichever you choose, it is most logical to insert the de-esser after any compression and EQ as these both change the relative level of sibilance (Walkthrough, page 214).

The trick with de-essing is **only to reduce the sibilance by as much as is necessary**. Remember that natural speech includes sibilants; if you pull them down too far you end up with an unnatural sound that has a lisping quality.

Tip / If you use a de-esser on a vocal track then you may also need to de-ess any reverberation effects that the vocals are sent to via an aux send – particularly where you're using a very bright vocal reverb.

Bright reverbs, particularly plates, have a tendency to accentuate sibilance. To reduce this sibilance simply insert a plug-in de-esser before the bus reverb. In some cases you may be able to de-ess the reverb send only, and not the main vocal.

Tip / There's a world of difference between a good de-esser and a poor one. A poor one may do more harm than good, unless used very sparingly. If you do a lot of vocal production and struggle taming sibilant frequencies then (only after trying to solve the problem at source) a good de-esser is a wise investment. Simpler de-essers reduce the gain of the whole signal when loud sibilants are detected whereas good ones only reduce the level of the frequency band where the sibilant sounds reside, leaving the rest of the vocal untouched.

VOCAL EQ

An 18dB/octave low-cut filter set at between 40–100Hz will take care of **low frequency** wind blasts and any mic-stand noise without noticeably impacting on the lead vocal. With some voices you may be able to push higher still; edge up the frequency until you start to hear a perceptible difference in the vocal tone then ease back a little.

Boxiness in the 150–400Hz region can lend an unpleasant tonality to a vocal line. To find the offending frequencies set up a parametric EQ with a narrow Q band and a 5–10dB boost and sweep it through the 150–400Hz band to locate the offending area. When the tone starts to sound unpleasant, apply a little dip at that frequency to tame it. Annoying peaks in the 2.5–6kHz **presence** region can be located and pulled back in the same way. It's also worth checking the 1–1.5kHz region if the vocal sounds too **nasal** or 'honky'.

PRO TIP

Some producers use more than one de-esser to tame sibilance. Where sibilant frequencies peak in different areas of a voice, simply add a second de-esser in series with the first. When using more than one de-esser, precision is key – if the target frequency is too wide, or the cut too deep, you can easily end up compromising what was a reasonable-sounding vocal line.

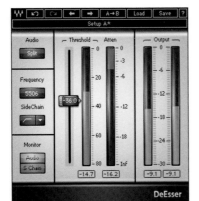

▲ Although it's much better to reduce sibilance at source, if you have to use a de-esser plug-in make sure it's a good one – like this one from Waves.

Setting up a de-esser

1 Open the de-esser in the vocal track. Insert it after any compressors and EQ.

2 Search for the target 'S' zone using the frequency selection button (unless this is preset). Some plug-ins have a monitoring option to allow you to solo the detected 'S' sounds.

3 Adjust the threshold and amount of sibilant reduction.

4 Consider automating the amount of de-essing if the problem is only evident on specific words or phrases. An alternative is to automate the de-esser bypass so that it only switches on when problem sibilance occurs, leaving everything else unaffected.

Where the singer produces unpleasant-sounding peaks in the audio spectrum on certain phrases only – for example, where the voice pushes hard in a higher register – a dynamic EQ plug-in might be more suitable as it only notches out the selected frequencies when they exceed a specified threshold level. You might also consider automating the EQ.

I wouldn't normally roll off the **extreme highs** (8kHz and above) from a lead vocal unless dealing with a track where the singer had been recorded with a poor choice of mic that added too much fizzy top end. That said, a gentle top cut can help **backing vocals** sit more comfortably behind the lead vocal and you can also try it on a lead line to get a more ribbon-like smoothness from a capacitor mic.

The majority of initial EQ tweaks are about cutting: cutting headroom-eating lows and awkward frequency spikes caused by the peculiarities of a singer's voice or a less than ideal choice of mic. But **boosting** can be useful too, particularly if the vocal needs additional definition to stand out in the mix. Like all EQ boost, it must be handled with care.

The key rule when boosting is not to do anything that makes the sound too aggressive. Boosting the **presence** area of a vocal (2.5–6kHz) can aid intelligibility, although more than the gentlest amount of lift can add an unpleasant edge to the voice. At the very least, ensure you're boosting with a wide bandwidth (low Q) so that you add a hump rather than a peak.

A more common strategy is to add brightness to the sound without making it aggressive. The trick is to use a simple high shelving EQ set at between 8–10kHz to add a few dBs of boost. This opens out the sound and makes it sound more airy (it's what engineers are referring to when they talk about '**air**' in a mix), but it avoids adding boost in that part of the vocal spectrum that can sound aggressive or sibilant.

Note / There's a big difference between the results you get using a good equaliser and a less good one – especially on as pivotal a part as the lead vocal. A poor equaliser may apply cut and boost where you want it, but anything more than a minor adjustment can produce an unfocused or nasal sound – no matter what you do the sound never seems quite right. By contrast, a high-quality EQ manages to retain a natural sound even when a lot of cut or boost is needed (this is particularly true of higher-end hardware boxes). If you're looking to expand your list of plug-ins, a good parametric EQ should come close to the top of the list, along with a nice compressor and a high-quality algorithmic reverb (page 57).

REVERB

Vocals always sound more comfortable when treated with reverb or delay. In most cases reverb is used to create a sense of musical interest and to give the impression of the vocal existing in a three-dimensional space rather than in the dead confines of a vocal booth. Even the current trend of dry-sounding vocal treatments uses ambience settings based mainly on early reflections (ERs) to place them in the mix.

Using reverb on vocals comes with its share of complications. The main one is that adding significant amounts of reverb has the psychoacoustic effect of making the vocal sound further away, pushing it further back in the mix. Yet this is precisely what we don't normally want to do; in the case of

THE ORDER OF PLUG-INS

EQ can be added before or after compression. I tend to think it makes more sense to EQ after the compressor as this avoids the compressor trying to fight any EQ boosts or dips you've added. The result sounds very subtly different; try both to see which you prefer. The de-esser, if you're using one, should be added after EQ.

Where an automatic gain levelling plug-in such as Vocal Rider is used, this should come first in the signal chain, although where very low frequency components in the vocal track are causing it to over-react in some places, preceding it with a low-cut, 18dB/octave filter set at around 80Hz can produce more reliable level tracking.

MAKE WAY FOR THE VOCALS

It can be easy to fall into the trap of endlessly tweaking EQ on the lead vocal only to find that nothing helps it sit in the mix. In these instances it's worth looking at the wider mix, arrangement and orchestration to see whether there is enough space for the vocal to do its magic.

In busy mixes the vocal is often forced to fight with guitars, keyboards, percussion, over-boomy drums and other instruments that inhabit the same part of the frequency spectrum. No matter what EQ work you to do the vocal, it just doesn't seem to sit comfortably in the mix.

In these instances take a step back to see where the problem lies. If you've done a good job on the arrangement, you may only need to tweak the electric guitar tonality to give the vocals the space they

need. More challenging problems can arise when you take on a project part way through, when you have no control over the initial arrangement or choice of sounds. A good first step is to try cutting frequencies from other instruments instead of trying to EQ more clarity into the vocal – an approach which can quickly generate harsh results.

The frequency range that you cut is paramount here. You're looking to cut in the general region in which the bulk of the vocal's most important frequencies lie – usually the ones that convey the intelligibility of the lyrics. A useful tip once you've decided on the EQ frequency is to adjust it while listening to the vocal rather than the instrument you are EQ'ing: that will help you focus on the effectiveness or otherwise of the adjustment.

A quick way of making cuts across a range of instruments if you've routed instrumental parts to group buses (page 39) is to dial in a gentle dip in the instrumental EQs on those buses and then – if you need to – potentially also boost the vocal EQ in the same area using a dB or two of wide boost. However, avoid making the vocal sound too aggressive. The mix should really be made to fit the vocal and not vice versa.

Other techniques for solving the problem include dropping conflicting instruments from the arrangement altogether, using a filter to roll away higher frequencies in, say, guitar or keyboard parts when the vocal is in or utilising a side-chain fed ducker (Walkthrough, page 234) on parts that are stifling the vocal.

---

the lead vocal we usually want it to sound as though it is at the forefront of the mix.

Of course there are exceptions to this rule: Enya's vocals were dripped in Lexicon reverb to create her trademark sound. But in contemporary pop the trend is to use less reverb – or at least a less-obvious reverb – so that the vocal line takes on a sense of space but doesn't recede in the mix. The producer's job is to walk a fine line between giving the vocal its own distinct space, with just enough liveliness to make it sound as though it belongs to the rest of the mix, but not so much that it gets pushed from its rightful place at the front.

The first question when picking a reverb for a vocal is 'What type?'. The usual suspects are plates, rooms and very occasionally halls. In many cases it is the plate that wins. We don't usually want to suggest any specific type of space to the listener – that is

distracting. This is where a fairly anonymous algorithmic 'ambience' reverb or plate simulation works well.

Convolution reverbs are great for emulating concert halls, cathedrals, car parks and caves, but unless you're preparing a Gregorian chant those cathedrals and caves are of little use in most vocal production. Coarse 'old school' reverbs can sound very flattering on vocals, but don't discount more modern **plate** emulations where you want a more natural sound.

Smaller **room** settings can create a convincing sense of space while adding almost no noticeable reverb – but be careful not to impose too much of a specific room character on the sound unless you have a good reason for doing so.

Overall I tend to consider reverb as more of a musical glue and a way of adding polish

PRO TIPS: SPACE

Ask a dozen producers how you get a vocal to sit correctly in a mix and most will say it starts with a good musical arrangement. After that there may be some juggling of levels and the use of EQ to carve spaces in the guitars and synths so the vocal stands out more, but it all starts with a good arrangement.

Producer Mick Glossop hands on the tip that if the tonality of the vocals changes in different sections of the song, it may be helpful to put the different sections on different tracks so they can be treated with different EQ and compression settings.

to a vocal than a means of making it appear as if it were performed in a particular type of environment.

When you've found a setting that suits the voice – and works in the context of the wider song – it is simply a case of altering the controls to shape the sound.

The controls you normally spend most time on are those governing the **decay time** and the balance of **ERs** with the **reverb tail**. The modern trend is against long tails, giving more prominence to less bright-sounding ERs to breathe life into the vocal in a subtle way. Where the early and late reflections have their own level controls or a balance control, skewing the balance in favour of the ERs can allow the use of a longer reverb tail as this will now be at a lower level.

Adding **pre-delay** to reverb helps separate it from the dry part of the vocal sound, which can help keep the vocal sounding close to the listener. Anything between 20–200ms may be added, depending on the song.

DELAY

Reverb on the lead vocal is by no means essential. There are many producers who use little or no vocal reverb and choose delay instead. This can be anything from barely noticeable **slapback delay** to long, cascading **tape-style repeats**, often using **ping-pong settings** to add stereo interest.

Selecting a **delay time** related to the tempo of the song helps reinforce the rhythm but it also tends to make the delay less obviously audible as each delay gets partly obscured by the beat of the song. Adjusting the delay time so that it is a little faster or slower than the song tempo can help it stand out more and make it a touch more interesting.

▲ The Massey TD5 tape delay plug-in for Pro Tools: a highly regarded tool with a vintage sound.

Try different **delay types** to see what sounds the most musically satisfying. A typical digital delay is capable of producing repeats that are as clean as the original, although this can give unmusical results, with the delay tails interfering with the ongoing vocals. An easy fix is to add a **high-cut EQ** after the delay line to warm the sound of the repeats. (A similar cut to the low end will reduce the risk of mix-clogging at the low end too).

A better option may be one of the many popular **tape delay emulations**, which make successive delays progressively more indistinct, as though they are receding into the distance. This characteristic was originally caused by the quality loss that occurred when the output of the tape delay (the tape loops tended to wear quickly) was fed back to the input and then recirculated to create repeating echoes (page 26). The results, particularly when used with subtle signal deterioration like flutter, can sound great.

Many producers marry the best of both worlds by employing both reverb and delay treatments to support vocals in the mix.

Tip / Often fairly long delay times, in the order of hundreds of ms with three or four audible repeats, work well, and while this might sound excessive in isolation, you may find that once the whole mix is playing the delays become almost subliminal, adding the necessary interest without the need for much – if any – reverb.

ADVANCED TECHNIQUES

Tip / One way to control the distancing effect of reverb is to adjust the **pre-delay**. A value of between 50–150ms will help pull the initial hit of the vocal line further forward and increase its clarity while little or no pre-delay and more reverb will help push backing vocals further back. Almost all reverb plug-ins include a pre-delay control. If yours doesn't then insert a simple delay plug-in set to 100 per cent wet before the reverb. Note that the pre-delay time can be set to work with the tempo of the track.

Tip / Give delay tails a slight blur by feeding a very short reverb from a repeating delay so that each delay has a subtle halo of reverb associated with it. This technique can be used alone or in combination with a second, non-delayed vocal reverb or ambience treatment.

Tip / To thicken a vocal without adding an obvious reverb tail, use a gated reverb, with a pre-delay if it suits, instead of an ambience or plate setting.

Tip / A convincing vintage slapback-style vocal echo can be created by using a reverb ambience program that comprises only a short burst of ERs and then delaying it by around 90ms so that it sounds like a slightly diffused echo. Reduce delay feedback to zero so that there's only one echo.

Tip / There are a number of emulations of the Roland Space Echo. Used sparingly on either a reverb or delay setting it can give vocals an ambient warmth that few other effects deliver. Don't overdo the effect.

Tip / Layer an echo with a reverse reverb effect (page 193) for a slightly other-worldly sound. Use it during a breakdown or to highlight a specific line as a spot effect.

Tip / Where you have two almost identically 'good' vocal tracks but only intend to use

one of them, try feeding the reverb from the (muted) unused one instead of the dry, unmuted lead. The slight variances in performance make the reverb sound more interesting.

Tip / Instead of relying on a simple delay plug-in, try feeding the delayed signal to a guitar amp set up in a lively-sounding room such as a bathroom, stairwell or large hallway, then put a mic in the room and feed that signal back into the mix. The colouration of the amp and room will produce a very organic-sounding delay with plenty of character. If you don't have a guitar amp or a mic cable that will reach the bathroom (or if there's someone in the bath), feed the delay from a guitar amp plug-in into a convolution reverb set to produce a small, bright room sound. EQ, then feed into the mix to taste.

DOUBLING AND LAYERING

One of the earliest multitrack vocal techniques was double-tracking, the practice of singing (or playing) the same part twice on two different tracks.

The natural thickening effect offered by double-tracking sounds the way it does because even the best performer varies their performance very slightly in terms of pitching and timing on each pass: think identical twins singing the same part at the same time – that's what a good double track should sound like.

Some singers are better at double-tracking than others. Ones that aren't invariably leave the producer with a lot of work to do at the edit stage.

Note / **Double-tracking a part doesn't necessarily make it sound bigger or more forward**, which is why the technique

TECHNIQUE: AD-LIBS

Ad-libs can be dropped into a song where the arrangement leaves space.

The treatment you give them is usually much the same as any other vocal, although you may choose to use more or less delay and/or reverb for artistic reasons.

EQ decisions are often influenced by a desire to keep the ad-libs from interfering with the lead vocal line – if playing at the same time as a closing chorus, for example.

Ad-lib takes can be pillaged for short vocal segments to provide rhythmic elements: I've taken laughs, breaths and other exclamations from after a take and then used them over an intro.

Time-stretching is often useful when doing this as it allows these accidental sounds to be made to fit the space available.

FAKING IT

Early attempts at faking double-tracks used a spare tape machine as a delay, recording onto tape via an aux send on the console and then returning the delayed signal from the playback head to the mix. The physical distance between the record and playback heads and the tape speed determined the exact delay time, which tended to be around 70–200ms, depending on which tape speeds were available.

This process doesn't replicate the varying time and pitch elements of a real double-track, so when solid-state delay devices became available

various designers added a little pitch modulation to the delay to try to get closer to the real thing. Predictably, none of these strategies managed to replicate real double tracking, although they did help establish slap-back echo and chorus effects that were useful in their own right.

Today there are numerous plug-ins that attempt to recreate the sound of real double-tracking by adding random elements to the delay modulation. They're certainly getting closer to the sound of two separate, layered performances, but to my ears there's still no substitute for the real thing.

is more often used for harmonies or other backing vocal parts where more complexity and texture is required. It does have its place on lead vocal lines – often to add interest to a voice or to provide a change of character in different sections of the song, but don't count on it for 'the big vocal' sound. Whether you choose to use it is ultimately a matter of artistic judgement: just check it's having the intended effect rather than adding unneccesary depth and complexity to the all-important lead.

Normally, double-tracked parts are balanced so that each is equally loud. The same effects are usually added to both tracks. In other words, the double-track is treated as a single voice.

Some producers have gone beyond double-tracking, experimenting with triple-tracking and beyond. This technique was used to create the opening for 10cc's 'I'm Not in Love', where massively layered vocals were recorded so that each layered vocal ended up on its own track.

Multi-tracked vocals were also reportedly used to good effect on many of Michael Jackson's early tracks.

With standard double-tracks both parts might be **panned centrally** (where there are other backing vocals panned left and right). Where there are few or no backing vocals, the two parts can be spread out right and left to add width to the sound. Often **panning to 10 o'clock and 2 o'clock** is enough. Going further risks divorcing the two parts and destabilising the mix.

EFFECTS ON VOCALS

Very subtle use of **chorus** or even **vibrato** (less than 10 per cent wet signal) can give a vocal a certain depth and texture, although I'm generally cautious about applying chorus or pitch detuning effects to lead vocals as it can detract from their immediacy. Where a lead vocal **delay** is used, adding subtle pitch modulation to the delays can be more effective – it adds texture without modifying the dry part of the sound.

While **stereo width enhancers** that use elaborate filtering or phase inversion may be used to good effect on **backing vocals**, they offer no real benefit on a lead vocal as the usual aim is to keep it up-front and in the middle. Such devices can also compromise mono compatibility to some extent (Stereo Width: A Warning, page 220). While the resulting small change in level or tonality might be acceptable in a backing part, it is best not to risk damage to the lead vocal.

Adding artificial **stereo width** to **harmonies** can be useful for pushing them outwards, away from the centrally-placed lead vocal, although where harmonies are layered, I usually favour panning the layers left and right of centre manually to create the necessary width.

ADVANCED VOCAL PRODUCTION TECHNIQUES

Tip / A common vocal thickening technique is to use a pitch shifter plug-in to add a slightly pitch-shifted version of the original signal to itself. A shift of between 4 and 7 cents (hundredths of a semitone) adds the necessary variance without making the vocal sound out of tune. Adding a delay of 20ms or so to the shifted version also helps thicken the sound. Plug-ins that can produce two pitch-shifted outputs at the same time can be used to add both positive and negative shifts (+6 and -5 cents used together is a popular combination), and if each output can be set to a slightly different delay time, so much the better. I tend to reserve this trick for backing vocals as, to my ears, it pushes a lead vocal too far back in the mix.

Tip / A variation on the above treatment is to combine it with any of the delay vocal treatments outlined above. By feeding the delay plug-in's input from a pitch shifter set as above but with a 50/50 wet/dry mix, the delays can be made to sound thicker and more textural without compromising the dry part of the sound.

Tip / One technique I devised using Auto-Tune as a pitch shifter in an attempt to replicate double-tracking failed to produce an authentic result but still created a useable and interesting musical effect. Make a copy of the lead vocal and place it on adjacent track on which is inserted an instance of Auto-Tune or similar. Set the musical scale then adjust the correction speed towards the slower end of the range. Played as is, the pitch variances between the tracks introduced by one being processed via Auto-Tune and one not creates a random phasing effect, not unlike the psychedelic tape

STEREO WIDTH: A WARNING

To my ears, artificial stereo enhancement plug-ins often sound a bit **too** artificial. If the results are appropriate on an artistic level then that's fine, but in my experience the 'naturalness' of a sound is usually inversely proportional to the number of plug-ins used.

If you do wish to add stereo spread, those processors that work by adding a polarity inverted version of the left channel to the right channel and vice versa are often safest as any added components cancel out when the mix is summed to mono.

Those that work by manipulating both EQ and phase (such as Q Sound, Spatializer or Roland's now defunct RSS system, sometimes known as 3D processors) to emulate the way the human ear perceives off-axis sounds can make the stereo width seem even wider than the speakers but note that mono compatibility often suffers.

It is also worth remembering that while dance mixes can sound spectacular in stereo, most club attendees find themselves closer to one of the stereo speakers than the other so any radical stereo effects can throw the overall balance out in situations where you can only hear one speaker. Worse still are those establishments that put the left speaker in one room and the right speaker in another!

As long as your main vocal and rhythm section is panned centrally, the damage done by ill-considered playback systems over which you have no control will be minimised.

Having issued these warnings, using one of the so-called 3D enhancement programs to place the occasional dry, bright vocal line right off to one side can add a nice surprise element – almost as though someone is whispering into the listener's ear.

phasing effects used in the '60s. The slower the retune speed, the slower the phasing effect. Try delaying the Auto-Tuned track by a few milliseconds for an augmented effect. You can also automate the retuning speed control to vary the amount of phasing at different points in the song.

Tip / If a vocal is too tame, add an overdrive or mild distortion plug-in into the track's effects chain. Those plug-ins that emulate overdriven valves, such as the PSP Vintage Warmer, produce a very natural and musical sound reminiscent of overdriven analogue tape. There are also plug-ins designed to emulate specific analogue tape recorders – right down to the choice of tape brand

and tape speed. You're unlikely to want anything too radical, but even a tiny amount can add a surprising degree of clout. The overdrive plug-in can be inserted anywhere in the effects chain – including in parallel compression and distortion setups. I'd normally avoid bit-crushers though as the distortion they add is enharmonic (although they can occasionally work magic on lo-fi downtempo vocals).

Tip / To turn a vocal into something that sounds more like a keyboard pad, set up a long reverb and feed its output through a rotary speaker emulator. The dense texture of the reverb will be coloured and modulated by the rotary speaker emulator giving it a non-vocal character. Try gently bringing up the effected signal underneath a sparse mix to add a bit of textural glue. You can try the same trick after a delay. Alan Parsons used a rotary speaker to add interest to the female backing vocals on Pink Floyd's 'Dark Side of the Moon'. John Lennon also sang through one to create the trademark trippy vocal sound used on The Beatles' 'Tomorrow Never Knows'.

Tip / You can add ghostly overtones to a vocal by asking the singer to whisper a double track instead of singing it. These whispered doubles can be effected to taste, often treated with an extra helping of reverb, and then added to the mix to re-enforce specific sung phrases for an effect that can sound both subtly haunting and ethereally chilled.

Tip / When parallel compressing a lead vocal line you don't have to stop at just one parallel bus. Mix engineer Michael Brauer (Rolling Stones, Coldplay) revealed to Sound On Sound that he sometimes routes lead vocals in parallel to five different compressors at once (page 175).

Tip / To create the classic 'telephone' effect, either use a convolution processor where a telephone (or radio) impulse response is available, or fake your own by adding a small amount of distortion and then bracketing the sound with steep high-and low-pass filters. Start with the low cut filter set at around 500Hz and the high at around 3kHz and then adjust to taste. A 24dB/octave slope usually gives good results. ●

AUTO-TUNE ABUSE

Despite its clichéd sound, the 'hard tune' Cher effect created when a pitch correction plug-in is set to its fastest retune speed seems reluctant to go away (page 196). Some plug-in manufacturers have even designed versions of the plug-in to exaggerate the effect.

The effect is easy to get. When working to a preset music scale with fastest retune the note will jump to the nearest note in the scale. This means a good singer has plenty of control over exactly when and where the note changes. All the natural slurs and vibrato are stripped

from the sound giving it a quality that is slightly robotic, not unlike a vocoder but without the loss of clarity.

The melody of the pitch corrected sound can be controlled with far greater precision using a plug-in that allows the pitch shift to be controlled live from a MIDI keyboard or MIDI DAW track. Here the MIDI track dictates the note that the vocal is shifted to, regardless of the singer's pitch. It sounds best when the singer is close to the right note, but even sloppy performances can be made to sound pretty good.

Very few tracks employ hard tune pitch correction all the way through. Most use it for select phrases – in which case just use automation to switch it on when you want it, or place the phrases you want hard-tuned on a different audio track with Auto-Tune on it.

A subtler technique is to use pitch correction alongside delay and/or EQ and/or reverb on selected vocal 'spins' to create wandering, perfectly-tuned delays that drift back in the mix. This is easy to achieve by feeding an aux send to a delay via a real-time pitch correction plug-in.

Auto-Tuned vocal spins

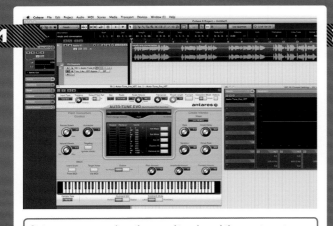

Set up an aux send on the vocal track and then automate this so that it only sends signal where required.

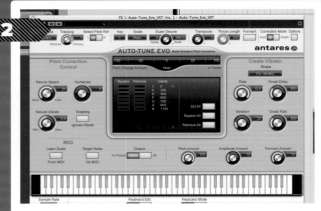

Insert a pitch correction plug-in before a delay plug-in (100% wet) on the aux bus, set the correct pitch scale then set the pitch correction speed to its fastest setting.

Adjust the delay line and any subsequent EQ or high end damping as required.

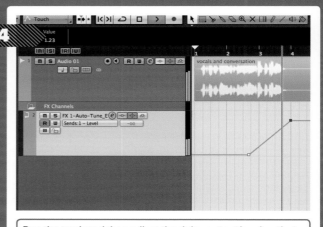

Run the track and then adjust the delay output level so that you hear the desired level of hard-tuned delays added to the natural vocal at the appropriate places in the song. Adjust the send automation timing and levels if necessary.

TIPS FOR A BETTER MIX

Don't compromise quality in the pursuit of loudness.
Excessive limiting and heavy mix compression make for a tiring mix. Where an extra 10 per cent of volume is required, leave the serious work to the mastering professionals: they're used to maximising loudness without ruining the sound.

COMMON MIX MISTAKES AND HOW TO AVOID THEM

The mix sounds too bright or too bassy.
A long mixing session can mess with your sense of perspective. Refer back to well-mixed commercial tracks regularly to keep the ears calibrated.

15
ELECTRIC GUITAR PRODUCTION

GUITARS IN THE MIX

Although synths and samplers rule supreme in today's dance music and a fair slice of pop production, the electric guitar remains a mainstay of many styles, from rock and metal to country, indie and power pop. It also plays an occasional but integral role in hip hop, R&B and noisy indie-dance tracks.

Given the sheer number of tones that can be generated at the recording stage (Recording Electric Guitar & Bass, Chapter 7), and the vast palette of sounds that a track might demand — from light jazzy plucks to full-on rock mayhem — attempting to generalise on how to make specific tones work in the mix is tricky.

What one can say is that in any typical guitar-led track, much of the producer's time — both when recording and mixing — will be spent sculpting and shaping the guitar tones so that they work in the context of the wider mix. This is particularly true for tracks with multiple distorted guitar parts — whether they are single tracks recorded in two or more ways, or multi-tracked guitars played by multiple players (often on different guitars).

While the kind of mild distortion used in blues tracks rarely presents significant mix difficulties, heavier distortion often does, especially when lots of dense chordal playing is involved. The reason behind this is the actual mechanism of distortion (see Jargon Buster, left).

The additional harmonics introduced with each new note compete for space with vocals and other instruments in the mid range — including other guitars — while the inherent compression effect makes the sound denser and more sustained.

Left to their own devices, heavily distorted guitars have a habit of dominating mixes, both in the frequency and time domains, with results that are typically muddy and aggressive, leaving little space for the producer to fit in other mid range instruments and vocals.

The problem is made worse if the guitar players rely on heavy distortion when playing live and feel they should be able to use the same settings in the studio — even when adding double tracks and overdubs that they don't / can't perform live.

The job of the producer is to engage any number of production (and psychological) approaches to improve the situation without having to resort to a pair of wire cutters. Some of these are engineering approaches, many are down to the musical arrangement (Chapter 18) and some hinge on the quality and style of the playing. For better or worse, most rely on the guitar player's co-operation, which is why the successful producer needs a good 'bedside manner', alongside their engineering skills.

BEFORE YOU START...

Before you begin pulling the different guitar tracks together in the mix, take a listen to some contemporary recordings in the style you're aiming for and see how the various parts fit together. Don't just listen to the guitars: see how they work within the wider arrangement and mix. What you hear may surprise you. Very often the electric guitar parts will be less bright and aggressive than the kind of tone the guitarist wants to use.

It's a fact of studio life that the inexperienced guitarist always want to create a huge sound all on their own, whereas the power in a well-produced

JARGON BUSTER: DISTORTION

Distortion adds a complex series of harmonics to the basic guitar sound while at the same time reducing the dynamic range of the instrument, much like a compressor.

This distortion becomes more complex with each additional note added to any chord,

This is because when a signal is distorted, sum and difference frequencies are generated that are related to the original frequencies; the more notes a chord includes, the more complex and confused these intermodulation products become.

If that sounds too technical, the practical outcome is that full chords create much more complex harmonics then single notes or 'root and fifth' power chords (page 226).

track comes from the combination of the various guitar parts and the bass.

The Who — a band that has inspired generations of guitarists — created songs that sound huge, even by today's standards. But if you listen to the different layers you find that the guitar sounds aren't nearly as distorted, bright or heavy as one might imagine. Add in the bass and in some cases the piano, though, and you get a result that is far bigger than the constituent parts suggest.

The truth is that when mixing, less is often more. Nowhere is this more true than when dealing with multiple guitar parts which, unless they are taking the centre-stage role in a solo, should be given supportive rhythmic and melodic roles, allowing the vocals to shine. Even in death metal, the vocal still manages to find a place above the guitars.

It's also worth re-iterating that golden mixing maxim: **not every track can shine**. In other words, don't process and EQ every track to sound fantastic in isolation or they will all end up at the front of the mix when you bring the faders up. **A well mixed track places the various sounds in a hierarchy of importance**, with the main sounds at the front of the mix and supporting ones placed further back.

Viewed in these terms, guitars should be mixed in the context of the whole song. The practical consequence of this is that guitar mixing is more often than not about reduction and control: reducing the EQ footprint and controlling the mid-range — in some cases discarding sections (and guitar parts) entirely.

All of this can be deeply troubling to the inexperienced guitarist who wants to dominate the mix. 'Less is more' is not a maxim welcomed by many guitarists — particularly those less experienced in studio work. If you can't persuade them to use what you feel is a more appropriate sound at source and you want to keep your mixing options open, plug their guitar into an active DI box feeding the Thru jack to the amp as usual and take the clean DI feed to a spare track on your DAW (page 230).

THE WAY THAT YOU PLAY IT
Getting a set of manageable (and malleable) guitar performances starts long before you turn the faders of the mix up. The recording method, and the way the amp is set up, play a pivotal role (Recording Electric Guitar & Bass, Chapter 7). But so do the playing techniques employed by the guitarist.

Over the decades a number of different playing methods have developed — some almost entirely for studio application. The use of **power chords**, **retuning**, **palm-damping** techniques and **part-playing** are all commonly used to give different sonic flavours to guitars. Used carefully these techniques can be used to create bigger, clearer and more confident guitar parts.

POWER CHORDS
The Who's Pete Townshend probably did more to establish the use of power chords than anyone. Today these chords are used in all manner of pop and rock styles.

Despite the name, a power chord isn't technically a chord at all as it only contains the root and fifth notes of the chord, along with octaves of these notes. Power chords are flexible; a 'root and fifth' power chord can be played in place of, or over, a major, minor or minor 7th (and a load of other

IN DEPTH: DISTORTION

Overdrive: The first level of guitar distortion is overdrive, which is intended to simulate the sound of an amp driven into mild distortion.

Distortion: has a more rocky, intense sound but it still sounds fairly natural – if distortion can ever be described as natural!

Fuzz: goes beyond normal distortion by clipping the audio waveform to produce something close to a square wave. Depending on any subsequent EQ, fuzz can sound raspy and bright or as mellow as a kazoo. Fuzz invariably sounds best on single lines or simple chords, and, because it can sound very dense, must be used carefully to avoid filling up all spaces in a mix.

And beyond: Today we have other distortion processes based on bit-crushing (where a digital signal is deliberately reduced in resolution until serious distortion is audible), ring modulators that produce dissonant tones by modulating the wanted sound with a second sound to produce only sum and difference frequencies, and phase distortion that uses the waveform of a signal to modulate its own delay time.

I sometimes use mild doses of phase distortion for adding a hint of 'fur' to bassy sounds, but other than that I feel these more extreme forms of distortion tend to sit rather better with synths and samples than they do with guitar!

chords too) with no musical conflict. The benefit of using power chords in the mix is that the root and fifth interval of the power chord produces far less aggressive intermodulation products when distortion is added than if full chords are used instead.

TWO-PASS TAKES

Another technique to create all the power without the sonic confusion is to record a single guitar part in two passes. On the first pass the guitarist might only play the top three strings of the chord, and on the second just the bottom three. Because there are fewer notes in each part, the intermodulation products are less complex. When the two parts are added together you get the full chord back but with less in the way of chaotic overtones: in other words, cleaner distortion.

The technique can be refined by varying the amount of distortion on the two passes to get, for example, a less dirty, more solid low-end alongside fizzier highs.

There's no need to stop with two passes either. Try recording three tracks playing two strings per track or even one note per track over six tracks: producers have tried them all. In most cases, though, splitting the chord in two achieves the desired result without changing the sound you would expect to hear from an electric guitar too radically.

If you have access to a Roland VG-series processor and a guitar with a GK pickup, try experimenting with guitar sounds that use a separate distortion processor for each string. The result is a distorted sound where every note retains its

separation and clarity – very different from the sound you get when all six strings go through a single distortion box in the usual way.

OPEN TUNING

An open tuning is one where the strings are tuned so that a chord is achieved without fretting (or pressing any of the strings). In the studio, open tunings can give a song a distinct character. Common variants include:

> tuning all open strings to Bs and Es so that any straight barre produces a power chord,

> tuning all strings to octaves of the same note to create more of a droning sound,

> tuning to an open major chord as 'Keef' does so often in The Rolling Stones (although he also removes the bottom E string when tuning to open G), and

> Nashville tuning (there are several variations on this), where you switch the bottom three strings of the guitar for strings half as thick and then tune them an octave higher than normal. This produces a ringing, 12-string type of sound but the lack of the low-tuned strings means the sound is always light and airy. This is a particularly useful sound for layering with other guitars.

Any of these tunings work on their own or on second parts when doubling a guitar line played in regular tuning.

DROP TUNING

Drop tunings use the familiar chord shapes, but with the guitar tuned to a lower pitch. Both Stevie Ray Vaughan and Jimi Hendrix regularly tuned to E flat rather than the plain old E that most of us use. In grunge, many players have tuned down to D or even used

TECHNIQUE: POWER CHORDS

Common power chord examples are the 'first shape' G major with the G string left open, the 'third shape' B major with the B string left open and the 'second shape' E chord with the bottom E, top E and B strings left open.

This latter chord is probably the most (over?) used power chord in rock music. The third shape A major, with first and second strings fretted at the fifth fret also features in many classic rock songs.

The way the power chord rings often means less distortion is needed to create an exciting sound. Free's timeless classic, 'Alright Now', for example, feels as if it is heavily distorted. But listen carefully to the record and you'll discover that the sound used is only very lightly distorted; it's the choice of chords that creates the desired effect, not brute-force distortion.

Baritone guitars with bottom B as the lowest note.

We also have specialised seven-string guitars that extend the lower range almost into the bass player's territory. At the same time, bass guitar designers seem intent on adding strings at both the top and bottom to allow them to play deeper low notes while straying into guitar range on the upper strings. Only good musical arrangement can avoid conflicts between these unnaturally high basses and low guitars.

Although drop tuning can make mixing a little tougher, it is an integral part of the sounds of certain genres – grunge and death metal being the most obvious examples.

DAMPING THE RHYTHM

If a distorted chord is simply strummed and allowed to ring until the next chord is played, you end up with a wall of sound that is hard for other instruments to break through. This presents particular problems in songs that feature prominent rhythm guitar tracks.

A common technique used in indie rock and metal to avoid this problem is for the rhythm player to employ subtle string damping using the palm of the picking hand or by an almost subconscious slackening of pressure on the fretted strings to create spaces in the sound and to give it a rhythmic shape. The technique is sometimes reffered to as 'chugging' when used to play an eight-to-the-bar rhythm.

DOUBLING PARTS

Double-tracking guitar parts (and sometimes tripling) is commonplace in modern guitar production. Doubling in this

context – playing the same part twice in two different takes – produces a very different sound from splitting a single guitar part and treating each 'split' in different ways. (See Layered distorted rhythm with DI signal walkthrough, page 230).

Before going any further here it's worth issuing a warning: **although doubling can add depth and texture to guitar parts, the double needs to be played very accurately to sound good**.

And unless the sounds of each part are chosen carefully, double-tracking can have the opposite of the desired effect: pushing parts further back in the mix rather than making them bigger. (Overall I tend to side with those producers who say that the more you layer a guitar part, the smaller-sounding it gets!)

If you do decide to double-track, the best results are usually achieved by:

> **Doubling the distorted part with a much less distorted part.** You might also use a different amp (or plug-in amp model) on the doubled track to introduce a greater variation in sound.

> **Switching guitars for each part.** Try a guitar with humbucking pickups for the first part and one with single coil pickups for the second. A variation of this technique is to use an acoustic guitar in place of the second electric guitar.

> **Using different chord inversions for the doubling part**, or even employing a capo to play chord inversions further up the neck so that you get a wider spread of notes in the combined track. If the sound is too thick, miss out the lower couple of strings of the layered chordal part. If you need more

weight, play only the bottom couple of strings on the second pass.

Tip / To reinforce a riff, have the guitar and bass play the same line. Although it's a familiar technique (whole lotta Zep anybody?) – and shouldn't be overused – it remains a goodie!

DI DOUBLES

If you've taken a dry feed from the guitar amp alongside the distorted sound during recording (page 123), try mixing in a compressed version of the clean feed alongside the distorted part. This is often enough to give extra clarity and definition to the guitar part, even when relatively little of the clean sound is added. This sounds very different from double-tracking – but is a useful ploy when you need to clean things up a little.

If the clean DI feed is a bit **too** clean, then use a guitar amp simulator to give it a more natural amp sound with a hint of edge and mix this with the original.

The two sounds can be panned to different sides of the stereo spectrum if the guitar part needs a wider spread – but this depends on whether any other guitars are playing at the same time. Where one of the sounds needs to be much louder than the other to give the required blend, you may need to adjust the pan positions of the two parts to keep the stereo image suitably balanced.

Tip / Many engineers get good results by mic'ing the strings of an electric guitar and mixing this signal in with the mic'ed amp sound. The guitarist must be playing in a quiet environment away from the amp for this to work.

GUITAR SEPARATION: ORGANIC METHODS

Treating a single guitar track is relatively easy. Where two guitar players are playing together, more attention has to be given to the parts they are playing and the sounds they use to help them fit in the mix.

Guitar separation is made significantly easier if you leave your options open at the recording stage.

Where the amp is recorded using **two mics**, one close and one out in the room, the balance of the two mics can be used to help position the sound appropriately; the close mic tends to pull sounds forward in the mix and the more distant room mic tends to push them further away.

Changing the balance between the two can be enough to provide separation between two guitars – especially where one plays an obvious lead role and the second provides support.

Mixing two guitar parts is made significantly easier if each player uses a different guitar and/or amp during recording to generate different tones. If one player is using a sound with a fair amount of low end grunt, the other can often be set to give a thinner sound.

The reason different guitars generate such different tones is down to their individual pickups, which exhibit resonant peaks that boost the sound of a specific part of the audio spectrum – rather like built-in EQ. A humbucker's resonant peak is at a lower frequency than that of a typical single coil pickup, for example.

One of the reasons for using different guitar types is to separate these peaks and

Layered distorted rhythm with DI signal

1 Record the mic'ed amp on one track while simultaneously recording a clean DI feed from the guitar onto a second track.

2 Use an amp modelling plug-in to shape the tone of the DI'd track.

3 Balance and pan the two tracks to taste.

4 If necessary EQ the mic'ed amp track and maybe add some compression to the DI'd version – especially if you're after a cleaner sound for that track. Using compression instead of overdrive adds the necessary sustain without adding dirt.

so organically stress different frequency ranges within each instrument.

EQ can be used to enhance this natural separation; simply cut Guitar A at Guitar B's resonant frequency and vice versa. This is easy to do by ear: just sweep the EQ between 1–4khz and listen for the stand-out resonant peaks (page 38).

Where you have two guitars that sound overly similar, you can use EQ cut to moderate the natural frequency peak in Guitar B and then use boost elsewhere in the same sound to create a new, artifical, peak at a different frequency. This has to be done carefully – you need both guitars to sound musical – but used effectively this kind of EQ treatment can really help separate similar sounds.

Tip / Although panning can be used to maximise separation, do your best to get the individual instruments in the mix to come through clearly when monitoring in mono first (page 287).

Tip / Remember that all panning decisions should be made in a full-mix context, with other instrumental parts playing. A guitar part panned to one side may work well counterbalanced by a synth part panned to the other.

Tip / Layered and doubled rhythm guitar parts are easier to control if fed via a single bus or controlled by a set of grouped faders (page 39). The bus route is also appropriate where you need to apply common processing to the whole rhythm guitar mix, such as compression or EQ.

EQ
The much-quoted golden rule of EQ is that cuts tends to sound more natural than

boosts, especially over narrow frequency ranges. This is largely down to the way the human ear perceives spectral balance; we are more sensitive to narrow peaks in a frequency response (like those made by a wah pedal) than to narrow dips like the kind produced using notch filters.

That's all well and good, but the electric guitar has never had a natural sound – it can be whatever you want it to be, so don't be shy of using more vigorous EQ to achieve the desired results.

Although the bottom string of a guitar generates useful frequencies as low down as 80Hz (lower with some tunings), you can usually get away with **cutting** everything below 50Hz, sometimes even 80Hz.

The unique **colouration** of the sound is most evident in the 400Hz–3kHz range. The higher end of this range is where you find a guitar's '**bite**'. Sweep a parametric EQ set to boost through this area to identify areas that sound interesting, as well as those that sound **boxy** or **aggressive**. Boost useful and characterful tones and reduce any rogue frequencies you find.

Check for **muddiness** in the 150–400Hz range, though be careful not to kill too much low-end **punch** if you're working on high-energy rock. The lower end of this range is best evaluated with the bass and drums playing; often what you think is a punchy guitar sound on a record is actually a combination of the guitar and bass.

Finally, one of the main uses of EQ when treating guitars – other than for altering the tonality of dual guitar parts to make them sound less similar – is for creating artifical dips in guitar parts to allow other instruments or voices to push through the mix.

Tip / Where EQ is used to cut guitars to create space for other elements, like vocals, consider automating the EQ so that it only cuts when the other instruments or voices are present.

ADJUSTING PHASE TO SHAPE THE TONE

I've warned about the perils of phase shift caused by time delays between signals before – for example when two different mics pick up the same source from different distances (page 74).

Phase shift introduces unnatural colouration caused by the comb filtering produced when a signal is added to a slightly delayed version of itself. Normally this is a bad thing, but in the world of electric guitars where the word 'natural' has no currency, phase-induced colouration can sometimes be used as a creative tone-shaping tool in its own right.

Where the guitar amp has been recorded with two mics – a close mic teamed with a second mic a metre or so out in the room – you can adjust the phase (and therefore the tone) of the combined signal by adjusting the distance of the room mic from the amp, its distance from the floor and the amp's distance from the floor.

If the tracks are already recorded, you can change the virtual position of the second mic using the track delay function in your DAW. Adding a millisecond (ms) of delay makes the track behave as if the mic was placed around 300mm further from the sound source, while a negative 1ms offset effectively brings the 'mic' 300mm or so closer. Each adjustment you make to the time (or the mic's actual physical position) influences the tone. You ears will tell you which setting works best.

You can get slightly different results by using a phase adjustment plug-in on the second mic. Unlike a simple delay, which affects all frequencies equally, phase adjustment plug-ins, modelled on analogue circuitry rather than digital delays, are frequency-dependent. As a result the colouration they introduce is slightly different.

GUITAR DUCKING

The technique of ducking, employed on a daily basis by radio DJs to ensure their speech remains louder than the music, can be used to keep chordal guitar parts out the way of the vocals. The ducker is inserted on the guitar track with its side-chain fed from the vocal track. The aim is to get the guitar level to drop by a small amount whenever the vocals are present.

Ducking is often performed using a compressor, with the lead vocal track triggering the compressor's side-chain. The compressor then pushes down the signal of the guitar when the vocal is present.

But using a compressor is not the only option, nor in my opinion is it the best. I've always found it fiddly to set up and it has a tendency to duck the guitar part most when it least needs it – specifically when the vocal part is at its loudest.

I prefer to use a gate for ducking instead, as you can set a precise amount of gain reduction to be applied whenever the vocal part exceeds the threshold you set.

You need a gate that allows the range of gain reduction to be set to a negative value as well as the more usual positive value. In other words, when the gate closes, instead of reducing the signal level, it increases it.

TECHNIQUE: CHOPPED GUITAR

One of the benefits of working to a sequencer grid is that effects can easily be synchronised to the tempo of the song, even where the song includes tempo changes. A classic technique that has found use in everything from rock and pop to dance is to set up a square wave tremolo effect set to 8th or 16th notes and then use this to chop sustained, distorted guitar chords.

Green Day used something similar on the opening to 'Boulevard of Broken Dreams' but I've sneaked this effect into lots of mixes, sometimes as a subtle rhythmic reinforcement, sometimes as a more obvious effect.

Most DAWs have a native plug-in that can recreate this effect, although you can just as easily use a gate triggered via its side-chain to achieve the same result. The side-chain is simply fed from a control track where you record a series of quantised drum hits in any pattern of your choice to control the chopping rhythm. See Chopped guitar walkthrough, page 237.

Using such a gate, simply feed the lead vocal into the gate's side-chain input then tweak the gain reduction range control to give the required amount of level ducking. Finally set the attack and release times so the ducking action feels natural, without becoming abrupt. The result is a gate on the guitar track that pushes the guitars up in volume when the vocal signal is not present. (Ducking using a gate walkthrough, page 234).

There are dedicated ducker plug-ins available if you feel more comfortable using something specifically designed for the job or if you don't have a gate plug-in with the features you need.

ROCK GUITAR

The early rock classics by bands such as Free, Led Zeppelin, Cream, The Who, Jimi Hendrix and The Rolling Stones – so often referenced by today's players – were mixed rather differently to today's tracks.

Back then the drums and bass guitar fulfilled a more supportive role, with guitar/s and vocal/s mixed up-front (although I always thought the Rolling Stones' vocals were too quiet!). Kick drums were all but inaudible and bass guitars sat at the bottom end of the audio spectrum well out the way of the guitars.

Today's rock producers tend to give drums far more prominence, with the bass mixed using much brighter tones to help it cut through. The resulting mixes feature busy mid-ranges, and specific care is required to stop them getting out of control.

Many rock and metal guitar sounds incorporate a mid-range dip or 'scoop'. This is partly due to the popularity of the Marshall amps used by so many guitarists.

The benefit of this scooped sound to the producer is that it allows the guitar to produce a solid chunk at the low end coupled with an assertive upper bite while the mid range dip helps carve a natural space for the vocals.

This scoop can be made deeper or wider with a subtle parametric EQ cut to suit the vocalist. Additional low cut can be used to remove some of the low cabinet thump from the sound if it is fighting for space with the bass.

GUITAR SOLOS

Guitar solos comprise mainly single note lines so are not usually hard to shape – although it may be necessary to pull down the level of any chordal guitar parts to make room for them. if this is necessary, set up a **ducker** controlled from the solo line. Any audible gain pumping in the chordal part will add to the track's sense of energy.

While some **EQ** may be required to fine-tune the tonality of the solo sound, an overdriven guitar rarely needs much additional processing other than, on occasion, some delay or reverb with pre-delay to create a bigger stadium rock sound.

As a rule, the faster the track, the less useful reverb will be, as it can muddy up the spaces between notes. **Delay** is often more flattering and need not be set extremely high in level. Delays of between 300–900ms can work well and are often set at or close to a multiple of the track tempo. Stereo delays, that bounce successive echoes from left to right, can add interest.

Reverb comes into its own in slower songs where there's plenty of space for it to do its magic without clouding the mix. Indeed

Ducking using a gate

1 Choose a gate that offers negative attenuation values (this example uses the native one in Logic Pro) and place it in the guitar track insert point.

2 Set the gate side-chain so that it is fed by the vocal track.

3 Use the threshold control to detect when the vocals are present and then set a negative attenuation value (here +5dB) to determine how much the level will increase when the vocal is not present.

4 Adjust the attack and release times so that the speed of the ducking sounds natural rather than too jerky.

TECHNIQUE: AUTO-TUNE SOLOS

Remember that where a solo is (largely) monophonic in nature – which is to say most solos! – you can shift notes into tune, or generate a more artifical sound, by inserting an instance of Auto-Tune or similar onto the solo track. See page 203.

slow blues songs, especially those in minor keys, can sound extremely evocative when dripping with reverb. Spring or plate settings usually work best with guitar unless you're specifically after a 'telecaster in the Taj Mahal' vibe.

Where a less distorted, or even clean sound, is being used for solos, **compression** helps keep the sound even and enhances sustain. Setting a longer compressor attack time can also emphasise the pick attack. Mark Knopfler's sound during his Dire Straits days is an excellent example of how well this can work. Simply increase the attack time by ear until you hear the distinctive pick attack and then set a fairly fast release time so that the compressor is allowed to reset between notes.

Guitarist John Mayer sounds as though he uses a lot of compression in combination with moderate distortion to produce an almost pedal-steel-like sustain in his blues-influenced style.

Tip / Mixing a guitar solo is often more about keeping other mix elements out of its way than modifying the sound of the solo itself. In most cases this isn't too difficult, as the guitar solo usually takes over from the main vocal and so can afford to be placed right at the front of the mix, with adequate level to cut through.

CLEAN GUITAR

With so many words given over to distorted guitars, it is easy to overlook those musical genres that use either clean or just very mildly distorted sounds.

Pop, folk, jazz and country styles frequently demand clean sounds, where a small amount of reverb and a touch of compression is often enough to sit the sound comfortably in the mix.

NEW TONES: THE E-BOW AND BEYOND

Although the E-Bow (right) has been on the market since the 1970s, this magical little sustain gadget is still relatively unknown. I've had countless guitar players come up to me at gigs to ask what it is and how it works.

The great thing about the E-Bow is that it can make single guitar strings sustain indefinitely. As you change its position over the string, the timbre also changes. It uses a sensing coil to pick up the string vibrations, which are then amplified and fed back onto the string via a second coil that provides the energy to keep the string vibrating. This is all powered by a nine volt battery.

As it focuses its magnetic field on only one string at a time, the E-Bow is strictly monophonic and some players adapt

to its quirks faster than others, but it produces a unique range of sounds rich in harmonically changing tones.

In the studio I've used multiple tracks of E-Bow to build up chordal pads, which sound very different from keyboard pads yet at the same time don't sound anything guitar-like. E-Bow-generated tones can also be used for spot effects, drones or simply to add texture to existing synth parts. Adding delay and modulation effects, such as chorus, adds useful movement and complexity to the sound.

If you like the idea of extended or even infinite sustain on all six strings at once, then the Fernandes Sustainer is a good choice. The down side is that it has to be retrofitted into a guitar (or you can buy a Fernandes guitar with one ready fitted).

At its highest setting the Fernandes Sustainer works rather like a polyphonic E-Bow, though at lower sustain settings it is extremely good at emulating the 'liveliness' of an instrument played at high volumes close to the amp, where notes close to feedback sustain for longer, with added harmonic complexity in the sound.

Modulation pedals such as **chorus** and **phase** (page 303) are often used during recording rather than being added at the mixing stage as guitar players often need to hear the effect to play appropriately.

Chorus was very popular back in the '80s with bands such as The Police, but it has now taken something of a back seat. in part this may be because chorus tends to push a sound back in the mix unless the song is very sparse – something that has fallen out of fashion in the current 'more of everything' production landscape.

Delay may also be used with clean guitar, the most significant historical example being the instrumental bands of the '60s, such as The Shadows and The Ventures. They used tape delay – it was all that was available at the time – so a tape delay plug-in or pedal might be appropriate if you're after this type of sound.

Other than a dedicated group of enthusiasts, this type of effect has largely been consigned to history, but its legacy can be be heard in the records of bands such as Pink Floyd and U2, where guitarist The Edge frequently uses synchronised delays to emphasise picked arpeggios played using a clean or slightly dirty guitar sound.

The amount of **EQ** work needed on a clean guitar part depends very much on the musical style and on the characteristic sound of the instrument and amp used during recording. You may only need to boost the 3–6kHz region to add **presence**, but in other cases you may also need to restrict the lows to produce a more focused sound that takes up less space in the mix – such as the accent guitar in a reggae mix.

▲ Echoes from Nomad Factory: One of a number of plug-ins that model original hardware tape delays.

SUMMARY

Getting multiple guitar parts, especially those involving distorted chords, to work in a mix is no trivial matter and can take a bit of trial and error – especially if you don't have the luxury of the clean DI'd guitar track/s to work with.

Life is a little easier if you're in at the recording stage. Invariably the best results start with a good musical arrangement, accurate tuning, solid playing techniques and careful attention to the choice of tonality and the placement of mics. Working closely with the guitarist to temper their natural inclination to dominate the mix can be important too.

But if you get it right, making a great guitar sound fit in a mix is one of the most satisfying parts of music production. ●

Chopped guitar

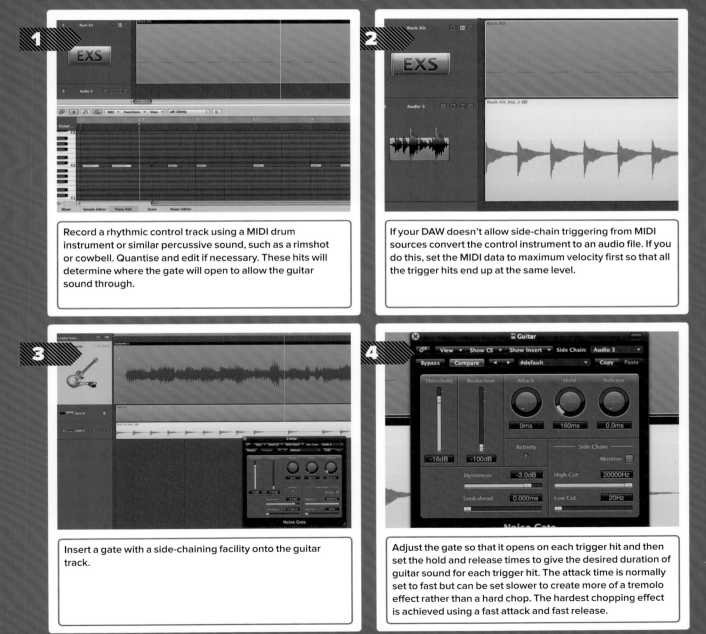

1 Record a rhythmic control track using a MIDI drum instrument or similar percussive sound, such as a rimshot or cowbell. Quantise and edit if necessary. These hits will determine where the gate will open to allow the guitar sound through.

2 If your DAW doesn't allow side-chain triggering from MIDI sources convert the control instrument to an audio file. If you do this, set the MIDI data to maximum velocity first so that all the trigger hits end up at the same level.

3 Insert a gate with a side-chaining facility onto the guitar track.

4 Adjust the gate so that it opens on each trigger hit and then set the hold and release times to give the desired duration of guitar sound for each trigger hit. The attack time is normally set to fast but can be set slower to create more of a tremolo effect rather than a hard chop. The hardest chopping effect is achieved using a fast attack and fast release.

16
DRUM PRODUCTION

> FROM A MIXING PERSPECTIVE THE SOURCE OF THE DRUMS IS TO SOME EXTENT IRRELEVANT; BOTH 'REAL' RECORDED ACOUSTIC KITS AND SOFTWARE-DERIVED DRUM SOUNDS ARE MIXED IN VERY SIMILAR WAYS.

THE SOURCES OF DRUMS

Drums in the mix come from one of three sources:

> **a recorded acoustic kit,** with any number of tracks for individual drums; can be as few as one, or as many as five or six plus overheads and room mics;

> **samples,** either triggered from hardware samplers, drum machines, software sampler plug-ins or from software instrument plug-ins such as BFD and Toontrack's Superior; or

> **a mix of the two,** with drum replacement and/or layering used to bulk up weaker recorded drum parts.

In some genres, including dance, urban, pop and some chillout/downtempo, the drums may be entirely **programmed**, the sounds sourced from samples or drum synth instruments such as NI's Maschine or Logic's Ultrabeat. Complete or part loops from commercial libraries may also be employed, either as the foundation of a groove or to add detail to a programmed backbone.

Meanwhile in rock, metal and some pop styles, drums are either sourced from live recordings, or by way of a software drum package based on high quality studio recordings of acoustic drums.

Sampled instruments from the likes of Stephen Slate, Toontrack, Native Instruments, XLN Audio and FXPansion all offer multi-mic'ed kits. These can be used as sound modules when programming drum parts or can be triggered from electronic drum pads via MIDI. Many include drum grooves as MIDI files.

Less natural and electronic drum sounds are well catered for by various sample libraries and plug-ins such as Spectrasonics' Stylus-RMX.

From a mixing perspective the source of the drums is to some extent irrelevant; both 'real' recorded acoustic kits and software-derived drum sounds are mixed in very similar ways, the main difference being that sampled drum instruments have the advantage of being recorded in world-class studios using a selection of great – and often rare – mics and pre-amps.

One practical difference is that for producers whose drums are provided by acoustic recordings, the preliminary task – before you begin tweaking any EQ or compression settings – is to assess whether any form of **drum replacement** or **layering** is necessary.

DRUM REPLACEMENT

You'll often have to work with bands that include an acoustic drum kit where the kit itself is less than ideal or where the drummer plays all the right beats in all the right places but doesn't hit the drums in the way needed to get a great sound.

Drum replacement is the process of using hits on the original drum track to trigger different sounds. It is an established part of modern drum production, its use ranging from the **specific** (underpinning a weak kick with an electronic one to add punch or replacing the snare drum with a different type) to the **complete-fix** (layering or substituting completely different drum sounds for the mic'ed sounds across a standard acoustic kit).

Drum replacement can be used on anything from kicks and snares to crash cymbals and toms. I'm not convinced that replacing ride cymbals is a good idea, though, as the process – as well as being

Drum replacement with a contact mic

1

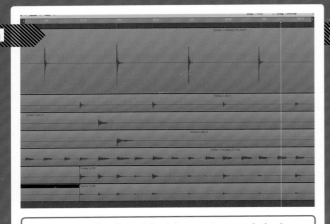

Audio screen showing original drum parts recorded using contact mics. The stereo overheads are shown on the bottom two tracks .

2

Clean up any parts to be replaced either by gating or editing out sections of spill to allow cleaner triggering. Don't worry about the gated signal sounding good — it only has to clean up the hits to make the triggering more positive. This is much easier when using contact mics as there is far less spill to worry about.

3

Insert a drum replacement plug-in. In this example Steven Slate's Trigger is used to replace the kick drum. The other drums are replaced in a similar way, but not the overheads as these include the cymbal sounds.

4

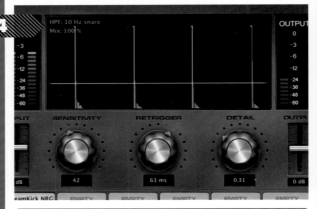

Adjust the Sensitivity and Retrigger time controls to reduce the amount of false triggering between hits. Retrigger sets a time after each hit during which additional retriggering is inhibited. This helps avoid accidental doubling caused when the plug-in is triggered twice from different parts of the same hit.

tiresome — strips away a lot of natural playing nuances. The same is generally true of hi-hats too.

Drum replacement is not only a problem solver, it can be used creatively too. It is routinely used in speed-metal production to create the relentless, punchy sound heard on records. Then there are layering tricks that add bulk to weak hits where a triggered sample is processed heavily and mixed with the dry, mic'ed drum sound to give a kind of layered parallel hit that makes use of both the original hit and the sample.

DRUM REPLACEMENT AFTER CONTACT MIC'ING

Where you know that drum replacement may be necessary, the best approach while recording is to fit contact mics to each of the drums (below) and record the signals from the mics onto separate DAW tracks.

There are various commercial contact mics, which either clip to the drum rim or are fixed to the head with adhesive so that they pick up the signal by direct vibration

rather than capturing the sound from the air. Rim-mounted contact mic triggers incorporate a transducer that contacts the edge of the drum head. The recorded sound is usually pretty bad, but the lack of significant spill from other drums makes it easy to derive a trigger pulse for triggering samples.

Where you intend to replace the entire kit's close-mic'ed sounds, but not the overheads, it can be useful to place commercial damping pads (for example, the rubber mat used for practicing) on the drum heads to minimise the sound of the hits being picked up in the overheads. The triggers will still work (though you may have to cut away a section of the damping pad to allow the trigger to still contact the head) but there will be little spill — all you get from the snare will be a damped click that will serve perfectly well as a trigger pulse.

If the drums are being recorded at the same time as other band members (Chapter 10), the sampled sounds triggered from the drums should be used to set up the monitor cue mix.

Where I know that drum sounds will need to be changed at the mixing stage, my own preference, if I can get the drummer to go along with it, is to set up real cymbals and a pair of overhead mics with a fully electronic drum kit — in my case a Roland TD12 kit. By using this setup you can record the cymbals using standard mic techniques (page 150) without too much noise from the pads, while also recording the MIDI data and some guide drum sounds from the V-Drum kit at the same time. It offers the best of both worlds — a natural feel to the overheads with the definition and flexibility of individually triggered MIDI drum samples.

TECHNIQUE: SNARE RATTLE

If snare rattle is a problem but you like the sound of the snare, record a few hits at different velocities with nothing else playing and create your own snare sample set. When you come to record the full kit you can then turn the snare off.

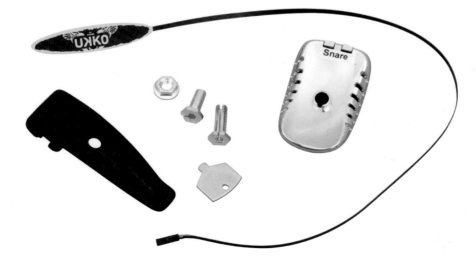

DRUM REPLACEMENT USING THE RECORDING OF AN ACOUSTIC KIT

Unfortunately, you don't always know in advance that replacement will be necessary. What do you do in situations where all you have is an audio recording of the drum kit? It is a common enough scenario, but be prepared to put in some work to get a good result.

The worst case is where you've got nothing to work with except a **single stereo (or mono!) file** of the entire drum kit. In this case there's not a huge amount you can do to mix in your own samples other than painfully programming in replacement parts to mirror the original drum track using MIDI or by pasting new samples into the DAW (Walkthrough, page 245). The waveform display will at least show you where the main kick and snare beats occur, giving you a visual reference to help you line up your samples. Be warned that this approach can take time, demand a lot of trial-and-error time-shifting and requires a careful choice of replacement or layered samples.

If you have the drums recorded on **separate tracks** then there's a lot more you can do. Software packages such as Drumagog, Avid's Sound Replacer, Toontrack's Drum Tracker, SPL's DrumXchanger (above right) and Stephen Slate's Trigger drum replacer are all designed to simplify drum replacement.

All of these require the drums to be recorded on separate tracks, ideally with as little spill as possible. Depending on the software, it may use a **real-time trigger** approach that detects the audio as it plays and then triggers the samples as the song plays, or an **offline process** where the

▲ SPL's DrumXchanger: One of the industry standard drum-replacement plug-ins. Simply set the Trigger and then choose a target sample.

mic'ed drum track is analysed by the plug-in before the trigger MIDI data is generated.

The difficult part in both approaches is getting the software to trigger accurately from the drum hits without generating spurious beats from any spill on the same track. Stephen Slate's drum replacer includes a means of summing the signals from the various mics to help cancel this 'crosstalk', but the less spill you have, the better the results will be.

HOW DRUM REPLACEMENT SOFTWARE WORKS

A typical drum replacement program uses gate-style threshold technology to identify individual beats while muting any remaining spill. It also translates the amplitude of each beat to a MIDI velocity value so that the MIDI data generated from the drum track triggers a series of samples that follow the dynamics of the original part.

Close-mic'ed **kicks** and **snares** are usually fairly easy to use as trigger sources as the amount of spill is typically fairly modest. EQ

> WHAT DO YOU DO IN SITUATIONS WHERE ALL YOU HAVE IS AN AUDIO RECORDING OF THE DRUM KIT? IT IS A COMMON ENOUGH SCENARIO, BUT BE PREPARED TO PUT IN SOME WORK TO GET A GOOD RESULT.

Drum replacement – mic'ed kit

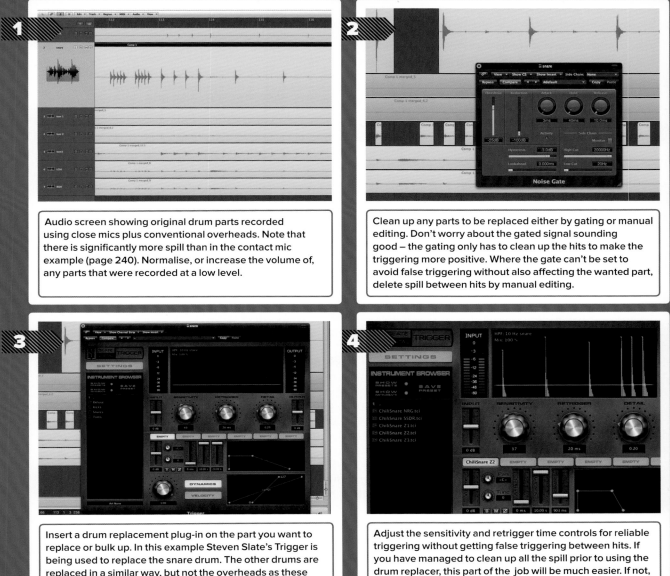

1 Audio screen showing original drum parts recorded using close mics plus conventional overheads. Note that there is significantly more spill than in the contact mic example (page 240). Normalise, or increase the volume of, any parts that were recorded at a low level.

2 Clean up any parts to be replaced either by gating or manual editing. Don't worry about the gated signal sounding good – the gating only has to clean up the hits to make the triggering more positive. Where the gate can't be set to avoid false triggering without also affecting the wanted part, delete spill between hits by manual editing.

3 Insert a drum replacement plug-in on the part you want to replace or bulk up. In this example Steven Slate's Trigger is being used to replace the snare drum. The other drums are replaced in a similar way, but not the overheads as these include the cymbal sounds.

4 Adjust the sensitivity and retrigger time controls for reliable triggering without getting false triggering between hits. If you have managed to clean up all the spill prior to using the drum replacer, this part of the job will be much easier. If not, you may need to return to Step 2 to further clean up the raw recording/s.

can be used to exclude remaining spill while enhancing the wanted sound. Remember it doesn't matter how nasty the drums sound at this stage – as long as the individual hits are clearly defined.

Tom-toms can be trickier to replace as they tend to suffer from a lot of spill. They also resonate in sympathy with other drums. Fortunately, few songs include more than a few dozen tom hits, meaning you can use the DAW's waveform editor to manually remove all unwanted material between the hits (page 257).

It might sound tedious but this manual editing clean-up operation usually only takes a few minutes and makes triggering much more reliable; just ensure that you cut directly before the attack of each hit to preserve accurate timing. If your DAW offers a tab-to-transient feature it makes identifying the individual beats a little quicker.

I don't often need to replace **hi-hats**. Where it is necessary, it helps enormously to use manual editing to split the closed and open hats to separate tracks so that they can be used to trigger separate open and closed hat samples. That said, I try to avoid hi-hat replacement: real hi-hats produce many different open, closed and part-open sounds that an automatic replacement plug-in simply can't differentiate. There's also likely to be a lot of hi-hat signal in the overheads.

Although dedicated drum replacement software usually gives the best results when you need to replace drums, an alternative **'old-school' approach** is to use EQ, gating and manual editing techniques to separate out the individual drum hits.

If your DAW offers it, you can use its audio-to-MIDI conversion routine to create

THE RIGHT REPLACEMENT

Just because the best sampled drums sound clean and punchy doesn't necessarily mean they'll fit in with the track in terms of dynamics, flavour or character. You need to ensure that you are introducing the **right** kind of sound in place of its lacklustre predecessor.

Because it's rare that the contribution of the overhead mics can be left out of the mix entirely, the sounds chosen for replacement must be selected to blend with what's heard in the overheads too. Equally you need to pick a sound that gels with the rest of the kit – that sounds as if it could be a part of the kit.

It's also worth remembering that drum sounds are pitched sounds – that is, they have a pitch which may occasionally relate to the key of the wider track, or more likely, to the other drums in the kit. Spending time auditioning replacement samples to find the right sound is usually time very well spent.

a series of MIDI notes with velocities corresponding to the intensity of the hits. You may need to shift the notes in the DAW's grid editor so that they correspond to the MIDI note number of the sound you want to trigger in the sampler.

The same comments about erasing sections of high-level spill still apply.

A QUESTION OF TIMING
Using automatic drum replacement software to generate MIDI data is often a relatively quick and efficient process, but it is not foolproof and requires some care from the producer to ensure that:

❭ **the timing of the replaced sounds is correct against the original recording**. To check this, open the original recording in the sample editor then check that the newly-generated MIDI hits are perfectly aligned with the original hits. If they're not, shift them accordingly.

❭ **the hit velocities have been correctly interpreted**. Again, if they're not, go into the MIDI file and adjust as required.

Drum replacement on a stereo file

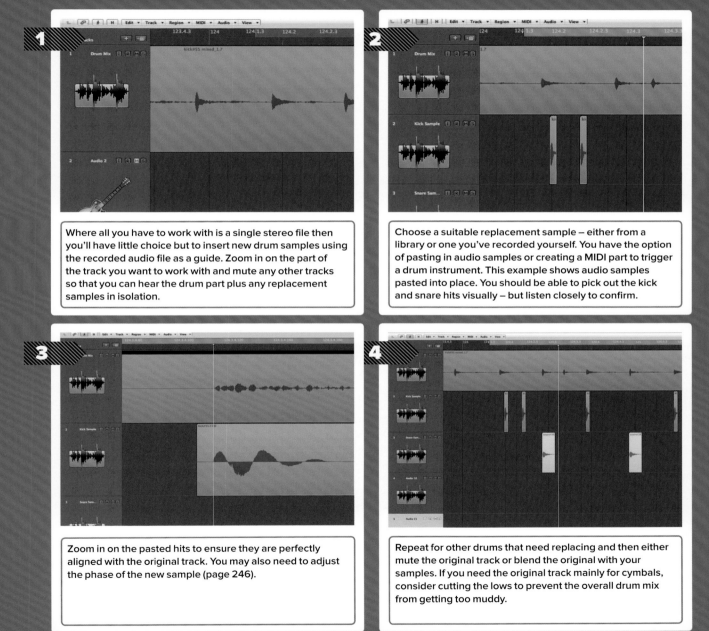

1 Where all you have to work with is a single stereo file then you'll have little choice but to insert new drum samples using the recorded audio file as a guide. Zoom in on the part of the track you want to work with and mute any other tracks so that you can hear the drum part plus any replacement samples in isolation.

2 Choose a suitable replacement sample – either from a library or one you've recorded yourself. You have the option of pasting in audio samples or creating a MIDI part to trigger a drum instrument. This example shows audio samples pasted into place. You should be able to pick out the kick and snare hits visually – but listen closely to confirm.

3 Zoom in on the pasted hits to ensure they are perfectly aligned with the original track. You may also need to adjust the phase of the new sample (page 246).

4 Repeat for other drums that need replacing and then either mute the original track or blend the original with your samples. If you need the original track mainly for cymbals, consider cutting the lows to prevent the overall drum mix from getting too muddy.

> **all hits are present**. Missing or weakly-played hits may need to be corrected.

> **there are no falsely triggered notes**. Edit the MIDI data to remove any present. Be wary of retiming hits that have been played with less than ideal precision unless you also edit the original drum recording or you'll end up with a flamming or doubling sound due to the timing difference between the new sample and the drum picked up by the close and overhead mics. If there is a timing problem it's often more effective to copy an entire bar of all drum tracks from elsewhere in the song and replace the wonky bar in full.

When the MIDI hits accurately reflect the hits in the original audio file and you're happy with the replacement samples then you can either leave the MIDI track as is, and treat the samples using plug-ins, or you can bounce the replacement sample track down as a new audio file to be treated that way. However, check out the comments about **phase**, below, before doing so.

Tip / When replacing drum sounds it can be beneficial to remove as much of the signal you're replacing from the overhead mics (and/or room mics) as possible to avoid blurring the definition of the new sample and introducing potential phase issues. To reduce the contribution of individual drum sounds in the overheads, use low-cut filtering to preserve the cymbal sounds while thinning out the low end of the drum hits as much as possible.

PHASE

When **layering** new drums with the original recorded parts rather than replacing them completely, it is essential to check that the phase of the original drum hits and the replacement samples is the same. Failing

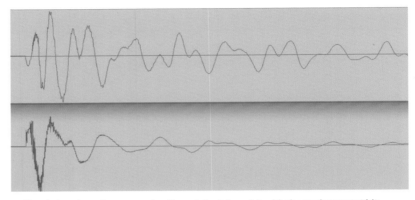

▲ Check the phase by comparing the original drum hit with the replacement hit. Ensure the start of the drum hits are aligned and that both waveforms set off in the same direction. In this example both waveforms set off in different directions.

to do so can result in tonal changes and a loss of low frequencies.

Even when **replacing** drums, it helps to align the phase of the new sound with what the overheads have picked up, although applying low-cut filtering to the overheads reduces the effects of comb filtering (page 74), which causes problems mainly at low frequencies.

To check the phase, start by ensuring the start of the drum hits (original and replacement) are aligned and that both waveforms set off in the same direction (see screengrabs, above). If one goes negative while the other goes positive, insert a **polarity inversion plug-in** on the track carrying the replacement drum part. The waveforms won't stay in phase after the initial hit as the drums will invariably be tuned differently, but if you can get the attacks lined up and in-phase, the sounds will blend much better.

You can fine-tune the sound by changing the timing of the replaced track by a tiny

TECHNIQUE: GROUPING

Use the DAW's grouping feature when editing single drum tracks you've recorded. The edit will automatically be applied to all drum tracks.

amount in either direction to see if you can bring about a further audible improvement or increase in low end. Rather than aligning the attacks, for example, you might try aligning the peaks of the first waveform following the attack instead.

MIXING SAMPLED KITS

Sampled kits generally present the least amount of work in the mix. They are typically well recorded in flattering rooms, and the plug-in instrument will usually allow you to bring in a little of the room sound to add the required ambience. Where this doesn't sound right for the track you can always turn down the virtual room mic channels and add your own reverb or ambience instead.

If you add your own **reverb** it helps to have the sampled instrument set up so that its multiple outputs, corresponding to the various mics, are allocated to separate DAW tracks. By running the different drum mics on separate tracks you can process each one differently.

While little corrective **EQ** is usually needed with anything as well recorded as a sampled drum kit, you may wish to add different amounts of **reverb** or ambience to the various drums.

The **kick** mic shouldn't need any extra reverb, but the other drums might benefit from some room ambience. Depending on the style of music, the **snare** might benefit from a little plate or other reverb. The **overheads** will already include a degree of room ambience. Unless you're after a particularly wet drum sound these can usually be left as they are.

In fact, 90 per cent of the time the secret to getting a good drum sound from a sampled drum instrument is not down to the treatment of individual sounds, but balancing the volumes of the various kit mics. This balancing process turns out to be much the same as that used to balance a live acoustic kit.

MIXING ACOUSTIC KITS

There are two main approaches to balancing an acoustic kit. Both give different results.

Close mics first: The first approach is to rely mainly on the close mics, adding just enough of the overheads to balance the cymbals with the rest of the kit. Concentrating on the close mics produces a tight, fairly dry sound that doesn't take up too much space in a mix, but which still delivers a solid punch. Reverb (often convolution) is used to generate the necessary ambience. If you

AWKWARD REPLACEMENTS: DRUM FILLS

Most automatic drum replacement plug-ins do a fair job where the drummer is playing a simple beat.

But they have a decidedly tougher time where a drum fill includes a lot of closely-spaced hits or flams. How successful you can be when tidying these kinds of fills depends largely on whether cymbals are playing at the same time or not.

With complex fills I generally let the plug-in do its work on the easy parts and then manually edit out the pauses between the other hits in the fill (and in some cases, shorten the hits so they don't run into each other). The hits are then moved into place so that the fill sounds natural. But while you can usually chop up and move individual beats in the overhead tracks, you can't always remove the

sounds between the beats, as the process disrupts cymbals audible in the overheads.

If you're still struggling you might have to copy a fill from elsewhere, slice it and then tighten up the timing, or in some cases lose the overhead mics altogether during the fill and program in a crash cymbal at the start or end of the bar to cover what's missing.

need more cymbals you can use EQ to lift them in the overhead mic/s, sometimes in combination with some judicious low cuts.

Overheads first: The second approach is based on early recording methods where only one or two mics were used to capture the whole kit. What you got was the naturally balanced kit, alongside the sound of the room it was played in. While this can sound nice for jazz, it isn't punchy enough for most pop work and there's no way to adjust or treat the individual drums if the balance is less than ideal. To get around these limitations, close mics are added on the individual drums and sometimes the hi-hat, but rather than these being used as the basis for the main drum sound, they are mixed in at a lower level – primarily as a means of balancing the main overhead signal.

Today's producers generally choose the latter 'overheads first', approach. The genre is key too: 'overheads first' gives a more natural kit sound, which suits some genres better than others. 'Close mics first' is often more effective with power pop and rock styles where punch is the order of the day.

EQ

If you recorded the drums in your own studio the individual drum sounds may benefit from a little EQ to get the best from them. As with any EQ, the overall effect should be judged in the context of the whole mix.

A common mistake is to mix the drums too bright in the mistaken hope that it will help them cut through the mix. Pushing up the highs and upper mids will help the drums cut through, it's true, but too much brightness generates conflicts with other instruments; before long you're left with a crowded, harsh and overbearing mix.

In fact, the secret to in-your-face drums isn't lots of high EQ. If you listen to well-produced pop tracks you'll notice that the drums are a lot less bright than you might have imagined. Drums are mixed to drive and underpin the track, not trample all over it. In underground dance the drum and percussion sounds are carefully chosen so that the cymbals don't dominate the high end. The same is true in urban productions, where hi-hats are either mixed low, or are absent altogether, their place taken by sparse mid-heavy shakers. Some artists eschew the high-end altogether: Peter Gabriel went through a phase of not using any cymbals at all; the resulting arrangements sound really open and clean because of it.

THE KICK DRUM

In modern production the kick drum is invariably the most important drum in the kit. It drives the rhythm and, alongside the bassline, underpins the groove. It provides a foundation upon which the other rhythmic elements sit, and on which all other melodic parts rest.

The kick's relationship with the bassline is paramount. No other mix elements share such a close space in terms of both their frequencies and dynamic impact. For this reason you should ensure that the bass part is playing when you make any major adjustments to the kick drum EQ or dynamics.

The main frequency areas of interest when dealing with kick drums are:
> **30Hz and below:** Unhelpful sub-bass frequencies
> **60–90Hz:** Fundamental punch

TECHNIQUE: PANNING

Where the overhead mics are recorded in stereo, the usual panning strategy for the close mics is to match the corresponding drum positions in the overheads but without making the kit seem unrealistically wide. Be careful not to pan the toms so wide that the drum kit stretches from the extreme left of the soundstage to the extreme right.

Whether you choose to mix the kit from the drummer's view or the audience perspective is up to you, but don't end up with the toms in the overheads panned one way and the close mic'ed toms the other or you'll dilute the stereo image of the kit.

Other than that there's not much to say about panning: the kick usually sits centre-stage, as does the snare, with claps and other ear candy a little left or right. Additional percussion is panned wherever feels right. The hi-hat is usually placed just slightly off centre to mirror its physical placement in the drum kit.

> **150–250Hz:** Tubbiness or boxiness
> **3–6kHz:** Click and clarity.

Typical EQ tweaks to the kick drum include **carving space for the bassline**, gently **cutting any boxiness** and easing up the upper mids to **bring out the click**. To beef up the kick sound without making it sound muddy **add boost at the fundamental frequency** of the sound (usually around 80Hz) and then use an **EQ dip** around an octave higher (around 160Hz) to avoid any muddy build-up. This works well in the 'fat kick, skinny bass' mixing scenario (page 293).

Before doing any compression ensure that the kick channel is gated to remove any spill. The **gate** must come before the compressor as once a signal is compressed its dynamic range is reduced, making it harder to set a gate threshold that effectively differentiates the loud sounds from the spill. If the kick rings on too long, a shorter gate release time can help clean it up. As with all drums, use a fast gate attack setting with lookahead where available.

Compression can be used to enhance the attack of the kick by setting an attack time long enough to let the initial 'click' transient through before the gain reduction kicks in. This can be anything between 10–50ms depending on the sound you're after. Set the release time to be as long as possible while still allowing the compressor to reset before the next kick comes along. The exact timing will depend on how busy the kick part is and on the tempo of the song; a 100ms release time is a good starting point. A ratio of between 3:1–5:1 combined with a peak (rather then RMS) setting, usually delivers good results. As a rule, the more evenly the kick is played, the less compression you're likely to need.

Before the advent of the sampler, weedy kick drum sounds were often bolstered by placing a gate on the output of an **oscillator** running at between 60–80Hz and then triggering the gate from the kick track to add a short burst of bass frequency to underpin the kick. The oscillator was usually tuned to the key of the track. It's a trick still used today, although you can just as effectively use a different (complementary) drum sample, or even a synth sound.

If the compressor is not giving the kick the kind of dynamic shape you want, try

KICK AND BASS: A PIVOTAL PARTNERSHIP

The sonic relationship between the kick drum and the bassline is probably the most important sonic relationship in most forms of dance, rock, urban and pop music. Not only does it define the groove, it also anchors everything that goes above it (page 293).

It is important to note that the bass should be playing while you make any key decisions relating to the kick – including on EQ, compression or drum replacement.

A common technique for ensuring that the kick and bass work together, rather than fight each other for space and clarity, is to pick sounds that complement each other. This usually means a low-end bassline with a bass-light kick or a less deep sounding bassline with a sub-heavy kick.

It can be helpful to mentally picture where each part is at its strongest in EQ terms while you mix the two; your job as

a producer is to ensure that they don't both peak at the same point in the audio spectrum. Arranging a ducker to drop the level of the bass slightly whenever the kick comes along can help improve separation as well as foster a sense of energy and power.

You'll know when you have it right as both the bass and kick will remain audible as distinctly separate sounds, with each supporting the other.

inserting a **transient designer** plug-in into the channel and further tweaking the attack and release times there. Use such plug-ins with care though: it's easy to generate unnaturally spiky results.

SNARE DRUM

Snare drums generate a wide range of frequencies due to the vibration of their wire snares. The main frequency areas of interest are:

> **120–180Hz:** Weight and punch
> **180–300Hz:** Boxiness
> **1–2kHz:** Snap
> **3+kHz:** Attack and presence.

Altering the snare's timbre may be as easy as giving it a gentle **EQ** cut or boost in the relevant frequency area. Often more useful are **distortion** or **harmonic enhancer** plug-ins for creating crisper sounds without the harshness.

Where you had a separate mic on the bottom of the snare (don't forget to flip the polarity to put it back 'in-phase' with the top mic), try adding **distortion** or **enhancement** to the **bottom mic** alone.

If the snare lacks weight and you can't EQ it back in, try using a **sub-octave plug-in** and mix in a little wet signal (start at 10 per cent and increase to taste) to add more weight to the bottom end.

Where a sub-bass plug-in doesn't produce the right kind of boost, try using **drum replacement** to layer another sound with the snare to beef it up. This might be a different sampled snare drum (one with the necessary lows), a purely electronic sound from a synth or even a different sample such as a short tom hit or some form of low-pitched ethnic drum. Use a **gate** on the snare close mic to close

down the channel between hits to reduce the effect of snare buzz and hi-hat spill, adjusting the gate decay time to follow the natural decay of the drum sound. Use a fast attack with look-ahead if the plug-in offers that feature (page 259).

Compression can be used to emphasise the attack of the snare drum using similar settings to those outlined for the kick (you may also want to re-read the start of **Compression & Dynamics 101, Chapter 11**, which includes a detailed outline of how compression affects a snare drum sound).

Reverb can be added to enhance the sense of space; today's fashion is for short, fairly dry reverb sounds rather than the expansive washes that dominated in the '80s. If you're using sampled drums that have room mics built in, a little of the room ambience may be all you need. A subtle application of gated reverb can also be used to stretch a skinny snare sound.

Tip / A classic trick for adding definition and character to an otherwise standard snare, made famous by a generation of house producers, is to trigger a second snare, or clap, sample (usually one rich in higher frequencies) slightly before or after the main snare hit. The result impacts both on the groove (making it subtly faster or lazier depending on where the second snare/clap hits) and the clarity of the snare itself, bringing into tighter definition the snare's contribution to the beat. Experiment with the stereo width and reverb settings of the added hit to ease it naturally into the groove. You can take the technique one step further by adding a reversed snare or clap sample immediately before the main snare hit for a 'breathing' snare sound that eases into the next beat.

TOMS

Editing out the spill spaces from between tom hits helps keep the resonating heads from muddying the drum sound. The tom signal in the overheads disguises these edits very effectively. If you can achieve this using a **gate** that's fine, but in many cases other drums hits cause the gate to trigger unnecessarily. Often it's best to **manually edit** the tom track (page 257). The main aim is to keep the tom tracks free of anything that isn't an intentional tom hit.

While it may be tempting to find the resonant frequency of a tom and boost that to add more punch, toms often sound better with some **low-cut filtering** to trim away anything below 80–100Hz and, where more definition is required, some gentle parametric boost in the 3–6kHz region. Excessive boxiness can usually be fixed by sweeping an EQ boost between 100–250Hz to find the fundamental frequency and then applying an EQ dip around an octave higher.

Tip / Always evaluate the final tom and snare sounds with the overhead mics turned up as these make a significant contribution to the overall sound.

OVERHEADS

Before you start mixing in the overheads, and if you have not already done so, try setting a **negative delay** on the overhead mic track (typically around 3–4ms) to bring the waveform into perfect alignment with the snare. This can result in a better sense of focus and clarity. You should hear the sound focus itself when you pass through the correct delay value.

If you've chosen the 'overheads first' approach when mixing the drums you may need to use an **EQ** cut to reduce boxiness in the 150–250Hz region. Trimming away

the very low bass below 60–80Hz can help keep the end result sounding clean and well-focused.

Unless the room in which the recording was made was very dry sounding you may not need to add **reverb** or ambience to the overheads. If it is required, use it sparingly.

If you've taken the alternative 'close mics first' approach, you can afford to trim significantly more low end from the overheads so that they are left to carry mainly the cymbals and the stick attacks on the drum heads. A gentle 6dB/octave sloping low-cut filter set as high as 200–300Hz usually manages this in a natural way. Not only does filtering out the lows from the overheads clean up the sound, it also avoids phase cancellation problems at the low end of the spectrum that might otherwise compromise the all-important bass end of the drums.

ROOM MICS

Room mics located further from the kit can add a significant amount of room **ambience** to the sound, which in some studios sounds fabulous. In others it just sounds messy. Sometimes adding a little of this room signal helps bring the kit to life and glue the constituent sounds together, but unless you want a 'drums in garage' effect, tread lightly.

While the room mic's contribution might sound impressively brash and exciting – especially if you **compress** the hell out of it – it also has the effect of filling in the spaces between drum hits, leaving less room for everything else in the mix. This can work in your favour when trying to get a big sound from, say, a three-piece rock band, but in a busy mix you may be better off opting for a tighter, more compact drum sound.

If you don't have space for room mics while recording but want to emulate the effect, take a send from the stereo overhead mics track, feed it via a delay of between 10–20ms and then add a **convolution reverb** loaded with an IR taken from a suitable room. Compress this for a more aggressive sound (try an SSL-style talkback compressor) and then mix the squashed signal back in with the rest of the drum mix, starting at a low level and then fading it up until the balance sounds right.

THE DRUM BUS

Once you have the kit balanced and you're happy with any reverb or ambience effects, leave the drums as they are and move on to concentrate on another aspect of the mix for a while. You might also play some commercial records to help recalibrate your ears. When you've had a good break, return to the drums.

How do they sound with fresh ears? Does the amount of reverb and ambience suit the rest of the mix? Too much will sound messy while too little can separate the drums from the other instruments, pushing them 'outside' the mix. Does the overall drum kit sound too bassy or toppy? Is there too much lower mid muddiness? If so, it's time to get out your highest quality **EQ** to see if you can strike a better tonal balance – though don't make any overall EQ decisions unless the rest of the track is playing.

It's worth noting here that life is much easier if all drums are routed via the same **group bus** (page 39). When they're bused you can do any necessary EQing and compression to the whole group – as well as easily changing the volume of the whole drum kit in relation to other mix elements – rather than going through each drum track to perform the same tweaks.

If the whole kit lacks energy, putting a **compressor** across the drum bus can help. Bus compression can also add a subtle (or not so subtle) sonic glue to the group – especially useful when a number of mics have been used across the kit.

To add a bit of 'squash' to the overall kit sound choose a 'drums' preset with a ratio of around 2:1 and then adjust the threshold until you see around 4dB of gain reduction, ensuring that your ears, not your eyes, make the final decision as to how much gain reduction sounds right. Increasing the attack will allow the transient hits to come through clearly. Leave the release time on auto or set to between 100–200ms.

Where even more power is needed, set up a **parallel compressor** (page 172) fed from an aux send on the drums subgroup. This can add serious bulk to a full drum kit, but be wary of pushing it too far. You can also use parallel compression to introduce a different flavour to a drum mix – enhancing its sense of power and energy.

LAST WORDS

Drum mixing doesn't happen in an audio vacuum. It happens in the context of the full mix, and specifically, alongside the bassline. Indeed many engineers start by balancing the drums, bass and vocals. Once they're right, the other instruments are brought into the mix around them.

When the drums are sounding good, and are working with the bass to provide a solid and well-defined rhythmic backbone to the track, then you're ready to start pulling the other constituent instruments into the mix knowing that any remaining tweaks to the drums will be about detail alone. Get these rythmic fundamentals right and the rest should fit neatly into place. ●

TOOLS OF THE TRADE

It's worth using the highest quality compressor you have on the drum bus.

1176 or dbx 160 models are popular for use with drums, as is the SSL Mix Bus compressor.

The spectacularly trashy SSL Listen Mic Compressor is less than ideal for bus compression but makes a great parallel compressor.

TIPS FOR A BETTER MIX

In the closing stages of a mixdown, remember to take regular breaks.
When you return to the mix you'll find it much easier to identify if it is sounding well-balanced.

COMMON MIX MISTAKES AND HOW TO AVOID THEM

Ear fatigue is resulting in poor mix decisions.
Don't mix with your monitoring set too loud, and don't mix for overly long periods – both will tire your ears quickly.

17
PRE-MIX
HOUSEKEEPING

Audio 4#06

Audio 5#02

Audio 5#03

THE BEST PERFORMED RECORDINGS MADE USING THE BEST EQUIPMENT STILL BENEFIT FROM A CLEAN-UP AND SOME TECHNICAL TWEAKING.

PLANNING THE MIX

When you have finished the recording process, hopefully with a selection of strong material, and when you've got a rough arrangement laid out, then you're ready to start planning the mix.

Before beginning the mix proper there are a few routine housekeeping tasks relating to the audio tracks and mixer setup that will make your life easier and the mix cleaner as you blend the various tracks into the final master recording. They include:

❯ **Cleaning up the audio**, removing apparently silent sections that may contain low-level noise,

❯ **Editing out unwanted spill during pauses**,

❯ Checking that any **drum replacement samples** are in time and in-phase with the original parts,

❯ **Reducing the level of guitar noise** at the starts and ends of phrases,

❯ **Cutting unwanted low and high frequencies** on selected tracks,

❯ Doing any **fine-tuning and editing** in Melodyne or other offline pitch correction software where applicable,

❯ Setting up **fader and/or bus groups**,

❯ Sorting out any **timing issues** – moving audio in time where necessary,

❯ **Consolidating MIDI instruments**,

❯ **Re-arranging** and **colouring tracks** in the DAW, and

❯ **Backing up** the project's audio files.

TRACK CLEANUP

Even the best photos benefit from some Photoshop tweaking: some brightening here, some sharpening there. These days digital post-production is part of the photographer's art and can help achieve results that are better than real life.

The same is true of audio. The best performed recordings made using the best equipment still benefit from a clean-up and some technical tweaking.

Top professionals let their assistants take care of these rather mundane jobs, but in the real world most of have to do it ourselves.

The first job is usually **removing any apparently silent sections of audio** that may contain noise; either electrical hiss or unwanted physical noises captured by the mic, like paper rustling, chair squeaks and performers breathing.

Even where the amount of noise between sections of wanted audio seems to be acceptably low, the cumulative noise from 24 or more tracks of audio can add up to be quite significant.

The DAW environment makes the cleanup process relatively easy. It's simply a case of using the scissors tool or equivalent to divide tracks into wanted and unwanted sections of audio before trimming them to length and removing or muting the unwanted sections (page 256).

The same editing technique can be used to remove unwanted spill from instruments like drums – although you have to be careful in situations where the level of spill is significant as the sudden disappearance and reappearance of spill at each edit point can be more obvious

WALKTHROUGH The audio clean-up

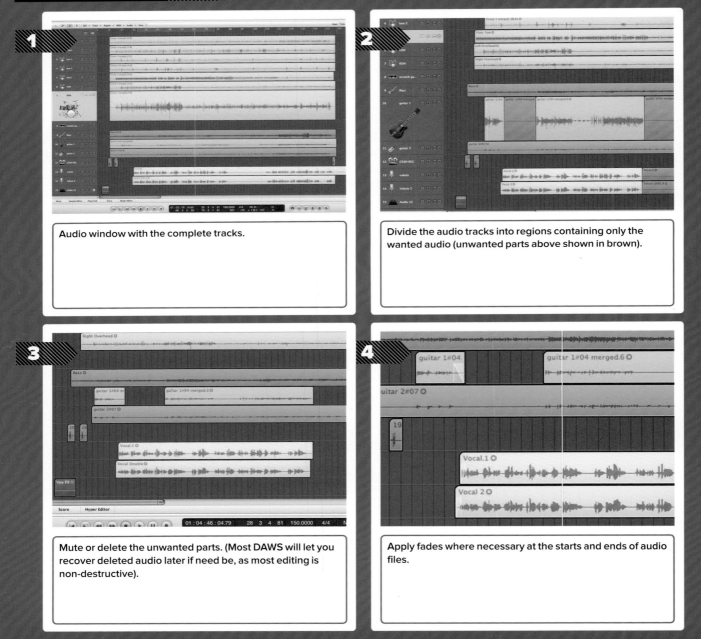

1 Audio window with the complete tracks.

2 Divide the audio tracks into regions containing only the wanted audio (unwanted parts above shown in brown).

3 Mute or delete the unwanted parts. (Most DAWS will let you recover deleted audio later if need be, as most editing is non-destructive).

4 Apply fades where necessary at the starts and ends of audio files.

than leaving it audible all the time. A good compromise in such situations is to use volume level automation to drop sections of exposed spill by a few dBs.

An alternative method, once you've divided the track into wanted and unwanted sections, is to move all the unwanted sections containing spill onto a new audio track and drop the new track's level as far as you can without the change in spill level becoming too obvious.

GUITAR NOISE

Other common noises that can require attention are **guitar amp hums** or **string noises** before the guitarist starts to play a section and again when they finish it.

You can usually hide the worst of these with careful editing, applying a fade as the last note dies away. It's also worth editing out or using automation to reduce the level of string noise between notes on exposed guitar solos where a lot of overdrive has been used (Fig 1); even the slightest finger movement can produce squeaks, clunks and bangs that are better removed, or at least reduced in level.

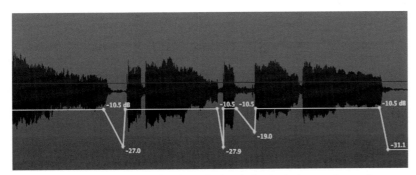

▲ Fig 1: Use of automation to bring down the level of noise between phrases in a guitar solo.

The offending noises usually show up clearly as short bursts of sound in the waveform editor and are easily distinguishable from the notes you want to keep.

Tip / Adding **delay** or **reverb** to an exposed guitar part while mixing will help disguise edits. It is one reason why guitar sounds to which you plan to add delay or reverb effects are best recorded as dry as possible: if you try to clean up a part that has had echo or reverb applied at the recording stage you have to wait until the effects have died away before fading out the section, which can leave noise exposed.

DRUM SPILL

Spill is almost always a problem with drum kits, especially on close mic'ed **tom tracks**.

It can be particularly troublesome where **double-headed toms** are used. Even when damping pads are used, double-headed toms have a habit of resonating along with every snare and kick drum beat, producing a near-continuous low-mid drone that really muddies the mix if left untreated.

Back in the day, when tape was the only recording medium, engineers would use noise gates on each tom channel, either while recording or during mixing, but even when set up carefully these had a habit of opening whenever the snare drum was struck.

In today's DAWs you can get a cleaner result by looking at the waveform display of each tom track in turn and then manually silencing the audio between hits using the track cleanup method described above for guitar. Unless you're editing a crazy drum solo this doesn't usually take long.

When solo'd the edited tom tracks can sound unnatural, but once the overhead mic tracks are added – which will include the full-length tom hits – chances are they'll sound fine. Adding a fade after each tom hit helps the spill to die gracefully rather than cutting off abruptly (Fig 2). I use the same tom cleanup technique if I'm planning to replace the tom hits with samples (page 239); it provides a much better defined trigger source than a simple noise gate.

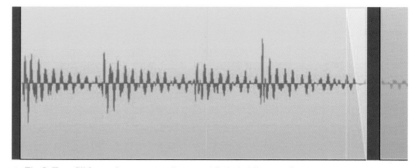

▲ Fig 2: Tom fill featuring a manual cut and fade (with muted next section).

Close-mic'ed **kick drums** and **snares** are usually better cleaned using a noise gate rather than the tom 'strip silence' method.

In this instance insert a noise gate on the kick and snare tracks, ideally one with a side-chain filter that can be used to set the frequency range that triggers the gate (see Walkthrough, right).

The aim is to tweak the lower and upper filter cutoff points to isolate the snare drum signal so that the gate only responds to the snare. If the full signal is allowed through, a bleeding hi-hat or tom hit can trigger the gate falsely, introducing unwanted noise into the mix and blurring the definition of the snare.

To avoid hi-hat spill from triggering the snare gate, reduce the upper filter cutoff frequency on the gate to allow the thump of the snare through while excluding as much hi-hat as possible. Then use the lower filter to exclude as much of the kick drum signal as you need to mitigate false triggering.

Note that the filter setting doesn't affect the sound passing through the gate – just the frequency range to which the side-chain is most sensitive. Most gates have a side-chain listen facility so you can hear the affect the filters are having as you adjust them.

To avoid affecting the attack of the snare, set the gate attack time to its fastest setting and also set a millisecond (ms) or two of **lookahead** if the plug-in offers it. Lookahead simply means that the plug-in reads the audio file a short time in advance so that the gate can open in anticipation of a hit rather than having to wait until the hit arrives before it starts to open. Set the release time as fast as possible without shortening the decay of the drum.

The same gating process can be used to isolate any other drums that are significantly louder than any spill on the same track.

EQ CLEANUP

After removing or muting sections of audio that contribute nothing to the mix (or worse, contribute unnecessary noise), it is time to trim away any unnecessary frequencies – usually found at the lower and upper ends of the audio spectrum.

In almost every track you record, from guitars to vocals, drums to bass, you'll end up not only with the desirable frequencies of the signal – those that define the character of the sound source – but also frequencies above and below them that contribute nothing useful, and indeed may add unwanted low-end rumble or high-end hiss

Gate on the snare

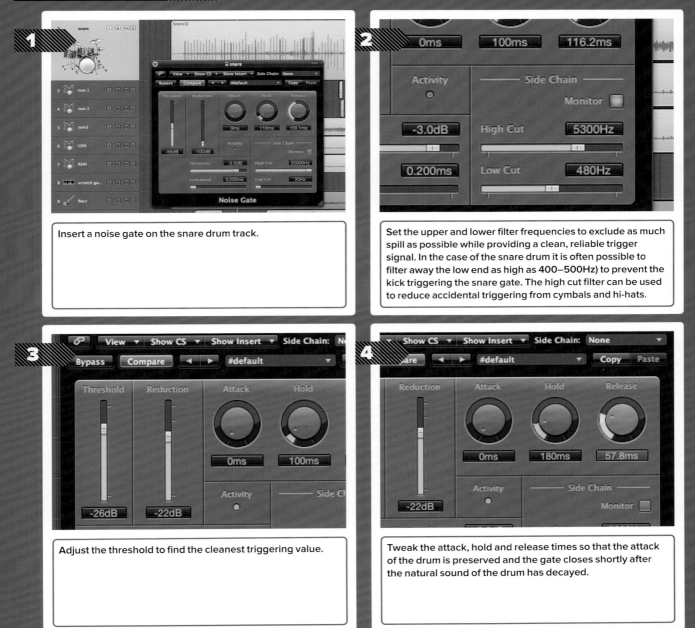

1 Insert a noise gate on the snare drum track.

2 Set the upper and lower filter frequencies to exclude as much spill as possible while providing a clean, reliable trigger signal. In the case of the snare drum it is often possible to filter away the low end as high as 400–500Hz) to prevent the kick triggering the snare gate. The high cut filter can be used to reduce accidental triggering from cymbals and hi-hats.

3 Adjust the threshold to find the cleanest triggering value.

4 Tweak the attack, hold and release times so that the attack of the drum is preserved and the gate closes shortly after the natural sound of the drum has decayed.

that compromise the upper end of the mix. Even in a well recorded **vocal** track made using a pop shield and solid mic setup, for example, some air blasts invariably get through the shield, causing the mic diaphragm to move at low frequencies.

A spectrum analyser can show up significant activity as low down as 20Hz, sometimes even lower, on even the best recorded vocal. This low-end – which can be inaudible on a less-than-ideal home monitoring setup – contributes nothing useful in audio terms. It eats valuable headroom and often interferes with other instruments that naturally inhabit the bass area, like the kick drum and bass.

To remove this unwanted low end, it is common to apply a low cut filter. Adjust it carefully so that you don't thin out the vocal part, and listen to the results both solo'd and in the context of the wider mix. An 18dB/octave low cut filter set at around 80–120Hz usually works fine, but every voice is different; try moving either side of 120Hz while listening for tonal changes in the voice. If the cut sounds obvious then reduce the filter cutoff frequency.

Electric guitars can also suffer from low frequency thumps and cabinet resonances. If they do, give them the same low-cut treatment.

At the other end of the frequency scale, high-end cuts are used to remove unnecessary high frequencies from instruments that don't have any really high harmonics, such as **mic'ed guitar** and **bass amps**. Upper cuts help reduce hiss and may also smooth out the tonality where the initial sound is too gritty – although detailed adjustment of the high filters should be left until you get to the mixdown proper.

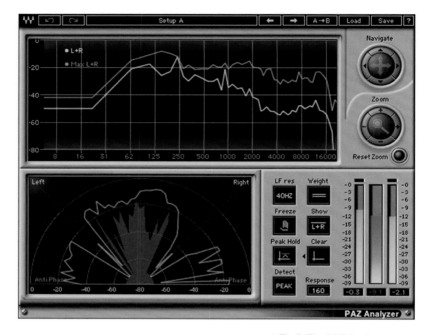

▲ Fig 3: The PAZ Analyzer from Waves: includes a useful spectrum analyser.

Tip / While a kick drum has a fairly well-defined pitch, the action of the beater pushing the head as it hits can send blasts of air at the mic which translate into very low frequency energy. Most kick drums concentrate the bulk of their energy in the 60–100Hz range so you can usually roll off the lows at 30–40Hz. Roll off higher in a 'fat bass, skinny kick' mix (page 293).

Tip / A spectrum analyser plug-in (Fig 3, above) is particularly useful for checking whether there is any unwanted low (or high) frequency energy in a track that doesn't need it – particularly if you don't fully trust your monitoring setup. Always set the spectrum analyser to its highest resolution.

VISUAL CLEANUP
Keeping your DAW's arrange window in good health is more to do with refining workflow and saving time than it is about aesthetics. To get the most out of the time

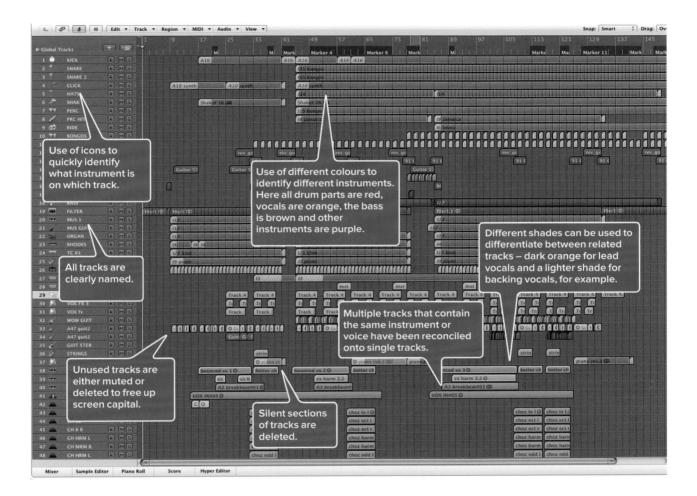

Use of icons to quickly identify what instrument is on which track.

Use of different colours to identify different instruments. Here all drum parts are red, vocals are orange, the bass is brown and other instruments are purple.

Different shades can be used to differentiate between related tracks – dark orange for lead vocals and a lighter shade for backing vocals, for example.

All tracks are clearly named.

Multiple tracks that contain the same instrument or voice have been reconciled onto single tracks.

Unused tracks are either muted or deleted to free up screen capital.

Silent sections of tracks are deleted.

you spend in the studio it's worth developing your own best practice around how you display the tracks in any given project – especially if you tend to use a lot of tracks.

Most DAWs let you rearrange the way tracks are displayed on the arrange page and many also allow you to change the **colours** of the various tracks or regions.

It helps to keep **similar parts on adjacent tracks**, such as drums, backing vocals, instrumental parts, FX and so on. I identify

these different types of sounds using colours so I know at a glance which tracks are which, for example red for drums, orange for vocals, purple for guitars and so on. Using different shades of the same colour for different kinds of the same sound can also help (bright orange for lead vocals and duller orange for BVs etc). Some DAWs also allow you to choose **pictorial icons** for each track.

At this stage you can also **remove unused tracks** and **consolidate multiple parts** that belong together onto the same track, for example, a guitar part that was recorded in sections over three of four tracks that has the same sound and requires the same mix treatment.

BUS GROUPING

In larger projects with multiple instruments, vocals, drum tracks and so on, it is often useful to assign sets of sounds that belong together to different 'mixing groups' (page 39).

All mainstream DAWs support bus grouping (named because the group of sounds is sent to a single mixer bus) in either mono or stereo. When you've identified groups of sounds that would benefit from grouping, all you need do is assign them to a specific group.

If you have an **acoustic drum kit** as part of a mix, for example, you might assign all drum tracks to a stereo group and label it 'Drum Bus'. Once you've balanced the individual drum tracks, you can control the kit's overall level in the mix using the Drum Bus group fader.

Grouping in this way, also sometimes referred to as creating subgroups, not only aids workflow (balancing a mix is much easier if you only have to adjust one fader for the whole drum kit, rather than eight or nine every time you want to change the kit level), it also allows the entire group to be processed using a single set of plug-ins, or even routed to an external processor using the group's insert point. **EQ** and **compression** are frequently used as group bus processors.

Other candidates for grouping include **backing vocals** and **chordal guitar parts** comprising two or more guitar tracks.

Assorted **percussion** can often be grouped, as can some **keyboard** parts.

In the dance music world producers typically group kick/s, 'rest of drums', bassline/s, all musical elements, FX and finally, if applicable, vocals (lead and backing are usually split).

With a bit of care you can set up a typical mix so that only a handful of faders are required to balance all essential components.

There is one key drawback of group bussing: if you change the level of a group by adjusting the group bus fader, any send effects relating to the individual tracks making up the group won't change unless the corresponding effects are also routed to the same bus. Fortunately there's a way of countering this drawback: using **fader grouping**.

FADER GROUPING

An alternative to group busing (or a companion to it) is fader grouping.

Here faders belonging to a logical group of tracks such as our hypothetical drum kit are assigned to the same 'fader group'. Moving any fader in the group causes the others to follow suit, so that the whole group level can be adjusted up or down using any fader in the group.

There's usually a key command to switch the group mode on and off so that if you need to change the balance within a group you simply turn off group mode, tweak the level/s, then turn group mode back on.

Fader grouping is useful where you don't want to apply common processing to the group mix (as with bus grouping) but still need control over several tracks at the same time.

A COMBINED APPROACH

To get around the limitations imposed by the use of either fader grouping or bus grouping alone you can combine both approaches by creating a fader group and then routing the fader-grouped tracks to a single mix bus.

This double-grouping allows level changes to the whole group to be made either using the individual track faders or the bus fader, and it also allows send effects to be set up which will work normally as long as you use the track faders to control the level; in other words, when you turn down any one of the grouped faders, all post-fade effects fed from the grouped tracks get turned down by the same amount.

The only thing to watch for is if you apply overall compression or some other form of dynamics processing on the bus, you'll need to readjust the threshold if you make any level changes using the track faders, as the level feeding the bus will have changed.

COMPING

Comping (short for compiling) is the editing stage that involves auditioning the various takes you've recorded and then choosing the best sections to produce a seamless 'best of' performance. The process is mainly used for vocals and instrumental solos and it should happen before you do any tuning tweaks.

Different DAWs provide different tools to help with the job, such as Logic's Swipe Comp, although you can do the same job with the usual cut and paste editing tools.

EVERY BREATH YOU TAKE

Take care not to cut off breaths prior to the start of a sung phrase without a good artistic reason for doing so as these are part of the natural performance and the vocal will sound odd without them.

If the breaths are too loud, use automation to drop them in level rather than removing them entirely, as shown in the image on the right – the dips are where the volume is pulled down.

Another approach taken by some engineers (those who like to make life difficult!) is to separate all the breath sounds and move them onto an adjacent track so that they can be turned up or down independently of the main vocal line using their own track fader.

A simpler approach is to use a dedicated breath control plug-in such as Waves'

DeBreath, which automatically detects breath sounds and allows their level to be changed relative to the vocal using a fader.

It should be noted that some styles – including dance, urban and chillout – celebrate unnatural vocal styles and the producer may deliberately choose to edit out breaths (or heavily increase their volume!) to move the vocal performances out of the ordinary.

It should also be noted that the treatment of breaths in lead vocal lines and harmony / chorus block lines is likely to be different. Where you may want to retain breaths in the lead vocal to

preserve the nature of the performance, breaths in big chorus blocks may need to be edited out or drastically reduced in level to avoid multi-layered and staggered breaths that sound messy and add nothing to the performance. A practical compromise is to leave natural breaths on a small number of constituent harmony or layered chorus parts to retain a natural feel, while reducing the overall number of layered breaths.

As a rule, avoid doing too much fine-detail work to breaths at this stage though, as their level will change when compression and EQ is applied when you begin mixing.

The ultimate aim when comping is a final vocal (or instrumental solo) that is (largely) in tune and delivered with the right degree of emotion and feel – something that you as producer have to judge subjectively.

My own approach when comping is to pick the one track that is the best of the bunch, then select from the remaining tracks to replace any sections of the main track for which there are better alternative takes, either musically or emotionally (page 265).

Once you have all the chosen vocal parts on a single track, use the DAW's crossfade tool to ensure a seamless join between each section. In most cases you'll be able to fade in and out during the silence between words (though if you do so, watch those breaths! (Every breath you take, page 263).

A more forensic approach is to audition every word or phrase in every take and select the best for the final comp, an approach that can yield technically good results, but can deliver a vocal that feels somewhat patchy from a performance point of view – a patchwork vocal made up of so many parts. Trust your ears: a slightly weaker region may work if the flow and feel of the whole comped verse works better.

Ultimately, it's up to you as producer to decide on any compromises necessary to maintain a strong sense of musical performance. The bottom line? What works, works.

Tip / Using the colour palette to shade audio parts according to how good they are can be useful when comping. You might choose to use darker shades for better takes, for example. Audition each part and colour away until you have a final comped take of the strongest (darkest) parts.

VOCAL FINE-TUNING

After you've comped the vocal or instrumental solo you should be left with a single track with a hopefully uniformly strong performance. But it's still unlikely to be perfect (whatever that means). This may be fine – there are plenty of musical styles that celebrate 100 per cent authentic performances. But many producers at this stage will reach for Auto-Tune, Melodyne or similar to perform any fine-tuning that needs doing.

There are two options here:
> **1: offline processing**, and
> **2: live processing in the mix**.

With the first option, the engineer takes the various comped vocal lines and works on them in an offline program like Melodyne to massage the tuning, and also treat any timing problems on the lead vocal and any other lines that need attention.

Everything from vibrato to note positioning can be amended, to the minutest degree, with tweaks made as the vocal plays alongside a roughly mixed backing track. The tweaked vocal lines are then bounced down after correction for use as final stems in the mixdown.

In the second scenario, a pitch correction plug-in like Antares' Auto-Tune is employed on the vocal track/s to shift off-pitch notes onto the desired note while the mix actually plays. The pitch correction process can either be subtle or extreme, with automation often used to catch specific notes only.

Both of these options are covered in depth in **Pitch Correction 101, Chapter 13** and **Vocal Production, Chapter 14**.

Comping the lead vocal

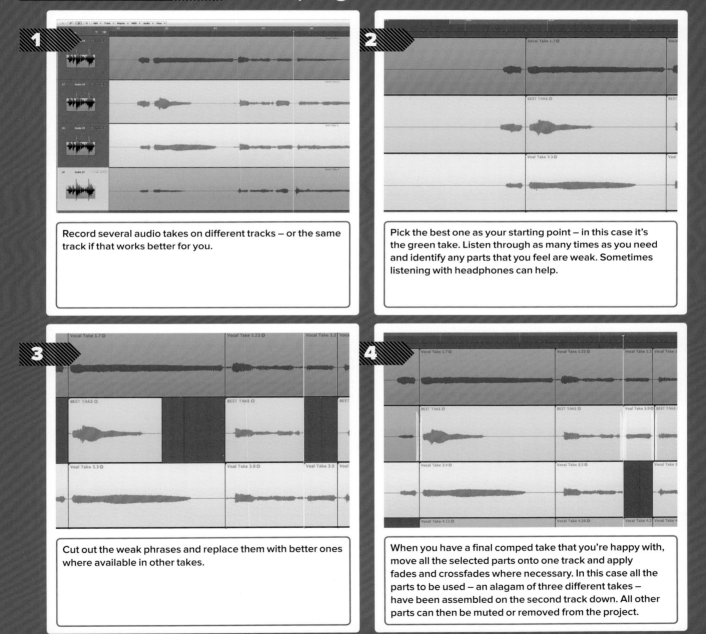

1 Record several audio takes on different tracks – or the same track if that works better for you.

2 Pick the best one as your starting point – in this case it's the green take. Listen through as many times as you need and identify any parts that you feel are weak. Sometimes listening with headphones can help.

3 Cut out the weak phrases and replace them with better ones where available in other takes.

4 When you have a final comped take that you're happy with, move all the selected parts onto one track and apply fades and crossfades where necessary. In this case all the parts to be used – an alagam of three different takes – have been assembled on the second track down. All other parts can then be muted or removed from the project.

'Cut and move' backing vocals

1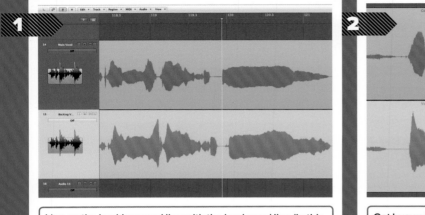

Line up the backing vocal line with the lead vocal line (in this example the backing vocal is on the bottom track).

2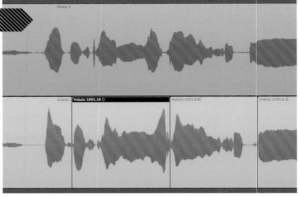

Get busy with the scissors on phrases that are out of time and divide the backing vocal parts into separate phrases.

3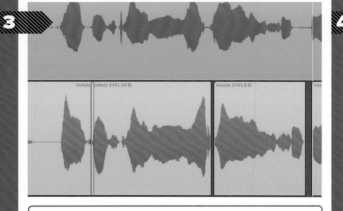

Move individual phrases so that their start points are aligned with the starts in the main vocal.

4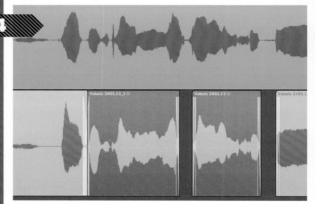

Apply fades if any edits take place mid-phrase. You may also need to use time manipulation to change the length of badly-timed phrases. In this example the two regions in red have been time-compressed slightly to shorten them. Most DAWs offer some way to do this. The result is a backing phrase that is now nicely aligned with the lead vocal.

BACKING VOCAL TIMING

It is highly unusual to find that all the raw recorded backing vocals perfectly match the timing and phrasing of the lead vocal – or indeed of the other backing vocal parts and/or harmonies.

Sometimes slightly misaligned backing vocals sound fine, in which case leave them alone. However, if you're aiming for a tighter sound there are several techniques you can use to improve matters:

〉 **Cut and move:** Where individual words or phrases simply need moving to line them up with the main vocal, divide the offending track into phrases using the scissors tool (or equivalent). Then slide the phrase backwards or forwards until it matches the main vocal. Any overlaps can be dealt with by shortening the sections to minimise overlap, then applying a short crossfade of around 50ms or so. See Walkthrough, left.

〉 **Time manipulation:** Where words or phrases are too long or too short, you may have to resort to using the DAW's time manipulation facilities – leaving a gap mid-word or between two words that are normally joined can sound unnatural. Timestretch algorithms tend to produce undesirable side-effects if used too heavily, but as a rule small adjustments don't compromise the sound greatly, and where the backing vocal sits behind the main vocal or is layered with other backing vocal parts, minor pitch manipulation artefacts are likely to be hidden.

In Logic you can use the built-in Flex Time editor to stretch or shorten regions without altering their pitch, although for basic tasks the Region Stretch command is more than adequate. Where an edit has been made in the middle of a word to stretch only one syllable rather than the whole word, listen carefully to ensure the edit is glitch-free. If it isn't, apply a short crossfade at the edit point to smooth over the transition.

〉 **Melodyne:** These kind of timing tweaks can also be made using Melodyne – still the tool of choice for those who frequently deal with complex vocal arrangements that require in-depth work. Not only does Melodyne allow you to move single notes and full phrases on any given track, the 'big guns' Studio version also lets you compare (and alter) note positions across different tracks to allow you to easily line up, for example, harmonies or chorus blocks. Note lengths can also be changed via the graphical interface.

With practice and patience Melodyne is a supremely powerful tool with the ability to pull huge multi-part vocal arrangements into time. Indeed the main danger is overdoing the edits to yield a result that is a little **too** perfect, the life and soul of the performance sacrificed to the gods of sonic perfection. And however good its algorithms, you still need to be aware of introducing audible artefacts where too much pulling and tugging is done.

Note / When performing any kind of detailed editing work, keep audio crossfades as short as possible (just long enough to hide the edit) to avoid phasiness or chorus-like modulation where two sections overlap. Avoid crossfading over breaths as you can end up with an unnatural sounding mix of two breaths. A good way of disguising fades is to locate them so they coincide with a snare drum beat to help disguise the edit. Where the crossfade editor offers a choice of equal power or equal level crossfades, try both to see which sounds most natural.

Melodyne timing tweaks

1

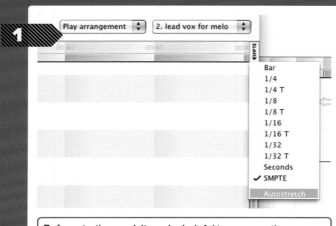

Before starting work it can be helpful to program the song tempo in the Transport Bar (100bpm in this example). This allows you to work against the Melodyne grid. To audition the vocal track double-click it so that it opens in the Editor window. To allow detailed edits ensure that Snap-to-Grid is set to SMPTE and that Autostretch is ticked.

2

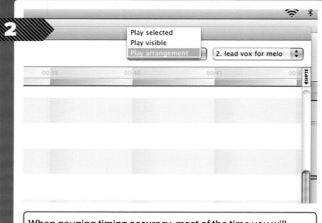

When gauging timing accuracy, most of the time you will want to work with the backing track playing. To do so ensure Play Arrangement is highlighted. The relative balances can be adjusted in the Mixer window – sometimes it can be useful to turn the backing track right down so that you can hear any artefacts that the program is introducing more easily.

3

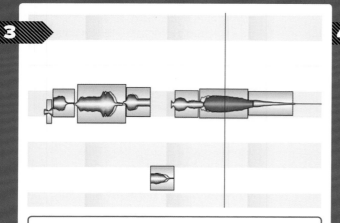

Altering phrasing is as easy as using the Time tool to shift notes in time. When a note is highlighted, the tool can be used at the start of the block to move the note forwards or backwards in time. Clicking and holding a note's end allows you to lengthen or shorten it. Note that edits will affect surrounding notes too – so be sure to check these don't suffer.

4

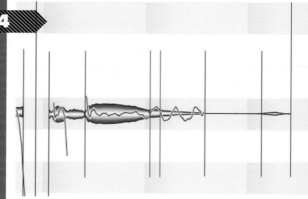

Sometimes you may need to artificially cut a note using the Note Separation tool. This can be useful when any changes you make with the Time tool are causing problems to surrounding notes, or when Melodyne's definition process has failed to correctly identify a note division.

WALKTHROUGH Timing harmonies in Melodyne

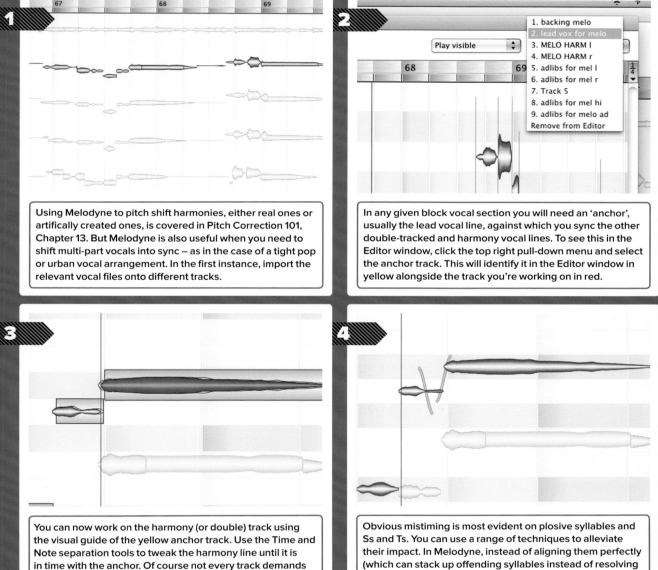

1

Using Melodyne to pitch shift harmonies, either real ones or artifically created ones, is covered in Pitch Correction 101, Chapter 13. But Melodyne is also useful when you need to shift multi-part vocals into sync – as in the case of a tight pop or urban vocal arrangement. In the first instance, import the relevant vocal files onto different tracks.

2

In any given block vocal section you will need an 'anchor', usually the lead vocal line, against which you sync the other double-tracked and harmony vocal lines. To see this in the Editor window, click the top right pull-down menu and select the anchor track. This will identify it in the Editor window in yellow alongside the track you're working on in red.

3

You can now work on the harmony (or double) track using the visual guide of the yellow anchor track. Use the Time and Note separation tools to tweak the harmony line until it is in time with the anchor. Of course not every track demands 100 per cent accuracy: this can sound too inhuman. But the choice is yours.

4

Obvious mistiming is most evident on plosive syllables and Ss and Ts. You can use a range of techniques to alleviate their impact. In Melodyne, instead of aligning them perfectly (which can stack up offending syllables instead of resolving the problem), you might prefer to cut a note or drastically reduce its volume using the Amplitude tool.

TIME AND PHASE FORENSICS

Where an instrument or ensemble has been captured using multiple mics set up at different distances, some engineers choose to compensate for the timing discrepancies before getting into the mix, while others consider that to be part of the mixing process.

A typical example might be the overhead mics on a drum kit where the sound arrives three or four milliseconds after it reaches the close mics on the individual drums.

In this case it can be sonically advantageous to slip the overhead track back in time to line up the waveforms of, for example, the snare hits on both the close and overhead mics. Where the two overheads were set up at different distances from the snare drum, it may also be advantageous to line these up too, although I'm always wary of changing the timing between the two halves of a stereo signal. Listen as you adjust the delay time and you'll know when the result sounds right.

Whether these adjustments are worthwhile or not depends on whether they improve the sound of the kit. Remember that when all those classic records were made using tape, there was no facility for this kind of hyper-detailed adjustment other than patching in external digital delay units, which few engineers did. Some engineers obsess over this kind of detail while others virtually ignore it – but if it tightens the sound of the mix and adds more weight to the kick drum, I'd say it's worth doing.

CONSOLIDATE MIDI INSTRUMENTS

Where you have MIDI tracks driving software instruments or external synth modules, it can be a good idea to bounce them down as audio stems with effects bypassed and then mute them – even if you plan to mix using the MIDI parts playing live.

The key reason for doing this (other than to free up DSP resources if you're on a lower-powered computer) is that if you ever need to revisit the track in the future you'll be able to fall back on the audio track if the MIDI instruments used in the song are no longer available to you. There's no guarantee you'll have the same hardware synths a few years down the line and it has also been known for software instruments to be discontinued where the task of rewriting them to work with a new OS has been deemed uncommercial.

Another reason for making every part available as an audio track is that it makes it much easier to transfer the project to a different DAW platform or to create stems for **remixes**: you simply save the song as a bunch of separate audio files that all start at the same time, then you can drop them into any DAW to mix.

It is also a good idea to make **project notes** and save them as a text file in the same folder as the song data, detailing the settings of any external equipment used, the sample rate and bit depth of the project and of course the tempo, along with locations of any tempo changes.

AND FINALLY... BACK UP!

Before starting work on the mix, back up all song files to at least one other place, and ideally more than one. Never use a **different partition on the same hard drive** to back up as a mechanical drive failure will lose all the data on all partitions of that drive. Back up to **separate drives** and also consider burning a **data DVD**. Online storage options like **Dropbox** can also be useful.

Make sure you power up any **backup drives** every few weeks as a drive left unused for a long period is more likely to fail than one that is used fairly regularly.

Now you've done this initial housekeeping and backed up your files, you're ready to start mixing. The work you've done so far will let you get on with this creative part of the producer's job without having to worry about mundane practicalities that can waste time and energy. ●

TIPS FOR A BETTER MIX

Listen to the mix from the next room with the door left open. Balance problems are often more obvious when the mix is heard in this way.

COMMON MIX MISTAKES AND HOW TO AVOID THEM

The faders keep creeping up. If a part feels too low in the mix, try bringing the faders of other elements down rather than turning the problem track up. It's one of the simplest ways of preserving headroom.

18
THE
ARRANGEMENT

stringz

○ piano rev.1   A6

bounced vs 1 ○   better choz ○   bounced vs

-2.7   -4.8 dB
-4.8 d   -6.7

vs harm 1 :   vs harm 1 end (

A3 breakbeat#01

*04 ○

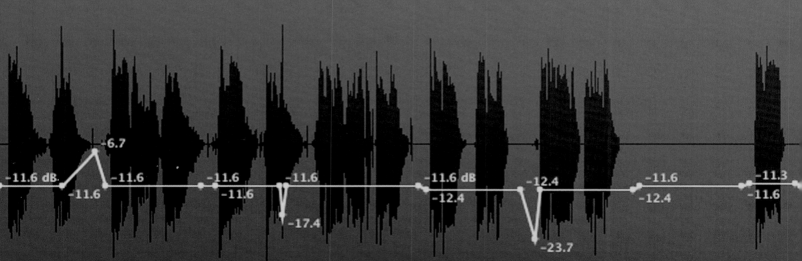

-6.7
-11.6 dB   -11.6   -11.6   -11.6   -11.6 dB   -12.4   -11.6   -11.3
-11.6   -11.6   -12.4   -12.4   -11.6
-17.4   -23.7

> **ARRANGEMENT AND PERFORMANCE ARE EVERYTHING... NOT ONLY IS A WELL ARRANGED SONG INVARIABLY A BETTER SONG, A STRONG ARRANGEMENT IS ALSO A PRE-CONDITION FOR A GREAT MIX.**

THE IMPORTANCE OF ARRANGEMENT

A chapter on arrangement? In a music production book? Surely some mistake! Ah, but if only the producer's job was as simple as setting up a couple of mics and tweaking the faders to get a balanced mix. The truth is that among the many qualities demanded of the modern producer, an understanding of the fundamentals of arrangement is all but essential. Not only is a well-arranged song invariably a better song, a strong arrangement is also a pre-condition for a great mix.

I've said it before in this book and I'll say it again here: arrangement and performance are everything. Knowing how much instrumentation should accompany the chorus, knowing when to cut the second guitar, knowing which vocal lines deserve a harmony and which parts can be doubled are the kinds of decisions that turn a good song into a great one. In the big band era, where band leaders had upwards of 50 performers on stage before them, arrangers were worth their weight in gold.

BUT SHOULDN'T THE BAND BE SORTING THE ARRANGEMENT?!

At some stage every producer has a 'Shouldn't the band be sorting the arrangement?' moment. And the answer – presumably – is yes. But few band members will have the mixing experience that you do, and many won't have as much songwriting experience as you might expect either. More often than not they'll simply come to you with the arrangement of the song that they play live.

The benefit of the ears and accumulated knowledge of the experienced producer means that they – often more than the band – will know what kinds of arrangement will work well before the mixdown starts. And which won't.

The great record producers, from George Martin and Quincy Jones to Craig Leon and George Massenburg, understood the importance of arrangement. When I asked George Massenburg how he got his vocals to sit so well in the mix during an interview in the '80s, he replied to the effect: "You have to arrange the music to leave space for them". EQ and processing came afterwards, he said. It's obvious in a way – space in the mix allows the pivotal parts to breathe – a fact that is all too easy to forget, especially in the era of the near-limitless track-count.

A poor arrangement can generate numerous problems for the producer during mixdown. Common examples can include:

Problem: **An important part is getting lost in the mix**. Specifically, the verse vocal, accompanied by a busy guitar part that peaks in the same frequency area as the vocal, is struggling to be heard.

Potential solutions: The producer might suggest **dropping the guitar part altogether**, or asking the guitarist to do a quick **re-write** so that the part takes a secondary role to the vocal, dropping in the odd phrase when the vocal pauses. If the guitar part has to stay, the producer might suggest picking a **different tone** – one with less high-end that subtly reinforces the vocal rather than interfering with it. **Notching out the frequency range** in the guitar that is competing with the vocal, usually in the 2–4kHz range, can also help, as can **ducking** the guitar part/s so that its level drops slightly when the vocal is present.

Problem: **The overall 'shape' of the song is confusing.**

Potential solution: Listeners expect certain things from their music; in dance music this is invariably blocks of 8-bar turnarounds, in pop it can be a familiar verse/chorus paradigm. By messing too much with the established traditions of a genre you risk alienating an expectant dancefloor / A&R man. **Tweaking an ill-considered structure** slightly may turn a miss into a hit. Having said that, there are exceptions to the rules – outlined below.

Problem: **The song is dynamically and emotionally flat**, devoid of highs and lows.

Potential solution: The builds and drops of emotion are almost entirely a product of arrangement and changes in orchestration. Examine the song structure to see how changes could be made. **Start by muting / unmuting certain tracks** to see what each part contributes to the mix, then **build the track from the loudest chorus backward**. Knowing which parts to cut and re-introduce for the build is essential. Dance producers are masters of this art: some tracks are little more than extended breakdowns and drops.

Problem: **The mix is overcooked** – a problem often found among unconfident bands, songwriters (and producers). In arrangement terms this often manifests itself as an **over-busy mix** (right), where multiple guitar parts underpin big block harmonies while organs, pads and other keys fight for space in the mids. Electronic drum programming is easy to overdo too, with MIDI-generated beats that no-one but the hypothetical eight-

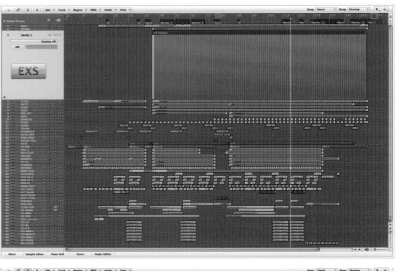

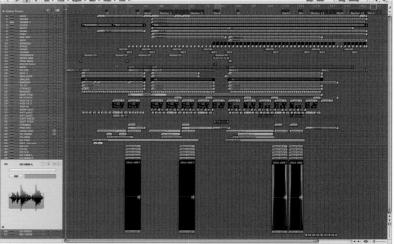

▲ Sometimes you can mute a surprising number of tracks to build a stronger arrangement and production. In this example a client came with a half-finished mix (top) that was over-busy, with too many parts fighting rhythmically and dynamically. Of the many tweaks made, six tracks were deleted from the song (shown bottom in black). These included an unhelpful bongo part, a chorus harmony that was added nothing important to the track, an occasional spot effect that didn't quite work, and an organ part that was unnecessarily doubling a pre-existing Rhodes line.

armed drummer could ever hope to master.

Potential solution: Remember that **less is often more**. Start from the beginning and ask what role each part plays and whether any can be dropped from the mix. **Everything has to have a reason to be there.** Try muting some parts while easing up others. It's surprising how much more solid a struggling arrangement can become when a few unimportant parts are dropped (no matter how loud the protestations of the guitarist / keyboard player / shaker shaker).

SOME KEY PRINCIPLES

Entire volumes could be written about the art and science of music arranging, and the classics can be analysed over and over, only to discover that for each seminal track there is a different arrangement, with different musical parts playing different roles.

But each of the classics invariably adheres to a few fundamental principles: foundations on which all else is built. These can be narrowed down to:

❭ **Groove**: The track must have a solid, hopefully infectious, rhythm. Even slow ballads have a rhythm.

❭ **Shape**: The track should have its ebbs and flows, highs and lows, builds and releases – a constant flow of emotion.

❭ **Colour**: The track must engage the listener from the first bar to the last; variation is paramount.

Rare is the hit track that doesn't feature all three of these fundamentals,

regardless of the artist, the genre, the instrumentation or the song structure.

ALL ABOUT THE GROOVE

Much modern pop is dominated by a clear beat, typically powered by an up-front kick drum. Take a listen to any urban crossover hit or top 40 pop production and you'll find the kick and snare anchoring the rhythm, supported by the bass, often with hats and other percussive part-mixed fairly low. These are dancefloor-friendly tracks with radio-friendly mixes that owe much to the production flavours of the underground club scene. The listener is left in no doubt when to move.

The head-nodding, toe-tapping business of groove is a fundamental cornerstone of dance music – dance in its loosest possible sense.

But it doesn't need to be so obvious or kick-heavy as the latest generation of pop producers might have us believe. I've always been intrigued by Phil Spector's records and all those Tamla Motown hits. They have irresistible grooves, yet when you break down the tracks you find that the drums are mixed low – often the singer's tambourine is louder than the entire drum kit and the bass guitar is recessed among the other instruments. It shows that rhythm doesn't have to be beaten into the listener by force. Indeed these old records are masterclasses in how to get all the instruments to work together to imply a groove that is effortlessly compulsive.

Aside from exemplary music performances, part of the reason these songs groove so well is that the drummer plays the rhythm that feels right for the song – not necessarily one a quantise grid would approve of. To create a sense of urgency the snare hits fall a few milliseconds ahead of the click. For a more laid-back feel the drummer holds the hit back for a fraction of a second. Deployment of subtle (or not so subtle) swing injects variation and 'feel' into a rhythm that at first listen sounds like a straight four-on-the-floor beat.

A great drummer will add this feel instinctively. For those working without a drummer, the introduction of **swing** into a programmed (or sampled) drum part can be achieved by imposing groove templates on either the MIDI or audio data (see Walkthrough, right).

Most mainstream DAWs are able to create custom groove templates based on audio or MIDI patterns played by real drummers. Where you need to tighten up other elements in the mix, you can use the drummer's original performance to create custom groove templates.

Groove templates really come into their own when **programming drum parts**, where they allow all programmed instruments, including the drums, to be locked to a grid that has a real groove to it rather than straight 16ths. Many of the sampled drum instruments on the market, such as BFD or EasyDrummer, come with a library of MIDI drum parts played by real drummers which can be very useful for extracting groove templates with feel.

Of course working to any grid – even one with feel – strips away the natural timing variations that a real drummer would add. It is possible to add some small random elements using the quantise humanise function included in most DAWs, but don't add too much or it

HUMANISE THE GROOVE

Working with **MIDI** has many advantages. Generating realistic drum parts is not necesssarily one of them – unless you have a drummer play the part using pads. Fortunately there are a number of techniques that can help inject some real-drummer feel to a programmed beat.

1 - Program beats live. This is easy with drum pads but is just as simple using a **MIDI** keyboard if you have a good sense of timing. Simply loop up a four-bar click, press record and then manually tap new sounds over the top. Keep all quantise settings off. You may need to do a bit of editing afterwards to correct the more noticeable errors, but you should end up with a nice human-feeling beat, with velocity differences and the subtle imperfections of a drummer. This technique works well when programming percussion parts too.

2 - Shift the sounds. If you prefer to program using a note or matrix editor, you can introduce timing imperfections by dragging notes a little before or after the bar/division, or by running a sequence through some kind of MIDI humanising algorithm.

3 - Learn how a drummer plays. Physical and kit limitations mean that only certain sounds can play at certain times, so, for example, a closed and open hat can't hit at once, nor can a snare, crash, closed hat and tom. Until the octapoid drummer is born these limitations provide useful pointers on how to program realistic parts.

4 - Choose your sounds carefully. If you want live-sounding drums, pick samples from real kits or use one of the many excellent libraries supplied for virtual instruments like BFD or EasyDrummer.

will make the performance sound sloppy. For other ideas on programming more realistic drum beats. (See Humanise the groove, above.)

SHAPE OF THE TRACK

In theory a pop song can be structured in any number of ways, as some of The Beatle's more wayward tracks have demonstrated. Or how about Queen's Bohemian Rhapsody? But in practice most songs use derivatives of a handful of tried-and-tested structures that have barely evolved since the demand for radio-friendly records first started. These structures have served songwriters well for generations and continue to meet the needs of emerging genres today.

Most radio-friendly songs have some form of intro, two or more verses, a chorus

WALKTHROUGH

Using custom groove templates

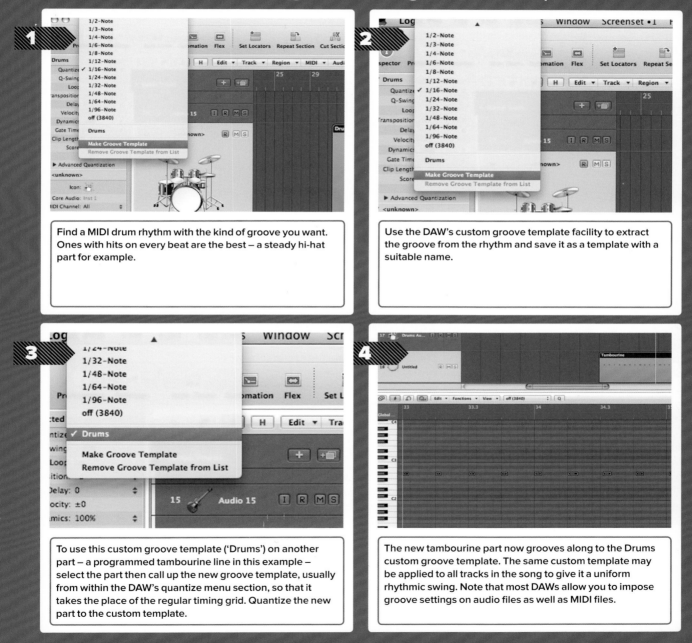

1 Find a MIDI drum rhythm with the kind of groove you want. Ones with hits on every beat are the best – a steady hi-hat part for example.

2 Use the DAW's custom groove template facility to extract the groove from the rhythm and save it as a template with a suitable name.

3 To use this custom groove template ('Drums') on another part – a programmed tambourine line in this example – select the part then call up the new groove template, usually from within the DAW's quantize menu section, so that it takes the place of the regular timing grid. Quantize the new part to the custom template.

4 The new tambourine part now grooves along to the Drums custom groove template. The same custom template may be applied to all tracks in the song to give it a uniform rhythmic swing. Note that most DAWs allow you to impose groove settings on audio files as well as MIDI files.

and sometimes a bridge or middle-eight section (See Terms of the trade, right).

To break the flow of the song, and clearly change the dynamics, a 'breakdown' section is often inserted before the final chorus, though not always. Not only does the breakdown provide a respite in energy, it allows the arranger to re-build the song all over again, toying with the emotions of listeners before returning all mix elements for one last blast.

These breakdowns and builds are especially important in dance music, where an understanding of the emotional state and expectations of the dancefloor is paramount. DJs' first-hand experience of what floats listeners' boats makes them some of the best arrangers around: they know where to bring in a breakdown and when to build up again. They are masters of the dancefloor's emotions.

Once you've decided the order of the verses, choruses and so on, and created a solid first arrangement, it is time to make the orchestration decisions, choosing which instruments will play during which verse(s) and which parts will drop where.

To do this I usually **work backwards from the point in the song where everything is in** – often the final chorus. Then I move towards the front of the song, dropping out parts and changing balances so that the song dynamic builds in a way that at the same time feels natural and also ever-engaging.

If you have guitar, keyboard and synth pad parts recorded in every verse, for example, you might decide that during the first verse the rhythm section and vocal is accompanied by the piano, or maybe

acoustic guitar. In the next verse the synth pad part might be added, or perhaps one of the instruments could be switched for another. A producer might also record a completely new instrument track after mixing has started if they feel the song needs it.

It should be noted that it is not usually enough to simply shuffle around a number of identical musical backing blocks and then dropping vocals over the top because the song will end up with the same dynamic in every verse, while every chorus will have the same weight as every other chorus. Although it's fine to build the basic song structure by block-shifting, instruments will need to be dropped out or rebalanced in the different 'copies' to give the song a sense of dynamic shape. Otherwise you risk losing the listener's interest.

COLOUR: MAINTAINING LISTENER INTEREST

The fact that our hearing systems have evolved as survival mechanisms means we're naturally highly attuned to changes in our acoustic environment; things that remain constant tend to get tuned out by our brains. This has a fundamental impact on how we make music.

It's so easy – and far too tempting – in our cut and paste world to take a section of a song, such as a chorus, and then copy it to wherever a chorus is needed. While this may work perfectly well structurally, using the same vocal take for every occurrence of the chorus won't engage the listener as much as if you use a different take for each one – even if the performance is very similar. You can sometimes afford to be a little more casual when repeating backing vocals or when adding layers, but for the

TERMS OF THE TRADE

Intro: Opening section of the track. In pop, the shorter the better – usually. (Remember Billy Joel's words of insider wisdom: 'If you're gonna have a hit / You gotta make it fit / So they cut it down to 3:05'.) On the flip side is that lovely long intro to Gerry Rafferty's 'Baker Street' and the opening drum opus on Dire Straits' 'Money For Nothing'. Remember the rules are there to be bent or broken.

Breakdown: Section where the main rhythm drops out and the track breaks down to its simplest elements.

Drop: The moment the track 'drops back in' with all parts playing, usually after the breakdown. The term is mainly used in dance music.

Build: A build in energy, typically at the end of the breakdown, where new elements gradually fill the mix, building tension to a climax before the drop. It's the moment for the drummer to have fun.

Fill: Anything from a drum break to a crazy noise sequence to round off a bar or phrase before a new section begins.

Middle eight: Annoying, or sublime, section that is different from the verses and chorus. Typically lasts eight bars.

THE POWER OF FOUR

Most pop music has a four-to-the-bar beat, which is easy to follow and can be interpreted as an echo of the human heartbeat. There have been a few successful departures from the more usual 4/4 time signature, such as The Stranglers' 'Golden Brown' and Dave Brubeck's 'Take Five', but I've often thought that people who write in 5/13 or 'pi over 9' time must suffer from some kind of heart arrhythmia!

Arrangements are also often built using a four-bar paradigm. That is to say, verses, choruses, intros and outros are often multiples of four bars. A typical verse might be 16 bars, and a chorus eight, for example.

Underground dance is almost religious in its reverence to this kind of structure: the DJ build must be 16 bars at least, with turnarounds every eight or 16 bars. The golden rule is rarely broken.

Of course there's no actual law to say that all musical elements must be two, four, eight or 16 bars long – even if the listener, on some kind of unconscious level, expects it. Slipping in an extra bar can work magic sometimes; that epic guitar solo at the end of Pink Floyd's 'Comfortably Numb' would not have been nearly so dramatic without the extra D major bar inserted as a launch point just before it starts.

In pop and dance productions a common trick is to insert a sneaky single-bar of silence after the build and before the track drops: a one-bar tension raiser that at the same time confuses the dancefloor and drives it wilder.

When working on the arrangement then, you must be ever-aware of the wandering attention span of the audience. Wagner didn't write his 'Ring Cycle' for today's pop music consumers, that's for sure. And while prog rock epics still have their fans, a commercial hit has to strike a balance between familiar repetition (choruses in particular) and making people switch off through boredom.

Getting this balance right can be particularly tricky when an artist or band brings a song into the studio when it was originally written with live performance in mind. In a live situation you might be able to get away with cycling around the same intro chords for a minute and a half while asking the gathered population of Neasden if they're having a good time (No!), but when it comes to a recording, a typical listener will lose patience if the same thing is repeated in the same way more than two or three times.

Much of this engagement is, as outlined above, down to the arrangement. Introducing a different guitar part into the mix for verse 2, or a funky clav line to accompany verse 3 will help to maintain interest. Avoiding the copy and paste buffers and ensuring repeated vocal lines are not repeated vocal takes will help too. But there are also a wealth of production tricks that you can draw on:

> **Pruning intros ruthlessly:** A pop track should be powering into verse one, or sometimes a shortened version of the chorus, within the first 20 seconds. Where an intro is extended, try adding accidental sounds into the mix such as breaths or guitar noises and then repeating them as rhythmic elements, or time-stretching them beyond recognition for use as ear candy.

lead vocal the audience craves something that sounds like a different complete performance (even if it was comped from half a dozen different takes) every time. If you don't have the material to make this work, at the very least aim for two different lead chorus lines which are repeated twice for some variation.

In dance music – where sampled loops dominate production – the finest producers are aware of the need for constant change. Any number of tricks, from synth layering to dynamic filtering and subtle rhythmic changes can break what could easily become a monotonous four-to-the-floor workout. Subtle percussive workouts are weaved in and out of the groove, while build FX have developed into an artform of their own, with any number of tricks employed to ratchet up the pressure.

> **Dynamic filter treatments** on synths, basslines and whole backing tracks have been used by dance producers for years. It's an old trick but one that doesn't really go out of fashion. Use different filters on otherwise repeating synth parts to meet the ear's craving for change. During verses, where the vocal needs to sit loud and proud above dense instrumentation, try adding a filter across the entire music bus, and pulling the high-cut filter way down into the 400–500Hz region, only opening it again at the end of the verse to build into the chorus.

> Some techniques have been done to death. At one time composers felt it useful to give a song a lift by introducing **a key change** just as things were about to get boring (it was something of a tradition among boy bands for the performers to rise from their chairs at this point). One example of this working rather better than it might have with a lesser performer is in Celine Dione's chart-topping 'My Heart Will Go On'. Although I've heard enough of that too! Thankfully the most crass examples of this musical device have died out, Eurovision songwriters being among the few endorsees left. If you must use a key change, instead of plumping for the old 'up by a semitone' routine try using a different interval.

> **Drum fills** present a time-honoured method of varying the beat (and allowing the drummer to show off). The occasional fill or open hi-hat motif helps draw in the listener. Drum fills are particularly useful in genres that use quantised drums as even the tightest live drummer invariably introduces some natural variation to the timing that helps stop the listener tuning out.

> **Automation** is your friend. In the old days producers would keenly ride the

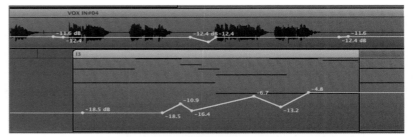

Fig 1: Automation is used on this pad part to gently change the volume during a verse, raising it towards the chorus; these subtle fluctuations – sometimes across several parts – help keep the mix fresh.

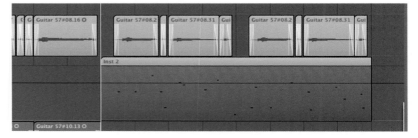

Fig 2: In this example, a guitar part is layered with a programmed Midi synth line, introduced in the second verse to introduce some variation to the arrangement.

faders of melodic backing parts, like synths, keyboards and guitars, to ease them in and out of the mix, introducing subtle – almost unconscious – change that ensured ongoing engagement (Fig 1). Automation makes the whole job much easier, and anything can be automated, from simple volume levels to pan position, to the amount of signal feeding effects sends. You can even automate individual effects settings.

> Try **layering** parts with different instruments at different points (Fig 2). A slinky guitar part may play alone in verse 1 and then be layered with a noodling synth line in verse 2. Neither has to stand out of the mix – just gently reinforce what's gone before and change the tonal feel of the verse.

SOME TECHNIQUES HAVE BEEN DONE TO DEATH. AT ONE TIME COMPOSERS FELT IT USEFUL TO GIVE A SONG A LIFT BY INTRODUCING A KEY CHANGE JUST AS THINGS WERE ABOUT TO GET BORING.

❯ Try **changing the character of the reverb** at set points during the song instead of maintaing the same ambience setting for the whole of a track. Experiment with a different type of reverb as a spot effect during a breakdown, for example, or using a different vocal treatment for the chorus.

THE SALVAGE OPERATION

Not all of your clients will play perfectly all the time (just as long as they *pay* perfectly most of the time!), and comping and/or copy/pasting sections of drum, guitar and bass parts to create the illusion of a tighter performance is commonplace. This kind of salvage work is considerably easier to do if the song was recorded to a click, but as I point out in Recording Bands, Chapter 10, working to a click doesn't always do the music any favours – it depends on the musicians involved and on the style of music being recorded.

Where there is no click it is still possible to edit using the waveform display of the drum part as a guide so that you can see where the beats are. Short sections can be copied and pasted into other parts of the song to replace flawed sections.

The inherent problem of working with audio that isn't nailed to a click track is that the tempo of the song has a habit of drifting slightly. Fortunately, all the serious DAWs now allow you to perform time-stretching of selected regions on the arrange page, so if the part you've copied is too long or too short to fill the gap that needs filling because of a tempo variation, you can easily massage it to length, disguising the edits with a short crossfade if necessary.

Note / If your recorded tracks suffer from a significant amount of spill, copy and paste editing may not work as the spill may not

match the new section. It's another reason to get your recordings as dry and free from spill as possible where you know extensive editing will be needed.

THE MAJOR SALVAGE JOB

Small copy and paste tweaks and gentle massaging of recorded audio into time is par for the producer's course, but what happens when the amount of work required is rather more significant? How far you go with this depends on the budget and the act you're working with. In the case of an inexperienced band where all the performances are sloppy, it is possible (with great patience) to rebuild the song from the ground up and force the various elements to sit on a quantise grid.

The first step in a major salvage project is to determine the nominal tempo of the song and adjust the DAW tempo to match it as closely as possible. Before attempting this make sure all the audio tracks are continuous from start to finish and that they all begin at the same time. If they don't, the relative timing of the various parts will move, making your life considerably more complicated.

If your DAW has an automatic BPM detector try it on the drum track to see if it can extract any useful information. Because of timing variations in the original performance, it won't line up with the grid at this point, but it might help to get the first beat of the song lined up with the start of a grid quantize bar. If the BPM detector fails to deliver, you'll need to beatmatch the old-school way. Set a click track running, loop through a section where the kick drum sits on the first beat of the bar and then manually increase/decrease the song tempo until the click more or less hits on the groove.

When you've found the nominal tempo start laying out a backing rhythm track by taking the best-played 'straight' rhythmic parts and copying them to new tracks in at least one or two bar sections – ideally longer – using the time-stretch tool to make them fit the grid.

Where the drums are recorded over several tracks (kick, snare, toms, overheads, for example), all the tracks should be grouped so that all the relevant parts stay together (page 283). Any time-stretching should be applied equally to all parts. Bars with fills should be copied separately and tweaked in length to fit. I've occasionally even had to divide fills into individual hits and then move these to get them sounding in time.

Having assembled a complete drum track and checked that it plays smoothly, it's time to do the same with the bass part(s), ensuring that they lock tightly with the drums. Rogue notes can be separated out using the scissors tool and then shifted into place using the drum waveform as a guide.

Once the bass part is complete and working with the tidied drum part, you might want to bounce it down so that you have a complete audio track. Not only does this guard against accidentally disturbing the edits, but where your DAW supports audio quantise, you may be able to tighten the timing further. If the rhythm of the song isn't straight, consider using a section of the edited drum part to create a custom quantise groove template (page 277) so that the quantised bass sits tightly with the drums.

Vocals can usually be cut into phrases and slid into position unless the timing of the original performance was extremely bad

– re-read Pre-Mix Housekeeping, Chapter 17 for more details on manipulating vocals.

I don't like using timestretch on lead vocals as even the best algorithms produce some undesirable side effects, although you can usually get away with it when making small adjustments.

Backing vocals are a little more tolerant of stretching as they're usually either layered or hidden behind the main vocal, but again do what you can by moving individual phrases around before stretching or squashing to fit. As a rule, keep all crossfades between edited sections as short as possible – just long enough to hide clicks or abrupt transitions.

MIDI instruments are easier to deal with as you can quantise or move the MIDI data without worrying about the effect on sound quality, but electric guitars, acoustic guitars, keyboards recorded as audio and so on each have to be dealt with individually, a section at a time employing time-stretching where necessary.

I don't like having to do this kind of 'demolish and rebuild' salvaging; the truth is that if you have to go to such lengths, it is often far better to get the players back in to replace their parts. But sometimes it's the only solution where the client needs a result and doesn't want to / can't get the original players back.

Yet however painful the process is, it can be good training to go through a track rebuilding exercise at least once in your career as it quickly teaches you what you can get away with and what will pose problems. It might also convince you that a career in plumbing is far more profitable and considerably less stressful! ●

The dreaded salvage operation

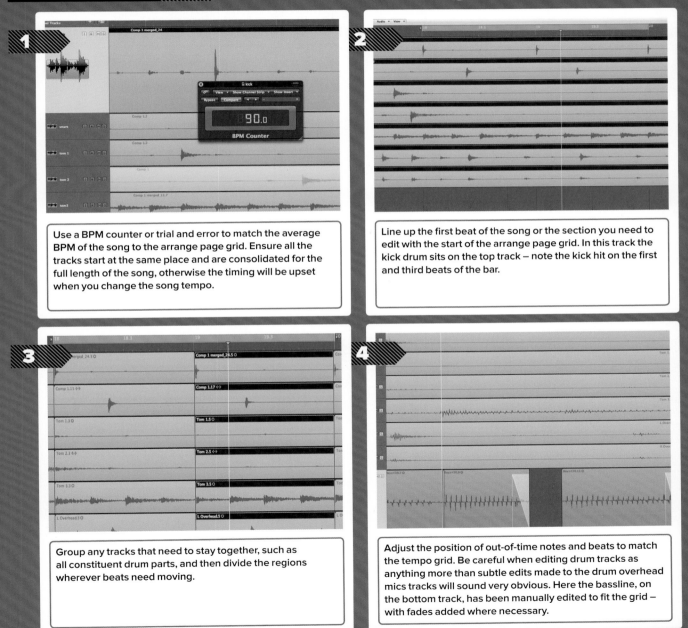

1

Use a BPM counter or trial and error to match the average BPM of the song to the arrange page grid. Ensure all the tracks start at the same place and are consolidated for the full length of the song, otherwise the timing will be upset when you change the song tempo.

2

Line up the first beat of the song or the section you need to edit with the start of the arrange page grid. In this track the kick drum sits on the top track – note the kick hit on the first and third beats of the bar.

3

Group any tracks that need to stay together, such as all constituent drum parts, and then divide the regions wherever beats need moving.

4

Adjust the position of out-of-time notes and beats to match the tempo grid. Be careful when editing drum tracks as anything more than subtle edits made to the drum overhead mics tracks will sound very obvious. Here the bassline, on the bottom track, has been manually edited to fit the grid – with fades added where necessary.

19
THE MIXDOWN

BEFORE YOU START

So this is it: the mixdown, the culmination of all your efforts so far – the placing of mics, the massaging of egos, the coaxing of performances, the comping of vocals, the tweaks to the arrangement.

A lot of work will have been done before you get to this point. Depending on the track being mixed, you will have done some or all of the following:

❯ Any **pre-mix housekeeping** (Chapter 17) – cleaning up audio, editing spill, cutting unwanted frequencies where appropriate, consolidating audio and MIDI instruments as audio tracks, tidying up the DAW's mixer page, and backing up data.

❯ Sifted through the various vocal and instrumental solo takes and **comped** the best parts, removing unwanted material (page 263).

❯ Done any **fine-tuning and editing** in Melodyne or other off-line pitch correction software where applicable (page 262).

❯ **Set up fader and/or bus groups** for groups of tracks that belong together, such as drums, backing vocals, layered guitars, bass parts and so on. The fewer faders you have to worry about, the easier the mix will be.

❯ Set up an **early rough mix balance**.

❯ You may also have done some work on the **arrangement** (Chapter 18).

❯ If you've **not** done anything to the arrangement yet, you may find yourself making changes to it as you proceed through the mixdown. These changes can range from the subtle (cutting a guitar line

to free up mix space or losing a couple of bars from an over-long intro) to more major interventions (inserting an additional chorus to add weight to the end of a song).

When making these last-minute arrangement tweaks you have a choice. Do you try to get a **rough working balance first** and then turn your attention to the arrangement, or do you **work on the arrangement first** and the balance afterwards? It's a chicken and egg situation, because changes to one has an inevitable impact on the other (cutting an unnecessary percussion line from the arrangement, for example, will free up mix space for the drum overheads).

Most producers aim to get the general arrangement nailed before they start balancing the mix.

But note that this is a general shape only: in practice you will find yourself continually tweaking the structure – editing fills, shifting ad-libs, and so on – as you progress. Arranging, like balancing, is an ongoing process that doesn't end until the master is signed off, especially with dance mixes.

Tip / At this stage there will probably still be more parts in the DAW's arrange window than you ultimately use. Until you set up a good initial balance, you won't know which ones will fit and which won't. Keep all of them until it's obvious which parts can go.

APPROACHES TO MIXING

The three broad approaches to mixing can be thought of as '**rhythm first**', '**melody first**' and the holistic '**all tracks up**'. The one you choose will depend on the material you're working on and your own instincts about what the focus of the track is, though much also depends on your level of experience.

PRO TIP: REFERENCES

Even experienced engineers and producers keep commercial material for reference on hand, ideally in a similar style to the music being worked on.

Not only does this reference material give the less experienced producer something to aim for, it also helps 'recalibrate' the ears during long mixing sections that can distort your perspective – no matter how experienced you are.

Rhythm first: This approach is about building the track from a solid foundation upwards. The solid foundation in this case is the rhythm section, comprising the drums and bass line. This is the usual approach for tracks built around a dominant beat — including dance, urban and many pop tracks. It is also often the best approach for the less experienced engineer or producer.

The initial mix balance should be performed on the loudest part of the song, leaving enough safety headroom (right) to accommodate the extra parts as you bring them in. Setting up the DAW's loop points around the loudest part — often a closing chorus — means you can tweak continually as the song cycles.

Whatever DAW makers tell you about the fancy maths used in their mix engines, I find that my mixes sound clearer if I keep the individual track and master mix levels under control and add any necessary make-up gain and processing when mastering. In other words, treat the top of the meter as an absolute limit, not a target! A final 24-bit mix that peaks at -6dB is fine.

Note / In a typical rhythm-led song the balance of the bass line and drums remains fairly constant throughout. Although there may be occasional level changes dictated by the dynamics of the song (a dropping of energy during a breakdown, for example), if you start making serious level changes to either the drums or bass then you risk destabilising the song.

Melody first: Where the rhythm plays a less pivotal role than the vocals, or a solo instrument in the case of a largely instrumental composition, it makes more sense to concentrate on the most important melodic elements first, before bringing in supportive parts later. This approach suits vocal-led jazz, folk and some more esoteric pop and downtempo indie and rock tracks.

With this approach, the producer might place a backing part or two in the mix — keys, guitar, pads etc — and then use them as a foundation against which to work on the pivotal melodic or vocal part/s.

All tracks up: This is for more experienced producers or engineers who try to get a complete mix balance, albeit not the final version, by bringing up all faders and then tweaking until they get a good balance. After this they work on the EQ, processing and effects before making any final mix adjustments. This approach isn't so different from that employed by the live sound engineer mixing a band at a festival or a multi-band gig where there's been no time for a sound check — something I do more often than I'd like!

The truth — of course — is that few producers stick to one method. Each has its merits, and the nature of the track will normally steer you in a particular direction; identify the core elements of the song and you'll know what to balance first.

One thing most engineers would agree on, whichever approach you take, is that **you should balance the loudest section of the song first**, then the next loudest and keep working backwards until you get to the quietest part. This allows you to get the levels set up correctly for the loudest part and then proceed through the mix without worrying about running into headroom problems.

JARGON BUSTER: HEADROOM

Headroom is simply the difference between the highest signal peaks and digital clipping (Digital Full Scale or 0dB FS). Because low frequency components in a typical instrument or voice tend to be much louder than higher frequencies, removing unnecessary lows has the effect of increasing the available headroom (or safety margin) as well as taking some load off the end-user's speaker system.

EARLY PREPARATIONS

When the levels feel like they're getting somewhere close to where they should be, it's time to do some important foundational legwork.

Group buses: We've talked about the benefits of using group buses before. The human brain struggles to concentrate on too many things at the same time. Breaking the mix into groups that can be balanced using group bus faders or grouped channel faders makes life considerably easier, especially on big, busy mixes. If you didn't do this at the pre-mix stage, do it now before you go any further.

Even a complex mix can usually be reduced to faders for drums, guitar, bass, synths, backing vocals and lead vocal — with perhaps another two for instrumental solos and spot effects. An even simpler reduction, commonly used in parts of the dance production world, is kick/s, other drums, bass, all music, FX, parallel bus/es. Where vocals are featured, additional buses are added for lead vocal and backing vocals. Once you see the makeup of a song, it is usually pretty obvious which parts can be grouped and which can't.

Any decisions you make on grouping at this stage don't have to be final: you can re-allocate individual tracks to different groups or change a track's relative volume within a group at any time.

Early balance in mono: Even in a predominantly stereo world, mono compatibility remains important, and I find it useful to set the initial balance with the monitor controller set to mono, before you give yourself the luxury of stereo.

Setting the balance in mono like this means you don't get a false sense of separation from the stereo panning, although **it's still worth setting the pan controls to where you think they'll eventually need to be**, as the level of the sounds can change slightly depending on the panning characteristics (the so-called 'panning law') employed by the DAW.

Why is this? For various technical reasons the signal level when the sound is panned to the centre (that is, fed to both the left and right buses equally) is usually not the same as when the pot is panned completely left or completely right. This means that a mono mix made with the pan pots in the centre will have a slightly different balance from one made with some of the pans centred and some panned extreme left or right.

By panning the sounds in the DAW and then using the monitor controller to let you hear a mono mix, you can avoid the situation where you balance the mix in mono with all the DAW pans set centrally to find that the balance changes slightly when you pan sounds to where they need to be.

Effects on the buses: Using effects on buses allows you to treat multiple channels with the same effect; all drum parts, for example, might be placed in the same ambient space, or all vocal parts given the same delay.

Even though you won't know what specific effects a part will need yet, it may be worth placing one plate or hall-style, and one subtler ambient-style reverb on different aux buses, with perhaps a tempo-synced delay on a third. All settings can be refined later, but adding some initial effects at

MONITORING 101

HOW LOUD TO MIX

While it is tempting to mix at high volumes, there are three good reasons not to do so:

> **the ears quickly tire** – making the process harder work, and mistakes more likely,

> louder volumes make it **more difficult to judge the balance**, and

> repeated high-level listening over a period of years makes **long-term hearing damage** more likely.

A better approach, for the mix and your hearing, is to turn up the monitors for short spells to check the mix is working at higher levels, but to do most work at a more modest volume – the kind of level the end user is most likely to listen at.

Having a second set of 'grot-box' speakers with a limited bass extension helps you evaluate how the mix will sound on a portable radio or compact hi-fi system. These small speakers are particularly important for judging how bass instruments will sound on consumer systems.

Most pro studios have at least two sets of speakers, often more, among which you'll find a set of grot-boxes – usually something like an old Auratone or a hard-wired Ghetto blaster. Yamaha NS-10s are also still popular as a real-world secondary reference. Indeed, some engineers rely on them almost entirely for mixing.

You can set up a cheap grot-box monitoring system using a portable music player with an aux input. Just feed this from one of the stereo outputs on the monitor controller and switch to it whenever you need to. In addition to revealing how the music will translate on smaller systems, it will probably also let you know if there's too much low end, as the speaker cones will flap around more than usual and the sound may distort excessively.

A practical alternative to a grot-box is the Focusrite VRM Box, which emulates the sound of several different types of speaker over headphones.

MIXING FOR CLUB RIGS

Not all tracks are destined for the radio, the iPod or the car stereo. Some go straight to the clubs.

When mixing for a club rig, most of the same monitoring rules apply: don't listen too loud, only do detailed work on headphones and so on.

But you might find yourself throwing the volume up more regularly – to check that the mix stands up when pushed loud.

Many dance producers also road-test their tracks in a club environment – either when DJ'ing themselves or by asking a friendly DJ for a favour – before bouncing out the final master to see that the arrangement and mix work on a big rig.

▲ The Yamaha NS-10: Probably the most widely used second set of studio speakers in the world.

USING HEADPHONES

While I'd be reluctant to mix anything entirely on headphones, they do play an important role in the mixing process, allowing the producer to do precision listening and to check that the mix translates properly to headphones or earbuds. **A solid mix needs to sound good on both speakers and headphones.**

Precision listening: I like to think of headphones as sonic magnifying glasses, helping you delve further into a mix to identify problems on a more forensic level. Headphones are particularly good when making delicate changes to EQ, compression, panning and some effects (reverb in particular).

For this work, semi-enclosed or open-backed phones are generally the best as they add less colouration to the low end. It is worth investing in a decent pair as higher-end models are good at revealing mix problems, such as digital glitches and mild cases of clipping, which budget studio monitor speakers may not reveal. As with speakers, take care not to listen at excessive levels – especially for prolonged periods.

Translation: Monitoring on headphones also allows you to check how the mix will sound when played on mobile devices and they may show up problems that you missed when listening on speakers.

The proliferation of iPods and other personal music devices means that a significant percentage of the listening public now experience their music via in-ear buds. As a consequence, just as you have a pair of grot-boxes to check the fidelity of a mix on low-end speakers, so it's worth having a pair of buds on hand to check how the mix will translate on consumer headphones. Several high profile producers have disclosed that they spend a lot of time optimising their mixes for earbuds. Don't spend too long on them though: they can tire the ears quickly.

Tip / Sometimes you get so involved with a mix that you lose perspective and can't tell what is too loud and what isn't. Listening at a lower level on the grot-box speakers will help, but it can also be useful to listen to the mix from the next room with the door between left open. A surprising number of engineers use this trick, which has a way of revealing balance problems that for some reason don't seem obvious when you're sitting in front of the speakers.

KNOWING YOUR SPEAKERS

In many ways it doesn't matter how you monitor, or which tools you use (as long as they are reasonably good). The most important thing is **knowing your speakers and/or headphones**.

Many producers have no choice but to mix in less-than-perfect rooms, with inexpensive monitors and no option of a second pair. These apparent limitations are less important than knowing the nuances of the system you work with.

Getting to know your speakers means listening to how commercial mixes sound in your studio and mixing your own tracks to get a sound that is as close to these sonically as you can.

And remember, again, that many successful producers keep commercial tracks parked on spare DAW channels for ongoing A/B referencing during mixdown. Referring back to these commercial mixes regularly allows you to 'reset' your ears to a sound that you know translates.

TECHNIQUE: BLIND LISTENING

Switch off the computer monitor every so often or activate the screen saver.

In the era of the arrange window it can be easy to think of a song in terms of a 2D visual construct when it is nothing of the sort.

Turning off the screen lets you concentrate on the music without visual distraction.

this stage will give you an early indication of how parts might sit in the wider mix with ambience applied. I tend to add these to my template song so whenever I start a new project they're ready to go.

Automation, Part 1: Although the really detailed automation programming usually happens later – when the mix is close to completion – some engineers find it useful to do some broad automation early on to help key parts, like vocals, sit comfortably in its surroundings for the duration of the track. The point here is that if you've taken a 'rhythm first' approach, and have balanced the loudest part of the track – with the vocals in – they may be noticeably too loud during quieter sections earlier in the song.

Automation on the vocals is typically used for:

> **ensuring the vocal line sits at the right level relative to the backing** across the song, and

> **ironing out major vocal level discrepancies caused by less than ideal mic technique** and by the level changes that often occur when singers change to a different vocal register.

Once this basic automation has been done, dynamic processing can be used to add density to the vocal part as well as tightening its dynamic range (Vocal Production, Chapter 14).

At this stage you might also introduce basic level automation to change the relative levels of key instruments or groups of instruments in the different sections, although a well-crafted arrangement will tend to build naturally, relying on the players' dynamics and the way the musical

LESS IS MORE

In the Studio SOS series, Sound On Sound writers help readers with problems in their studios. One of the most common issues is the excessive use of plug-ins for no good reason. Sometimes the reader will go out to make a cup of coffee while we tinker with their mix. When they get back they ask what we've done to make it sound so much better.

In fact the only thing we've done is bypassed all plug-ins other than the reverb – and we've dialled in rather less of that! Ironically, thinking too deeply about which effects to use, and adding too many plug-ins, is one of the major reasons home recordings end up sounding a mess. If you're struggling, try simplifying things a bit.

arrangement introduces instruments at different points in the song.

Then...: Only once the balance is close to how you finally need it should you switch back to stereo monitoring and start thinking about effects and EQ.

BASS IN THE MIX

Alongside the drums (Drum Production, Chapter 16), the bass line is the most important element in the track's foundation. So fundamental is it to the track's rhythm and mix foundation that **it should be present whenever key mixing decisions are made to the drums** – particularly the kick drum. If you are mixing using a 'rhythm first' approach then the bass should be introduced to the mix immediately.

The bass line is either supplied by a bass guitar, a sampler or a synth, sometimes in combination. From an engineer's standpoint, **synth and sampled bass** parts are the easiest to deal with, offering a range of benefits:

> The player's keyboard technique doesn't affect the sound of the notes – only the level and timing.

> Where the bass line is available as MIDI data, any level discrepancies can be

fixed in the MIDI editor. The timing can be tightened using the DAW's quantize facilities or by lining up the MIDI data with specific drum beats viewed in the drum track waveform.

❯ Where the MIDI data powers a plug-in instrument, you can simply change the patch, or the instrument, to create a whole new sound. The same data can be used on other channels to create stacked layered basses. It can also be used to generate new upper synth lines on higher octaves to reinforce the lower (often sub) bass.

Despite the inherent flexibility of having the MIDI data, beware of changing the original sound too much. Sticking close to the original is often best from a feel perspective as the player's performance (particularly note duration) is invariably influenced by the sound being used during the original recording. A radical change to the sound's attack and release settings can throw the track's wider rhythm and destabilise its foundation. Where a new sound is too different from the original, try adjusting the note lengths or the envelope of the new sound, paying particular attention to how the bass and drums work together.

Some styles of sampled bass guitar can be interchanged without causing problems as long as the samples feature a similar style of playing. However, switching from a conventional finger-played bass to a 'slap and pull' style sound probably won't work as the playing approach is very different.

Life is slightly more difficult when dealing with **real bass guitar lines** as the engineer is at the mercy of the recording, and the technique of the player. The majority of bass guitar recordings are now made using some form of DI technique (page 124),

often straight from the instrument using a DI box, so what you get to work with is the raw sound straight from the bass guitar.

Sometimes you only need to compress and EQ a well-played DI'd bass part to make it sit comfortably in a mix.

If you need to give the sound a different flavour, the proliferation of bass amp modelling plug-ins has given the producer a wide choice of tonal characters that sound more complex, and often more rounded, than applying basic EQ.

As with guitar amp modelling, each combination of amp and speaker has a unique tonal colour so it should be easy to find one that works for the track; pay particular attention to how the bass sound sits with the kick drum.

Getting the right sound from a well-played bass is usually straightforward, but too often engineers are faced with a bass guitar recording that's either uneven, lacks attack or is beset by string rattles. Some fret noise is part of the sound of the instrument, but when played poorly even the best bass guitar can lack power and sound messy. Adding compression exacerbates the problem, making the sound even more messy and emphasising any rattles and squeaks. Cue the bass salvage job.

BASS SALVAGE

String rattle: **High-cut EQ** can be used to reduce the level of offending string rattle, but it will also rob the bass of definition; there's only so far you can go before compromising the tonality of the bass part. An 18dB/octave high-cut filter is perhaps the best option: simply reduce its cutoff frequency until you get the best compromise between clarity and noise.

Using a suitable **amp model** plug-in, or even just a **speaker model**, can often sound more convincing than EQ. As a rule, 15 inch speakers (and their models) filter out more top end than smaller speakers, making them a good choice for cleaning up a messy bass sound. A combination of high-cut filtering and a suitable amp model often delivers a better result than either alone.

More balls: Under-assertive bass lines can be given an energy injection with a healthy dose of **compression** from a dbx160 compressor or other 'compressor with attitude'. An attack time of around 20ms with a release time of 60–100ms can help. Adjust the amount of compression to show a gain reduction of up to 10–12dB. Because compression brings up noise, it may be necessary to employ a **gate** prior to compression.

Adding some **parallel compression** (page 172) can also fatten up an insipid bass sound: try routing some signal to a parallel bus with an aggressive compressor before resorting to more drastic measures.

Layering or replacing: Where the performance is too messy to rescue, or where compression can't make up for a lack of playing technique, you're often left with little choice but to replace the bass part completely, either using a different player, or programming the line as best you can using a sampled bass guitar, or – and this can be a life-saver – layering the less-than-ideal existing part with a new synth bass part.

Layering retains the character of the original performance while bulking it up so that it stands up in the mix. Where string rattles are a problem, the new layered part can be pushed forward and the rattling part eased back so that its essential character remains, with the rattles much lower in the mix.

When layering, a **bass synth** often works better than a bass guitar sample as it doesn't end up sounding like a double-tracked bass guitar part. Using a synth also allows you to adjust the new bass sound's envelope so that if, for example, only the attack part of the bass guitar sound needs beefing up, you can use a shorter synth tone that decays before the natural decay of the bass guitar. Analogue synths work well at beefing up basses; the MiniMoog is a particularly good candidate for the task. Using a pure sine wave is also great for adding bulk to the bottom end – and can be mixed at a surprisingly low volume.

Generating a new layered line from the original bass part can be time-consuming. Some DAWS provide an **audio-to-MIDI** function that attempts to create a MIDI part from a monophonic audio line. This is always worth a try, although you may have to spend a little time deleting false notes and correcting errors where the software didn't establish the correct note. However arduous, this process may still be quicker than working out the part, learning it and then replaying it. Melodyne also offers good audio-to-MIDI facilities – but be prepared to spend some time cleaning up the end result.

The key to successful layering is precise timing: get the timing wrong and you can end up with a bigger mess than you started with. This often means getting busy with precise MIDI editing, performed with the original audio file open at the same time.

Tip / It pays to check the **phase** of the two layered parts to make sure you're not losing any low end. Flip the polarity of the new part and see if the subjective level of bass increases or decreases. Pick whichever has the most low end. If it changes from note to note, try **rolling away all lows** from the original part below around 120Hz and rely on the new part to provide the necessary low end bulk. Also check the waveforms of both parts on screen to see that the sounds are correctly aligned and that they at least start off in phase (page 246).

Tip / Dance music makes frequent use of live / programmed bass combination lines, with a programmed bass line complemented with live samples to provide real-feel slides, string-snaps and fretboard noise. Deciding which parts play when is important: for example, you probably wouldn't want to layer a fixed pitch synth note with a sampled slide. Some sample libraries contain dedicated folders full of bass string sounds and effects purposefully designed to be layered with programmed sequences.

Tip / Where the layered bass line is being used to disguise string rattle, an envelope modifying plug-in such as the SPL Transient Designer can be used to shorten the original sound, disguising some of the rattles, with the layered sound being extended to whatever length the note needs to be. Most of the character of a sound comes from its attack section so keeping a shortened version of the original sound may be all that's needed to fool the ear.

KICK AND BASS

If there's a single relationship in the mix that the engineer needs to get right, it is the one between the kick drum and the bass.

The low end of the kick and bass occupy the same, hugely important part of the sonic spectrum. A large amount of a mix's energy is concentrated in the lower frequencies, and both parts need to be able to do

their job there, each maintaining its own character, energy and definition.

This relationship is even more important in dance music, where many of the melodic mix elements are simply afterthoughts to the kick/bass relationship. **Its importance cannot be overstated: the kick and bass supply the foundation for the whole mix – get it right and the rest of the mixdown becomes a whole lot easier.**

Fortunately, there are a few surprisingly simple techniques that can be used to keep the two parts from fighting, and to forge a solid alliance between them instead. They all have the same goal: giving each part its own space to work. Which technique is right will depend on how the bass line interacts with the kick in the given track.

'Fat bass, skinny kick': In tracks that have relatively simple drum parts and a solid, rhythmic bass line, it is often easiest to accommodate a big bass sound in the low end underpinning a well-defined, but not excessively fat, kick.

In this scenario, the bass line does its work in the lower frequencies, with the kick drum's lows shaved so that it delivers more punch and high-end energy than depth. Visualising the two parts in the frequency spectrum, **the bass sits beneath the kick**.

'Fat kick, skinny bass': Where the bass line is busier and the song is beat-driven, it is often better to use a big, defining kick and tailor the bass line to keep it out of the kick's way.

The bass can be pulled away from the kick in two ways; through **clever programming**

PRO TIP

Every pro engineer has their own way of balancing and blending the elements that make up the mix, but almost all stress the importance of getting the bass and kick drum working together, both tonally and rhythmically.

Vocals are also crucial, the concensus being that if you can nail the vocals and rhythm section, everything else can be slotted into place without too much trouble – providing you have a good musical arrangement.

(in the case of synth basses, shorter notes with a fast attack help the kick drive the song, whereas longer, fatter sounds are more likely to cloud the low end of the mix) and/or by **using EQ** (the frequency range that determines the character of the bass is often in the 150–350Hz part of the spectrum. Try using subtle boost in this area to emphasise the core sound of the bass while using a gentle low-cut filter to trim the low end just enough to keep it out the way of the kick.) Visualising the two parts in the frequency spectrum in this approach, **the kick sits beneath the bass**.

'Scooped bass': Where there is no obvious candidate for the fat and skinny roles you need to do some judicious EQing to both parts to create space in one for the other.

EQ can either be used to carve a dip in the bass part to accommodate the kick drum or vice versa. To open up some space for the bass line, for example, you might use a parametric filter to create a scoop in the 80–100Hz range of the kick drum, where most of its energy resides. This allows the bass to push through the scooped hole, consolidating its own place in the mix. The same approach can be used in reverse to make space for the kick.

It's worth noting that picking the right frequency to scoop is key: you need to be sensitive to the **fundamental frequencies** (right) of both to work out what needs to push through and what can be scooped.

An additional trick – that can be used with all three methods, but most commonly with the scooped bass approach – is to set up a system that allows you to **duck the low end of the bass when a kick drum is present**. **Multiband compressors** or **frequency-dependent duckers** can both be employed

DRUMS AND BASS: THE RADIO PERSPECTIVE

Where a track is intended for radio or domestic play rather than the club market, it is often more important to resolve drum and bass conflicts that occur in the 100Hz–250Hz range rather than lower down. Not only is this the more audible range on most car and domestic playback systems, it is also where the actual **character** of the sounds resides (the fundamental pitches lie further down).

While the thump of most kick drums lies around 70–90Hz, the character of the drum is often more audible in the 150–180Hz zone, while its defining click can be as high up as 3–4kHz. It is important to ensure that the peak in the bass line doesn't occur in the same places.

If the bass projects its tonal character in the 200–250Hz range and the kick around 150–170Hz, they'll probably sound more distinct than if they both have their character in the same area – even if their fundamental frequencies (the really low frequencies below 90Hz or so) overlap. In either case, you may still need some help from EQ to cut into the kick spectrum in the area where the bass character needs to project.

for this job. The aim is a bass that sounds big and fat between kick beats but which the ducker makes skinny whenever a kick is present (see Walkthrough, opposite). The amount of this ducking treatment you apply depends on the style of the music. Sometimes an obvious tonal change adds to the energy of the track – rather like compressor gain pumping – while other mixes demand a less obtrusive approach.

A final trick (really a simpler take on the above technique, and employed across the board in the dance world) is to use a **compressor on the bass line whose side-chain is triggered by the kick drum** so that every time the kick hits, the bass is pushed back in the mix.

Driven hard, this basic ducking technique can create obviously pumping mixes, with the kick and bass breathing heavily against each other. Used less obviously, the technique can ease down the bass line's energy when the kick is present without requiring too much in the way of EQing.

JARGON BUSTER: FUNDAMENTALS

Any pitched musical sound is the result of something vibrating, whether it be a string, a metal bar or the loudspeaker cone used to reproduce the sound of an electronic keyboard.

A typical note comprises the lowest resonant frequency that the vibrating element of the instrument can produce for any given note – known as the fundamental frequency – plus a series of harmonics above.

A low A has a basic frequency of 110Hz, for example, but unless the instrument produces only a sine wave, this fundamental frequency is accompanied by a series of harmonics at multiples of the fundamental frequency, musically related to it but higher in pitch.

The balance between the fundamental and the various harmonics is what creates the timbre of an instrument.

Frequency-dependent bass ducking

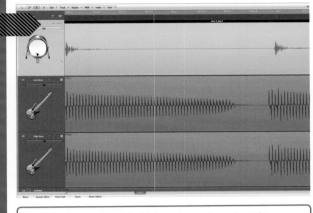

1

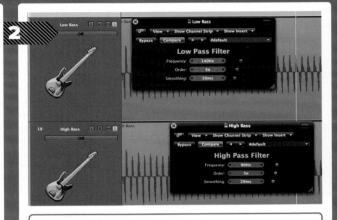

2

Copy the bass part so that it is on two adjacent tracks. Although omitted here for clarity, routing the two bass tracks via a bus makes level adjustment easier. Overall bass EQ and compression may then be applied to the bus insert point.

Use high and low pass filters so that one track is filtered below 120Hz and the other above 120Hz. When combined, the resulting tone should sound essentially be the same as the original. Note that you may have to adjust the filter frequencies so that they overlap slightly in order to retain the original tonality.

3

4

Set up a ducker (a compressor or a gate with a negative attenuation range) on the low-pass filtered track (the bassy sounding one) and key the ducker side-chain from the kick drum track. Where conflict in the mid-range characters of the two sounds is causing a problem, try placing the ducker on the high-pass filtered (brighter) bass part instead.

Adjust the amount of ducking to taste and then readjust the balance between the two bass tracks so that you get the full original sound when the kick is not playing. Set a fast ducker attack (3–10ms) and a release time of 40–80ms. Adjust by ear for the most musical results.

WHERE BASS IS BOSS

While the usual job of the bass line is to work with the kick to support the track, there are some musical styles that feature the bass in a more prominent role.

The Stranglers were one of the first bands to use the bass as a lead instrument in its own right, where its bright, distorted sound allowed it to sit forward in the mix without burying everything else. This type of sound is easy to achieve using a guitar amp plug-in on the bass track rather than a dedicated bass amp plug-in, adding overdrive on the amp or inserting an overdrive pedal model before the amp.

'Bass as lead' is also a feature of underground house, electro, nu-rave and dubstep tracks, where the bass (most often a synth) doesn't play an anchor or support role, but rather delivers the central riff. Stacked synths generate the tones, which extend well into the mids (and highs).

Electric bass can generate a range of tones. 'Slap and pull' bass playing has a typically wide dynamic range, demanding more assertive compression to regulate it. Gain reduction amounts of up to 10dB may be required and, where that isn't enough, a peak limiter can be used after the compressor. An automatic gain riding

plug-in such as the Waves Vocal Rider may also be useful before the compressor to help level the sound prior to processing.

A bass equivalent of auto-wah may be used to give a bass guitar a sound not unlike a synth's filter sweep. Electro-Harmonix pioneered this kind of effect with their Bass Balls pedal back in the '70s. Today we have plug-ins that can emulate auto-wah pedals and recreate classic synth filter sections. Placing a compressor and limiter after the filter helps suppress any excessive resonant peaks that might otherwise cause clipping.

Tip / When mixing the kick and bass, keep A/Bing with the grot-box speakers to get a 'real world' picture. Remember that however pivotal the sub 100Hz frequencies are, the 100Hz–250Hz zone plays a key role too: if the kick/bass relationship only works below 100Hz then you've probably failed a lot of radio listeners (Drums and bass: The radio perspective, page 294).

Tip / Sometimes a bass line just doesn't have the low end punch the track demands. In situations where EQ fails to improve things try a **sub-bass plug-in** set to generate a lower octave. Used in moderation these plug-ins can help thicken a weak sound.

Tip / An alternative – and one many engineers prefer – is to simply **layer the existing bass part** with a synth playing the same notes an octave lower, using a sine or triangle wave. Where the part is already a MIDI track this is trivially simple: just copy the track, assign it to a new doubling instrument and then drop it by an octave.

Tip / To add more punch to the kick and bass combination without spoiling the separation you've struggled to create, try sending a small amount of signal **from each** to a single **(parallel) bus compressor** and then squash them hard – try a high ratio and as much as 20–30dB of gain reduction. Feed this very squashed signal back into the mix at a low level, typically 15–18dB below the dry sound. It helps give added girth to the rhythm section, as well as gelling the two sounds together in a way that still retains their individuality.

Tip / In situations where you just can't get the kick and snare to work as you need them to, don't be afraid to **change the sound/s**. Using a drum replacement technique (page 239) to introduce a new kick drum sample to the mix, for example, may solve the problem.

Tip / If you need to add low end EQ boost to beef up a kick, typically around 70–90Hz, use a **low cut filter** to reduce subsonic activity in the kick and also try putting an EQ dip around an octave above the EQ boost

TECHNIQUE: FRETLESS BASS

A well-played fretless bass can sound wonderful and fortunately few players bring one into the studio unless they know how to play it pretty well. However, the lack of frets can mean the occasional pitching problem.

Applying pitch correction set to a fairly low correction speed (with automated bypass if necessary) can pull sustained notes into pitch without stripping away any natural slides and nuances. Where the plug-in has a dedicated bass mode, use it as it improves the pitch tracking part of the process.

As with fretted bass, compression may be used to even out the sound and add density. Although it is unusual to add effects or reverb to conventional bass parts, fretless bass may be treated to some slow chorus, and where the arrangement is very sparse, some reverb too.

to keep the mids clean. An 80Hz boost can work nicely coupled with a 160Hz dip, for example.

PANNING

There are two reasons a producer uses (or doesn't use) panning when mixing, the first **creative**, the second **practical**.

A major practical reason for **not panning** is to make the best use of low frequencies. High-energy **bass** sounds and the **kick** are very rarely panned anywhere but the centre. This allows the load to be shared over both speakers rather than just one. It is also where we have come to expect these sounds to be placed in a balanced mix. At lower frequencies, sound becomes more omnidirectional; in other words, bassy sounds tend to provide fewer positional clues to the listener so they may just as well be in the middle as not. The **lead vocal** is also generally positioned in or near the centre as it tends to be the main focus of the song.

Panning other sounds tends to be more a matter of artistic taste and creating balance, so dual **guitars** tend to get moved to opposite sides, layered **backing vocals** spread across the stereo field and so on. The **drum kit** is usually panned according to how it is set up (page 248).

I tend to avoid panning **pianos** and **drums** too widely as they can sound unnaturally wide but ultimately you have to use your ears to judge what is right.

Listen to the mix using headphones to check the stereo compatibility in detail: remember the majority of listeners nowadays use earbud-style headphones that make panning seem more dramatic than when heard over speakers.

Ultimately you should try to keep a nominally even left/right balance as you pan sounds – something easily checked by viewing the stereo mix meters in your DAW.

Before committing to any panning decisions, hit the mono button again and ensure the instrument balance and bass energy stays much the same in mono as it does in stereo.

POLISHING THE MIX

This is the stage at which a professional producer would become more involved with a mix, although the convergence of mixing and production often means the same person executes both roles – especially in the project studio. Where the same person is engineering and producing, taking **regular breaks** to help regain musical perspective is essential. This final part of the mix is best approached on a new day when the ears are fresh.

By this stage the mix should be sounding pretty solid, with any timing and tuning errors taken care of. The panning should be more or less where it'll be in the final mix and you'll have some effects set up on sends for adding to the drums and vocals as well as any other instruments that need them.

Now is the time for polishing and fine-tuning levels, EQ and effects, and for testing the mix on as many speaker systems as possible.

A/B REFERENCES

Before you start the final polish it's important – if you haven't already done so – to get some reference material to help you establish a guideline benchmark as to balance and tonality. Even top producers have a few tracks that they A/B their mixes with: it's not something to be ashamed of.

Having reference tracks is particularly useful when mixing a style of music that you may not be overly familiar with, giving you a chance to hear what's happening in which frequency area, what roles are given to each instrument, how up-front certain elements are, and so on.

The one vitally important thing to bear in mind when A/Bing against reference tracks is that the commercial material will have been professionally mastered, while yours is not yet at that stage. What this means is that when A/Bing you will not be comparing like with like, and will therefore endlessly be aspiring to an impossible goal.

A useful strategy to make a more level playing field is to introduce some **temporary compression and limiting** on the master mix bus.

Although you can't second guess exactly what the mastering engineer will do, a generic mastering setup will give you a better idea than no processing at all. If you're planning to do a small scale release where there will be no commercial mastering, it can also form the basis of the final 'end-of-line' processing.

Mastering (Chapter 20) generally involves low ratio, low threshold compression, which has the effect of squashing the dynamic range of the whole track by a few dBs rather than beating the louder peaks into submission, which is what we tend to do when compressing individual audio tracks.

Use your best-sounding **compressor** plug-in set with a ratio of around 1.1:1 or 1.2:1. An attack time of 20–40ms will prevent the transients being softened. Choose an

auto release time if possible; if not, a 100ms release time should be close enough. The crucial part is to bring down the threshold to register just 4–5dB of gain reduction on the loudest sections.

Follow the compressor by a **limiter** (again, the best you have) adjusted to bring the peaks up to 0dB full scale (pages 34–35), or just below, and with the limiter input gain set so that the loudest peaks indicate up to around 3dB of gain reduction.

Mastering tends to include a little **EQ** too, but there's no formula for this as EQ is generally used to compensate for imperfections in the monitoring system of the studio where the material was mixed. No matter how good the studio, the mastering engineer will almost always have better monitors and acoustic treatment.

This temporary master bus processing is not – in theory at least – designed to be in place when you bounce the final master recording. It's there to give you the best possible guide as to how the finished mastered mix might sound. But it's worth noting that the trend for strapping a compressor and limiter on the master bus for the final bounce is growing in many areas of dance production, where extreme master bus processing is often employed to bestow loud, noisy and deliberately home-grown flavours to the final mix.

Just remember that if you do overdo things in the master bus processing department, the mastering engineer will be left very little space with which to work.

Note / Adding compression to the master bus is likely to change the subjective balance of a track somewhat. You may need

▲ **An example temporary master-bus chain set up to allow the producer to compare like with like when A/Bing against commercial mixes. Note the compressor and limiter, plus various meters to give you a good visual indication of what's going on in the mix.**

to go back to individual tracks and groups to refine some of the earlier mix settings to take these changes into account.

PROGRESS REPORT

Whether you ultimately choose to keep or mute the master processors, you should now be hearing something pretty close to how the song will sound to the public. If you've done a good job so far, the mix will have good front/back perspective as well as a healthy left/right stereo spread. The vocal should sound forward and confident, but not so loud or dry as to appear as if it has been awkwardly stuck on top of the backing track. It should feel as though it belongs in the track, not separate from it, but it should still be the main focus of the mix and it should be intelligible (page 301).

Now it's time to consider which tracks need further tweaking.

COMPRESSION IN THE MIX

You don't always need to use compression. There's sometimes a tendency to use it because of an expectation that certain sounds always need compression. Sometimes it is simply used, as George Mallory once famously said of Everest, 'because it's there'. But as with any other processing, you should have a good reason to reach for the compressor.

In most cases some compression on the **lead vocal** will keep it at the front of the mix (page 208), but when it comes to other instruments the choice of whether or not to compress is often less clear.

Even top engineers have different views on this. Some love their compressors and use them liberally to make a sound

bigger. Others, like Alan Parsons, made a point of using virtually no compression on the drums on Pink Floyd's 'Dark Side of the Moon' as he believed compression made the sound smaller.

Like all processing, compression can play a valuable role when used properly, but too much reverb, too much compression and too much unnecessary high-end boost on lots of tracks makes for messy, oppressive and aggressive-sounding mixes. Music is about the interaction of notes and the spaces around those notes. If poor arrangement and over-processing fill up the spaces there's little room left for a mix to breathe.

Note / When making any decisions relating to compression, remember to take into account **all instances of compression** that affect any single sound. In some mixes a snare drum, for example, may be compressed as many as four times – on its original track, on the drum bus, on the master bus, and then during mastering, And that's before the radio station stuffs it through its own transmitter compressor! The effect of this cumulative compression can be to significantly alter your original sonic plans for the humble snare.

BUS COMPRESSION

Bus compression is either applied across the master bus or to subgroups within the mix. It is a highly effective tool for helping mixes (and submixes) to gel and it can also be employed alongside parallel compression – as long as you don't overdo the processing. It is not the same as mastering.

Bus compression affects the dynamics of multiple tracks on a shared bus in a different way from compression on individual tracks. When you compress a complete mix or sub-mix, the louder elements affect the low level elements too, pushing them down slightly.

Using modest levels of bus compression can help make the mix sound more cohesive; a characteristic exploited by SSL when they developed their bus compressor (right).

Applying more intense bus compression results in audible gain pumping. This has the effect of enhancing the sense of loudness and power of the mix, possibly because it emulates the way our own hearing protection mechanism works when sound is really loud. This assertive type of compression is frequently used in dance and rock production.

Compression doesn't just alter dynamics. It also colours the signal, and the subtle distortions and frequency/phase response changes imposed by certain compressor designs can enhance the musicality of a mix. The elements at play here are tube circuitry and audio coupling transformers, although certain optical and FET compressors can also have a significant effect on the tonality of the end result. It's worth experimenting with different models to hear how they impact on the mix.

For **gentle 'glue' bus compression**, ratios of less than 2:1 are often used – sometimes as low as 1.1:1 if the compressor has that range of adjustment. A medium attack time with auto release works well; bus compressors with no time constant adjustment are invariably preset to appropriate values.

For subtle processing, I'd aim for a gain reduction amount of between 2–4dB.

If you want to hear the **gain pumping as an obvious effect** then anything up to 10dB of gain reduction can work; you might also want to try a higher ratio. Where pumping is used as an effect it is important to adjust the attack and release times to get the compressor breathing along with the tempo of the track.

In all cases, if the results of the compression start to become counter-productive, adjust the threshold level to reduce the amount of gain reduction.

Reminder / When deciding whether a type of processing improves the sound of a mix or not, arrange it so that you can audition the process-in and process-out versions at the same subjective level, otherwise it's human nature to assume that loudest is best (see page 165).

PARALLEL COMPRESSION

Parallel compression (page 172) is the technique of mixing a dry signal with a heavily compressed version of itself. It can be incredibly powerful at the mix processing level, adding weight and density to a track that is otherwise well-mixed but still sounds lightweight.

Parallel compression can be used on **individual tracks** (the kick drum, the bass, the vocal), on **group buses** (the drum bus, the vocal group bus), and sometimes even the **main stereo bus**. The simplest way of generating parallel compression is by using a compressor with a wet/dry mix control such as PSP's Vintage Warmer (far right). Just insert it into the relevant track's insert point and adjust the wet/dry balance to taste (usually around 5–10 per cent wet). Where no mix control is provided, feed the compressor from a post-fade send.

▲ The SSL Stereo Bus Compressor Module for the X-Rack modular rack system – also available in plug-in form: can be used to make a mix more cohesive.

Using a high compression ratio (10:1 or more), reduce the threshold to give up to 20dB of gain reduction and then add just enough of the compressed signal to thicken the mix by the desired amount. As with heavy bus compression, the attack and release times should be set so that any gain pumping pulses along with the song tempo.

When employing parallel compression, ensure that your DAW's plug-in delay compensation is switched on – both for the tracks and buses – to avoid phase cancellation problems cause by a delay between the dry and processed sound.

Tip / **Drum parts** can benefit from parallel compression. One technique is to run the drum bus through a 'gel' compressor, with some moderate overall compression to help glue the kit together. An aux feed from the 'gel' bus is then fed to a second parallel bus with a heavily squashed compressor inserted to add bulk and energy.

Tip / Other tricks include parallel compressing a **kick/bass** hybrid (send a small amount of bass and kick to the same parallel compressor). Parallel compression can also help firm up lead **vocal** parts.

Tip / A timid **mix** can be thickened by employing parallel compression across the master output. Just add the parallel compressor on the master bus and adjust the wet/dry balance until it's thick enough. If you want to keep certain elements out of the parallel process you'll need to set the bus compressor on a spare aux bus (not the master) and feed it using spare post-fade sends across the track. To exclude specific mix elements from the parallel compression process, simply turn their respective compressor aux sends to zero.

▲ PSP's Vintage Warmer 2: Use the Mix control to alter the balance of wet/dry signal when using parallel compression.

BACK TO THE VOCALS: INTELLIGIBILITY

Vocal intelligibility (the 'Can I hear almost every word?' test) can be difficult to judge in a track you've been working on for hours or days. As a consequence, it can be helpful at this stage to invite listeners who are unfamiliar with the song to comment on it (the intelligibility of the vocals rather than the quality of the song, of course!).

The reason I say this is because there's an intelligibility test I've tried that uses heavy filters to reduce the human voice to a set of distorted tones that seem to convey almost no information. Listen to the filtered examples and you have no idea what is being said – they're that distorted. Next, you get to hear the original undistorted recording played through just once. Then you go back to the distorted version and for some reason you can hear what is being said quite plainly – even though it is the same distorted sound that you first heard. It would appear that knowing what **should be there** prepares your brain to make sense of the sound that **is there** — a sound that would be unintelligible to a fresh listener.

By this stage in the mixing process you will have heard the vocals so many times that, for better or worse, you'll probably know the lyrics back to front. This means you're unlikely to be the best judge of whether the lyrics are intelligible or not. You need a fresh pair of ears to decide that for you.

Tip / If you don't have anyone on hand to give you the benefit of a fresh pair of ears, the 'outside the room' listening test (page 289) is surprisingly effective at identifying whether vocals are too high or low in the mix.

Tip / Getting the vocal part to be exactly the right level is something even the pros struggle with. It's why some mastering engineers ask you to supply them with several mixes, with the vocals supplied at slightly different levels (page 325).

LOUDNESS, AND THE MIX

No subject generates as much emotional debate in pro mixing and mastering circles as loudness.

The trend over the past decade or more has been for mastering houses to squeeze ever more volume from the final mix to ensure that 'their' mix is the loudest.

It's a trend that has been fuelled by the explosion in home mastering, where the producer comes to the mastering job with different ears and desires to the seasoned mastering professional. The underlying maxim in the movement has been 'loud is better'. But there are many who disagree and who are vocal in their criticism of

a mastering treatment that can end up, paradoxically, damaging the audio fidelity of the final mix.

But it's not just in mastering that loudness wars are fought: producers have been refining techniques for maximising their pre-mastered mixes for years.

An understanding of how the listener perceives different kinds of sounds is essential to an innate understanding of loudness.

The louder something is, the more likely it is to drown out other elements in the mix. And the more harmonically complex a sound is, the more overlap there will be with other instruments vying for the same spectral real estate.

Beyond this, **we also perceive longer sounds as being louder than brief ones**, which provides us with one obvious means of using loud sounds without them clogging up the mix: **keeping them short**.

Drums clearly fall into the category of loud, short-duration sounds. But there are many others; synth blips, gated pads, stabs and plucked arpeggios are all easy to incorporate into a mix. These short, fast-attack sounds can be used like tuned percussion, playing simple melodies that reinforce both the chordal progression and the rhythm of the track. Rhythm guitars — with their spiky transients play a similar role. The more of these non-drum instruments that contribute to the rhythm of a track, the less you have to rely on the drums to carry everything.

A practical outcome of the same theory is that **short sounds which are getting lost in the mix can often be given more definition**

MY VIEW: LOUDNESS

My view on mix loudness is that trying to make your mix sound as loud or louder than anything that has gone before trades away a significant amount of audio quality in exchange for a bit more level when your track is heard on the radio (where it will be compressed even more by the unsubtle dynamic processor in the transmission chain).

If you can moderate the amount of compression and limiting you use to achieve a good balance of loudness and sound quality, then that's as far as you should go.

After all, the typical music listener has been evolving for millions of years — they are perfectly capable of operating a volume control!

MODULATED DELAY FX

A number of popular studio effects work by adding a slight delay to a signal and then modulating the delay time using a low frequency oscillator (LFO) or other source. As the delay time is modulated, the pitch of the delayed sound wavers up and down. The type of effect produced depends on the delay time, whether or not feedback is applied and whether the dry signal is mixed in with the modulated signal or not.

CHORUS

Chorus is created by adding an equal amount of delayed and dry signal, where the delayed signal has no feedback. The nominal delay time is below that needed to create an audible delay – typically 30ms or less. The effect was originally designed to approximate the sound of two instruments playing the same part at the same time, as happens with double-tracking, the slight pitching and time differences between the wet and dry sounds producing a richer sound than a single instrument. In fact, the regular LFO modulation of the effect means the sound doesn't come across as particularly natural, but as is so often the case, the effect was accepted as a treatment in its own right and is often used on clean guitar and fretless bass. Perhaps the best-known user of chorus was Andy Summers during his days with The Police.

Today we have stereo chorus plug-ins that apply slightly different settings to the left and right channels as well as multi-voice chorus plug-ins that sound like several individual chorus units, each with slightly different settings, running at the same time. Roland's classic **Dimension D** box is a close relation of the chorus device.

Chorus-like circuits were used to produce the lush, layered sounds of early analogue string machines. Chorus adds movement (stereo width where the effect is in stereo) and texture to a sound but also has

the effect of pushing it back in the mix, which can be useful for adding interest to keyboard pads while sitting them behind the lead vocal and other instruments.

VIBRATO

Take away the contribution of the dry sound from regular chorus and you're left with an imperceptibly short delay to which pitch modulation has been added. This is vibrato. Vibrato is occasionally used to add interest to electric pianos and electric guitars.

FLANGING

Reduce the nominal delay time on a chorus device to around 15ms, add feedback and you have a flanger. Its distinctive whooshing sound caused by the intense comb-filtering of the combined straight and delayed sounds intensified by the feedback applied from its output back to the input. As flanging is a very strong and instantly recognisable effect, it is often best to use it occasionally rather than have it running all the time. However, it can be used before a reverb unit to add extra sparkle and texture to the reverb sound. It can also sound great used alongside telephone EQ on effected vocals, and occasionally across the whole mix for short sections.

ROTARY SPEAKER

The rotary Leslie speaker developed to accompany the electric organ can be thought of as a kind of mechanical vibrato effect, although there's also an amplitude modulation component in there too (tremolo). Separate treble and bass speakers are modulated in different ways and at different speeds, the bass end by means of a rotating baffle that acts as a reflector and the highs by means of a spinning horn. The Beatles are often credited with using the Leslie cabinet for processing guitar and even John Lennon's voice.

A defining characteristic of the mechanical Leslie is the time the speed takes to change when switched from high to low. This ramp-up, ramp-down effect is emulated in plug-ins and can be automated along with other parameters.

PHASING

Phasing is based on an analogue circuit that modulates the phase (as opposed to the time delay) of an audio signal and mixes that back with the dry version of the same sound. The end result is much milder than chorus or flanging but can be made to sound more resonant with the application of feedback. Phasing goes hand-in-hand with electric pianos such as the Fender Rhodes, but is also routinely applied to guitars and synths.

by lengthening them. Synth parts can have their hold or release times augmented, while individual samples can be time-stretched. Another option is to add a gated reverb or short delay to the sound to give it additional length.

Because our ears are more sensitive to mid and high frequency sounds than to low ones, **adding harmonic complexity to a sound can also help it stand out**. A limp snare drum, for example, can be given a new lease of life by applying some controlled distortion, while a bass guitar can be given more mid-range projection by using parallel distortion (page 178) followed by EQ to emphasise the frequency range that needs bolstering.

Although mastering engineers routinely make use of compression and limiting to enhance the loudness of a mix, some mix engineers even resort to hard analogue clipping on occasion. On rare occasions, digital clipping can work, as long as it is confined to very short transient peaks, such as snare drum hits, although it is not a technique I recommend as the type of distortion produced can make a mix sound very fatiguing. (If clipping is to be used, I'd rather feed the mix into an analogue processor of some kind, or via an analogue mixer that distorts in a kinder way.)

Tip / The human hearing system is particularly sensitive to sounds in the 2–4kHz range. Boosting here can make a part appear significantly louder. Keep boosts wide to avoid getting overly aggressive results.

AUGMENTING AND POLISHING

By this stage your mix should be 95 per cent of the way there, and any final work should be about refining details to help the balance and separation rather than disturbing it to any great extent.

Ear candy: You may feel that the track could benefit from additional 'ear candy' elements: fills, FX, filter automations and so on (page 278). These can be inserted / copied and then faded up until they sit comfortably in the mix. If the new elements need extra processing, such as compression or EQ, or if they need their level/s automating to maintain their balance as the track progresses, make the changes now. Where artificial reverb or ambience is needed, you can usually use one of the send reverbs you've set up.

Automation part 2: If you find yourself constantly fiddling with the same faders to re-adjust the balance, it may be a sign that you need to alter a track's balance over time. Level fluctuations at this stage are often controlled using forensic level automation, EQ automation and additional compression/limiting – frequently a combination of all three.

When levels don't work: One tip for establishing the best level for a problem track is to turn it down until you can say for sure that it is too quiet. Make a note of the fader setting then move the fader up until the track is obviously too loud. The space between the two settings gives you an indication of the level window in which the fader should sit. A good starting point is to split the difference and position the fader mid-way between the two points.

Are the reverbs right? Now that everything in the mix is playing, does the amount of vocal reverb still sound right? Furthermore, has adding the reverb changed the fundamental tonality of the vocal? If you think it has, mute the reverb for a moment and see if the vocal tonal balance is better with the reverb off. If it is, try placing an EQ before the vocal reverb and adjusting it so that the reverb tonality more closely matches that of the dry vocal.

Adjustments to the reverb pre-delay can also help, as phase cancellation between the dry sound and the initial reverb reflections can occasionally cause tonal changes. A good strategy is to first set the approximate pre-delay time according to where you want to place the vocal part in the mix – a longer pre-delay keeps the vocal up-front while a short or zero pre-delay will push the vocal further back, as might be more appropriate for a backing vocal or distant choir. Once this is established, make tiny 1ms changes to the pre-delay time to see if the tonality changes in any significant way. If it does, use your ears to decide how much pre-delay works best.

Tip / The rather nasty reverb plug-in that came bundled with your DAW might sound surprisingly good in the context of a mix when used to add a short tail or ambience to a part to help it stand out more clearly. Using reverb to isolate or give definition to a part is essentially using it as a tonal control tool rather than as a means to place a sound in a sonic space.

I rather like Logic's Platinumverb for this purpose as you can alter the early reflections/reverb tail balance control to give early reflections only, then mix these in with the dry sound to make a sound more dense and add a little length at the same time. Because the ER pattern ends quite abruptly, the sound still stays up-front in the mix. Keep the reverb in mono to avoid spreading out the sound you are trying to focus.

An eye on the art: When you get to this stage of the mix it can begin to feel as if you're dealing more with forensic sound design rather than a living, breathing piece of art. Always remember to evaluate each decision you make in terms of its creative impact as well as its sonic fidelity; you may have massaged the sound to work as part of the mix balance, but does it still convey the right emotional message? Do the vocals, for example, have that confrontational edge you had planned, or have you inadvertently given them a warmer, more friendly sound as you've been mixing? And does the guitar sound pump in the way you had wanted, or did you settle for a more stable tone in the interests of the wider mix? Of course every sound needs to work in its context – but always keep at least one ear on the art.

Keep it simple / It is worth remembering – especially during this final polishing process – what I said earlier in the book about some of the Sound On Sound reader mixes I've helped with (page 290). Their main problem is frequently excessive processing. Where possible, approach compression, and especially EQ, with as light a touch as you can.

Re-re-re-evaluate / Re-evaluate the mix regularly, because although in an ideal world you'd start with the foundation and then add parts, every single tweak you make to one part of a mix affects the way everything else sounds. This means you'll invariably find yourself making further tweaks to parts that you thought were done and dusted as you get towards the end of the process.

OVERALL TONALITY

Because of the way our ears become acclimatised to a particular sound, it is

PRO TIP: SEPARATION

A popular approach to maximising separation among the pros is to work on conflicting groups at the same time – with everything else muted. You might work on the kick drum and bass guitar together for a while, for example, to get them to work together.

You might also pull up just the electric guitars and the vocals to see what you need to do to give them maximum separation. Only when you've separated them do you bring back the whole mix.

COMMON MIX PROBLEMS:
SPILL, ROOM, BRIGHTNESS AND BEYOND

PROBLEM: TOO MUCH SPILL

Spill from drums and other instruments that finds its way into vocal and instrumental tracks can be your friend or foe while mixing, depending on how much of it there is and its tonality.

A modest amount of nice-sounding spill can help mix elements blend, but where the spill doesn't sound great (usually the problem is muddiness) or there's too much of it, you might have to fight to get the mix sounding decent.

There are a few common techniques that can be used to control spill:

> Some engineers experiment with **expanders or gates to pull down the level of spill on specific tracks** during pauses in the wanted sound. Often this doesn't work as well as it might do though: if the spill is high enough to warrant such surgery it's hard to set a threshold that differentiates the wanted sound from the unwanted sound.

> The **SPL Transient Designer** (or similar) sometimes works better than a gate or traditional expander in hiding spill between notes as it works independently of the input signal level.

> Although it takes a little longer, setting **manual level automation points** to pull down pauses by a few dB can be more effective than simple expansion or gating if you don't have a transient designer.

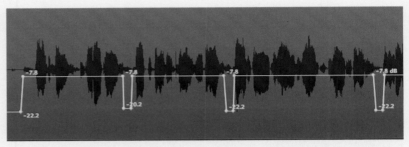

▲ **Automation is used here to manually lower the volume of spill between passages.**

> It is sometimes possible to use **dynamic EQ** to subtly brighten the wanted sound, though again, setting a reliable threshold can be tricky – using a conventional EQ and automating it can yield better results.

> Another technique is to **reduce the stereo width of the offending track/s**. Sometimes this reduces the level of spill due to phase cancellation. If this helps, consider putting the problem track in mono or at least severely reducing its stereo width.

> So-called **'bracketing' EQ** (cutting the highs and lows) can sometimes bring about an improvement if the track in question doesn't occupy the whole of the audio spectrum. Try using 18dB low-cut and high-cut filters to isolate the wanted sound without changing its character too much.

> If you've added **reverb** onto any tracks that have spill, it may be better to pull back on it and let the spill take a greater role in blending the sounds, rather than the reverb.

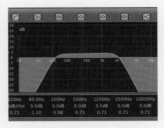

▲ **So-called 'bracketing EQ' – used to simultaneously cut both highs and lows.**

▲ The SPL De-Verb: Surprisingly good at reducing room sound on full drum mixes, individual tracks and overheads.

❯ In very extreme cases you may have to **overdub any seriously impaired parts**.

PROBLEM: TOO MUCH ROOM

A common problem that makes it difficult to sit the bass (or indeed any other instrument) alongside the drum kit in a busy mix is a kit that has been recorded with too much room ambience in the overhead mics.

A very live sounding kit can work brilliantly in a sparse mix but can generate serious challenges when there's a lot going on.

Taking some of the ambience from a drum kit can do a surprising amount to clear mix space but it is not particularly easy without resorting to specialist plug-ins.

While we're still some way away from a plug-in that separates a sound from its added reverb, SPL have a De-Verb plug-in (above) that imposes a faster release envelope on percussive sounds making them sound drier. The Release control on their Transient Designer does a similar thing.

Both plug-ins work well on complete drum mixes as well as on individual drums or stereo overhead mics.

A drier drum sound is far easier to fit into a busy mix without causing congestion so if you find yourself facing this type of problem, give a de-verb plug-in a try: you might be surprised at how well it works.

PROBLEM: LAYERING

Doubling vocals or guitars is a popular production trick, but care is needed when treating doubled parts. Experience has shown that less reverb is needed on layered parts than on single parts unless you specifically want them to recede into the background.

Layered sounds that are heavy in the lower mid range (like vocals) can also contribute to mix muddiness. If you can thin out layers and keep them fairly dry they'll retain their integrity within the mix much more effectively.

PROBLEM: BRIGHTNESS

Adding more top EQ helps a track stand out in a mix but it can also make it sound aggressive and unpleasant if overdone.

A common mistake is to listen to each part in isolation and EQ it to make it sound great on its own. The inevitable outcome is that everything ends up being too bright with all parts battling for attention.

Accept that some parts are more important than others and that some will have to sink further back into the mix.

PROBLEM: TOO MUCH VERB

Another common problem is a mix that, even if not swimming in excess reverb, has more than it needs. An easy way to check whether you've gone too far is to turn the reverb faders down to zero and then gently ease them up until you can just hear the reverb's impact on the mix then stop the fader. The difference between the old and new fader positions may surprise you.

possible to arrive at a situation where the mix sounds nominally well-balanced but is slightly too bright or too bassy when compared against a commercial track.

If this tonal imbalance is only slight, it is usually best fixed at the mastering stage using a good quality equaliser. Set up a temporary EQ across the final mix to provide an indication of the corrections that need to be made. You can then make a note of these, either to pass on to the mastering engineer or to inform your own mastering.

Comparing with commercial reference tracks again can help at this stage. You may also want to compare the spectrogram of the two recordings using a spectrum analyser plug-in. This can give a useful indication of the comparative positions of tonal humps and dips across the audio spectrum.

If the tonal balance is mainly a problem in the low end you can use what you learned from the temporary EQ to apply the appropriate EQ fix to the bass instruments in the track (after removing the temporary EQ from the master stereo insert). This 'bass fix' EQ is either placed on the stereo bus, or the relevant bass-heavy buses (the bass line and maybe the kick drum).

I would advocate using a really good EQ plug-in to do these final tweaks rather than the DAW's native plug-in/s. The UA models of the Pultec and Manley Massive Passive produce sonically smooth and classy results, but there are many good equalisers available from third-party companies such as Sonnox, Waves and PSP. If you've taken care with the mix so far, the amount of adjustment needed should be fairly small.

Tip / Listen to the mix with the computer screen off – bring up a screen saver after starting playback if you have to. Without these visual distractions you'll be able to concentrate more closely on the overall sonic balance.

AND FINALLY...

When you think you've nailed the mix, take a last break and then come back to it for a final close-listening session.

On the first play just sit back and enjoy the track without concentrating on any specific element of the mix. See if anything jumps out as not being right.

On the second, third and fourth plays, focus on pivotal parts of the mix. If it's a vocal-led track concentrate on the lead vocal

▲ The Oxford EQ from Sonnox – use the best possible EQ you can for any final tonal changes.

and how it sits in the mix. Does the vocal tonality sound right and does it have the right amount of reverb? Where the reverb sounds too obvious, try darkening it by rolling away some high end or simply turn it down in level.

If the track is rhythm-driven, focus on the drums and bass instead. Are the kick and bass well balanced, and do they leave space for each other? Does the rhythm pump or punch in the way you want it to? If not, try some (very gentle) compression tweaks, continually A/Bing to ensure you're not making the mix worse. You might also try altering the balance between compressors where you've employed parallel techniques.

If all's good then listen again, but from outside the room with the door open this time. Check that the vocals still come through and that the tonal balance holds up.

Then take a listen on headphones. Does the stereo balance work? Do any sounds poke out of the stereo spectrum awkwardly?

Next, audition the mix on the pair of grot-box speakers with limited bass response. Can you still hear the bass? Is the kick still present? If you've beem mixing using both the main studio monitors and the grot-boxes, the low end should hold up fine.

These final auditions shouldn't be rushed. If the bass isn't present on the grot-boxes then you have a problem, and however sick you may be of the mix by now, it's not too late to sort it out.

Finally, if you can listen to the mix in the presence of a friend / partner / the band without feeling self-conscious when certain sections are playing, then you've probably gone as far as you can before you turn the song over for mastering. Bounce it down and close the project. If you feel as though you have to check it again, do it another day when your ears have recovered and you're able to be more objective.

The mix is finished when you get to the point that further adjustments won't affect sales. ●

EXPORTING THE MASTER

When you're finished with the mix then it's time to export the master, either to pass on to the mastering engineer, or for your own self-mastering.

Export or bounce the master at the highest sample rate and bit depth to maintain the best possible quality – usually 24-bit WAV or AIFF files suffice.

The mastering engineer (or your mastering software) will be able to convert whatever you give them down to 16-bit, 44.1kHz for CD production, or to provide suitable resolution mp3s for internet distribution/streaming (page 326).

Some mastering engineers like to have a choice of mixes with the vocal up or down by a dB or so to allow them to get the best balance (page 325). Others will even accept a separate vocal stem and balance the vocals for you with appropriate processing.

If there are plans to **remix** the track, it is common practice to bounce down the individual group buses as separate 'stems'.

In these cases much will depend on the genre and the demands of the remixer: speak with the record label to find out what they want.

Although every case is different, remixers often like to have the main stems – including those for the lead vocal/s – dry, so that they can add their own effects.

Where effects play a pivotal role in the sound of an important part (an electric guitar that was effected using plug-ins, or a particularly hooky bit-crushed synth line, for example) then you may want to bounce down one stem with the effect/s and one without.

When submitting stems for remix it can be helpful to include information on the track bpm and any key / tempo changes too.

20 MASTERING

WHAT IS MASTERING?

Mastering is the process that takes the final recorded and mixed material and prepares it in any number of ways for full release and distribution. Its purpose is to create a single 'master' track (on whatever medium) from which all subsequent copies are derived. Beyond that even mastering engineers themselves disagree on what their role is – and should be.

It is easier to describe what a mastering engineer did in pre-CD days. Back then they were technicians with the vital – but unglamorous – job of ensuring that the final mix would transfer to the notably unforgiving medium of vinyl.

When pressing vinyl there are certain level and phase issues that have to be accommodated to keep the stylus from jumping out of the record's groove. Summing the low frequencies to mono and applying EQ were common mastering tasks. There was little or no artistic input: it was mainly a matter of getting the music from a piece of tape to a metal stamper and then a piece of vinyl with the least possible damage along the way.

Mastering today is still about ensuring that the material is appropriate for the delivery medium – usually CD, DVD or mp3. But modern mastering is also a creative process, with the mastering engineer playing a key role in how the final track sounds. And although the unglamorous parts of the job still exist – the engineer must balance levels and add track IDs and other subcodes relevant to the specific release medium – much more is also demanded, including:

❭ In an album project, ensuring that **all tracks sound as though they belong together**, even if they were recorded at different times or in different studios, sometimes by different producers and engineers.

❭ **Ensuring the track is a certain volume:** With commercial material the label is likely to demand that the engineer makes the track as loud as similar commercial tracks out there (no-one wants their mix to sound weak in comparison to the competition when played on radio or iPod). But the issue of loudness is a contentious one (page 315).

❭ **Bringing a fresh set of (impartial) ears to the final mix** in a monitoring environment that is generally more accurate than most studio control rooms, and often kitted out with very sophisticated speaker systems. This allows the mastering engineer to identify both frequency spectrum problems and minor distortions that may not have been evident when the material was mixed.

❭ Using a range of high-end (and often esoteric) outboard equipment and plug-ins to **remedy any obvious problems** and, where necessary, **add a sonic polish** to the recording to make it sound as commercially attractive as possible.

NOT A FIXED PROCESS

Given the many new and evolving roles that the modern mastering engineer may be expected to fill, it is sometimes easier to outline what mastering isn't.

First and foremost, it is **not a fixed process**. There are no magic pieces of outboard or plug-ins that 'master'. Similarly, there are no standard settings. **Mastering is a process that must meet the individual needs of the specific source material.**

Secondly, mastering is **not a subscribed set of steps** (1. Compress, 2. Check frequencies, 3. Limit and so on). The

MASTERING IS A PROCESS THAT MUST MEET THE INDIVIDUAL NEEDS OF THE SPECIFIC SOURCE MATERIAL.

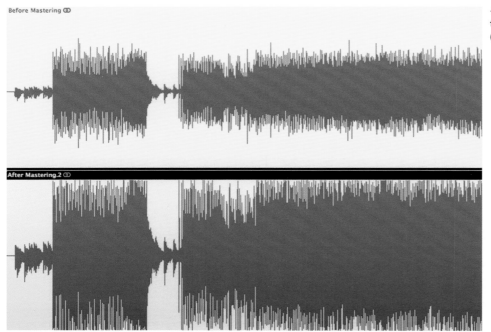

Before Mastering

After Mastering.2

◀ Waveforms for the same track, both unmastered (above) and mastered.

process changes for each project, although similar processes are often applied to some degree. In this respect mastering – like mixing – is personal. It is about bringing the best out of the given material, and so will differ from track to track; on a banging house number the aim might be to maximise loudness and tweak the sonic balance to work on a full-scale club sound system, while on a sultry folk number the mastering engineer may choose a much subtler approach, tweaking for warmth and clarity, perhaps adding a little top-end to help the vocals breathe.

It can be useful to compare music to other art forms when considering the role of the mastering engineer. In film, one of the final post-production stages, after shooting and editing, is grading, the process of altering and enhancing the colour of a film, both to ensure that it is maximised for the end medium (TV, cinema, etc), but also for artistic reasons – to add a certain visual flavour to the whole movie. The original material might have been wonderfully shot, with beautiful locations, great performances and a fine edit. The grading process ensures that a great film **will look great, and will translate properly, wherever it is seen**. The grading engineer in this respect stands between the eyes of the public and the intention of the film's producer and director.

The mastering engineer plays a similar role: they are the last person to tweak the master before it reaches the ears of the public. They stand between the record's intention on the one hand and the global audience on the other. They must therefore at the same time meet the expectations of the client/s and the listening audience, and deliver the necessary technical requirements. But most of all they must be sensitive to the 'soul' of the record – what it is trying to say to the listener – and be able to make the most of this using their ears and technical expertise. A good mastering engineer is able to bridge the gap between art and technology.

THE HOME MASTER

Given the skills needed to become a top mastering engineer, and the budget required to kit out the room and signal chain, the barriers to home mastering can sometimes seem overwhelming. Is it ever possible to master material in a home studio and, if so, is it a good idea?

The answer is that it depends both on your setup and the destination of the music. I certainly wouldn't advocate attempting to master recordings in an untreated room using tiny desktop speakers, and where the record is destined for commercial release it is almost certainly worth having it mastered professionally. Indeed part of the producer's job can sometimes be choosing a mastering studio and engineer with a

reputation for getting good results, ideally with projects in a similar genre to the one you are working in.

But that's not to say you can't master at home. Where you have invested in decent monitoring, are able to listen critically and have a room that has been acoustically treated to damp unwanted reflections and produce a reasonably even bass end (**Studio Acoustics, Chapter 5**), it is certainly possible to master your own mixes in cases where the scale or budget of the project doesn't merit a professional job.

While commercial mastering studios use expensive and specialised processors alongside fabulous monitors, you can do your own home mastering if you have access to a minimum of a good quality equaliser, compressor and limiter – either hardware or software. These are the basic tools of the trade, along with good quality, full-range monitors and high-end headphones.

COMPARING THE MASTER

Tonal defects due to imperfections in your monitoring system may be difficult to spot if you're mastering using the same speakers and room as you use to mix in, but you can learn a lot by burning a CD copy of the mix and playing it on different systems, including in the car, on a cheap music system and over headphones.

You can learn even more by A/Bing your own mix against one or more commercial tracks in the same genre as your own for comparative reference. Even the pros compare their own mixes with commercial tracks that they admire, or that their client has given them to show how they want their mix to sound.

CULT OF THE MASTERING ENGINEER

In certain production circles a small number of mastering engineers have taken on near-mythic status. Their understanding of sound and music, alongside truly golden ears – and often outspoken views on the art of engineering – have marked them, and their skills, out.

Lower down the food-chain, individual genres, labels and producers have their mastering engineers of choice, often for specific musical styles: individuals who

have built a reputation for doing the best job possible and producing a more commercially viable result. Word of mouth recommendations build reputations, and there can be tremendous loyalty towards some engineers from artists and producers.

Although this chapter concentrates on gear and processing, it's worth remembering that the most important asset of any mastering engineer is their ears. That's what makes a mastering engineer truly great.

EQ

Some EQ tweaks are almost inevitable during mastering. A mix may have too much or too little bass end, the bass frequencies may not punch in the right areas of the frequency spectrum, the lower mids may be too muddy, and the top end may be dull, too bright or downright aggressive. There may also be some remaining frequency peaks that cause harshness that weren't spotted during the mixdown.

Comparing the **spectrogram** of the track alongside that of a reference track using a **spectrum analyser** plug-in can be informative, although don't worry about the fine detail as that will always look different due to the specific sounds and musical keys of the individual instruments and voices. What you're looking for is a similar overall shape. A typical mix will show most energy at the low end of the spectrum (but not too much in the sub-40Hz region), tailing off fairly evenly towards the high end.

Mastering requires the **best equaliser you have**. The pros often opt for passive designs for general tone shaping, frequently used alongside a good quality active parametric dealing with more localised problems such as overly strong but narrow peaks. Manley's Massive Passive and modern clones of the old Pultec passive EQ are often used for the job as even very small adjustments can really sweeten the sound without losing clarity or focus, something that can be a problem with lesser equalisers. Plug-in emulations of these classic hardware equalisers can get very close to the real thing.

Bass: **Excessive low bass** can be tamed using a low cut filter with a slope of

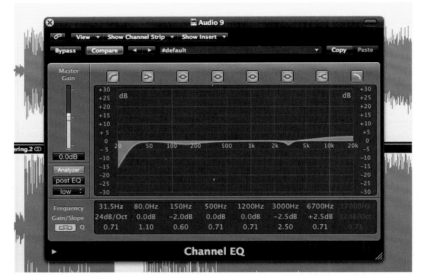

▲ EQ settings for a typical mastering job: note the low-cut, wide dip at 150Hz, slight notch at 3kHz and then the gentle high-shelving boost to add air.

between 6dB–18dB/octave. The steeper the filter slope, the more likely it is that undesirable audio side-effects will creep in, so choose the gentlest you can get away with. I'd rarely venture above 18dB/octave. Listening while adjusting the cutoff frequency will allow you to judge the point at which you start cutting into bass frequencies you want to keep. When you reach this point, back up a little.

The musical genre also affects the amount of bass you leave in a mix. Material intended for playback on club PA systems with powerful subwoofers might extend right down to 25Hz or below, while a domestic playback system is usually happiest with little or no energy below around 40–50Hz.

Lower-mids: Muddiness arises when the upper end of the bass region or lower end of the mid region is too crowded, usually in the 150–400Hz range. Use the

EQ 'boost and sweep' technique (page 38) to find the centre frequency of the muddiest zone and then apply a little cut in that area, adjusting the filter bandwidth to give the smoothest result. With a good equaliser, cuts and boosts of as little as 1dB can make a significant difference. Don't do anything too radical.

Presence: **Harshness** is usually associated with the so-called 'presence' region of the audio spectrum (the 2–5kHz range), where the human ear is very sensitive. Any narrow peaks in this region should show up on a spectrum analyser but it's also important to boost and sweep manually to identify aggressive areas. Again, EQ application should be done sparingly; cut is more natural-sounding than boost. Above 5kHz the sound conveys transient detail but tends to sound less harsh – although **vocal sibilance** might be audible in the 4–7kHz area.

Highs: Boosts above 8kHz add a sense of **airiness** and **transparency** to a mix with little risk of making it aggressive or bringing up **vocal sibilance**. Boosts in this region should be wide and gentle. In most cases a high shelving filter set anywhere from 8–12kHz works as well as anything if you just need to open the sound out a little.

Tracks recorded at different times can sound very different, most often at the bass end of the spectrum, so if you're working on a mastering project that involves more than one track, as well as ensuring each song is well balanced from a tonal perspective, you may also have to use EQ to massage the various tracks closer to what you perceive as being the correct tonal 'mean' for the album. Having a good reference 'anchor' against which to compare each of the other tracks helps to shape a common tonal character across the album.

VIEWING THE STEREO MIX

You can learn a lot from a stereo balance meter (often called a jellyfish or Lisagous Figure display), which shows the stereo spread of energy as the mix plays back.

In most cases you need to keep the overall mix looking and sounding fairly symmetrical so that sounds panned to one side are balanced by sounds panned to the other. This doesn't mean some parts can't be left-heavy for a few moments and others right-heavy for a while, but the average balance should be pretty symmetrical.

Note / While spectrum analysers are useful for showing the general profile of a mix, it is what you hear that really matters. Your ears should always be able to tell you more about a mix than even the best meters.

LOUDNESS

Record companies invariably push mastering engineers to make their mixes sound as loud as possible to compete alongside other over-loud mixes on the radio and in the clubs. But there is currently a backlash against this 'race to the top', with a range of high-profile mastering engineers speaking out against what they see is an insipid trend that is slowly killing music.

The desire for loud mixes is understandable – and if we subscribe to the market maxim that 'loud is good' then for some mixes it might be considered a commercial necessity. But nowhere in music production is the law of diminishing returns so clearly evidenced. Pushing a mix too loud does double damage: it kills dynamics and makes a mix unpleasant to listen to – the very opposite of what most musicians aspire to.

The problem is exacerbated when tracks receive airplay. Radio stations add further dynamic compression, often quite unsubtle, to make their stations sound louder than everyone else's. The cumulative effects of excessive compression and limiting at the mastering stage (to make your track sound louder than anyone else's) combined with the extra processing piled on by the radio station (to make their station sound louder than everyone's else's) can result in a sound that is – ironically – considerably worse than the original mix.

The political slant to mastering means that the engineer often has to make a judgement call on the best way of getting the track sounding adequately loud and punchy without squeezing the life from it. It's a tricky knife-edge to walk and I sometimes feel mastering engineers should have their own version of the Hippocratic Oath, which starts out by saying: 'First, do no harm'!

Tip / Related to loudness is the way the track builds. This should have been worked on at the mixing stage but it has been known for mastering engineers to apply subtle level automation to create a dynamic build-up throughout the track. This needs to be kept very subtle though if it is to sound natural.

COMPRESSION

Compression is routinely used in mastering, both to enhance the sense of loudness and density of a track and to help glue together the various musical elements.

Where the track has been mixed using bus compression, little or no additional compression may be necessary, but you'll have to use your ears to decide this.

A typical mastering setting for a compressor employs very low compression ratios, often as low as 1.1:1. Low threshold values can be adjusted to achieve the desired amount of gain reduction. Gain reduction seldom needs to be set higher than 4–5dB. Often it is set as low as 2–3dB.

A medium attack time of around 20ms allows transients through before the gain reduction kicks in, which helps retain the clarity and transient detail of the track. The release time should be set by ear so that no gain pumping is audible – unless you want it as an effect. The release time should be short enough to allow the compressor to return the gain to normal before the next strong beat comes along.

This can be difficult to hear with such a low ratio setting. If it is, try temporarily increasing the ratio to 2:1 or higher so that the gain pumping, which should now be very audible, pulses along with the beat of the song. Adjust the attack and release settings if required. When the pulsing works with the bpm of the track, revert the ratio back to its original low value.

Note / The subjective result of putting the compressor before or after the EQ is a little different so try both to see which sounds best. I usually start by compressing prior to adding EQ and then switch the two around to see what gives the best result.

The type of compressor used during mastering will depend on whether you only want to control the dynamic range or whether you also want to add some kind of

> THE POLITICAL SLANT TO MASTERING MEANS THAT THE ENGINEER OFTEN HAS TO MAKE A JUDGMENT CALL ON THE BEST WAY OF GETTING THE TRACK SOUNDING ADEQUATELY LOUD AND PUNCHY WITHOUT SQUEEZING THE LIFE FROM IT.

tonal character. A good VCA compressor, or its plug-in equivalent, will provide the least obtrusive processing. Tube compressors or those based on optical gain control circuits tend to impose more tonal colour.

It can occasionally be useful to use two compressors in series, one with a very low ratio, as described above, and a second one set to squash the top few dBs of a mix using a higher ratio, perhaps 2:1. However, I've rarely found this necessary at the mastering stage.

Where some parts of the audio spectrum need to be compressed more than others (as may be the case if the bass instruments have already been heavily compressed), then a **multi-band compressor** (page 170) is sometimes a better option.

In a mastering context, multi-band compression allows you, for example, to apply more compression to the lows than to the mids and highs. It may also help improve the balance of a track in which the vocals have either been mixed too high or too low. In this case, the mid band can be programmed to cover the vocal range and then its ratio and amount of compression adjusted in level as appropriate.

Parallel compression (page 172) can play a role in mastering too. I have used it when mastering dance or rock tracks that have lacked raw energy, which EQ and conventional compression have been unable to fix. Parallel processing can be used at the same time, or even instead of, gentle overall compression and when mixed in at between -15dB and -20dB relative to the main mix can add attitude and weight without compromising the all-important transients.

You may even want to add a touch of mild **distortion** after the parallel compressor. On its own this heavily compressed, lightly distorted signal will probably sound awful, but mixed appropriately low it can make a mix sound bigger and more punchy.

LIMITING
The EQ and compression applied so far will add a modest amount of loudness and may make the mix sound more cohesive, but it will do little to control peaks such as pokey snare drum hits.

For that you need to insert a limiter after the compressor, and although you could set the limiter output ceiling to 0dB FS (Digital Full Scale) for the maximum possible peak output level, it is often better to reduce it to around -1dB to allow a little headroom for the mp3 conversion process needed for online distribution or to load the song into an mp3 player.

Increase the limiter input gain until you see around 3dB of gain reduction on the peaks; your track will have gained another 3dB in subjective level, even though the peak level may be no higher than before.

The actual amount of limiting you can apply has to be determined by ear but I rarely go beyond a maximum of 5dB on peaks.

Specialised limiters, such as the Sonnox Inflator (overleaf), are available that are designed to squeeze out a little more loudness from a mix while doing the least subjective damage to the audio. These often use soft limiting, emulating the way analogue tape or valves saturate at higher levels, prior to a hard limiter stage. An alternative would be to use one of the new generation of tape emulation plug-ins followed by a limiter.

Although not uncontroversial, some mastering engineers allow the peaks of certain transients to clip briefly, arguing that the clipping distortion helps the beats cut through the mix. **Such an approach needs to be handled very carefully** to avoid making the track sound unpleasantly aggressive and I avoid it myself unless a client insists on even more loudness than can be achieved by conventional means. A good test to see if you've pushed a mix louder than might be ideal is to play the mastered mix at a slightly higher level than you'd normally listen at and see if the tonality makes you want to turn it down. If it does, your mix has probably been over-processed.

MONO BASS AND M/S

When cutting to vinyl, it is very important that there are no radically out-of-phase sounds in the bass end of the spectrum as these can cause cutting and tracking problems. Such problems can arise when layering bass sounds or when applying modulated delay, such as flange, to bass instruments.

There are hardware and software solutions that allow you to narrow the stereo image (or even sum it to mono) below a certain frequency only. One of the best solutions comes from the now-discontinued (but still available on the used gear market) Drawmer Masterflow 2476 mastering processor (below), which allows the stereo width to be adjusted over three frequency bands so you can set the bass to mono without affecting the mids or highs. Some mastering engineers address

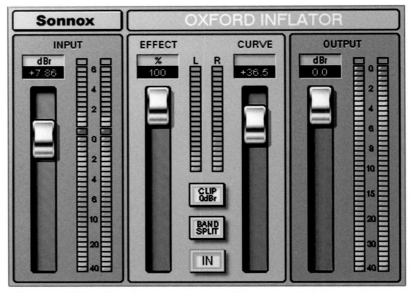

▲ The Oxford Inflator from Sonnox: squeezes a little more loudness from a signal.

the problem using Mid/Side processing, where the stereo signal is first split into its sum and difference components using a matrixing circuit and then low-cut applied to the side (difference) signal before returning the signal to its normal stereo format.

M/S processing can also be used to adjust the balance between centre-panned sounds and those panned to the sides. There was a time when mastering engineers would have specialist M/S devices built for them but these days there are plug-ins that make the process considerably easier. IK Multimedia, for example, offer a range of classic compressor emulations with an added M/S feature to allow the mid signal to be compressed and level-adjusted independently of the side signal.

First steps in the home master

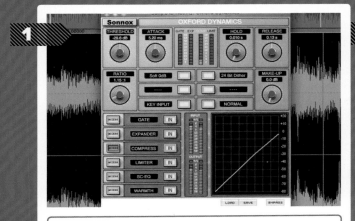

Where the dynamics of the mix need to be reduced or where you feel the sounds needs 'gluing' together, apply gentle compression using a single band compressor with a ratio of around 1.1:1–1.2:1. Bring down the threshold until you see around 4dB of gain reduction on the peaks. An attack time of around 20ms and auto release is a good starting point.

Use EQ to remove subsonic lows and to balance any tonal issues you can hear. Often it is necessary to dip the lower mids slightly in the 150–300Hz range to reduce congestion. A dB or so of additional high-end at 10kHz can add some air to the mix. Try the EQ before the compressor rather than after to see what sounds better for the track you're working on.

Add subtle warmth using a tube emulation plug-in or by passing the mix through a processor with valve circuitry and audio transformers in the signal path. The emphasis here is on subtle.

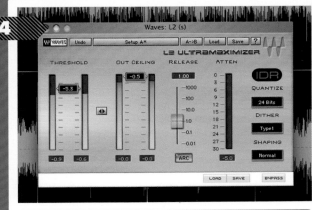

Limiting always comes last. You should not need to trim any more than 3–4dB from the loudest peaks to get the mix sounding tighter and louder. Some styles can stand more limiting: let your ears decide.

NO SINGLE APPROACH

Having outlined the key processes employed during mastering, it is worth reiterating the point that mastering can never follow a fixed recipe; every track has to be processed according to its own individual needs, and in rare cases no processing at all may be the best solution.

For this reason, presets in mastering plug-ins can only ever be considered as starting points.

If a track turns up that can't be improved on, a good mastering engineer should be professional enough to do no further unnecessary processing on it.

Also don't let the current obsession with loudness compromise your end result – try to talk sense into the client if they want to go further than is good for the song.

Tip / Listen to the finished mix on headphones as these often reveal clicks, hums and distortions more readily than speakers. They'll also show you how the stereo panning is working for playback over headphones and earbuds.

Tip / If you're doing a DIY mastering job and obvious problems become clear as you master then it is never too late to return to the mix and tweak it, turning down a vocal line or reducing a honky bass.

Tip / Although the overall dynamics of the song should have been established during mixdown, it has been known for mastering engineers to apply a little subtle level automation to bring out the choruses or final verses a little more strongly.

Tip / In dance music, automation is sometimes used rather less subtly to slowly lower the volume during breakdowns before returning the volume to 0dB as the track drops back in: a great way of upping energy on the dancefloor.

Tip / No matter how good your speakers are, check the finished master on as many systems as you can to ensure the mix translates both to low-end and high-end systems as well as to personal music players. If it is a dance mix, try to play it back over at least one club system before signing off on it.

TECHNICAL CHORES

The more glamorous parts of the job out the way, the mastering engineer will now turn their attention to the more mundane business of preparing the master for its end medium. Tasks include:

> **Trimming the starts of tracks** if they haven't been trimmed at the mixing stage to eliminate any unwanted sounds being audible immediately before the track begins.

> **Working on the closing seconds**, adding a gentle fade to the tail end of the final sound in the song to allow it to fade gracefully into perfect silence. Take care not to truncate the natural fade of any instruments, delays or reverb/s.

> **Ensuring adequate space between tracks**. Before saving the file, still as a 24-bit file at this stage (and at 44.1kHz when a CD will be the final delivery format), I routinely paste half a second of silence to the front of it to avoid any audio being missed when a slow CD player cues up the track for playback.

> **Dithering the track** down to 16-bit (for CD) or encoding to the desired kbps (for mp3)

**TECHNIQUE
CREATING MP3S**

When creating mp3 files for internet distribution I'd recommend a bit rate of at least 128kbps and ideally over 256kbps for the best results. Any lower than this and the audio quality will be compromised in a way that even the most tone deaf can hear.

Most DAWs and CD burning programs include the ability to convert standard WAV or AIFF audio files to mp3.

Next steps in the home master

1

Parallel processing: You can employ parallel compression techniques (page 172) while mastering to beef up a track that lacks energy. A parallel distortion process, feeding a guitar amp emulation with a little overdrive, can also add attitude. In either case check that you aren't making the mix too aggressive.

2

A little distortion: Distortion applied during mastering should generally be very subtle and is often best catered for by the analogue circuitry in mastering compressors and EQs (or their plug-in equivalents). Some mastering engineers copy a digital mix to analogue tape and then transfer it back to digital. These days you can get a similar effect using plug-ins.

3

Reverb: Reverb is not normally added by a mastering engineer unless the main vocal has been supplied as a separate stem and has to be treated in the mix. However, some simulated ambience can be useful for breathing life into a live recording that was mixed too dry. Convolution reverbs let you choose from a range of real-room acoustics.

4

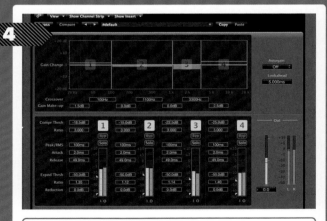

Multi-band compression: While a good mix should not generally need to be processed using a multi-band compressor, these devices make it possible to apply compression to selected parts of the frequency spectrum only, which can help suppress aggressive peaks or lift out mid-range detail.

Sonnox offer a nifty plug-in that can be used to monitor and compare the effects of different data compression processes and bit-rates in real-time.

> **Embedding the relevant PQ codes** and meta data (for CD and mp3s).

The order in which you accomplish these tasks is largely down to the software you use to prepare the final CD master. I still like the simple approach of Roxio's original Jam program, which follows a simple playlist format with the ability to adjust the relative levels of the various tracks, the spaces between them, and to apply additional fade-ins, fade-outs and crossfades.

There are many equivalents for both Mac OS and Windows — there may even be one built into your DAW. Stereo editing software such as Bias Peak or Steinberg's Wavelab also include playlist assembly tools.

The reduction from 24-bit to 16-bit is also handled by the program, with dither applied as the final process to maximise the dynamic range of the final project. So-called PQ codes that allow individual CD tracks to be cued up are also added by the program, along with any necessary copyright and titling data.

Where you need to have commercial CDs copied from your master, ensure the CD-burning software can produce so-called 'Red Book' compatible discs for playback on commercial CD players. The Red Book standard applies to pressed commercial CDs so the CD-R you make has to adhere to the same format, although strictly speaking the CD-R format needed to do this is known as Orange Book.

Tip / I'd recommend using the best possible CD-Rs when burning the master and blasting them with aerosol-compressed air to remove dust before use.

Tip / Always listen to the burned master all the way through using headphones in case a flaw in the CD-R has caused data corruption. Also check you can cue the start of each track from a domestic CD player without missing the starts of any tracks. Label the master once you've confirmed it is OK and then pack it carefully for use as a duplication master.

BURNING ISSUES

One problem with burning an audio CD as a master is that it will invariably contain some errors that are concealed by the error correction circuitry of the player.

Unfortunately there's no easy way to establish the error rate using project studio gear and as a consequence it is not unusual to have a master disc returned from the duplication plant because it has a high 'block error rate'. In this case the simplest course of action is usually to burn another master and re-send it.

Another option is to submit your master/s as data files. Check that the duplicating house offers the facility to accept uploads — many have a public ftp server which you can upload to. If they do, see what file formats they support and make sure a complete description of the master accompanies it.

Some CD mastering programs can save in specialised file formats created for the audio industry but you need to check the duplicating company can work from these as not all can. ●

WARNING: COMMUNICATION

Communication is key when dealing with all aspects of the mastering and/or duplication process.

I have heard horror stories of people sending off a folder of 24-bit computer audio files on CD-ROM to have a straight copy of the disc come back rather than an audio CD — purely because they hadn't clearly explained what they wanted doing.

If there are no instructions, you can't blame the duplicating company for making a straight duplicate of whatever you send them.

WALKTHROUGH Compiling the CD master

1 Place the 44.1kHz trimmed tracks (ideally 24-bit where your CD burning program automatically converts to 16-bit) in a playlist program in the desired order. Ensure there is a half second or so of silence at the start of each audio file to avoid slow CD players missing the track start.

2 Adjust the track spacing so that the transition from one track to the next feels natural. This will vary depending on the track tempos and the length of fade; go with what sounds right.

3 Adjust the level of any tracks that sound too loud in comparison with their neighbours.

4 Fill in any required metadata fields, such as for ISRC codes, then burn the master disc. Use a high quality, clean blank disc and only handle it by the edges. When it has been burned, play it through while listening on headphones to check for audible errors caused in the burning process.

MASTERING:
THE PRO ROUTE

CHOOSING THE WORLD'S BEST CLASSICAL MASTERING ENGINEER FOR YOUR TERRORCORE BANGER IS UNLIKELY TO YIELD THE RESULT YOU WANT.

CHOOSING A MASTERING HOUSE

If you decide to send your tracks off to be mastered professionally, the first task will be to choose the right mastering house/engineer for the job.

Most producers work from personal recommendations, but you can also look at sleeve credits to see which mastering house looked after a specific mix.

One thing that is essential when choosing a mastering house and engineer is that they have expertise in the area of mastering you seek.

Knowing the expectations of your audience and A&R demographic is important; choosing the world's best classical mastering engineer for your terrorcore banger is unlikely to yield the result you want.

Tip / Mastering is cheaper and more accessible to the home producer than ever before. Top studios – including Abbey Road – offer special rates for producers who upload their mixes online. Rates are usually flexible, with reductions if you want a number of tracks mastered at the same job.

WHAT THE MASTERING HOUSE NEEDS

There are a number of things that will make the mastering engineer's job easier and ensure a better end result for both you and them:

〉 A clear brief. Communicating your vision for the track and its final mastered incarnation is essential. The mastering engineer should have great ears and a wealth of experience, but none have the gift of foresight. Don't expect them to second guess what you want them to do. Clear instructions like: Loud, Open, Warm, with an indication of the audience (clubs, radio, iTunes) are all useful. Equally useful and just as essential is...

〉 A commercial reference (or two). Any number of adjectives are not as useful to guide the engineer towards understanding your vision as a couple of commercial tracks that you want your own track/s to sound like. A good mastering engineer should be able to tweak your mix to give it a similar sonic characteristic to the commercial reference – providing the mix is a good one to begin with.

Most mastering houses will advise clients to submit the mix peaking at around -2 to -5dB. This isn't only to allow them space to add volume but also to ensure that the file hasn't been accidentally clipped. Even if the meters show no clipping, it is sometimes possible for clipping to exist between audio samples when the data is returned to an analogue signal.

Depending on the genre, it may be wise to go easy on any master bus processing: if

▲ Online mastering has become very easy and – in some cases – good value for money. Among the high profile offerings are those from Abbey Road (left), Metropolis Studios (middle) and Mastering World (right).

you push it too far the mastering engineer won't be left with much space in which to work. That said, master bus processing plays an integral part in some genres, with the master compression affecting the perceived balance of the track.
In such cases it may not be possible or desirable to omit it – or even significantly reduce it.

In general, getting a mix 'loud' should not normally be the job of the producer: the mastering engineer will usually do a better job of it, with better tools and better monitors.

Where heavy bus processing **is** part of the genre style, the mastering engineer might ask for a second version without any master bus compression or limiting so that they can use their own equipment for the job. Indeed one of the traits of a good mastering house is its willingness to ask the original producer for a less processed mix if they feel they'll be able to do a better mastering job with it.

Tip / If you're unsure whether you've overcooked a mix and worry that your compressed track may leave the mastering house with little to do, then bounce two versions to send them, one with bus compression and one without. This gives the engineer the freedom to work on the one they find most useful. Because any overall compression can affect the vocal balance, sending a couple of extra versions with the vocals mixed at slightly different levels gives the mastering engineer more scope to do their job.

VOCALS

Although a track can be mastered as many times as you like, time and budget restraints usually mean you only want it done once, which means you want to send the mastering house the proverbial perfect mix.

One part of the mix that you may still not be totally convinced about is the level of the vocals – something that even the best producers can struggle with.

Using the mastering engineer to give a third-party opinion on this can be useful, and it is not uncommon these days for mastering engineers to be presented with a separate mix minus the main vocal and a separate vocal track so that they can balance and process the vocal in a more

appropriate way. This isn't something I'm totally comfortable with: it feels like offloading production decisions onto the mastering engineer.

A better solution is to submit several mixes with slightly different lead vocal levels, for example, one you feel is right, one with 1dB less vocal and one with 1dB more, to the mastering house. They can then pick the one that they feel is right for the final master. If you don't do this, some mastering engineers might ask you to re-submit a mix with the vocals mixed up or down before they begin mastering.

To learn (a lot) more about mastering, I'd recommend Bob Katz's excellent book 'Mastering Audio: the Art and the Science'.

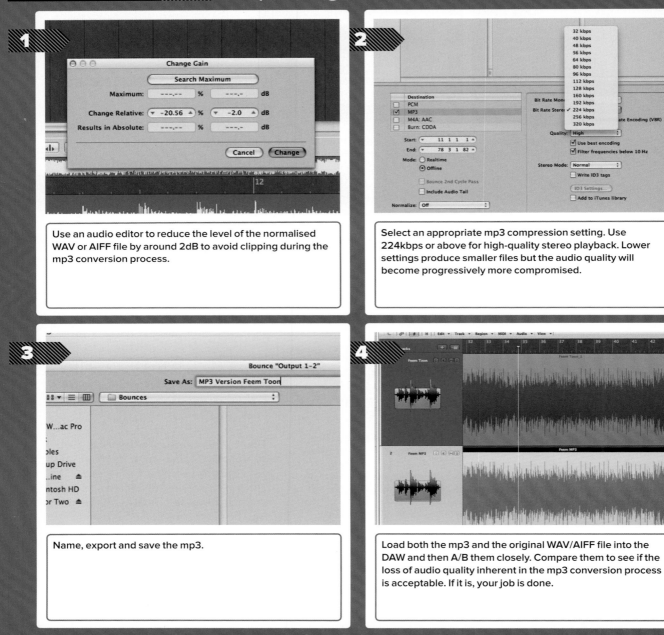

1

Use an audio editor to reduce the level of the normalised WAV or AIFF file by around 2dB to avoid clipping during the mp3 conversion process.

2

Select an appropriate mp3 compression setting. Use 224kbps or above for high-quality stereo playback. Lower settings produce smaller files but the audio quality will become progressively more compromised.

3

Name, export and save the mp3.

4

Load both the mp3 and the original WAV/AIFF file into the DAW and then A/B them closely. Compare them to see if the loss of audio quality inherent in the mp3 conversion process is acceptable. If it is, your job is done.

SECTION FIVE
FADE OUT

- Outro
- Glossary
- Index

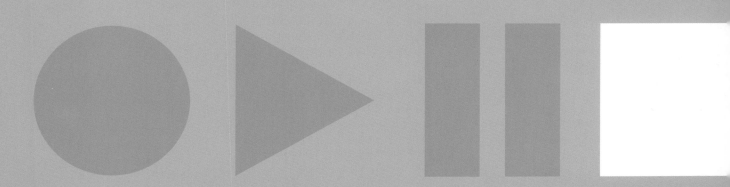

OUTRO
NEVER DONE LEARNING

So, we're done. 327 pages, 35+ walkthroughs, 150+ photos and illustrations, and 2,000+ index references later we're at the end of our journey through modern recording and production techniques.

We've tracked the history of recording from scratchy old cylinders to super-fast computers. We've outlined some of the finest pieces of equipment (still) found in studios worldwide. We've name-dropped a few of the true geniuses of production – from way back, to the kings of tomorrow. We've looked at the kit, and the mics, and the recording techniques used every day in large and small studios worldwide. And we've looked at how to create a solid mix, detailing the processors used and the processes the producer goes through to get it there.

What else is there to say?

First and foremost, you're never done learning. Every time I talk to a professional engineer or producer I pick up something useful that I add to my own personal repertoire and pass on to readers of Sound On Sound. You can learn something from everyone you come across whose work you admire: just keep asking those questions.

Second, talent is important. Having a great studio filled with bad musicians is like having a top-of-the-range camera with nothing to photograph.

Third, the interpersonal skills of a seasoned producer are as important as any other. Getting the best performance from a singer, a band or a mastering engineer is not something you learn from a book. Nor is the patience sometimes demanded during those stressful situations when the session is not going as planned. Creative people under pressure can be volatile – I sometimes think a producer is best defined as the guy or girl who stops the bass player killing the drummer!

Fourth: be prepared. It's the key to great music production. This prepping can be as simple as ensuring you've got the right vocal mic for a session. But it can start long before that. If you're working with a band you believe in, go to their gigs to see how the audience responds. Listen to recordings made at rehearsals to see if the musical arrangements can be improved upon. Compare their music with commercial material in a similar style. Then plan the recording. How many parts do you need to record to create an arrangement that will best carry the song? Should they play together as a band, or should you record the rhythm section first and then overdub all the other parts? Can (or should) they play to a click or will the track sound better played free? The best producers start their mixes long before the band even reaches the studio door.

Fifth: keep an open ear. Our passions as music lovers often influence our skill sets as producers, and metal production

> I SOMETIMES THINK A PRODUCER IS BEST DEFINED AS THE GUY OR GIRL WHO STOPS THE BASS PLAYER KILLING THE DRUMMER!

THERE'S VERY LITTLE THAT MATCHES THE FEELING YOU GET WHEN A MIX COMES TOGETHER, BRISTLING WITH ENERGY, LIFE AND SOUL.

– though it may share many common techniques with hip hop production – is a different beast, that requires a different mindset, and different knowledge. But that doesn't mean a metal producer is lost when faced with a hip hop act. Time and again in this book I've outlined production methods commonplace in one genre that have been 'borrowed' from another. The cross-pollination of genres is what keeps music moving; the same is true of production methods.

The beauty of the producer's world is that techniques can be borrowed from anywhere. How do you make a big guitar sound without dominating the mix? Listen to the rock bands of the '60s and '70s who walked the line with absolute confidence. How do you create larger-than-life stacked vocal arrangements? Take a listen to Brian Wilson's work with the Beach Boys or anything that Quincy Jones was involved in. How do you incorporate complex textures and found-sound montages into a musical work? Check out Alan Parson's work on Pink Floyd's seminal 'Dark Side of the Moon'. How do you big up your kicks? Just turn to the underground Parisien dancefloor and see what a generation of bass-loving producers armed with cheap compressors did.

At the same time, never forget the early pioneers; Les Paul or the many classics cut at Chess Records using equipment that seems almost prehistoric when viewed today. If nothing else these records reinforce the universal truth that the musical performance is far more important than the technology used to record and mix it. (It's not about the plug-in; it's about the idea, and the performance!) In the mixes of the legends there are ideas at work that provide the foundations for what we do today.

Last – but never least – there's no substitute for experience. Reading is good, talking is good, (good) courses are good, YouTube videos can be good. But none of them are the same as getting your hands dirty with a mic in front of a singer.

To expand that experience you need to work with as many musicians as you can, covering as many styles, even if you have to work for free – at least until you get good enough to justify a fee.

You need to learn the mics, and their positions, and their interactions, and a thousand techniques for getting the most from those recordings in the mix.

And even if you only ever want to record and produce yourself in a small home studio, you owe it to yourself to be the best engineer you can be – with a skill set wider than you think you'll ever need.

There's very little that matches the feeling you get when a mix comes together, bristling with energy, life and soul, with each instrument playing its role in a wider picture that is so much bigger than the sum of its parts.

Enjoy that moment.

But if complacency ever threatens to set in, remember to play a commercial album that you admire to remind you what else is possible. Because there will always be more.

And that's my last word: the truly great producer is never completely satisfied with their end results.

Anyone who is didn't set their sights high enough. ●

GLOSSARY

A /

Ableton Live: DAW with a difference, well-suited to live performance, dance music production and for matching the tempos and pitches of otherwise disparate musical elements.

AC: Alternating Current. The electricity mains supply uses an alternating current, usually with a frequency of 50 or 60Hz depending on the country. Audio signals also take the form of an alternating current at audio frequencies.

Active circuit: Circuit that includes components capable of providing amplification and which requires power to operate. Typical active components are valves, transistors, FETs and integrated circuits.

A/D or Analogue-to-digital converter: Circuit for converting analogue waveforms into a sequence of equally-spaced samples, each of which has a numerical value corresponding to the instantaneous signal voltage. For the sampling process to work correctly the incoming audio frequency must not exceed half the sampling frequency.

ADAT (Alesis Digital Audio Tape): Refers both to the recorders that use the format (now largely obsolete) and to the optical data connection protocol used to connect the machines. The ADAT connection protocol, licensed to many other companies by Alesis, is widely used for audio interfaces and other devices. One ADAT connection can carry up to eight audio channels at sample rates up to 48kHz or, by employing the additional S.MUX protocol, higher sample rates with correspondingly fewer channels.

ADSR: Acronym for the Attack, Sustain, Decay and Release parameters found in the envelope generator of many synth designs. Attack, Decay and Release refer to times while Sustain refers to the level at which the signal is sustained prior to the release phase.

AES/EBU: Two-channel, balanced interface used to transmit digital audio between devices, normally using 3-pin XLRs. The signal carries two digital audio channels plus clocking data at resolutions up to 24-bit.

AFL (After fade listen): Means of monitoring a signal within a mixing console post-fader. In other words, the fader position also affects the level of the AFL monitored signal.

Aftertouch: Part of the MIDI control protocol that produces a control signal based on the pressure applied to the keys of a MIDI keyboard. Most instruments use a single sensor to cover the entire keyboard, but specialised instruments provide independent sensors for each key to give **polyphonic aftertouch**. Aftertouch may be used to control any function to which it is assigned, such as vibrato depth or filter frequency.

Algorithm: Set of instructions designed to perform a specific task. For example, a digital reverb plug-in is based on a reverb algorithm. More complex software may comprise multiple algorithms.

Aliasing: The process by which ambiguous data is generated when a waveform is sampled at less than twice the rate of the maximum frequency being sampled. Aliasing results in non-harmonically-related frequencies being added to the audible

signal. **See Anti-aliasing.**

Ambience: Sound reflections in a space, such as a room, where the decay time isn't long enough to produce an obvious reverb decay.

Amp: Ampere, the standard unit of electrical current.

Amplifier: Electronic circuit capable of adding gain to an electrical signal.

Amplitude: Level of an electrical signal or sound.

Analogue: System that handles electrical signals in the form of continually changing voltages or currents rather than as a series of discrete measurements, as in a **digital system**.

Analogue synth: Musical instrument that creates sounds using analogue circuity to provide oscillators, filters, envelope shapers and so on.

Anti-aliasing filter: Filter used to treat an analogue waveform prior to A/D conversion to ensure that no frequencies higher than half the sample rate are allowed through.

Apple Loop: Proprietary format of sample loop file that contains metadata that allows it to be changed in tempo or pitch over a fairly wide range before the audio quality suffers unacceptably. Typically include short sections of musical performance such as drum rhythms, bass riffs or guitar chordal sequences.

Arpeggiator: Generator of sequence of notes, in a variety of orders, based on a user-defined chord. Can be soft- or hardware-based.

Attack: In the context of an **audio signal**, attack is the time taken for a sound to achieve maximum amplitude. Plucked strings and drums have fast attacks, while bowed strings have a much slower attack. In the context of a **compressor**, the attack time (more easily thought of as the 'response time') sets the rate at which the compressor changes its gain once the input signal has risen above the threshold.

Attenuate: To reduce the level of an electrical signal.

Audacity: Freeware, open source audio recording and editing software for Mac OS and Windows.

Audio: Any sound that falls within the human hearing range. **See Audio frequency.**

Audio frequency: The range of frequencies over which air vibrations are audible as sound to a human with optimal hearing. Although it varies from person to person, the accepted range is 20Hz-20kHz.

Audio interface: Device for digitising audio and sending it to a computer as data. Most interfaces also take audio from the computer and turn it back into an analogue audio signal. An interface with the ability to convert in both directions is said to be bi-directional or full-duplex.

Aural Exciter: Device that adds upper harmonics to an audio signal to enhance and brighten it. The Aural Exciter name is a trademark of inventors Aphex.

Automation: Means of recording time-stamped fader moves, or other parameter changes, that are then automatically played back along with the song to perform the desired changes. Automation is available on some hardware mixing consoles and virtually all DAWs.

Aux: Control on a mixing console channel or DAW mixer designed to send a variable amount of the channel signal to an aux bus. In a typical console there are one or more aux sends, each feeding separate aux buses. Some are sourced before the channel fader (pre-fade) for the creation of monitor mixes that are independent of the channel fader level. Others are arranged after the fader (post-fader) for feeding effects.

Aux return: Mixer inputs used to connect to the outputs of external effects units.

Aux send: The output from an aux send bus. On a hardware console this would be a physical output connector. In a DAW mixer, pre-fade sends can be routed to a physical output on the audio interface while post-fade sends would normally be used to feed effects plug-ins such as delay or reverb.

B /

Back-electret: Type of capacitor mic where a permanently charged material is fixed to the back-plate of the mic capsule. **See Electret microphone.**

Backup: Duplicate of digital data (often on hard drives, memory sticks, writable optical discs or cloud-based storage) for safety purposes.

Balance: The relative levels of the left and right channels of a stereo mixer channel or stereo mix. Mixers with stereo channels have a Balance control in place of the usual Pan control. Balance may also refer to the relative levels of the individual channel sources in a mix.

Balanced connection: System based around two out-of-phase conductors enclosed by a common screen. Both the sending and receiving device must have balanced I/O for the noise cancelling aspect of the connection to work.

Bandwidth: The range of frequencies that a device can pass measured between the -3dB points.

Bell filter: Cuts or boosts frequencies within a particular frequency range. The frequency response diagram is roughly bell-shaped, hence the name. The technical term for a bell filter is band-pass filter.

Band-pass filter: Attenuates frequencies above and below the filter's pass-band frequency while passing or boosting those within the pass band.

Binary: Mathematical system used in computing where data comprises ones and zeroes. This is well suited to switching circuity which has only two states, on or off.

Bit: Individual element of digital data comprising a one or a zero.

Bouncing: In the days of tape, the process of mixing two or more recorded tracks together and re-recording them onto another track. In the DAW environment bouncing can mean mixing the whole project to a single audio file or re-recording a single track to a new file to include any plug-in processing.

BPM: Beats Per Minute. Numerical indication of tempo.

Buffer: Circuit designed to amplify a signal without significantly loading it and to present a low impedance to the destination device.

Bug: Term for software fault.

Bus: Path along which signals travel and into which other signals may be mixed. A mixer includes buses for the stereo mix, any mix groups, the various aux sends and for the channel solo/PFL signals.

Byte: A single element of digital data made up of eight bits.

C /

Capacitor: Electrical component capable of storing an electrical charge. Also describes the type of microphone that uses a capsule based on electrical capacitance effects. Also known as a condensor.

Capsule: Part of a microphone that converts sound into an electrical signal.

Cardioid: Derived from the the Latin meaning, heart-shaped, cardioid describes the polar response of a unidirectional microphone, which when plotted out is very roughly heart-shaped.

CD-R: Recordable type of Compact Disc for storing audio or computer data. Can only be recorded once.

Channel (MIDI): One of 16 data channels over which MIDI data may be transmitted or received.

Channel (Mixer): Part of the mixer that handles an input signal prior to it being fed to a mix bus. A channel typically includes controls for adjusting gain, EQ, send levels, routing and overall output level

Chip: Integrated circuit.

Chorus: Effect created by adding a pitch modulated, delayed version of a signal to the original.

Chromatic: Musical scale comprising all 12 semitones.

Click track: Regular audible click corresponding to the tempo and quantisation grid set in the DAW.

Clipping: Distortion that occurs when a signal attempts to exceed the maximum level a piece of equipment or software can accommodate. Because the signal amplitude can never exceed this level, the tops of the waveforms become flattened or clipped.

Clone: Exact copy of digital data.

Comb filter: Filtering effect created when an audio signal is added to a slightly delayed version of itself. Some frequencies add while others cancel, producing a response with many peaks and dips, rather like the teeth of a comb,

Common mode rejection: Means of specifying how effectively a balanced circuit rejects a signal that is common to both the hot and cold balanced input conductors (usually noise and interference).

Compressor: Signal processor designed to reduce the dynamic range of audio signals. The usual mode of operation is that signals exceeding threshold set by the user are reduced in level.

Conductor: Material that facilitates the transmission of electrical current.

Console: Term used to describe a hardware mixer, but can also refer to a desk used to accommodate all components of a DAW system.

Continuous controller: Type of MIDI message used to convey a continuous change (actually a series of fine steps), for example, to vary a synthesiser parameter such as filter frequency.

Copy protection: Anti-piracy measure taken by software manufacturers to prevent the use of unauthorised copies of their software.

CPU or Central Processing Unit: Part of the computer that manipulates data.

Crash: Malfunction of computer program, sometimes requiring a computer restart.

Cubase: Popular DAW software by Steinberg.

Cut, Copy and Paste: Terms derived from word processors but also applied to the DAW environment where sections of audio can be duplicated, moved or divided into smaller section.

Cutoff frequency: Often associated with high- and low-cut filters, the cutoff frequency is the point above or below which attenuation begins, often measured at the -3dB point.

Cycle: One complete vibration of a sound wave or electrical signal. In the 1970s the logical term 'cycles per second' was replaced by **Hertz**, abbreviated to Hz.

CV: Control Voltage, a varying voltage used in analogue synthesis, to control parameters such as oscillator pitch (VCO), filter frequency (VCF) or amplitude (VCA).

D /

Damping: In **acoustics**, the way sound energy is absorbed to control reverberation time. In an **artificial reverberation device**, control able to emulate the way damping occurs in a real environment.

DAT: Digital Audio Tape. DAT tape machines were based on a similar principle to video recorders insomuch as they had rotating heads in order to achieve the required data density. Made obsolete by more modern storage media such as hard drives and solid-state memory.

Data compression: Not to be confused with a system for reducing dynamic range, data compression is a means of reducing the amount of data needed to represent an audio signal. Lossless compression allows the original audio to be reconstituted with no loss of resolution but the amount of data reduction possible is relatively small. More common are the consumer and broadcast compression formats, such as **mp3**, which work by discarding audio information that is being masked by more prominent sounds and is unlikely to be noticed by the listener. Using these systems an audio file can be reduced to less than a tenth of its original size. However, excessive compression does introduce unpleasant audible artefacts.

DAW or Digital Audio Workstation: Commonly used to describe an Audio and MIDI recording and mixing environment based on computer software.

dbx: Tape noise (hiss) reduction system that applies dynamic compression and high frequency boost during recording and the opposite process during playback. Also the name of the company.

Decibel or dB: Unit used to describe the relative levels of two electrical voltages, powers or audio levels. The dB itself only expresses a ratio – it has no absolute value – although 'spin-off' units are used where it is necessary to put numbers to signal levels. Some of these values may seem arbitrary but that's because they had their roots in the telegraphy industry.

dBm: Describes the signal level obtained when a power of 1 milliwatt is dissipated into a 600 Ohm load. 0dBm corresponds to 0.775 volts.

dBv or dBu: Again, 0dB = 0.775 volts, but this time the need for a 600 Ohm load is removed – we are only interested in the signal voltage.

dBV: A slightly more intuitive system where 0dB = 1 volt.

DC: Direct Current, essentialy a constant rather than alternating voltage.

DDL: Digital delay line used for various purposes, including the creation of echo effects.

Decay: Reduction in amplitude over time such as occurs when a plucked string loses energy.

De-Esser: Device for reducing the level of sibilance (S,T and F sounds) in vocal signals.

Destructive editing: Any process that changes the original file.

Detent: Physical click position to denote the centre of a rotary control, usually where the centre position is the default for 'no action' or neutral, as in the case of a pan control or EQ cut/boost knob.

Digital Performer: Popular DAW software from MOTU.

DI or Direct Inject. Process of recording an electrical signal without the aid of a microphone; the output from the back of a bass amp, the pickup of a guitar or from an electronic keyboard for example.

DI Box: Device for matching the signal level and impedance of a source to allow it to be connected directly to a mixer or audio interface. May be active or passive. Active models are powered either by batteries or phantom power.

Digital delay: see DDL.

Digital reverb: Digital processor or plug-in for producing a reverberation effect. The two common methods are **algorithmic** (**synthetic**), where delays and feedback loops are used to simulate the effect of natural reverb, and **convolution**, where an impulse response recorded in a real space is used to impose the acoustics of that space onto an electrical signal.

Dither: Process of adding low level noise to a digitised audio signal in such a way as to extend its low level resolution. Although this increases the level of noise very slightly, it allows very low level audio signals to remain smooth rather than spluttering into extinction when the amplitude isn't high enough to trigger the least significant bit in the audio converter. Using correctly applied dither, low level audio disappears smoothly into the noise floor much as it would with an analogue system.

Dolby: An encode/decode tape noise reduction system used with analogue tape. To oversimplify somewhat, low level, high frequency signals are boosted during recording and then the reverse of this process applied during playback so that any tape hiss is reduced in level. There are several variants on the Dolby systems: types B, C and S for domestic and semi-professional machines, and types A and SR for professional studio machines. Recordings should be replayed using the same Dolby system.

Driver: Software that handles the data stream between a computer program and a hardware peripheral, such as a printer, USB MIDI keyboard, MIDI interface or audio interface.

DSP: Digital signal processor, a computing microchip used to process digital signals, though the term is now also often used to describe audio signal processing in a computer DAW system.

Dry: Unprocessed signal that has had no effects added.

Dubbing, usually known as **overdubbing**: Recording additional audio tracks to an existing audio project.

Ducking: Automatic means of controlling the level of one audio signal with another using a side-chain system. In radio, ducking is often used to dip the level of the music when the announcer speaks. In mixing it can be used to drop the level of instruments that might otherwise conflict with the main vocal part.

Dynamics: Term describing how the levels change throughout a piece of music or other audio.

Dynamic microphone: Type of microphone that works using a coil of wire or a conductive ribbon moving in a magnetic field.

Dynamic range: Range in dB between the highest signal that can be handled by a piece of equipment with clipping at the upper extreme and the level at which small signals disappear into the noise floor at the lower extreme.

E /

Early reflections (ERs): The initial sound reflections from walls, floors, ceilings or other solid objects following a sound created in an acoustically reflective environment. These re-reflect and quickly build up into a dense reverb reverb decay.

Effects loop: System of using an aux send to feed an external effects unit or plug-in which is then routed back into the mix.

Effect return: Mixer input designed to accept the output from an effects unit (or its virtual DAW equivalent).

Electret microphone: Type of capacitor microphone that uses a permanently charged capsule rather than charging it from the phantom power source or valve mic power supply. The charged material may be fashioned into the diaphragm or fixed to the stationary back-plate.

Encode/Decode: System, such as Dolby or dbx noise reduction, that requires a signal to be processed prior to recording, then the reverse of that process applied during playback.

Enhancer: Usually describes a device capable of brightening audio material using a variety of techniques that go beyond conventional EQ. These might include dynamic equalisation, phase shifting and harmonic generation through controlled distortion. The **Aphex Aural Exciter** is probably the best known example of this type of device.

Envelope: The way the level of an electrical signal changes with time.

Envelope generator: Circuit or software designed to generate a control signal which in turn controls the level of an audio signal to impose a level envelope on it. The most common example is the **ADSR generator** used in a typical synthesiser.

Equaliser (EQ): Device for selectively cutting or boosting the levels of selected parts of the audio spectrum. These vary in complexity from simple bass and treble controls to multi-band parametric designs.

Event (MIDI): A unit of MIDI data, such as a note-on or note-off message or a program change command.

Exciter: See Aural Exciter.

Expander: Dynamic control circuit or plug-in designed to decrease the level of low level signals, rather like a compressor in reverse. The result is an increase in dynamic range of the signal being processed.

F /

Fader: Potentiometer controlled by a slider.

FET: Field Effect Transistor.

Figure-of-eight: Polar response of a symmetrical microphone where the diaphragm is open to the air on both sides. These are equally sensitive both front and rear but reject sounds coming from 90 degrees off-axis.

File: Collection of digital data stored so as to appear as a single item, for example an audio recording.

Filter: Electronic circuit that can cut or boost a specific range of frequencies or frequencies that occur above or below a specified cut-off point.

Firewire: High-speed data connection for computer peripherals such as audio interfaces. Also known as IEEE 1394.

Flange: Effect originally created by running two tape recorders slightly out of sync, now more commonly created using a modulated delay line with feedback. The delay time is usually only a few 10s of milliseconds maximum so the resulting comb-filtering creates a distinctive sweeping sound.

Flash memory: Type of solid state memory that retains data even when the power is removed. Flash memory is used in tablet-style computers, smart phones and many portable stereo and multitrack recorders, but is also making inroads into mainstream computing as its capacity increases.

Flutter echo: Resonant echo that occurs when sound reflects back and forth between two parallel, reflective surfaces. The closer the surfaces, the higher pitched the resonance.

Foldback: Also known as 'Cue Mix' in the studio. Means of setting up one or more separate mixes to be fed to the performers' headphones for use while recording and overdubbing.

Formant: Fixed frequency component or resonance that defines the character of instrument or voice. For example, the body resonance of a violin or acoustic guitar.

Format: Can describe a file type, such as WAV or mp3, but is also used to describe the process of initialising a digital storage device such as a hard drive to make it compatible with the connected computer.

Frequency: Measure of how many cycles of a repetitive waveform occur in one second. **See Cycles**.

Fundamental frequency: Usually the lowest frequency component of a sound, such as the pitch of a vibrating string.
Most instruments produce a fundamental frequency plus a series of harmonics and partials at higher frequencies.

FX: Short for Effects.

G /

Gain: The amount by which a device amplifies a signal, usually measured in dBs.

Garage Band: Entry-level DAW software for Apple Mac and some iOS devices.

Gate: In the context of **analogue synthesisers**, a gate signal is generated whenever a key is depressed. This is used to trigger envelope generators and other sound-shaping parameters. A gate can also be a **device designed to attenuate or mute signals** falling below a user-defined threshold to hide noise during pauses.

General MIDI or GM: Part of the current MIDI specification that defines a sound set to assure a minimum level of compatibility when playing back GM MIDI song files. The GM spec defines which sound types correspond to which program numbers, minimum levels of polyphony and multi-timbrality, response to controller information and other factors.

Glitch: Often used to describe a momentary corruption of a signal (such as a click or gap), or unexplained software/hardware behaviour.

Graphic EQ: Equaliser able to adjust several narrow and adjacent regions of the audio spectrum using individual cut/boost faders. The fader positions provide a graphic representation of the EQ curve, hence the name.

Ground: Electrical earth; the ground cable in a mains power system is physically connected to the ground via a conductive metal spike. The metal cases of equipment are usually connected to ground via the ground wire of the mains cable.

Ground loop: Where multiple ground connections exist between pieces of audio equipment, audible mains hum may result due to circulating 50/60Hz currents induced into the resulting loops. Ground loops are sometimes also referred to as earth loops.

Group: Can describe the **method of submixing specific mixer channels** by routing then to separate mix buses in a mixing console or DAW mixer. May also describe a **number of mixer channel faders 'grouped' together** so that adjusting any one fader in the group adjusts all of them.

H /

Harmonic: High frequency component of a complex waveform that is a multiple of the fundamental.

Harmonic distortion: New harmonics added when a waveform shape is changed by a distorting mechanism, such as clipping or a non-linear circuit.

Head: Part of a tape machine or disk drive that reads and writes data to and from the tape or disk in a magnetic form.

Headroom: Can be thought of as a safety margin (usually expressed in dBs) between the highest peak level of a signal and the maximum level the equipment can handle before clipping.

High-pass filter (HPF): Filter that attenuates all frequencies below its cutoff frequency.

Hiss: Noise caused by random electrical fluctuations in electronic components or by the magnetic tape used in analogue recording.

Hum: The unwanted addition of low frequencies related to the mains power frequency.

Hertz: Abbreviated to Hz, the unit of frequency that describes the number of cycles of a repeating waveform in one second.

I /

IC: Integrated circuit.

Impedance: The AC equivalent of electrical resistance, which may change with frequency.

Inductor: Reactive component, usually a coil, where the impedance increases with frequency.

Insert point: Connection point in a mixer or other device that allows an external processor to be patched or 'inserted' into a signal path so that the signal flows through the external processor.

Interface: In the world of DAWs we deal mainly with audio and MIDI interfaces, both hardware devices that allow signals from the outside world to be handled and then output by a computer. A **MIDI interface** enables a computer to communicate with MIDI instruments and keyboards. An **audio interface** provides a means to get audio signals in and out of a computer.

Intermodulation distortion: Form of distortion that introduces frequencies not present in the original signal based on the sum and difference products of the original frequencies.

I/O: The part of a system that handles inputs and outputs.

J /

Jack: Commonly used audio connector. May be mono or stereo and available in consumer 'mini' formats and more common quarter inch type used in music studios. There are also specialised Bantam and post office jacks used in some professional patchbays but these are not compatible with other types of jack.

Jitter: Measure of the instability in a digital clocking system, usually measured in parts per million.

K /

Kilo or k: Abbreviation for 1000. For example, 1kHz = 1000Hz.

L /

LCD: Liquid Crystal Display, often used for displays on synths and FX processors.

LED: Light Emitting Diode, common type of solid state lamp that emits very little heat.

LFO: Low Frequency Oscillator, often used as a source of modulation to create effects such as chorus or vibrato.

Limiter: Device similar to a compressor but with, in effect, an infinite ratio and a very fast response time to prevent signal levels exceeding the threshold.

Linear: Device or circuit that changes only the level of the signal being passed.

Line level: Slightly vague term that applies to non-microphone signals with a peak level measured in volts rather than millivolts. Nominal line level is around -10dBV for semi-pro equipment and +4dBu for professional equipment.

Load: Electrical or electronic circuit that draws power from the circuit feeding it.

Logic Pro: Popular DAW software for the Apple Mac platform.

Loop: Can describe a **signal path** where the output of a device is connected back to the input, or a **segment of audio** that can be repeated continually in a musically meaningful way, such as a bar of drums.

Low-pass filter (LPF): A filter which attenuates all frequencies above its cutoff frequency.

M /

M and m: Lower case m denotes milli, meaning one thousandth. Upper case M denotes Mega, meaning one million.

Memory: Computer memory usually describes RAM memory used to store programs and data while the computer is running, although a hard drive is, technically speaking, also a form of memory. RAM data is lost when the computer is switched off. Flash memory is similar to RAM but retains its data when the power is switched off.

Mic level: Somewhat vague term that describes the level available from a typical microphone, which must be amplified many times, up to 60dB or more, to increase it to line level.

MIDI: Musical Instrument Digital Interface.

MTC: MIDI Time Code; a MIDI sync implementation based on the SMPTE time code developed for the film and TV industries but transmitted over a standard MIDI connection. It measures time in hours, minutes, seconds and film/TV frames.

MIDI controller: Term used to describe the physical music instrument interface used to input a musical performance as MIDI data. Keyboards are the most obvious examples but there are others, including drum pads, wind synths and MIDI guitars, that also output MIDI data.

MIDI sound module: A hardware, MIDI-controlled sound generating instrument with no integral keyboard.

Multi-timbral: The ability of a MIDI sound source (hardware or software) to produce several different sounds at the same time where each can be controlled by a different MIDI channel.

MIDI Note On: MIDI message transmitted when note is played on the MIDI controller.

MIDI Note Off: MIDI message transmitted when note is ended or released on the MIDI controller.

MIDI In: Connection used to receive information from a master controller or from the MIDI Thru socket of another slave unit.

MIDI Out: Connection used to send data from a master device to the MIDI In of a connected MIDI device.

MIDI Thru: Connection on a slave unit used to feed the MIDI In socket of the next unit in-line. This passes the MIDI In signal through without change.

MIDI Port: MIDI is limited to 16 MIDI channels, but by using a MIDI interface with several independent MIDI ports, it is possible to have several groups of 16 MIDI channels operating at the same time. A multi-port MIDI interface must be supported by the host DAW software.

Mixer: Hardware or software device for combining two or more audio signals.

Monitor: Can refer to a **reference loudspeaker** used for mixing or to a **computer display screen**. It may also describe the action of **listening in to a specific audio signal**, such as a mixer solo output or to a performer's headphone mix.

Monophonic: One musical note at a time with no overlaps or chords.

Multi-sample: Usually refers to the way individual musical samples are arranged as a playback program in a musical sampler. Many instruments sound wrong if the note samples are moved far from their original pitch and the sound also changes depending on how hard the instrument is played. To create a natural-sounding piano, for example, multiple samples are needed, often a different one for each note repeated at many different intensities. These hundreds of samples make up the multi-sampled piano program.

Multitrack: A recording device or DAW capable of recording several separate parts or tracks alongside each other which may then be mixed to produce the end result.

N /

Nearfield: Also known as 'close field', this term describes a loudspeaker system designed to be used close to the listener. Less level is needed to achieve an adequate monitoring level and the reflected sound from the room is also less in proportion to the direct sound from the speakers.

Noise reduction: System for r**educing level of hiss or other unwanted continuous sound** (such as camera noise) present in a recording. The term also covers **encode/ decode tape noise reduction systems** such as Dolby and dbx.

Noise shaping: System used when creating digital dither to move the small amount of added noise into a part of the audio spectrum where the human hearing system is least sensitive.

Non-destructive: Process that applies changes without actually changing the original audio data. For example, cutting, copying and pasting audio doesn't change the original audio file but simply uses different parts of it for playback.

Non-linear recording: Describes a digital recording system where material doesn't necessarily have to be played back in the order it was originally recorded. Segments of audio from any position can be played back seamlessly; it is this capability that makes copy and paste editing possible.

Normalise: When talking about sockets and patchbays, a normalised connection is one that is arranged so that **the original signal path is maintained unless a plug is inserted into the socket whereupon the signal is diverted via the connected external device**. In the context of digital audio, normalisation is the **process of changing the level of an audio file so that its loudest peak corresponds to digital full scale**, in other words, the level is as high as it can be without clipping.

Nuendo: Steinberg's flagship DAW in a similar style to Cubase but with more professional features.

Nyquist Theorem: Named after the researcher who proved it, this is the rule which states that a digital sampling system must have a sample rate at least twice as high as that of the highest frequency being sampled to avoid aliasing. In practice, anti-aliasing filters aren't perfect so the sampling frequency has to be a little more than twice that of the maximum input frequency to provide some safety margin.

O /

Octave: Musical frequency or pitch that is double the frequency of the original.

Off-line: Process carried out in non-real time, such as converting a WAV file to an mp3.

Ohm: Unit of electrical resistance.

Omnidirectional: Microphone type that is equally sensitive to sound regardless of the angle it approaches the microphone.

Open circuit: Break in an electrical circuit across which current is unable to flow.

Open reel: Tape machine where the tape is wound on removable spools.

Operating system: Host software that enables a computer to load and run programs. Common examples are Windows and Mac OS.

Opto electronic : Device where an electrical parameter, such as resistance, is affected by a variation in light intensity, such as light falling on a photocell.

Oscillator: Circuit designed to generate a repeating electrical waveform.

Overload: Term commonly used to describe the action of either feeding too much signal level into a device or applying too much gain. Distortion results in either case.

P /

Pad: Resistive attenuator for reducing signal level, often found in microphones, DI boxes, mixer input stage and mic pre-amps.

Pan pot: Short for panorama, this control enables the engineer to steer a mono signal anywhere between the left and right mix buses to create the illusion of stereo positioning.

Parallel: In terms of signal flow, parallel means connecting two or more circuits together so that their inputs are fed from a common source and their outputs are then mixed together.

Parameter: A variable value, such as an EQ frequency, that affects the performance of an audio device or software.

Parametric EQ: Equaliser with separate controls for frequency, bandwidth and gain, which can apply both cut and boost. Most parametric EQ plug-ins include two or more stages that can be tuned to different frequencies and often high- and low-cut and high and low shelving filters to provide a comprehensive EQ tool kit.

Passive circuit: Circuit with no active elements.

Patchbay: Rows of panel-mounted connectors used to bring mixer and external processing device inputs and outputs to a central point. This enables them to be routed using plug-in patch cords.

Patch cord: Short cable for use with patch bays.

Peak: Maximum level of a signal, no matter how brief.

Phase: Offset between two sine waves expressed in degrees where 360 degrees corresponds to a delay of exactly one cycle.

Phaser: Common effect which combines a signal with a phase shifted version of itself to produce tonal filtering effects. The phase shift is modulated by an LFO to create a cyclic tonal change.

PFL or pre-fade listen: Means to monitor an audio signal prior to the fader controlling its level.

Phantom power: A DC supply, usually 48 volts, for powering capacitor microphones and active dynamic microphones. It is transmitted along the signal cores of a balanced mic cable so needs no extra cabling.

Phono plug: Simple push-in, unbalanced hi-fi connector developed by RCA and used extensively on semi-pro equipment and also for connecting S/PDIF digital audio signals.

Pitch: The musical interpretation of audio frequency where, in Western music, each octave is divided into 12 semitones.

Pitch bend: MIDI control message designed to produce a change in pitch in response to the movement of a pitch bend wheel, fader, ribbon controller or lever.

Pitch shifter: Device for changing the musical pitch of an audio signal without also changing its length.

Polyphonic: An instrument able to play two or more notes simultaneously.

Portamento: Pitch gliding effect between notes used in synthesisers and sample players.

Post-production: Work done to a music mix, film or TV program after the initial mixing is complete.

Power supply: Hardware unit able to convert mains electricity to the voltages

necessary to power a device such as mixer or valve microphone.

Post-fade aux: Aux signal sourced after the channel fader so that the aux send level follows any channel fader changes. The most common use of a post-fade aux is to feed effects devices so as to maintain the same balance of dry signal and effect regardless of the channel fader position.

PQ coding: Process for adding Pause, Cue and other subcode information to a digital master recording in preparation for CD manufacture. This is often accomplished in a CD burning program where the final album playlist is assembled.

Pre-fade: Aux signal taken from before the channel fader, usually for setting up foldback/monitor/cue mixes.

Preset: Effects unit or synth patch provided by the manufacturer. Often these factory presets can't be changed by the user, though they can usually be edited and then resaved as a user patch with a different name. Many software plug-ins come with presets for specific applications.

Processor: Term used to describe an audio device designed to treat an audio signal by changing its dynamics or frequency content. In most cases (other than the special cases of parallel compression and distortion) the whole signal passes through the device rather than being added to the dry signal. Examples of processors include compressors, limiters, gates, distortion devices and equalisers. While effects such as reverb and delay are created by signal processing, it helps avoid confusion if such devices are referred to as **Effects**. As a very general rule, processors are normally used via track, bus or master insert points whereas effects can be used both in insert points and in the aux send/return loop.

Pro Tools: Widely-used DAW, originally from Digidesign but now branded as Avid. The system comes in several variants, including

the high-end TDM system requiring Avid's own DSP cards and other hardware to operate, and the Native version introduced in 2010 that can run using a number of third-party audio interfaces. There are also lighter versions that run with M-Audio interfaces (also owned by Avid).

PPM: Peak Programme Meter; a meter designed to register signal peaks.

Punch in: The action of switching an already recorded track into record during playback, so that a section of the existing material may be replaced or added to. Most old-school engineers still call this process 'dropping in'.

Punch out: The action of switching the recording device out of record after executing a punch-in.

PZM: Pressure Zone Microphone. Also known as a boundary microphone, this type of microphone is designed to be used flush with a large surface where it is able to avoid capturing any sounds reflected from that surface.

Q /

Q: An alternative means of defining the **bandwidth** of a filter or parametric equaliser. The higher the Q, the more resonant the filter and the narrower the range of frequencies that pass through. In other words, a narrow bandwidth equates to a high Q value and vice versa where Q is defined as the filter's centre frequency divided by the bandwidth of the filter measured at the -3dB points.

Quantise: The process of moving events, such as musical notes recorded in a MIDI sequencer, so that they line up with a fixed timing grid, such as subdivisions of a musical bar.

R /

RAM: Random Access Memory. Data stored in RAM is lost when the power is turned off.

Real time: An audio process that can be carried out as the signal is being recorded or played back without having to stop playback and process the file.

Reaper: Low cost but powerful DAW software.

Release: Time taken for a level or gain to return to normal, for example, when the signal level falls below the threshold in a compressor. Release is also used to describe the rate at which a synthesised sound falls in level after the key has been released.

Resistance: A material's opposition to the flow of electrical current, measured in Ohms. A good conductor has a low resistance whereas a poor conductor will have a high resistance.

Resolution: The accuracy with which an analogue signal can be represented in a digital system. This is reflected in the number of bits used for encoding and the stability of the sample clock, but it also relates to the accuracy with which signal processing and mixing takes place within a DAW.

Resonance: Ability of a circuit or mechanical structure to store and release energy at a specific 'tuned' frequency.

Reverb: The audible effect of multiple sound reflections in a confined space.

RF: Radio frequency. RF interference exists above the range of human hearing.

Ribbon microphone: Microphone where the element that moves in response to sound is a thin conductive ribbon suspended in a magnetic field. As the ribbon vibrates, a small electrical current is generated within the ribbon.

Roll-off: Rate at which a filter attenuates a signal once it has passed the filter cutoff point, usually expressed in dBs per octave.

ROM: Read Only Memory. Rom contains data that can't be changed. The memory remains intact when the power is removed. An **E-PROM** (Erasable Programmable Read Only Memory) operates in a similar way to ROM, but the information on the chip can be erased and replaced using specialised equipment.

Ring modulator: Effect that takes two input signals and then processes them so that the output contains only sum and difference frequencies but none of the original frequencies. Depending on the relationships between the input signals, the results may either be musical or extremely dissonant. Can be useful in producing textural and aggressive effects.

RMS: Root Mean Square. Method of specifying the behaviour of a piece of electrical equipment under continuous sine wave testing conditions.

Rex file: Developed by Propellerhead, the Rex file is a widely-supported loop file format for use in DAW software. The name comes from 'ReCycle EXport' (Recyle was the original processing software designed to turn audio into Rex files) where the file is intelligently sliced into individual beats so that the playback tempo can be adjusted over a wide range without recourse to pitch shifting. Individual slices are triggered via MIDI notes giving scope for changing the loop by editing the MIDI data. Rex2 supports both mono and stereo files.

S /

Safety copy: Copy or clone of an original recording.

Sample: When an **analogue signal is converted to a digital data stream**, it is measured as a stream of samples. For example, CD audio is sampled at 44.1kHz. Can also refer to **a short section of digitised sound** used as a musical sound source in a sampler or in some types of synthesiser.

Also commonly used to describe **audio segments copied from other recordings** that are used in a new composition.

Sample Magic: Publishers of this book and an award-winning sample design company :-).

Samplitude: Powerful DAW software from Magix.

Sample rate: Rate at which an A/D converter samples the incoming waveform.

Sawtooth wave: Resembling the teeth of a saw, this waveform contains both odd and even harmonics.

Sequencer: Device for recording, editing and replaying MIDI data, usually in a multitrack format. Sequencers were the forerunners to today's DAWs.

Short circuit: A low resistance path, usually undesirable, that allows electrical current to flow when a fault occurs.

Sibilance: High frequency whistling sound that affects some vocal recordings (caused by airflow around the singer's teeth), specifically on F, S and T sounds.

Side-chain: That part of a circuit that follows the envelope of the the main signal to derive control signals for processing, such as gain control in a compressor.

Signal: Electrical representation of input such as sound.

Signal chain: The full route taken by a signal from the input to the output of a system.

Signal-to-noise ratio: Ratio in dBs of maximum signal level (before clipping) to the residual noise.

Sine wave: Pure tone with no harmonics.

Slave: Device controlled from a master device.

SMPTE: Time code developed for the film industry but also used in music and recording, often in its guise as MIDI Time Code or MTC.

Sound card: Internal computer expansion card that does the same job as an audio interface, facilitating the input and output of audio signals to and from a computer. Most internal sound cards are unlikely to give as good results as a dedicated external audio interface. See **audio interface**.

Sound On Sound: An early recording technique used before the availability of multitrack tape machines. It involved disabling the tape machine's erase head and then recording new audio on top of the old. If you made a mistake there was no going back. Also refers to a rather splendid recording magazine.

S/PDIF: Pronounced 'Spidiff' and standing for Sony/Philips Digital Interface, the S/PDIF digital data format is very similar to the professional AES-EBU standard although it is unbalanced and operates at a slightly different signal level. It is a two-channel system and can accommodate up to 24-bits of audio data as well as track start flags, source identification information, and timing data needed by consumer CD players and other devices.

SPL: Sound Pressure Level, measured in dBs.

Square wave: Symmetrical rectangular waveform comprising a series of only odd harmonics.

Sub bass: Very low frequencies below the range of typical monitor loudspeakers, typically 40Hz and below.

Subtractive synthesis: The analogue paradigm of starting out with a complex waveform and then using filters to remove various harmonic components.

Sustain: That part of the ADSR envelope that determines the level to which the sound will decay to if a key is kept held down. When the key is released, the sound decays according to the Release setting.

Sweet spot: The optimum position to place a microphone for the best results, or for a listener relative to the position of the monitor loudspeakers.

Sync: Process of forcing two or more pieces of equipment to run in synchronism with each other.

Synthesiser: Electronic musical instrument employing various methods of sound creation to allow it to produce a range of abstract and emulative sounds.

T /

Tempo: Speed of a piece of music measured in beats per minute.

THD: Total harmonic distortion.

Thru: MIDI connector which passes through the signal present at the MIDI in socket.

Thunderbolt: Ultra high-speed data connection.

Timbre: The tonal 'colour' of a sound determined by its harmonic complexity and the way those harmonics vary with time.

TOSLINK: Optical connector use for S/PDIF and ADAT format digital data.

Track: Term dates back to multitrack tape but now refers to a single part of a multitrack recording; each 'track' can be modified, edited and effected independently of the others.

Tracking: Old-school term for recording to multitrack tape.

Transient: Abrupt part of a sound where the harmonic content and level changes abruptly, such as the start of a drum hit, the onset of a picked guitar string or the tap of a hammer on a triangle.

Transparency: Subjective term used to describe clear, uncoloured audio quality that sounds true to the original source.

Tremolo: Regular modulation of the amplitude of an audio signal under LFO control.

Transducer: Any device for converting one form of energy to another, such as a microphone or loudspeaker.

Transpose: To change the key of a musical signal or performance by shifting it up or down by a fixed number of semitones.

Triangle wave: Symmetrical triangular shaped wave that contains odd harmonics, but at a much lower level than in the case of the square wave, giving it a purer tonality.

TS jack: Mono jack with Tip and Sleeve connections only. Used for unbalanced signal connections, such as guitar leads.

TRS jack: Stereo jack connector with Tip, Ring and Sleeve connections, often used to carry stereo signals, balanced mono signals or to get signals in and out of a console inert point.

U /

Unbalanced: A two-wire signal connection where the inner signal conductor is most often surrounded by a tubular screen, which also doubles as the return signal path. The screen helps reduce interference problems but it not nearly so effective as balancing.

Unison: To play or layer the same part using two or more different instruments (or voices).

USB: Universal Serial Buss, a serial communications protocol used to connect many computer peripherals including audio interfaces, MIDI interfaces, external hard drives and keyboards.

V /

Valve: Vacuum tube amplification device known also as a tube.

Velocity: Rate [speed] at which a key is depressed on a MIDI keyboard, used to control loudness.

Vocoder: Signal processor that takes the music spectrum of one signal, such as a voice, and uses it to control a bank of filters to impose the characteristics of the voice on a second sound such as a synth pad.

Voice: Aside from the obvious, the term voice is also used to describe the ability of a synth or other electronic instrument to play multiple notes at the same time. For example, an 8-voice instrument is able to play 8 notes at the same time.

Vibrato: Pitch modulation, which may be a playing technique used with stringed instrument or, in the case of electronic instruments and effects, controlled from an LFO.

VU meter: Meter designed to average out and interpret signal levels in approximately the same way as the human ear.

W /

Warmth: Subjective term used to describe sound with enhanced low end or processed using subtle distortion and compression to make it sound a little larger than life.

Watt: Unit of electrical power.

Waveform: Visual representation of an electrical signal.

White noise: A random signal where the energy distribution produces the same amount of noise power for each Hz of the spectrum.

Word clock: The accurate clock that regulates the A to D and D to A conversion processes. Embedded information also identifies the start and end of each digital word or sample, and which samples belong to the left and right audio channels. While AES-EBU and S/PDIF embody clock signals within their data streams, it is often necessary (and sometimes beneficial) to connect a discrete word clock between equipment via their separate Word Clock In and Out connectors, usually BNC connectors.

Write: To save data to a digital storage medium. Also used as a term when recording mix automation data.

X /

XLR: Type of connector commonly used to carry balanced audio signals from microphones. Various pin configurations are available though microphones use the three-pin convention, other than some valve mics, which require more pins.

Y /

Y-Lead: Cable with a TRS jack at one end spitting out to two unbalanced TS jacks. Often used to connect patchbays or outboard equipment to console insert points.

Z /

Zero crossing point: Place where a signal waveform crosses from being positive to negative or vice versa.

Zipper noise: Audible steps heard when a parameter is being varied in a digital audio processor that doesn't include sophisticated data smoothing algorithms to avoid it.

INDEX

ABOUT
SAMPLE MAGIC

Sample Magic is an award-winning **sample p**
catalogue that spans house, electro, dubste

It is the publisher of the best-selling **Secrets o**

Sample Magic runs **courses** on music produc

You can find out more about us at
www.samplemagic.com